The Magic Arts
in
Celtic Britain

Lewis Spence

green=interest
orange=mithras
pink=ritual

DOVER PUBLICATIONS, INC.
Mineola, New York

Bibliographical Note

This Dover edition, first published in 1999, is an unabridged republication of the work as published by Rider & Co., London and New York, n.d.

Library of Congress Cataloging-in-Publication Data

Spence, Lewis, 1874–1955.
    The magic arts in Celtic Britain / Lewis Spence.
        p.   cm.
    Originally published: London ; New York : Rider, 1945.
    Includes bibliographical references and index.
    ISBN-13: 978-0-486-40447-9 (pbk.)
    ISBN-10: 0-486-40447-1 (pbk.)
    1. Celts—Religion. 2. Magic, Celtic. 3. Great Britain—
Religion. I. Title.
[BL900.S57   1999]
299'.16—dc21   98-37461
                                                                      CIP

Manufactured in the United States by Courier Corporation
40447106   2014
www.doverpublications.com

Preface

FOR the greater part of a lifetime I have awaited the appearance of a work especially devoted to the consideration of the occult arts as they were practised among the Celtic peoples of Britain. Essays, articles and other fugitive contributions to our knowledge of Celtic arcana have appeared in considerable profusion from time to time, but no volume as yet purports to examine in its entirety the whole range of British-Celtic Magic. Here, I may say parenthetically, I employ the term "Magic" as usefully describing in a more or less comprehensive manner all the occult arts, and even Mysticism itself, which has, I believe, intimate associations with it, in the historic sense at least.

Having long awaited such a book, and beholding no signs of its appearance, I at last resolved upon the somewhat desperate expedient of writing it myself. I realize that to some extent my claims to authoritative knowledge in certain sections of Celtic lore might not pass muster among Celtic purists. My acquaintance with the Celtic tongues is confined to a considerable vocabulary of its modern dialects alone. But I happen to be a Celt, I can lay claim to a fair share of the Celtic temperament, and I can truthfully aver that my knowledge of Magic in all its forms has more than half a century of research to recommend it. I have with care, and I hope with understanding, perused practically every page which has been written on the subject of Celtic belief, as it was known to these islands, which is now available in print. In short, in writing this book I have been actuated by a desire to provide my readers with the kind of volume which I had always hoped might eventually appear from more competent hands. I have set down nothing in these pages without the sanction of superiority, and if their record is not a flawless one, it is, I believe, free from anything in the shape of gross misdirection and careless statement.

But I have by no means slavishly followed the explanatory declarations of my superiors in Celtic lore. Indeed, in more instances than one I have ventured to differ sharply from their conclusions. Quite a number of Celtic scholars are by no means well versed in Anthropological science and in folk-lore, and where I have considered them inaccurate in these respects I have said so plainly and have ventured upon elucidations which have seemed to me more in keeping with the canons and spirit of these twin sciences.

Perhaps this book might have been entitled *The Idea of the Supernatural Among the British Celts*. In that case, however, it would have been necessary to include a description of that vast mass of common superstitions which are generally believed to have had their origin in the Celtic mentality, that flotsam and jetsam of popular lore which is to be encountered over the length and breadth of these islands—warnings, minor domestic superstitions, proverbial sayings and rhymes—in short, the minutiae of popular credence. But the majority of such beliefs and customs cannot appropriately, in my view, be associated entirely with Celtic belief, appearing as they do to have their source in the great storehouse of a common European body of superstition. Even so,

I have included many such beliefs in these pages for the sake of completeness. Moreover, the caption to which I allude would have made essential some more or less exhaustive account of Celtic mythology and rite, which would have carried me far out of the course I had set for myself.

Nor will the reader find much in these pages concerning witchcraft proper, which was in no sense a system of Celtic provenance alone, and which, as practised in Celtic communities, reveals very much the same features as it did elsewhere. Only here and there, too, in such places as comparison has seemed to make it necessary, have I alluded to the Magic of ancient Gaul, a more exhaustive description of that allied, though in some respects sharply dissimilar, system demanding a demonstration much too extended for the space at my disposal. The whole intention, in brief, has been to supply a readable and accurate account of the Magic arts as found among the Celts of the British Isles which might be comprehensible to the wayfaring reader.

I have thought it well to include a fairly comprehensive statement concerning the Mysticism of the British-Celtic races, without which such a book could scarcely have fulfilled its legitimate intention. In venturing upon several novel and strictly personal theories respecting the origins of Druidism, and its associations with the cult of the Divine King, the British belief in Reincarnation, the cultus of Arthur, the mystery of the Grail and the problem of Second Sight, I have, though respecting the views of genuine authorities, adhered more particularly to my own individual conclusions, some of which, it will be seen, are entirely at variance with those of other writers, and reflect the results of long and careful consideration. If they are erroneous, legitimate criticism will doubtless make plain where I have stumbled and I shall be the first to accept the discipline of its strictures. At the same time I would plead that the framing of a first essay on the vexed subject of Magic as known to the insular Celts is a most onerous and complicated task—one, indeed, in the course of which it is scarcely to be expected that errors more or less salient will not obtrude themselves.

I should add that what I have written concerning modern Welsh criticism is set down in no spirit of cavil, but in the hope that the truly extraordinary achievements it has made will be still more widely appreciated and that its efforts will be released from a certain diffidence of attitude and a vein of apology which, it seems to me, is inappropriate to a scholarship so able and so distinguished.

                                                                    L. S.

Contents

CHAPTER I

THE MAGIC ART AMONG THE CELTS

CHAPTER II

THE MAGIC ART AMONG THE CELTS (continued)

CHAPTER III

THE PROBLEM OF DRUIDISM

CHAPTER IV

THE PROBLEM OF DRUIDISM (*continued*)

CHAPTER V

CELTIC SPELLS AND CHARMS

CHAPTER VI

MAGICAL BOOKS OF THE CELTS

CHAPTER VII

THE CELTIC SPIRIT WORLD

CHAPTER VIII

NECROMANCY, PROPHECY AND DIVINATION

CHAPTER IX

THE CELTIC BELIEF IN REINCARNATION

CHAPTER X

CELTIC MYSTICISM

CHAPTER XI

CELTIC MYSTICISM (*continued*)

CHAPTER XII

THE CULTUS OF ARTHUR

CHAPTER XIII

THE MYSTERY OF THE GRAIL

CHAPTER XIV

THE SECOND SIGHT

List of Illustrations

List of Drawings

CHAPTER I

THE MAGIC ART AMONG THE CELTS

THE tradition of the arcane and the mysterious cleaves to certain races so naturally as to make it seem an inherent and inalienable possession. The Magic of Arabia, the secret doctrines of India and the runic mysteries of Scandinavia are salient expressions of racial affinity with the mystical and the marvellous. But to no race, I maintain, was it given to cultivate a higher or keener sense of spiritual vision or of the fantastically remote than to the Celtic. It has indeed justified the claim by the production of a literature which casts back to the seventh and eighth centuries of our era, and is unsurpassed in fantasy and weirdly delicate invention. Later Celtic popular stories and folk-tales reflect and continue this distinction in the primitive yet brilliant simplicity and remote strangeness of their subject-matter and narrative quality. And as if unexhausted by the conception in its Irish sphere of a series of sagas unmatched for magical charm among the world's mythologies, the Celtic tradition addressed itself in its later heyday in the island of Britain to the transformation of these older materials into a body of romance which, because of its noble excellence, its amazement of marvel and incident and its almost divine sentiment of chivalry, made every land in Europe its spiritual tributary. To the Celtic sense of wonder and the generous ideals which accompanied it as expressed in the Arthurian epic, the folk of the Empire of Britain, both in these islands and in the Britains oversea, are vastly more indebted than even the wisest among us suspects. To the great lessons it inculcates we can trace our national enthusiasm for the qualities of freedom, mercy, chivalry, fair play— all those virtues which, I dare to say, still in great measure distinguish us from the rest of mankind, and which, in the sight of the whole world, have made this island a refuge for the oppressed and the unprotected in days of darkness.

It is not necessary that I should trace in these pages the pre-history or the later progress of the Celtic race as situated in its regions of settlement— in Britain, in Ireland, in Gaul or in the Lesser Britain of Armorica or Brittany. That has been done so frequently and with such acceptance by a cloud of gifted witnesses as to render further demonstration of it needless and supererogatory. In these pages it is the Magic and Mysticism of the Celtic race, its arcane and occult practice and ideality, I wish to describe. The subject is indeed one which, although copiously treated, has not so far been separately and particularly examined in a work especially devoted to its consideration. That I shall succeed in my endeavour to present a satisfactory account of a theme so vast and complicated is a hope beyond my expectation, but I may, through long acquaintance with its subject-matter, be enabled to supply an acceptable account of its more outstanding principles.

The writers of antiquity were at one in realizing the native superiority of the Celtic mind in the science of Magic. Pliny remarks that the Britain of his day (the first among the new centuries) "celebrates them with such ceremonies that it might seem possible that she taught Magic to the Persians". Diodorus Siculus, Timagenes, Hippolytus and Clement of Alexandria were unanimous in believing that Pythagoras had received his mystical philosophy from the Celtic priests of Gaul, rather than they from him. Valerius Maximus, in the Second Book of his "Stromata", issues a warning that if one should jeer at the notions of the Druids respecting immortality, he must also laugh at those of

Pythagoras. The ancient world was assuredly almost as deeply impressed by the doctrines and mysteries of ancient Britain as it was by those of Egypt or Chaldea.

That a very complete system of Magic, associated with a definite body of mystical dogma and arcane thought, was practised by the Magi of ancient Britain and Ireland is apparent from trustworthy evidence. In the pages that follow it will be my endeavour to make more clear than has yet been done the type of arcane belief to which it actually belonged. It is important that we should seek to estimate its more precise status among the magical systems of the world; that we should realize wherein, if at all, it differed from other similar systems; that, in short, we should be enabled to state conclusively what were its salient characteristics and qualities. It has been said that in no sense does it differ from other Aryan bodies of occult belief. It has even been urged that it cannot be distinguished from the Magic of the primitive medicine-man or witch-doctor of savage races. If this be so, the evidence will either substantiate such a theory or will dispose of it entirely, although it must be added that any just consideration of its more profoundly philosophic mysticism totally overthrows the notion that its practitioners were merely a body of crude and unlettered aboriginal jugglers—and indeed the accounts of Julius Caesar, Pliny, Strabo and Cicero, among others, reveal the falsity of such a view.

Before proceeding farther I must explain what I imply by the term "Magic", an expression which certainly has different meanings for different authorities, from some of whom we may seek for guidance. Tylor, the initiator of the modern school of Anthropology, defined Magic as "occult science", and subdivided it into the "spiritistic" and the "natural"; that is, he believed certain kinds of Magic were wrought by the aid of spiritual entities, while others were induced by "sympathetic Magic"—that species of sorcery which believes that like causes bring about like results through the employment of mimetic or theatric action, or ritual.

But Magic is now held by many authorities to proceed from what is known as *Mana*, a Melanesian word which expresses a mysterious energy or essence issuing from a reservoir of arcane power. This magical essence is thought of by some savage peoples as pervading the whole world, and if the magician can attract a sufficiency of it he can employ it for his mystical purposes. It seems not improbable that the belief in spirits may have been developed from this belief at a later period—that is, *Mana* came to be "personified" in spirit-form, to take on the shape of individual spirits.

But types of Magic exist which, in my opinion, fall under the heads of neither of Tylor's categories, nor of that of *Mana*. I cannot, for instance, explain such obviously magical acts as the transformation of men into shapes other than their own, human or animal, or the changing of a landscape by lliusion, as being due either to the influence of spirits or to mere sympathetic Magic. Some other factor, acquired or separately developed, appears to enter into the tradition of Magic in such cases. Here we have a belief associated with an innate potency in humanity unguessed or ignored by the modern anthropologist. Yet it was recognized by the Arab sage Avicenna, who long ago gave it as his belief that there exists in the human mind a certain power of altering objects, and that such objects obey that power when the sorcerer is inspired by a sense of extreme supernatural might. Paracelsus also believed that "all the wonders of Magic are performed by will, imagination and faith", and such must unquestionably have been the attitude of the Egyptian and Babylonian magicians when they supplicated the gods to grant them power to engage in magical acts. It is this third phase of Magic, then, by which we must seek to account for such instances as appear to be outside its other two categories, that is if we desire to understand the primitive idea of arcane practice in its entirety.

It is necessary to say at once that such records as we have of Celtic Magic in the region which is now known as England furnish us with only scanty clues to the magical ideas or practices of the Celtic race. For such information it is necessary to appeal mainly to the literatures and traditions of Wales, Ireland and Scotland. Certain parts of these records are acceptable as being of the nature of genuine chronicle and folk-tradition, and are not easily disposed of. In the lands alluded to we find the mysterious caste of the Druids wielding powers of illusion, raising winds and tempests, casting mists over the landscape for the confusion of their enemies or for reasons of defence. They are masters of the arts of shape-shifting and bodily transformations, they are capable of vision at a distance. We find them united in magical colleges for the instruction and furtherance of arcane knowledge. By a draught of mysterious elixir they can induce forgetfulness. They can dry up watercourses and employ their sorcery on behalf of their native rulers in battle. They engage in magical contests with Christian saints and missionaries. They can annihilate time through prophecy and the divination of omens. An understanding of the language of the animal world is vouchsafed them. Indeed, there is no department of the magical art in which, apparently, they are not versed.

An account of the great contest of St. Patrick, the apostle of Ireland, with the Irish Druids, as set forth in his Tripartite Life, well exemplifies the contemporary belief in those magical potencies which the Druidic brotherhood were said to be able to wield, and to a certain extent summarizes them. On the eve of *Bealltainn*, when the great bonfire of the god Beli was lit, a fire was seen to be burning in the direction of Tara, the Irish religious capital. This was irregular, as only by the hands of the Chief Druid could such a fire be kindled at that festival. In some dismay the Archdruid proceeded to the spot where the blaze appeared, and in angry surprise discovered St. Patrick and his followers chanting their psalms round a camp-fire. The Druid ordered the offending Saint to accompany him to the Assembly at Tara, where he eloquently defended his mission of salvation before the King, with arguments so damaging to the Druidic faith that the wrathful pontiff challenged him to work a miracle which would justify those powers he claimed on behalf of his divine Master. The Saint refused to disturb the order of Providence to gratify mere curiosity, whereupon the pagan priest, to display his occult powers, chanting spells and brandishing his wand, plunged the landscape in a heavy snowfall. This illusion Patrick dispersed by simply making the sign of the Cross, on which the Druid, not to be defeated, caused a thick darkness to fall upon the countryside. But the Saint, resorting to prayer, dissolved the gloomy cloud.

The King, anxious for further proofs of the relative powers of the rival priests, commanded each of them to cast his book into the water, so that he in whose volume the letters remained uninjured might be declared the minister of truth. To this the Druid would not consent, and he further refused a similar trial by fire. The King then ordered each of the rivals to enter a tent filled with dry boughs which would be set alight. "Nay," said the Saint, willing to display the superiority of his divine Magic, "let one be filled with green branches, and this I resign to my opponent." St. Benin, who accompanied Patrick, besought his leave to enter the tent of dry boughs, and did so, bearing the Druid's mantle, while the Druid, carrying his, as fearlessly entered the tent of green twigs full of sap. Both huts were fired at the same moment, and in the twinkling of an eye the shelter of green boughs, containing the Druid, was reduced to ashes with all that it held, save the young saint's mantle. In the other nothing was consumed except the Druid's cloak.

If we seek among the Celtic languages for expressions relative to the Magic Arts we find that the noun employed to describe the spoken word of Magic, or the spell, among the Gaelic-speaking Celts of ancient Scotland and Ireland was *Bricht*, which has been equated with the Icelandic *bragr*, "poetry", that is "magical rhyme".[1]* A term commonly in use among the Gaels to denote any magical act, or sleight of sorcery, is *Druidheachd*, which only too readily reveals the actual source of its inspiration.[2] The word *Eolas*, "knowledge", is also frequently still in use as signifying magical potency in the more popular and general sense of the term.

If we look for examples of the type of sorcery implied by the word "Drúidry" we shall most easily discern them in the records of Irish Druidism. To induce confusion, or to conceal themselves, the Druids were in the habit of casting dense fogs over a landscape. To cover their approach from the sea, such a method was employed by the leaders of the Tuatha Dé Danann, or Children of the Goddess Danu, an early race of Celtic magicians, when they first invaded Ireland. These immigrant sorcerers spread "druidically-formed showers and fog-sustaining shower-clouds" over the countryside, causing the heavens to rain down fire and blood upon its defenders, the native aboriginal race of the Fir-Bolgs. But the Fir-Bolgs had Druids of their own, whose counter-enchantments put a period to the disastrous exhalations.[3] Another instance of this species of smoke-screen is to be found in the tale of Cormac, who, seeking for his wife Eithne and his children, kidnapped by Manannan, the god of the sea, passed through "a dark magical mist" in the course of his successful efforts to discover them.

The raising of artificial windstorms was also a prominent feature of Druidical sorcery. When the Tuatha Dé Danann, in their turn, hopelessly endeavoured to repel the onset of the Milesians, the last of the Hibernian races to seek settlement upon the soil of Ireland, they sent a "druidical" tempest against the invaders, which made it impossible for them to reach the shore. Donn, one of the Milesian leaders, discovered that the atmosphere was quite unruffled above his galley, and realizing that the storm was magically induced, invoked "the power of the land of Erin" against its violence, whereupon it subsided. But the Danann sea-god, Manannan, shook his magic mantle in the direction of the Milesians and a fresh tempest wrecked some of their craft before they succeeded in making a landing.[4]

Inspired by all the hate of Celtic feud, the Druid Mog Ruath of Munster, when he opposed King Cormac and his Druids, drove them by his magic fire and storm-spells from that kingdom. We learn, too, that the Druids of King Loegaire sadly persecuted the early Christian missionaries by sending heavy snowfalls and thick darkness upon them.[5] Broichan, the Druid of King Brude, a Pictish monarch who ruled over a part of Scotland, caused so dire a storm and such fell darkness to descend upon Loch Ness that St. Columba found navigation upon its waters impossible for a time.[6] The god Lugh bore off Conn of the Hundred Battles in a magic mist to an enchanted palace, where he prophesied to him concerning the fortunes of his royal descendants.[7] The tales regarding such magical interference with the elements are so numerous as to make possible reference to the most typical only.

Shape-shifting and the transformation of persons into forms other than their own are equally the common themes of Celtic magical story. It is necessary to discriminate between these forms of enchantment. The first is, of

---

* See references at end of this work.

The Wicker COLOSSUS of the DRUIDS,
Wherein Malefactors, Prisoners of War, and sometimes Innocent Persons
(when there was a deficiency of the former)
Were Burnt as Sacrifices to their Deities.

STONE AT KINNELLAR, ABERDEENSHIRE, SHOWING DRUIDIC SYMBOLS

DRUIDIC ALPHABET

R	B	Boibel		B	Beth
十	L	Loth		L	Luis
メ	F	Foran		N	Nuin
ﾉ	S	Sain		F	Fearan
弓	N	Neaigadon		S	Suil
ﾒ	D	Daibhoith		D	Duir
ﾁ	T	Teilmon		T	Tinne
ﾁ	C	Casi		C	Coll
戈	M	Moiria		M	Muin
ﾁ	G	Gath		G	Gort
ﾁ	P			P	Peith
⊖	R	Rube		R	Ruis
↑	A	Acab		A	Ailim
ﾒ	O	Ose		O	On
ﾃ	U	Ura		U	Ux
ﾖ	E	Esu		E	Eachta
ﾖ	J	Jaichim		J	Iodha

1st Col. : Bobileth alphabet
2nd Col. : Beth-luis-non alphabet

LVRNE trouvee dans le tombeau

URN CONTAINING THE ASHES OF THE ARCH-DRUID CHYNDONAX

course, descriptive of the guises into which a magician can transform himself. The second implies his transformation of another person into any shape, human, animal or inanimate. The Irish Druid Fer Fidail abducted a girl by transforming himself into the shape of a woman, while another Druid deceived Cuchullin, the Irish Achilles, by assuming the shape of the Lady Niamh. The "Rennes Dindsenchas", an ancient Irish tract, informs us that an enchantress named Dalb the Rough transformed three men and their wives into swine, while in the famous tale of "The Children of Lir", the three children of that god are changed into swans by their stepmother Aeife. The Druid Fear Doirche, furious with the maiden Saar, changed her into a fawn, in which shape she became the mother of Ossian. In many instances of transformation it appears to be the rule that a person's shape may not be magically altered unless he or she is without clothing at the time of the metamorphosis; but it is certainly a rule which has numerous exceptions, and it does not seem to apply to shape-shifting. The examples I have given above refer both to the first class of transformation and the second, and I have placed them side by side for the purpose of contrast and comparison, as they are frequently confused by writers on Magic and folk-lore.

Transformation is also frequently to be remarked in connection with that series of tales which deals with the supernatural personage known as "the Loathly Lady"—a hideous hag who seeks deliverance from an enchanted condition (the result of some spell laid upon her) by union with a self-denying hero. In a Scottish Gaelic tale, *The Daughter of King Underwaves*, Diarmid, a Fenian hero, encounters such a hag, who begs for shelter and a share of his couch. When the request is granted she is transformed into a damsel of surpassing loveliness.[8] We shall encounter this type of story later on in considering the topic of the divine sovereignty in Ireland.

In the adventures of Pwyll, Prince of Dyved, as related in the Welsh *Mabinogion*, we find it recorded that that hero assumed for a year the shape and outward seeming of Arawn, King of Annwn or Hades, while his plutonic highness took on the bodily guise of the mortal prince for reasons mutually beneficial.[9] This is rather an unusual case of transformation, illustrating as it does an incident in which two magicians agree to exchange their outward identities for a political reason. But we are not led to believe that they exchanged their bodies and they certainly retained their personalities.

In the Irish *Book of Invasions* we find the Milesian hero Amergin vaunting that it is possible for him to change his shape "like a god". He can become even "the wind that blows upon the sea, the ocean wave, the surge". He can transform himself into "a strong bull", an eagle, a herb, a lake.[10] The elucidation of this passage is of the utmost importance for the comprehension of Celtic Magic. Remarking upon the quality and character of the magical science which enabled Amergin to accomplish these metamorphoses, M. D'Arbois de Jubainville declares that according to the tenets of Celtic philosophy it consisted in making oneself identical with those forces of nature which the magician desired to wield. "To possess this science was to possess nature in her entirety." The process is "sympathetic" to some extent—that is, it corresponds to that modern scientific idea of Magic which believes that like causes are capable of bringing about like results. But it would be absurd to refer it to merely sympathetic notions alone, for it is clear that a vital and overmastering desire also enters into the conception of it. We find a similar passage eloquent of the ability of the knowledgeable magician to assume the appearance of any given object or force or quality in one of the poems of the Welsh bard Taliesin, who tells us that he is "a vulture upon the rock", and that he has been an eagle, the fairest of plants, the wood in the covert, the word of science, the sward itself.[11] Now this passage might be, and has been, referred to a belief in reincarnation, but I consider erroneously so. It is indeed a wonderful proof of the recognition by the Celtic imagination that all matter is indeed one and that the assumption of its various forms can readily be achieved through the spiritual and mental potency of the magical initiate, as expressed by Avicenna and Paracelsus. As M. D'Arbois indicated, this doctrine was reflected in the teachings of the Celtic philosopher John Scotus Erigena at the court of Charles the Bald, King of France, in the ninth century.[12]

It is indeed extraordinary that anthropologists should have relied for so long upon the narrow hypothesis that all Magic is capable of being classified either as sympathetic or spiritistic. Nor is the classification at all a scientific one when we consider the stress laid upon magical personal potency, either natural or acquired, by Egyptian and Babylonian arcane texts and by mediaeval magicians.

In the tale of "Art and Balor Beimenach" collected by Jeremiah Curtin and included in his *Hero-Tales of Ireland* (pp. 331 ff.) we are told how Balor, the one-eyed god of the Fomorians, was transformed into a white horse through the enchantments of his wife, who had eloped with a cripple. In this equine form Balor was forced to carry grain to the mill, but he succeeded in escaping and dwelt in the hills until his wife discovered his whereabouts, had him brought to her and transformed him once more, this time into a wolf. In this guise he avenged himself by killing his wife's cattle, but was hunted, and was about to be despatched, when his father-in-law, to whom he made signs, took pity on him and spared his life. His wife, who knew him for her husband, pretended that he had slaughtered one of her children, whereupon the King, his father-in-law, angrily struck him with his wand, thus inadvertently causing him to take human shape once more.

In the same volume (pp. 367 ff.) Curtin also furnishes us with the story of the King of Lochlin, an interlude in the much longer tale of "The Cotter's Son and the Half-Slim Champion", in which the injured monarch recounts the manner in which he was bewitched by his wife when he discovered her with her paramour. When surprised by her husband, the lady, who was evidently a sorceress, struck him with a rod and changed him into a wild deer. She turned a pack of hounds upon the luckless king, and he was hunted by them into the fastnesses of the mountains, where he succeeded in eluding them. He then indulged his vengeance by making raids upon her gardens and fields and destroying her crops. But one day, as he was engaged in his work of mischief, she sprang up from behind a wall and once more struck him with her magic wand, whereupon he became a wolf. Shortly afterwards he fell in with a she-wolf, a woman under enchantment. She had been placed under spells when about to become a mother, but could not bear her child unless she received her mortal form again. One day the wolf-king, awaking suddenly from sleep, and confused by a dream, bit her in the side, when there emerged from her body an infant who grew to the stature of a man in a single moment. The wolf-woman died from the wound, but her son survived and nourished enmity for his mother's slayer. He chased the enchanted king from place to place and in one of these encounters the latter once again came face to face with his treacherous queen, who, terrified at the sight of him, dealt him a blow with her wand, upon which he regained human shape. The now disenchanted King of Lochlin snatched the wand from her and by its aid transformed her into wolf-shape as a punishment for her misdeeds.

In his useful work *Legendary Fictions of the Irish Celts* (p. 153) Patrick

Kennedy alludes to the weird legend of Earl Gerald Fitzgerald, a renowned practitioner of the Black Art and an inveterate enemy of the English. His wife, cognizant of his powers of enchantment, begged him to display them for her diversion, so to please her he transformed himself into a goldfinch. But while he disported himself before her in this guise he was attacked by a hawk and immediately killed. Once in seven years he rides round the Curragh of Kildare on a steed whose silver shoes were half an inch thick at the time of his disappearance, and not until these are worn down to the thinness of a cat's ear will he be restored to human society. He and his warriors await the hour of their liberation in a great cavern beneath the Rath of Mullaghmast, until a miller's son with six fingers on each hand shall awake them by blowing a horn. The tale is similar to those told of Arthur, Thomas the Rhymer and Barbarossa.

In his familiar work on *The Topography of Ireland* Giraldus Cambrensis alludes to several instances of the transformation of people into animal shape which occurred in his own time, the twelfth century. He tells how a priest, journeying from Ulster to Meath, through forest country, encountered a wolf which addressed him in human speech and led him to where a she-wolf lay grovelling in agony beneath the shelter of a tree. These animals informed him that they were natives of the province of Ossory, who had been transformed into their present shapes by an enchantress named Natalis. At the end of seven years the enchantment would cease and they would be restored to human form, when two other persons would be substituted in their stead. The she-wolf, who appeared to be at the point of death, begged the priest to afford her the comfort of the Sacrament, but as he thought he was not provided with its elements, he could only refuse her piteous request. But the he-wolf reminded him that he carried a few wafers in his missal. The creature then tore off a part of the skin which covered his mate, thus revealing her as an old woman, whereupon the holy man, doubting no longer, administered the viaticum. He parted with the enchanted animals in the morning, and reported the adventure to the Bishop of Meath, who later consulted Giraldus himself as to the propriety of placing the matter before the Pope!

When Ceridwen, a nature-goddess of the British Celts, brewed a draught of poetic inspiration in her magical cauldron, she left it in the keeping of a certain Gwion, upon whose fingers some drops of its contents fell. He thrust his scalded hand into his mouth, whereupon he suddenly acquired universal knowledge. Enraged that such a boon should be conferred upon so undistinguished a mortal, the goddess attacked him, whereon he took refuge in flight. She pursued him, and to escape her fury he transformed himself successively into many shapes —a hare, a fish, and a grain of wheat. In order to destroy Gwion the more easily, the offended deity assumed in turn the appropriate forms of a greyhound, an otter, and lastly a hen, in which most unromantic guise she swallowed the luckless Gwion, later to bear him as an infant, whom she abandoned to the waves in a coracle. Yet he survived, to become the inspired bard Taliesin.[13]

Manannan, the Celtic god of the sea, somewhat resembled the Greek Proteus, also an oceanic deity, in his ability to change his shape as easily as does the element over which he ruled and which he personified. He was wont to cast thick fogs round his chief dwelling in the Isle of Man, and by the power of his magics was able to make one object seem a hundred, while little chips which he cast into the water assumed the proportions of great vessels of war. Like certain Eastern gods he had three legs, and these are still represented on the coat-of-arms of the Isle of Man. Some authorities believe them to be a form of the swastika. It seems to me much more probable that in the case of a sea-god they are a memory of that symbol known as "the churning of the ocean", which represented the primal flood or the power of the sea. A weird legend of the island, mentioned by Miss Eleanor Hull in her *Folklore of the British Isles* (pp. 182–3), tells how two fishermen mending their nets on the shore saw Manannan rise from the sea to the accompaniment of thunderous uproar. The weather had been foggy and they had lit a fire with flint and steel, but at the first spark from their tinder-box the fog began to move up the mountainside, closely followed by a revolving object resembling three legs spread out like the spokes of a wheel. The tale is also recounted in Moore's *Folklore of the Isle of Man*.

In the Scottish Highlands most of the tales which allude to shape-shifting are associated with enchantresses who take the form of deer. In a tale from South Uist entitled "The Widow's Son" (collected by J. F. Campbell in his *Tales of the West Highlands*, II., pp. 307 ff.), and narrated by a crofter, we are informed that the hero, a simple youth named Iain, was engaged in shooting deer. He espied a hind, and took aim at it. But when he was about to pull the trigger she suddenly changed her appearance, and he beheld "the finest woman he ever saw". He therefore refrained from shooting, and as suddenly the maiden changed once more into a deer. The animal scampered off at last and Iain followed in its track until it leapt on the thatch of a cottage, calling out to him that if he were hungry he might enter the house and eat his fill. The house turned out to be a robbers' den, and the bandits, entering, surprised and slew the young hunter. But when they left the bothy the hind made her way inside, and shaking wax from her ears upon the dead man, restored him to life. In the sequel the hind turns out to be a king's enchanted daughter, and she and Iain are duly united.

A similar tale from Cowal, in Argyllshire, tells how a forester in the army of the Earl of Argyll, when that nobleman was in the field against the great Marquess of Montrose, was ordered to fire at a hind which persisted in following the army. It was observed that the forester refrained from firing, and when rebuked for doing so he piteously exclaimed: "I will fire, but it will be the last shot that ever I will fire." Scarcely was the charge out of his gun when he fell dead. The enchantress, who was the forester's sweetheart in deer-form, reassumed her human shape, uttered a terrific shriek, "rose like a cloud of mist up the shoulder of the neighbouring mountain", and vanished among its heathery slopes.

The late Mr. J. G. McKay, an approved Celtic scholar, was of the opinion that deer-transformations in the Highlands are to be accounted for by the manner in which the priestesses of a deer-cult attired themselves in the skins of hinds, suddenly discarding them, or reassuming them while on the moors. In his notes to the recently published fifth volume of J. F. Campbell's work under the title of *More West Highland Tales*, Mr. McKay particularly directed attention to cases of magical sex-shifting in Highland superstition. He indicated that the form of the Gaelic adjective in all recorded tales of metamorphosis into equine shape shows that a female animal is intended. No matter what the sex of the person transformed, he or she becomes a female when enchanted into animal shape, more particularly the equine. He adds: "There are three other Highland tales, however, in which sex-shifting occurs, but on the part of women. In one, a queen and her attendant maidens are all changed into white stags; in another, a white stag becomes a woman; and in a third a woman becomes a water-horse."

Perhaps the weirdest Celtic tale of animal transformation is that Welsh instance of such a change to be found in the Mabinogion story of *Math, Son of Mathonwy*, Prince of Gwynedd. Gwydion and Gilvaethwy, his nephews, had conspired to compass the ruin of Goewin, his foot-holder, and the maiden was outraged by Gilvaethwy. In order to punish the miscreants, Math, who was a magician of might, by aid of his magic wand turned Gilvaethwy into a hind and Gwydion into a stag, dooming them to be paired together and to have young while in this condition. Next year he turned them into a sow and boar, only on this occasion he changed the sex of both. At the beginning of the third year he again transformed them, this time into a wolf and a she-wolf, again changing their sex. In each transformation the unhappy pair brought forth offspring, which were later transformed into human children. The story has received a very complete and indeed most elaborate treatment at the scholarly hands of W. J. Gruffydd, Professor of Celtic at the University College of South Wales, under the title of *Math vab Mathonwy*, a study which constitutes a veritable mine of British Celtic lore, and which, if somewhat laboured in its manner, must be classed as one of the most notable productions of contemporary Celtic research.[14] Still, Professor Gruffydd's statement that a change of sex and species is unknown in transformation tales is certainly belied by the examples furnished by McKay, as given above.

In some West Highland tales transformation into horse-shape is achieved by shaking a bridle at a person. George Willox, a sorcerer of Strathavon, was the possessor of a kelpie's bridle, by means of which he enchanted many people. There is also a tale from Galloway in which a woman farmer changes one of her labourers into a pony by shaking a bridle over him while he sleeps. Three Irish magicians with whom a certain Cian falls in get the better of him in playing a game, then strike him with a magic wand and turn him into a pillar of stone, as Jeremiah Curtin recounts in his *Hero-Tales of Ireland* (pp. 28–9). In J. F. Campbell's tale of "The Battle of the Birds", which is to be found in the first volume of his *Popular Tales of the West Highlands* (p. 26), a young man is transformed into a raven, but is released from that shape by a king's son. But in view of the great number of such instances I must append other literary notices of Celtic metamorphoses in a note.[15]

More than one anthropologist has tried to account for the belief in shape-shifting or transformation. Mr. Sidney Hartland sought to do so on the ground of the animistic theory, which suggests that savages or primitive people credit animals and objects with possessing a soul and mentality of their own. "It matters not to the savage that human form and speech are absent. These are not thought to be necessary, or, if they are, they can be assumed at will, or under certain conditions. For one of the consequences, or at least one of the accompaniments of this stage of thought, is the belief in change of form without loss of individual identity." Alfred Nutt was of opinion that the belief might have originated in the Zeus legend. Zeus, the shape-shifting father of the shape-shifting wonder-child Dionysus, may have supplied the model upon which the sagas of Manannan, of Lugh and Cuchullin, of Ceridwen and Taliesin, were framed, though a little later on in his *Voyage of Bran* he suggests a community of origin for these similar beliefs rather than any direct Classical influence upon Celtic thought.

Lord Raglan, in his admirable essay *The Hero* (pp. 261 ff.), opines that the idea of shape-shifting arose out of primitive ritual, in which men disguised as animals were familiar figures. At the same time he scouts the notion that savages are unable to distinguish between animals and human beings, as Professor Gilbert Murray and Sir James Frazer assumed. The notion "is quite untenable by anyone with any real knowledge of savage mentality". The savage may believe that people can take the form of animals, "but that is a very different thing from confusing men with animals".

But, these views notwithstanding, we must, I feel, once again make allowances for the theory of magical potency, which is not dependent upon either animistic or ritual associations, but which arises out of a belief that by inherent power spirits or magicians could achieve such a metamorphosis as shape-shifting. Arising probably from the idea of the fluid nature of spirit, it was imagined that spirits could assume any form they chose with ease because of the plastic essence of which they are composed. From this view it is but a step to the further assumption that a sorcerer is able to transform a person into any shape he may will him to take, for by primitive man body and spirit are frequently regarded as one and the same.

Nor may we ignore the evidence that the savage actually beholds certain transformations which appeal to him as magical. As Miss Cox remarks in her *Introduction to Folklore* (p. 87), he "sees a motionless egg suddenly turn itself into a bird, or a chrysalis into a butterfly, without any external agency. . . . He accepts these facts without surprise, and, with a mind naturally credulous, is not disposed to limit his belief in metamorphosis to just those instances of it he may chance to witness."

We now approach another department of Celtic Magic, that art of illusion which lent to the normal aspect of a place or building an entirely different appearance during a greater or less period of time. In Lowland Scotland we find this described as "glamourie", and in the Gaelic tongue as *sian*. Through this agency a hut or shieling might be transformed so as to appear as a lordly palace or castle, while a pool of water or puddle took the form of a surrounding moat. Rags might be temporarily glorified as resplendent attire and leaves or beans take the semblance of golden coin. When King Conchobar of Ulster and his men set out to drive away certain mischievous birds which were destroying his crops, they found themselves nightbound during the chase, and sought shelter in a magnificent mansion standing in a moorland waste. During his stay there the king became enamoured of the owner's wife, but was disappointed in his suit. In the morning he and his courtiers found themselves under the clear sky of heaven upon the desolate heath.[16] In a West Highland tale, too, we are told how a sorceress to whom Diarmid, the Irish hero, paid his addresses, built a resplendent castle on a hilltop for his delectation. "There was not a shadow of thing that was for the use of a castle that was not in it, even to a herd for the geese." In this delightful abode the happy pair resided for three days. But Diarmid moped and grieved for his comrades and hounds, so one fine morning he awoke to find himself in a moss-hole, deserted by the lady, who had grown tired of his petulant complaints. "There was no castle, nor a stone left of it on another."[17]

In the Irish tale of *Koisha Kaya* it is recounted how a certain Irish knight, O'Kroinikeard, when shooting at a hare, beheld it change into a most beautiful woman, who promised to marry him under certain conditions. Her presence utterly altered his home and estates, glorifying them out of all knowledge. But he broke his promises one after another. She punished him by mauling him frightfully and his house and land returned to their former condition, much of his domain degenerating into bush and ditches.[18]

The number of such tales of glamourie in Celtic tradition is legion, and those which I have cited above are merely standard examples of this very numerous class. They are, I think, to be accounted for not so much as examples of "sympathetic" Magic, but rather as issuing from that inherent power of the will which primitive folk believe exists in magicians and in spirits—a species of

Magic unscheduled by anthropologists. In some cases, however, they seem to imply a kind of hypnotic power directed upon the person who beholds these wonders as a magical interference with his vision.

This is perhaps the place to consider what has come to be regarded as another distinctive section of the Celtic magical tradition associated with that mystic ornament which the Druids were wont to carry suspended from their necks as a mark of their office—"the serpent's egg", so called, an oval ball of crystal said to be produced from the foam of a number of serpents meeting in congress. I might, perhaps, more appropriately have included it in the chapter which deals with charms and spells, but its importance appeals, I think, for early treatment.

The elder Pliny, writing of this amulet, tells us that, as the snakes twined together in a mass, they threw off these globes, which were formed from their viscous slime. By their hissing the ball was cast into the air, and if a Druid could catch it in a cloth before it fell he might, if mounted upon a swift horse kept in readiness, succeed in making off with it. The snakes followed after him in speedy and venomous pursuit, but could he succeed in crossing a running stream before they made up with him the prize would remain in his possession.[19]

This magical amulet was known to Celtic tradition as the *Glainnaider* or the *Glain-nan-Druidhe*, the Druid's glass, and Pliny informs us that it was chiefly employed for counteracting incantations. He had himself seen a specimen. This act of the snakes, says Dr. Owen Pughe, was only performed at one season of the year—in summer—and on the occasion of a given moon. The Welsh bard Aneurin alludes to it in one of his minor poems as:

> The quick-glancing ball,
> The adder's bright precious produce,
> The ejaculation of serpents.

He who possessed it was certain to gain any lawsuit in which he might engage and would be "well received by kings". Algernon Herbert was of opinion that the "serpents" were none other than the Druids themselves, and that the process of manufacture was one of simple glass-blowing.[20]

The Druids, says Davies in his *Mythology and Rites of the British Druids*, "are called *Nadredd*, adders, by the Welsh bards", and he believed that they owed this title "to their regenerative system of transmigration", which was symbolized by the serpent, which cast its skin and returned to a second youth. These "eggs", he thought, were manufactured by the Druids when "they assembled at a stated time in the summer", and he quotes Camden as saying that in many parts of Wales, Scotland and Cornwall people retained superstitious ideas concerning the origin and virtues of these "eggs" similar to those which Pliny recorded concerning them. This statement is interesting as it reveals the continuance of a belief from Druidic times until those of recent popular memory. The island of Bardsey, remarks Meilyr, an old Welsh poet, was known as "the holy island of the *Glain*", or Druidic egg, "in which," he adds, "there is a fair representation of a resurrection".

"These *Gemmae Anguinae*," says Camden, "are small glass amulets, commonly about as wide as our finger-rings, but much thicker, of a green colour, usually, though some of them are blue, and others curiously waved with blue, red and white." "Such beads," says Mr. Kendrick in his work, *The Druids*, "were called 'snake-stones' in Cornwall, Wales and Scotland and it is said that in Wales and in Ireland they were also sometimes called 'Druids' Glass'." Many of them date from the first two or three centuries before the Christian era.   Pliny, he thinks, may have seen a fossil, an echinus, "a conglomeration of tiny ammonites".   The persistence of the belief seems to have impressed Mr. Kendrick, and with good reason.

It is impossible to study Celtic magical science for any length of time without encountering frequent allusions to that famous race of wizard-gods known to Irish saga as the Tuatha Dé Danann, or Children of the Goddess Danu.   In practically every one of the tales and sagas which so frequently mention them incidents of a magical character are to be observed with such frequency as to distinguish them as a caste profoundly addicted to arcane dealings.   From the glowing pages of Keating we learn that the ancient home of this divine tribe was in Greece, and that while sojourning there they had come timeously to the assistance of the harassed Athenians in their wars with the Syrians.   For, by their powers of necromancy, they sent demons into the bodies of those Greeks who had been slain, resuscitating them so that they might once more engage in combat.   At a later time they migrated to the north of Europe, where they dwelt for some generations in the four enchanted cities of Falias, Gorias, Finias and Murias.   Thence they took ship for North Britain and Ireland, bearing with them four of the most potent magical talismans conceivable—the Lia Fail, a stone which hailed the king of the race by roaring under his feet at his coronation; the sword of the sun-god Lugh; the spear of the same divinity and lastly the cauldron of their chief deity, the Dagda.   That all of these arcane symbols reappear in the emblematic history of the Grail has long been acknowledged.

"It is difficult to resist the conclusion," remarks Mr. W. C. Mackenzie, in his *The Races of Ireland and Scotland* (p. 55), "that the Irish Druids were either Dananns themselves, or had learned their wizardry in the Danannic school."   In the Irish *Book of Invasions* we are informed that in the four cities of the Tuatha Dé Danann there presided four celebrated magicians, Moirfhais, Erus, Arias, famed for his skill in charms, and Semias, equally renowned as a spellbinder, and these, it is said, instructed youth in the several departments of the Magic Art.

I waive here the familiar circumstance that the Tuatha Dé Danann came to be regarded at a later time as a race of earthly monarchs and heroes.   The Irish chroniclers, at a loss for the actual material of history, seized upon the myths of this divine race and transformed them into mundane occurrences— though of a nature so marvellous that it is easy to discern their supernatural associations.   This experiment in pseudo-history, as D'Arbois de Jubainville indicates, had no actual relationship to the primitive traditions concerning the children of the goddess Danu.   The more ancient myth of their origins narrated their descent from heaven, although later Christian belief regarded them as "devils".[21]

It is scarcely necessary at this time of day to dissent from the sour and unfriendly verdicts which our godly forefathers pronounced upon the deities of the vanished races.   In this particular case the aspersion was peculiarly stupid and unsympathetic, for the Tuatha Dé were not only gods of light whose magical powers were for the most part wielded for good, but, as is now well understood, they imposed upon the peasantry of Ireland a most rigid rule of decency and morality, and are still regarded by them with affection as the fairies who dwell in the mounds and raths of romantic Eire—for to such a degenerate condition has modern folk-lore reduced this great and potent pantheon of wonder-working divinities!

But I do not propose to speak of the Tuatha Dé in their rôle of gods, nor in this place shall I allude to their religious or mythological nature, concerned as I am almost entirely with their magical status and history, the details of which will frequently appear in passages appropriate to its various activities in this volume. For it was chiefly from the Tuatha Dé that the Irish Druids would appear to have received their magical inspiration. We find their British kindred, the Children of Don, who, in some respects, are one and the same divine pantheon, intimately associated with the secret doctrine of later British Druidism, so that it is reasonable to assume that the earlier Druidic brotherhoods, both in Britain and Ireland, regarded this family of divine beings as the fount of all Magic. It is, however, not to be denied that at a later period, when degeneration of the Celtic religion occurred in Ireland, the gods at intervals appear, through one or other of their representatives, to have expressed their displeasure with Druidic motive and policy. When a beauteous lady from the Land of the Gods sought to beguile Connla, the son of Conn of the Hundred Battles, to the Land of the Living, Conn requested his Druid Coran, "of the mystic arts and the mighty incantations", to save his son from a fate so obnoxious to his father's unromantic prepossessions. At this the lady waxed wroth and declared that "the faith of the Druids has come to little honour among the upright, mighty, numberless people of this land. When the righteous law shall be restored it will seal up the lips of the false black demon: and his Druids shall not longer have power to work their guileful spells."[22] This passage is probably an interpolation from the hand of some later priestly scribe, who seized the opportunity to belittle the Druidic caste, even at the expense of justifying the pagan divinities.

It is also on record that King Cormac, "the Magnificent", whose historical era is placed at A.D. 177, attempted to put down Druidism, in revenge for which a Druid, one Maelcen, conjured up an evil spirit who placed a salmon-bone crossways in the King's throat as he sat at meat and so brought about his death.[23] How far these sentiments, unfriendly to the Druidic brotherhood, were dictated by Christian opinion we can only guess, but the aspersions of the supernatural lady in the tale of Connla certainly appear to me as a pious invention. This is scarcely surprising, as most of the ancient Irish manuscripts which treat of the Tuatha Dé were edited or rewritten by priestly scribes of the early Irish Church, who at times seem to have been unable to restrain their quite natural bias against a tradition which appeared to them to reek of the abominations of ancient sorcery. In any case, a marked difference in treatment is apparent in the accounts of the character of the Tuatha Dé at those various periods when the Irish sagas were copied and redacted.

But the Tuatha Dé Danann were not the only Irish race to indulge in Druidical practices. The Nemedians, who competed with the Fomorians for the soil of Ireland, had Druids of their own, as indeed had the Fomorians, whose spells proved too powerful for their enemies. It was these Nemedians, who had withdrawn to Scandinavia, we are informed by one text, who later returned under the designation of the Tuatha Dé Danann. While in the Northland they became expert in all the arts of divination, Druidism and philosophy. And the Milesians, who ultimately overthrew the Tuatha Dé, and who arrived in Ireland from Spain, had also Druids who proved more efficacious in their sorceries than those of the elder caste. But what we are able to glean from these confused stories of invasion proves one thing very clearly—that by the term "Druid" the Christian priesthood of Ireland intended to convey a caste of magical practitioners rather than a religious sodality. This view, however, largely arose out of prejudice, as it cannot be doubted that Druidism in Ireland was a religious as well as a magical cultus.

The early Irish Druids appear to have been grouped together in magical colleges or seminaries devoted to the study of the arcane. *The Book of the Four Masters* refers to the existence of a settlement known as Mur Ollavan, "the City of the Learned", as early as the year 927 B.C., which date, of course, may be regarded as distinctly hypothetical.[24]   Tradition speaks of "Isles of Women" in both Ireland and Scotland, where Druidesses dwelt apart from their husbands at certain seasons.   Indeed, several ancient nunneries in Ireland are conjectured to have been originally the retreats of Druidesses.   At Kildare, afterwards the shrine of St. Brigid and her sisterhood, there was in more remote times a community of Druidesses, who, like the Vestal Virgins of Rome, were charged with the upkeep of the sacred fire which burned there, and who in virtue of their office were known as *Ingheaw Andagha*, or "Daughters of Fire".   Of this sacred establishment the twelfth-century Welsh churchman Giraldus Cambrensis gives some account, laying stress upon its sanctity, yet failing to disguise its semi-pagan character, as he tells us that the holy fire was surrounded by a hedge which no male was permitted to surmount.   Nor was any plough suffered to turn a furrow in the adjoining pastures—a certain sign of pagan associations recalled in days when the earlier character of this shrine was half forgotten.[25] Tuam, with its nine-score nuns, may also originally have been a seat of Druidic women.[26]

In his *History of the Druids* Toland remarks in a note (p. 44) that a tradition existed that a Druidical college at Derry was converted into a monastery by St. Columba and he cites place-names in Anglesey as revealing the former existence of Druidic colleges in that island, particularly Tre'r Driu, "the town of the Druid", and Caer-Dreuin, "the city of the Druids" (p. 60), etymologies which, however, have been severely censured by modern authorities.   The Rev. W. L. Alexander states that a college of Druids existed in "the isle of the Druids" among the Western Isles until A.D. 563-4, when Columba arrived at Iona. Martin found that many circular hut-foundations in the Western Isles were still known in his time as "Druids' Houses", although in this connection tradition may well have been at fault.

But Ireland appears to have nourished a type of sorcerer who had no Druidic associations.   A prominent figure in Irish magical legend was the wizard Calatin, the parent of a brood of twenty-seven monstrous sons.   This family, who were known as the Clan Calatin, also embraced several female members of a peculiarly fearsome type.   Their spears, which dripped with poison, were directed by magical means so that they never failed to reach their mark. When Calatin himself was at last slain by the hero Cuchullin, Maeve, the Queen of Connaught, dispatched the wizard's daughters, three in number, to Scotland and then to Babylon, to be instructed in Magic.   When they returned some years later they were expert in every sleight of sorcery.

Maeve, on their reappearance in the island, kept them at her court until such time as she thought her old enemies of Ulster might be taken unawares. Then she let them loose with all their deadly arts upon Cuchullin, the slayer of their sire.   The three grisly harpies descended upon the meadow before the house where the hero was in conference with his allies.   They gathered grass and, mixing it with thistles, puff-balls, and withered leaves, they transformed this vegetable substance into the likeness of an armed host by the aid of their sorceries.   Suddenly the air in the vicinity of the dwelling was rent with war-cries and the boasting of trumpets, and Cuchullin, believing that his enemies had surprised him, rushed out-of-doors sword in hand.   But the Druids present assured him that the hubbub was only the result of a base enchantment made by the daughters of Calatin, which was intended to lure him to his destruction.

The party thought it well in the circumstances to withdraw to a glen which had the property of shutting out all sound, but they were followed there by the daughters of Calatin, who once more proceeded to conjure up phantom battalions. Then one of the sorceresses took the form of a woman to whom Cuchullin was much attached, and entering the place where he lay, cried out that the entire province of Ulster was ravaged and undone. This was too much for the hero, and in high wrath he seized his weapon and hastened from the silent glen, only, after being reduced to weakness by a series of magical stratagems, to meet his death on the battle-plain.[27]

In a search through Celtic literature for magicians of the more celebrated sort, we meet with the statement of Dafydd ap Gwilym, a Welsh poet of the fourteenth century, who avers that the three most famous sorcerers of Britain were Menw, Eiddilic the Dwarf (an Irish enchanter) and Math, the monarch, who appears in the *Mabinogion* tale of *Math, Son of Mathonwy*. The Welsh triads also speak of Gwydion and Uther Pendragon as practitioners of the Magic Art, and of a certain Rhuddlwm the Dwarf, whom Davies calls "the red, bony giant". The magicians of the Tuatha Dé Danann I have already alluded to, and concerning Merlin special treatment is essential. In a poem attributed by some to Taliesin, that bard vaunts his powers as an enchanter, and (if it be correctly translated) he tells us that he has associated with men skilled in the Magic Art, with Math, and with Govannon. Indeed, he describes himself as having been created by the Magic of Math, or by magicians resembling Math. In treating of the magical powers of the Celtic gods, later on, I will deal with the great thaumaturgical reputations of Gwydion and Pryderi. Gwydion, indeed, appears to have superseded Math as "druid of the gods", and certainly Llew, his son, cannot be omitted from the rôle of conspicuous Celtic wizards. Most of the outstanding Irish magicians I have alluded to in connection with incidents which reflect their arcane reputation, and these are described either in this chapter or in that which follows it.

Those mysterious regions which lay beneath the seas, and which were known to the Gaelic-speaking Celts as Lochlann and Sorcha, appear to have been the natural homes of Magic. The former seems to have been originally a peaceful enough demesne, inhabited by spirit-folk who brought fertility to the land, ensuring it plentiful harvests and numerous herds of cattle. These obscure spirits were probably the gods of a more ancient people, but later Celtic traditions regarded them as cunning and evil magicians, known as Fomorians, who dwelt in a gloomy sphere fulfilled of dark and gruesome sorceries. In short, the Celts conceived them as devils, precisely as the Christian missionaries at a later time regarded the Celtic deities as fiends or demons. In these submarine provinces Magic meets the invader at every turn, and he is much at a loss to vie with its inhabitants, who have the power to resuscitate the dead, to raise armies by a word, and change their shapes with such protean facility as to baffle the most ingenious magicians sent against them. For the original stories which narrate these florid adventures I must commend the reader to the *Popular Tales of the West Highlands*, by J. F. Campbell, the *Hibbert Lectures* of Sir John Rhys, and to the *Waifs and Strays of Celtic Tradition*, by the Rev. D. MacInnes, the Rev. James McDougal and others, as they are much too lengthy and complicated for appropriate summary in these somewhat crowded pages.

But I must not close this chapter without some more particular reference to the nature of the darksome spirits who populated the submarine localities of which I have spoken. As I have said, these were the Fomorians. The word implies "Dwellers under the Sea", and they are perhaps best described as the gods of an ancient and discredited pantheon, who were in opposition to the deities of light, as represented by the Tuatha Dé Danann, who were worshipped by a later race. They are alluded to as monstrous and misshapen forms, deformed and frequently equipped with but one leg or arm apiece, and with the heads of bulls, horses or goats. The chief of this band of demon-like creatures was that Balor, the one-eyed, of whom more than one mention has already been made. They appear to have waged continual war against the Tuatha Dé Danann, by whom they were conquered in the terrific battle of Moytura. But they were by no means crushed by this defeat and continued to harass the gods of light for generations chiefly by employing their undoubted powers of sorcery. At last they were finally routed and, says D'Arbois de Jubainville, "left Ireland and retired to their own country, that mysterious land across the ocean, where the souls of the dead find a new body and a second dwelling-place". For the gods of a conquered race almost invariably become the rulers of the Land of the Dead in the mythology of a conquering folk. Normally, they are represented in Irish literature as giants, that is they seem to have resembled the Titans of Greek myth who warred with the immortal gods of Classical tale. Their Magic does not appear to have differed in kind from that of their conquerors, yet it seems to have held for the earlier Irish tribes a terror which even the darker superstitions of Druidism could scarcely arouse. But here I must pause, and leave for another chapter the description of Celtic magical traditions as yet unrecorded.

Before closing this chapter I consider it proper to remark that quite a number of books, both "ancient and modern", purport to describe very fully, and even minutely, the entire ritual and magical circumstance of the Druidic faith and its arcane proceedings. A few of these originated with the Neo-Druidic movement in Wales and America which had its inception in the 'eighties of last century, and the greater number of them are inspired by a spirit of invention, or rely on the shaky foundations of the "Barddas" of Williams ap Ithel. Some of the older treatises are frankly imaginative to a degree. Still others of more modern provenance are simply concoctions specially written to appeal to popular credulity.

CHAPTER II

THE MAGIC ART AMONG THE CELTS (*continued*)

As in the case of Greek tradition, we find the draught of forgetfulness or healing a prominent feature of Celtic sorcery. Finn, or Fionn, leader of the Fenians, better known in legend as Finn MacCoul, possessed this virtue—that a drink given from his cupped hands would heal any wound or cure any disease. When his wife Grainne eloped with Diarmid, and that hero was wounded almost to death by the boar of Ben Gulban, he begged Finn to save him, "for when thou didst get the noble precious gift of divining at the Boinn, it was given thee that to whomsoever thou shouldst give a drink from the palms of thy hands, he should after that be young and sound from every sickness". But Finn, almost insane with jealousy, tarried so long in bearing the healing draught to his foe that when at last he approached with the life-giving water he found the Celtic Adonis beyond his aid.[1]

When Cuchullin, grieving for the beauteous Fand, the wife of the sea-god Manannan, felt no longer the urge to live, the Druids gave him a draught of forgetfulness, so that her memory troubled his mind no more.[2] Another version of the legend tells how Manannan shook his mantle of oblivion between the lovers. In the Scottish Gaelic story of *The Daughter of King Underwaves*, already alluded to, "a little man" tells Diarmid, the hero, that if he proceeds to a magic well he will there find a draught which will have the property of freeing him from his infatuation for the supernatural woman who has so greatly disturbed his life. He must put this water into a certain cup which possesses arcane virtues, dropping into it at the same time "a gulp of blood". When she drinks it he must refill the vessel and after quaffing it a second time she will be free of an ailment which torments her, while Diarmid, on his part, will lose his affection for her. All this he accomplishes, and accordingly frees himself from her spells.[3]

The magic wand wielded by the Druid magicians is a constant factor in Celtic tale. O'Curry tells us that the Druid's staff was generally made from the wood of the yew tree. In the story of Diarmid and Grainne we are informed that Reachtaire, a sorcerer, struck his son with a magic wand, thus transforming him into "a cropped pig having neither ears nor tail". Illan, a comrade of Finn, had a fairy sweetheart who was jealous of his wife. She struck her rival with a Druidic wand, turning her into the most beautiful wolf-hound which eyes ever beheld. In this condition she became the mother of the two world-famous hounds, Brann and Sceoluing, but was later restored to human form upon her husband's promising lifelong fidelity to the fairy.[4] The children of Lir were changed by strokes from a magic wand into four swans that flew over Loch Dearg for three hundred years, until released by St. Caemhoc.[5]

Dr. MacBain, writing on the subject of the magic wand of the Celts, remarks: "The Druidic wand plays an important part, a blow from it causing transformation and spells [sic]. It must be remarked, too, that the wood used for wands and Druidic rites and fires was not the oak, as in Gaul: sacred wood among the Irish Druids would appear to have been the yew, hawthorn, and more especially the rowan tree."[6] There is an allusion to a magic wand in Welsh tradition. In a song ascribed to the ancient British bard Taliesin, which is to be found in the collection known as *The Myvyrian Archaiology* (p. 62), mention is made of "the magic wand of Mathonwy, which grows in the wood, with more exuberant fruit, on the bank of the river of spectres". Mathonwy was one of the rulers of the British Underworld and thus a master of Magic by native right, though in the *Mabinogion* his son Math is styled Prince of Gwynedd in North Wales. But Math's magic wand had one association with Welsh myth, for in the tale in the *Mabinogion* which bears his name he employs it as a means of divination to discover whether the lady Arianrhod was a virgin or otherwise. The lady protested, doubtless as many another had done before her, that she was; but Math insisted that she should step over his wand, whereupon she left a child upon the floor, the famous Llew Llaw Gyffes. As she made her way, full of confusion, to the door, another child made its appearance. This was Dylan, who was later to become a marine deity. In Yorkshire they still say that "if a girl strides over a broom-handle she will be a mother before she is a wife", and it seems not improbable that the proverb may be a recollection of some such belief as we find in the above story that the chastity of a maid could be tested by stepping over a magic wand. Mr. Hartland also observes that "the broomstick is an obvious symbol such as would exactly fit the purposes of mimetic magic", and is there not a saying in some northern

English shire that if an unmarried woman has a child, "She has jumped o'er the besom"?

But it was not by aid of a wand, but rather with a javelin, that a Druid brought about the cessation of a magical drouth. A certain rebel chief conspired with another Druid in plaguing the King of Munster and his folk of the Irish south-west. One of the most harmful enchantments the magician inflicted upon this community was a spell by means of which all the water in the country was dried up. Man and beast perished and the crops began to wither, when the King succeeded in discovering a Druid of greater magical capacity than the former, who, by the expedient of casting his spear into the soil, opened up a bubbling spring at the spot where the weapon had fallen.

The raising of magical obstacles to hinder or check pursuit by an enemy was certainly a Druidic art. One of the best illustrations of it is to be found in the Scottish tale of *The Son of the King of Eirin*. This young prince vowed that he would never marry a woman whose hair was not as black as the raven's wing and whose cheek as red as its blood—a vow which seems to have been common among the Celtic aristocracy. He discovered such a maiden in the daughter of the King of the Great World, and promptly eloped with her. Her father pursued them, but the girl proved to be a sorceress of considerable resource, for she raised a forest in his path by means of working magic upon a piece of thorn, so that the pair succeeded in eluding pursuit.[7] In another tale of similar character the heroine escapes from a giant by plucking a hair out of her head and transforming it into a bridge by means of which she crosses a river.[8] In the Morayshire tale of *Nicht Nought Naething*, a giant's daughter with whom the hero has eloped, espying her father hot on their trail, takes a comb from her hair and casts it behind her. "From every one of its prongs there grew up a fine thick briar in the way of the giant." She contrives other obstacles successively with her hair-dagger, which sprouts into a *chevaux de frise*, and with a magic flask, the contents of which swell into a vast wave, which drowns the giant, "so that he was dead and dead indeed"![9]

In the occult lore of old Ireland we learn of the existence of a marvellous silver branch or bough, by virtue of which the gods lured favoured mortals to their joyous country. In some accounts of Celtic magical arts this important arcane device is frequently ignored or only partially described, and as it was the especial property of the god Manannan, who is so intimately associated with Druidic art, it appears essential to make good this deficiency and to provide a reasonably full description of it in these pages. This bough was, in effect, a link with the unseen world, a talisman by the aid of which certain mortals with whom the gods desired to establish communion and fellowship were enabled to make entrance into the overseas paradise of these divinities while yet alive.

This bough, or branch, was cut from a mystical apple tree and gave forth a magical music which none might resist. The apples which it bore served the pilgrim for meat and drink while in the Land of the Gods and during the whole period of his sojourn therein. The tree from which it had been cut grew at the door of the Court in Magh Mell, "The Plain of Honey".

> A silver tree upon which the sun shines,
> Like unto gold in its splendid lustre,

so it is described in the incident known as "The Sick-bed of Cuchullin".

Perhaps the most illuminating of the tales concerning it is that which recounts the manner in which Cormac MacAirt, the High King of Ireland, was lured to the Paradise of the gods by its agency. As Cormac was walking in the plain adjacent to his palace he observed a young man who held in his hand a wonderful branch which had nine golden apples depending from it. When the youth shook this branch, the apples, beating against each other, made sweet and mystic music, so that·he who heard it straightway forgot his sorrow and care. It had also the property of lulling folk into a magical oblivion. Cormac asked the young man if he would sell the branch, and to his dismay the youth demanded his wife, son and daughter in exchange for the bauble. The King, temporarily deranged by the music it gave forth, agreed to the bargain. At first his wife and children naturally expressed .themselves as horrified by his rashness, but after Cormac had shaken the silver branch and compelled it to discourse music, they at once forgot their dismay at the manner in which he had disposed of them and departed with the young man joyfully enough.

But after a year had passed, Cormac longed to see his wife and children once more, and set out to find them. A magic cloud enveloped him and soon he found himself in a wonderful plain, where he entered a fine house, in which he encountered a supernatural pair whom he knew by certain tokens to be Manannan, the god of the sea, and his wife. After some delay Cormac's wife, son and daughter entered the hall, and Manannan admitted that it was he who had taken them away from Cormac, as it had been his main intention to lure him to his happy country by this means. Cormac and his wife and family slept that night in the house of Manannan, and when they awoke in the morning it was to find themselves in their palace at Tara, with the silver branch and other magical articles beside them.[10] The magical properties of this branch were also brought to bear upon Bran, the son of Febal, who was likewise decoyed through its agency to the country of the gods, where he sojourned in an island solely inhabited by women.[11]

The Silver Bough is a salient feature of Gaelic legend as the Golden Bough is of Classical myth. So far as the Golden Bough of Italic tradition is concerned (that is the Bough of the Arician legend immortalized by Sir James Frazer), Andrew Lang has made it self-evident that that particular branch was not, as Frazer believed, identical with the Golden Bough which the Trojan hero Æneas used as a passport to the world of the dead, as narrated by Vergil, but a talisman of a very different character. The likelihood is that it was merely a token plucked by the successful combatant in a struggle for the office of priesthood to the deity of the Arician grove. The Celtic Silver Bough, on the other hand, appears as the equivalent of the *genuine* Golden Bough mentioned by Vergil as a passport to the Land of the Gods and has no association in folk-lore with the Arician bough, although Mr. Cook has intimated his belief that it possessed such associations.[12]

The magical stone of the kings of Ireland which was situated at Tara, and which recognized the true High King of that island by emitting a loud shriek when he stood upon it, has also Druidic associations. It is identified by knowledgeable writers with the Lia Fail, and is indeed the original Lia Fail, as I hope to make plain in my remarks upon it in another chapter. One of the earliest tales concerning it tells how King Conn of the Hundred Battles repaired one morning at sunrise to the battlements of the Ri Raith, or royal fortress at Tara, accompanied by his three Druids, Mael, Bloc and Bluicné, and his three bards Ethain, Corb and Cesare, for the purpose of watching the firmament, so that no hostile being from the air might suddenly descend upon Erin unknown to him. While perambulating the battlements, Conn chanced to tread on a stone, which immediately shrieked under his feet so loudly as to be heard all over Tara, and throughout all East Meath. He asked his Druids to explain the omen to him, and so profound was its significance that they required fifty-three days to arrive at a decision respecting the phenomenon. At length they told him that the name of the stone was Fal and that it hailed from Inis Fal, or the island of Fal. "It has shrieked under your royal feet," they said, "and the number of shrieks it has given forth is the number of kings that will succeed you."[13] Later, a supernatural being, no other than the god Lugh, led Conn away to his residence to inform him of the length of his reign and the names and fortunes of his successors.

This stone, the Lia Fail, was one of the four precious things brought to Ireland by the Tuatha Dé Danann. Rhys associates it with the property of light, and this he refers to its connection with a sun-god "in his earlier identification with the sun. In other words, it was a fetish connected with his worship". He further identifies the stone with the worship of Nuada, the principal Gaelic sun-god, and thinks that Tara was his high-place. The recognition of Conn by the stone was the last instance of its functioning as an oracle, as, at the birth of Christ, its "heart" sprang out of it as far as the village of Tailltenn, where it was known as "Fal's Heart". Now Tailltenn and its sun-festival were associated with the god Lugh, and this would seem to imply "nothing less than the eclipsing of the older god's glory by that of the younger", that is that Lugh superseded Nuada.[14] Some pregnant observations concerning the Lia Fail may also be found in Professor Macalister's work *Tara*, one of the most notable essays upon the supernatural and ritualistic associations of the ancient Irish kings yet forthcoming, and which reveals the high standard maintained by Celtic scholarship in our time.

I now wish to draw attention to a passage in British magical narrative which raises certain problems in connection with the personal identity of the Druid Merlin, some of which it will be more appropriate to deal with at a later stage when considering the arcane position of that important figure. In this place I shall follow the account as it is to be found in the seventeenth chapter of the Sixth Book of Geoffrey of Monmouth's *Histories of the British Kings*. The British ruler, Vortigern, dismayed at the result of his unworthy conspiracy with the invading Saxons, through which the nobility of Britain had been decimated at Stonehenge, consulted his Magi (in all likelihood the Druids are intended here) as to his personal safety. They advised him to build as a refuge a tower of exceeding strength on Mount Eryri, or Snowdon. He assembled a large number of masons at the spot and the work was duly proceeded with. But the building of the stronghold was nightly interrupted by some occult force, the foundations being swallowed up by the soil so that no man knew what had caused such an upheaval. The King's soothsayers arrived at the conclusion that only by seeking out a fatherless boy, slaying him and sprinkling his blood over the foundation stones could the building of the tower be carried on—a memory of the ancient belief that by an act of human sacrifice alone could the powers who disturbed the soil be placated. After a long search they succeeded in discovering such a lad, whose mother was a daughter of the King of Demetia and a nun.

The boy in question, whom Geoffrey calls "Ambrosius Merlin", indicated that Vortigern's wizards were in error, and assured him that the real cause of the nightly disturbance of the foundations of the tower was the presence of two dragons beneath the site, which did battle one with the other, thus overthrowing the structure. Vortigern commanded that the site should be excavated, and it was found that the monsters actually had their lairs in a pool beneath the soil. All were naturally confounded at the wisdom displayed by the boy, and deemed that he was "possessed by some spirit of God".

In the Prophecies of Merlin, as given by Geoffrey in his Seventh Book, we

STONEHENGE RESTORED

DANCE OF FAIRIES
(From an old English chap-book—Fairy hill, with door on left)

CAVALIER ENTERING A FAIRY MOUND
(Olaus Magnus, "History of the Goths")

find that the leviathans who had overthrown Vortigern's castle in its early stages were red and white in hue, the former being symbolic of the Britons, while his rival represented the Saxons. The latter, predicted Merlin Ambrosius, would prevail for a time, but in the end the white dragon should be "rooted out". The red dragon was immemorially associated with the British race. It was the crest of Uther, the father of Arthur, who, in the mythological sense, was himself a dragon, and bore the title of "Pendragon", that is "Chief" or "Great Dragon". Algernon Herbert translates the name as "The Terrible One with the Dragon's Head",[15] while Mr. R. Briffault describes Uther as "a dragon".[16] There does not, however, as Mr. E. K. Chambers remarks, appear to be any ground for the assumption that Uther was the father of Arthur, or that this descent is drawn from genuine ancient Celtic sources, Geoffrey being the first to allude to it, although such a view cannot interfere with the identification of Uther with the dragon in a symbolical sense.[17] In the story of "Llud and Llevelys" as given in the Welsh *Mabinogion* we find that these dragons had disturbed the isle of Britain five hundred years before the events narrated above and that King Llud, to put an end to their strife, dug a great pit at Oxford, in which he placed a large tank of mead, concealed by a covering of satin. In time the dragons appeared in the air, and fought frantically until they fell upon the satin cloth and duly sank into the mead. Llud then wrapped them in the cloth and buried them upon the site in the Snowdon district, near Beddgelert, still known as Dinas Emrys.

Raising the dead, or bringing them back to life, appears to have been included among the principles of Celtic Magic. We have already seen that the Tuatha Dé Danann were able to resuscitate those Athenians slain in battle with the Syrians by sending spirits into their dead bodies. When Bran, the great British god-enchanter, invaded Ireland for the purpose of liberating his sister Branwen from the tyranny of her Irish husband King Matholwch, he found that a magic cauldron which he had given to his brother-in-law was being made use of to restore to life those Irish warriors who had been slain in the course of the combat betwixt the Britons and the Hibernians. But his crafty brother Evnissyen disguised himself as an Irish champion and lay on the ground as though dead. He was duly placed by the Irish in the cauldron, when he stretched himself spasmodically, and with one mighty effort burst both the magic vessel and his own heart.[18] We also learn that the British gods Manawyddan and Pryderi, rulers of the Underworld, had among their treasures the Three Birds of Rhiannon, which could sing the dead to life and the living to death.[19]

Among the gods of the Celts we find the practice of Magic continually recurring. The British god Math, brother to that mysterious Don, on whom the entire British Pantheon of light looked as a mother, was regarded as a ruler of the Underworld, although he appears to have lacked any of the usual affrighting characteristics of plutonic deities. In the *Mabinogion* he is represented as a magician *par excellence*, and as passing on his arcane gifts to his nephew Gwydion, who, through the knowledge thus attained, became the "Druid" of the gods, the master of illusion and phantasy, and the instructor of mankind in all the useful arts of life.[20] In the same way the Irish hero Cuchullin was instructed by Cathbad the Druid, who had, he said, "made him a master of inquiry in the arts of the god of Druidism or magic and rendered him skilled in all that was excellent in visions". Here we should particularly remark the term "*dé druidechta*", which means in Gaelic "of the god of Druidism". This phrase, thought Rhys, "doubtless meant the divinity with whom the Druids had to do, and with whose aid they practised their magical arts. We are not, unfortunately, told the name of the god; but it is natural to suppose that it was the chief of the Goidelic pantheon, and this is practically settled by the kind of miracles which the Druids are usually represented as able to perform with most success in their competition with the early saints engaged in the task of Christianizing Ireland. These miracles may be described as mostly atmospheric, consisting of such feats as bringing on a heavy snow, palpable darkness or a great storm."[21] Rhys equates the British god Math with the Goidelic "god of Druidism" alluded to above, who was probably Nuada. Math was able to hear without difficulty "every sound of speech that reached the air", he was utterly righteous and just in his dealings with gods and men, he was the great diviner, teacher, and master of omens.

As we have seen, Gwydion appears to have succeeded Math as "druid of the gods". Gwydion wed with his sister Arianrhod, who disowned the only surviving son of the union, the great British sun-god, Llew Llaw Gyffes, "the Long-handed one of Light", and refused to give him a name. Llew was also gifted with Magic.[22] But the chief arcane triumph of the British gods was certainly the creation of the famous damsel Blodeuwedd, or "Flower-face", whom Math and Gwydion made out of flowers, the blossoms of broom, of oak, and meadowsweet, the most exquisite creature whom mankind had yet beheld. She was given to Llew as his wife. But she betrayed her too trusting husband, and the manner in which she did so has become, more by reason of its obscurity than anything else, one of the most famous passages in British arcane literature.

The story of Blodeuwedd is to be found in the *mabinogi*, or tale, of *Math, Son of Mathonwy*. The faithless flower-maiden fell in love with Gronwy Pevr, Lord of Penllyn, and the pair resolved to rid themselves of Llew. Blodeuwedd beguiled her husband into a revelation of the one and only way in which he might be despatched. The spear which alone could slay him must be a year in the making and could be made only on Sundays, during the time when Mass was being celebrated. Llew could not be killed either in a house or in the open, nor on horseback, nor afoot. Being of the seed divine, his life had been most carefully environed with magical prohibitions and safeguards. But, he confided to his wife, these difficulties might be overcome "by making me a bath on the bank of a river, and making a round roof above the vat, and thatching it well and snugly after that, and bringing a he-goat and placing it beside the vat, and by placing one foot on the back of the he-goat and the other on the edge of the vat". Whoever should smite him with a spear prepared in accordance with the above instructions and while he was in such a position would compass his death.

It is plain that here we are confronted by an example of that simple cunning which appears to have been associated with early Magic. The gods might, by their divine powers, decree the safety of a great hero or demi-god, yet it was possible for any crafty little nonentity to overthrow and bring to naught all their designs by the exercise of low cunning, and, by some tricky device, worthy of the "Philadelphia lawyer" of tradition, to overreach them and cause the ruin of their most illustrious favourites. Gronwy, advised by the treacherous Blodeuwedd, set about making the fatal weapon which was to take the life of her husband, and when the time was ripe she caused him to take up a position of vantage under the lee of a hill. She then begged Llew to give her a practical demonstration of the lethal position which he had described to her. In answer to her request he betook himself to a bath which she had built to his "specifications", thus displaying less of divine acumen than most mortals would have credited him with. All the accessories had been carefully prepared. Llew bathed, reassumed his nether garments, and placed one of his feet on the edge of the bath, the other on the back of the goat. Gronwy, espying his opportunity, cast the fatal spear. But Llew, instead of falling dead, was changed into an eagle and flew away with discordant cries.

His uncle Gwydion at once went in search of him and at last discovered him in what seems to have been an advanced state of decomposition. Gwydion struck the eagle with his magic wand, so that he reassumed human shape, but the hapless Llew had lost flesh and was now nothing but skin and bone. With the assistance of the best physicians in the country he regained his health within a year's time. Gwydion transformed Blodeuwedd into an owl, while Llew compelled Gronwy to assume the same position at the bath which had been so nearly fatal to himself, and while he was in that attitude, slew him.

In his notable essay *Math vab Mathonwy* Professor W. J. Gruffydd reveals at great length and with surprising ingenuity, which, however, is fortified by the soundest reasoning, the sources and origins of this tangled mythic scheme. He makes it plain that in the first instance the plot was drawn from early Irish sources, probably imported by Hibernian immigrants into North Wales, yet greatly garbled by time and circumstance until it has assumed a form almost entirely dissimilar from the original models whence it was drawn. He shows that the adjuncts of the bath, the he-goat, and so forth have all been assumed either from Irish or other European story-incidents which have more or less commonly recurred in early fiction. But I cannot hope in the course of a brief statement to demonstrate the extraordinarily thorough and painstaking skill with which he has unwound this ancient skein and has so dissected it that all its factors and component parts are made visible to the reader.

Diancecht, the Irish god of leechcraft, was also a distinctly magical figure. He treated a certain well with magic herbs and every wounded warrior who was plunged into its water overnight was fit for combat on the morrow. Manannan MacLir, the Irish sea-god, is said to have been a Druid, one Manannan Mac Oirbsen, who rose to a position of godhead.[23] He could "transform himself into many shapes by wizardry". He travelled in his magic boat made of copper, the "Wave-sweeper", which needed neither oar nor rudder.[24] He was the possessor of a famous magical mantle, which, if shaken between two persons, made it impossible for them to meet again. This may be an allegory of the fog which sweeps across the Irish Channel, fit symbol of severance by Magic. Vivien, the Lady of the Lake, possesses a similar mantle, symbolizing the mist which rises from water. The god Angus, another Irish deity, is also the owner of a magic cloak which could render him invisible, while Caswallan, the British hero who robbed Manawyddan, the British sea-god, of his lands and sovereignty, was the wearer of a magical tartan which conferred invisibility upon its wearer.[25]

The combats between the British gods of light and darkness are fulfilled of magical incidents. The hounds of Manawyddan and Pryderi, we are told, one day roused a white boar which took refuge in a magic castle, and was followed by the pack. The gods entered the castle, but signs of neither boar nor hounds could they perceive. In the courtyard stood an exquisite fountain, to which was attached a rich golden bowl. Pryderi raised the bowl to examine it, whereupon his hands cleaved to it so that it was impossible to disengage them. Manawyddan returned to his wife Rhiannon, who accompanied him to the castle, where she did her utmost to free Pryderi from his embarrassing position. But despite her efforts her hands also adhered to the bowl, and with a clap of thunder the castle vanished, along with the two captives.

Later Manawyddan found that the wheat growing upon his lands was disappearing, ear by ear. Convinced that the same enemy who had carried off Pryderi and Rhiannon was the author of this fresh outrage, he kept watch over the grain. At midnight he heard a great tumult, and beheld a host of mice biting off the ears of grain. He succeeded in catching one, decided to hang the animal, and had just made a small gallows for the purpose, when a man dressed like a travelling scholar accosted him and asked what he was about to do. On being informed of his intention, the stranger offered Manawyddan money to liberate the mouse, but this was refused. Still other men addressed him in the field, offering him considerable bribes to free the creature, but to the last of these, who was habited like a bishop, he declared that the only price he would entertain for the animal's life was that Pryderi and Rhiannon should be set at liberty, for naturally his suspicions had been aroused by his visitors' manifest anxieties as to the fate of the mouse. The "Bishop" turned out to be Llwyd, a magician, and the mouse his wife, whom, with his servitors, he had transformed for the purpose of stripping Manawyddan of his harvest to wipe off an ancient grudge he had against the god. Rhiannon and Pryderi were at once trans- ported to the spot, the fields resumed their prosperous appearance, and the mouse returned to human shape. All of which we learn from the *mabinogi* of *Manawyddan the Son of Llyr*.

The Irish saga of *The Fate of the Children of Tuirenn* teems with magical incidents. Lugh, the sun-god, had slain certain Fomorians who oppressed his people as tax-gatherers, and in revenge his father Cian was slain by the sons of Tuirenn—Brian, Iuchar and Iucharba. In vain did Cian assume the form of a pig, for the brethren penetrated his disguise and killed him. Lugh, to punish them for the crime, extorted from them the heaviest fine he could think of—that they must filch and present him with three apples from the Garden of the Hesperides; the skin of a pig belonging to King Tuis of Greece, the touch of which cured wounded persons; the spear of Pisear, King of Persia; the horses and chariot of Dobhar, King of Sicily; the seven pigs of Easal, King of the Golden Pillars; the hound-whelp of the King of Ioruaidhe, which could catch a wild beast on seeing it; and the cooking-spit of the women of the isle of Fian- chuive, which lay at the bottom of the sea between Scotland and Ireland. It was also ordained that they must give three shouts on the hill of Cnoc Miodhchaoin, in the land of Lochlann, a most dangerous proceeding when the character of its inhabitants fell to be considered. These seven objects, animals and performances appear to have constituted something in the nature of the seven wonders of the world according to Celtic tradition, and all of them have doublets in Celtic lore. The apples are found in Celtic stories of the Overseas paradise, the lance approximates to that of the god Lugh, the hound resembles Brann, the famous dog of Finn, the pigs are similar to those of Manannan and the British god Arawn, the horses equate with the steeds of Manannan, and the cooking-spit is reminiscent of that made by the god-smith Gobniu.

The adventures of the trio are much too long and complicated even to summarize, but in the course of them the brethren transform themselves into divers birds and animals, wage many combats, descend into the depths of the ocean, and at last succeed in achieving all but one of the labours set them. But before they had time to give the three shouts on the hill of Miodhchaoin, Lugh wove a Druidical spell round them so that they utterly forgot this part of their task and sailed back to Ireland, whereupon the cunning god challenged them with the omission. At the hill in question they were so sorely wounded that they had much ado to return to Eire, where they gradually succumbed to their injuries.[26] The reason for the inclusion of this tale in the present chapter is that not only does it reveal certain magical traits, but it is also associated with a series of weapons and other objects which we will encounter once more when we come to consider the implications of the Grail legend.

Let us consider briefly some other magical weapons as they are described in Celtic lore. The magical spear is usually manufactured by a certain smith and for a certain purpose. The Celtic smith is almost invariably an arcane figure with uncanny associations, a wizard capable of making supernatural weapons, an idea that may have descended from the Bronze or Iron Ages when metals were novel elements and appeared to possess supernatural attributes of sharpness and life-taking quality. It is a smith who prepares the spear which takes the life of Balor, the Fomorian cyclops-god with one eye, into which Lugh, his grandson, plunges the weapon in revenge for the slaying of his sire, MacKineely. That smith is the Irish god Gobniu, and brother to MacKineely. Llew, as we have seen, was discomfited in great measure by the casting of a magic spear from the hand of his wife's paramour Gronwy. This spear was wrought on Sundays only, during the time of Mass, and it was essential that its making should occupy an entire year. Thus it seems to have some arcane association with time, astrological or otherwise. That the atmosphere was full of spirits associated with the luminaries of heaven who were at particular seasons of the year supposed to strike down mortals with darts or arrows which communicated diseases such as epilepsy is a very ancient superstition, common to many countries so far apart as Britain and ancient Mexico, and the magic spear may indeed have been a confused reminiscence of this belief.

The Irish sun-god Lugh was also the possessor of a magical spear which seems to have symbolized a ray of the sun. It was gifted with an individual life of its own and was so thirsty for blood that it could be kept from slaying only by steeping its head in an infusion of poppy leaves which acted as a narcotic upon it. On the day of battle it was taken out of this brew, when it called out mightily, lashing itself into a frenzy and emitting flashes of fire. When freed, it launched itself against the ranks of the enemy in a tireless orgy of slaughter.

We also encounter numerous references to magical swords in Celtic romance. The Irish sea-god Manannan had three such weapons, "The Retaliator", "The Great Fury", and "The Little Fury". His compatriot divinity, Nuada "of the Silver Hand", possessed that particular blade which is associated with the traditions of the Tuatha Dé Danann. Finn MacCoul was the owner of a notable sword, the Macan Luin, which had been made especially for him by his grandfather. It was of so fine an edge that a second blow with it was needless. It had been tempered in the blood of "a living thing", to wit that of a hound. It is scarcely necessary to mention Excalibur, the sword of Arthur, in a catalogue of Celtic magical weapons, nor does its fame require that one should do so.

From time immemorial the Celtic peoples have retained the custom at religious and other ceremonies of walking in procession right-handwise, that is "with the sun", or keeping to the right in a circular motion. That this custom proceeds from an ancient cult of sun-worship is scarcely questionable. In Irish and Scottish Gaelic this motion is known as *deiseal* (pron. dyāsh-al), that is "right-handwise", and is regarded as propitious because in harmony with the movement of the sun. Its opposite, *tuathal* (pron. tŭae-al), or circling to the left, is considered ominous, and is known in England and Lowland Scotland as "widdershins", or "withershins", derived from the Anglo-Saxon "wither" meaning "against" and "sith" or "sins", "to walk". Toland says that the common people in the Western Isles of Scotland in his day (the late seventeenth and early eighteenth centuries), invariably walked round cairns when they had occasion to be in their neighbourhood, three times, from east to west, Protestants as well as Catholics. "This custom," he says, "was us'd three thousand years ago, and God knows how long before, by their ancestors the ancient Gauls, of the same religion with them, who turn'd round right-handwise when they worshipped their gods."[27]   The people of Colonsay, be-fore any enterprise, passed "sunways around the church" and turned their boats about in the same direction.   Wedding processions in the Highlands and baptismal parties frequently passed round the church in this direction, and herdsmen danced three times sunways around the fire at the *Bealltainn* festi-vals.[28]   To proceed in the opposite way was almost invariably the habit of the practitioners of the Black Art.   A Scottish witch, Jonet Forsyth, who was refused corn by a neighbour, walked round a stack "contrair to the sunis cours", with consequent injury to the grain, as did many others of the sister-hood when thwarted.[29]

I must now say something concerning one of the strangest figures in Celtic sorcery, one indeed whose appearance in its records is fraught with a certain mystery.   This was none other than the celebrated Simon Magus, the sorcerer alluded to in the eighth chapter of the Acts of the Apostles, who bewitched the people of Samaria and led them to believe that he was possessed of divine power.   St. Peter angrily repulsed him when he sought to purchase his con-version with money.   Later tradition averred that he betook himself to Rome, where he once more came into collision with Peter, parading his magical power by flying through the air in public.   The apostle breathed a vehement prayer for judgment upon him, whereupon the magician crashed to earth. Tradition adds that he died from the effects of the fall.

In Irish legend Simon Magus is said to have aided the Druid Mog Ruith in making his celebrated wheel, the *Roth Fail*, which had the property of bear-ing the Druid through the heavenly spaces.   But, like the flying machine of the British god Bladud, of whom we read in Geoffrey of Monmouth's *History*, it met with an accident.   Mog Ruith's daughter Tlachtga conveyed some of its fragments to Ireland, one of which she erected as the pillar-stone of Cnam-choill, near Tipperary.   In Celtic tradition its conveyance to Eire was looked upon as a dire calamity, and as fraught with extreme danger to the island's destinies.   Rhys was of opinion that the fierce denunciation of Christianity by the Irish Druids resulted in the apostate Simon Magus becoming identified in a manner with the pagan Druidic caste.   Again, the word "Druid" was trans-lated into Latin as "Magus", or magician, and as it was so frequently associated with Simon, the terms "Druid" and "Simon Magus" appear to have become interchangeable.   Indeed, Simon was familiarly known in Ireland as "Simon the Druid".

But the *Roth Fail*, "the wheel of light", was symbolic of the sun and as such came to be confused or identified, as in the story of Bladud, with a magic flying-machine which traversed the heavens, and therefore with the machine by which Simon is said to have aided his flights in Rome.[30]   The myth, on the whole, is similar to the Greek tale of Icarus, whose father Daedalus con-structed a pair of wings by which the youth flew through the air.   But the heat of the sun melted the wax which held them together, so that he fell to his death into the waters of the Ægean Sea.

At least one Roman author, Varro, tells us that the Druids practised walking on fire at some of their annual festivals.   They walked slowly, he tells us, over a bed of burning coals, but he adds that they were able to accomplish this by the aid of a certain ointment with which they previously besmeared the soles of their feet.   The practice, a very ancient one, has an almost world-wide recurrence.   The *Gabha-Bheil*, or trial by Beli, a later Irish ceremony, compelled a suspected person to pass three times with bare feet through a fire as a proof of innocence, and at the *Bealltainn* festival young men leapt through the fire, doubtless a "memory" of human sacrifice. Otherwise, I cannot find any justification for the statement of Varro, although it appears to me not at all improbable.

In some Irish and Highland tales we find mention of magical cups possessing occult properties. Thus in the West Highland story of *Finn MacCoul and the Bent Grey Lad* the hero is dispatched in search of "the quadrangular cup of the Fenians" which the King of Lochlann had filched from them.[31] Any drink a man desired might be had from it, in which quality it seems to resemble the Grail vessel and the magic cup given by King Oberon to Huon of Bordeaux. In the tale of Uistean we encounter a cup which had the property of curing the dumb.[32] Good fortune accompanies the cup known as the Luck of Edenhall, but if it ever be broken the luck fails. Peace and plenty are the portion of the family which retains the cup of Ballafletcher, in the Isle of Man, but serious consequences associated with spiritual visitation would ensue did it meet with an accident.[33]

The act of compassing the death of an enemy by means of magic wrought upon an image or effigy in his likeness was known to and practised by the Celts both in ancient and modern times. Boethius (Hector Boece) alludes to a case of this description in his *History of Scotland* in connection with a conspiracy said to have been directed against the life of Duffus or Odo, one of the early Scottish kings, who flourished towards the end of the tenth century. This monarch was seized with a nameless distemper without any ostensible cause. He could not sleep and wasted away because of painful and incessant sweatings. Certain sorceresses in the town of Forres were suspected of a design to destroy him, and the miscreants were at last discovered in the act of basting an image of the king at a fire, reciting occult verses the while. When arrested, they confessed that their art had been revealed to them by demons and that the leading men of the province of Moray had employed them to slay the king by the means described. The image was destroyed—a risky proceeding in the circumstances, as we shall see—and the sorceresses expiated their guilt in the flames. Meanwhile the King recovered the exercise of all his normal faculties, leading an army against the rebel chiefs who had conspired against his life and punishing them as they deserved. The occurrence is not alluded to by other Scottish historians with the exception of Buchanan, who merely quotes Boece, and having regard to the general untrustworthiness of its original recorder, it may perhaps be quite apocryphal. At the same time it seems to reveal that the practice to which it alludes was known and recognized in early Scotland.[34]

Images of this kind were, in the mediaeval period, usually made of wax, which would readily melt at a flame, thus presumably causing a wasting of the flesh in the hapless victim. But the specimens of such images—"pictures", as the older witches weirdly described them—known to later times, were generally modelled in clay, and were known in the Highlands as the *corp creidh*, or the "clay body". This effigy was placed on a board before a large and constantly replenished fire. Thorns, pins and needles were pushed into the still yielding clay, "elf-arrows" or primitive flint darts were cast at it to the accompaniment of dreadful oaths and imprecations, and finally the image was broken in pieces, upon which the victim was thought to yield up the ghost, blue flames issuing from his mouth![35]

This terrible instrument of Celtic vengeance, the invention of a sentiment unrestrained in its ferocity in remoter ages, and perhaps at times even in our own, has only of late been more generally discarded. Not so many years ago a *corp creidh* was discovered in a Highland burn, where it had been so disposed that the action of the water might wear it slowly away—the inference being that the unfortunate person who had earned the hatred of its maker might suffer the pangs of a lingering decline.

Rhys, writing on the subject of such figures, describes a *corp creidh* housed in the Pitt-Rivers Museum at Oxford. It is made from clay and stuck full of pins and nails. The specimen in question hails from a neighbourhood in Inverness-shire and is the gift of a Major G—— of that county. "It was intended for the Major", and was discovered by workmen at his front door. A similar experience, Sir John remarked, happened to a minister in the Highlands, who was observed to be wasting away. His friends instituted a search, when a *corp creidh* was discovered in a stream hard by his house.[86] It is impossible, when dealing with such a topic, to repress an exclamation of disgust and regret that proceedings so abominable could happen in a country confessedly Christian. It is not the insane idea that such dastardly means are actually effective that depresses one so much as the hateful and treacherous state of mind which prompts their use. But most students of the occult and of folk-lore are only too well aware that abominations of the kind are still occasionally indulged in, not only by the ignorant, but by persons in the higher ranks of society upon whom an enlightened training has evidently been wasted. Within recent years, too, sheeps' hearts stuck full of pins have been discovered in the chimneys of cottages in the Highlands and in Wales, revealing a comparatively recent resort to a practice intended to do mortal hurt to an enemy.

The minutiae of Magic are well illustrated by Celtic tale. In the West Highland story of *The Three Soldiers* their three supernatural sweethearts bestow upon them a towel or napkin, a magic whistle and a purse. The first contains "every kind of meat" on each occasion it is spread; the second, when blown, ensures that the blower will be in the midst of his regiment; while the third will be found full of gold and silver every time its strings are unloosed. The three articles are beguiled from the soldiers by the stratagems of a king's daughter. But the napkin also possesses the property of a magic carpet, resembling those known to Oriental tale, for when one of the soldiers stands upon it in company with the Princess and wishes to be in "the uttermost isle of the deep", the pair speedily find themselves in such a locality. The Princess, once more placing herself upon the napkin, wishes herself back in Dublin, while the soldier sleeps, and on awaking he finds himself marooned on the island. He feels the pangs of hunger and discovers two kinds of apples in an orchard. One variety causes horns to sprout upon the eater's head, while the other as swiftly removes them. A vessel conveniently passes the island and bears the soldier back to Dublin, where he assumes the guise of a vendor of apples, and sells some of the harmful variety to the Princess, who partakes of them, with the result that horns appear on her head. Her hand in marriage is offered by the King her father to anyone who will rid her of this deformity, and the soldier effects the cure by supplying her with the antidote, but prefers to accept a large fee for his services rather than risk matrimony with a lady of a disposition so equivocal.[87]

There is indeed no end to the minor marvels of Magic in Celtic tale. The ears of friendly horses and bulls are the repositories not only of food and drink, but magical toys of the most fantastic description are also to be found there, concealed in fruit—golden cocks that crow, diminutive women who sew and spin, magic shears which function of themselves.[88] And here I may appropriately remark upon the bizarre character of Celtic story no less than upon its delicate spirit of invention, which equals that of any body of similar fiction and far surpasses all in its remote loveliness and quality of elfin magic, repaying the imaginative reader a millionfold. In its record, indeed, the entire gamut of magical potency is expressed and in such a manner as to make it clear that the incidents it details are not donations from alien fiction or importations, but are rather descended from a common and greatly ancient fabric of human tradition, which its inherent spirit of marvel and craftsmanship has raised to a keener level of artistic performance.

I will not here forecast the ultimate conclusions I have arrived at on the subject of Celtic magical origins, as considerations associated with the material still to be discussed in future chapters make it incumbent that such a theory of origin must embrace them also. Speaking in a general sense, however, I may remark that only as regards a few essentials do we discover in Celtic Magic any marked difference from that of other European races. Most of the magical data I have already reviewed is familiar in the records of nearly all European magical systems—the raising of fogs or mists, change of scene by illusion, transformation and shape-shifting, the draught of healing or forgetfulness, the magic wand, the raising of magical obstacles, magical practice on the part of the gods—indeed all the arcane apparatus of the Celt appears to be of the selfsame species as that known to other European peoples and indeed to Asiatic and American races. Yet the treatment is vastly different in its superior aesthetic presentation. It is only when we approach the deeper questions involved in the discussion of Celtic mysticism that a marked difference becomes apparent in the spirit and *materiel*. It is in connection with such questions as reincarnation and metempsychosis, the legend of the Grail and the vexed topic of Neo-Druidism that the insistence of the Celtic mentality in placing its own stamp and seal upon mystical thought is fully revealed. Indeed, the seeming lack of any distinction between Celtic exterior or technical Magic and that displayed by other races and the sharp differentiation betwixt Celtic mysticism and the arcane thought of other European systems make it plain that the Celtic mind realized the relative unimportance of the former and expressed a fuller preference for the latter because of its greatly more vital significance for the human spirit. It is appropriate, now as ever, that the would-be initiate should realize that the Magic of the material and the outward is but a vain thing when compared with that great body of arcane knowledge which treats of the divine and lofty mission of the soul, whether it be associated with the Celtic race or with any other section of humanity.

CHAPTER III

THE PROBLEM OF DRUIDISM

THE protracted controversy concerning the nature and origins of Druidism may be said to date from the first appearance of John Toland's *A Critical History of the Celtic Religion and Learning*, containing an account of the Druids, written in 1718–19. Numerous highly debatable and ancillary questions were associated with the main theme, and the arguments aroused by these resolved themselves into a *kulturkampf* of such heat and violence that by the middle of the Victorian era "reasonable people" came to regard Druidism as a topic to be avoided because of the militant attitude of those who so fiercely discussed its

problems.   It appeared to provide a platform upon which the retired Anglo-
Indian officer, the village rector and the social bore, indeed every description of crank and eccentric, might rant and vapour to his heart's content.   The
very difficulties of elucidation it presented appeared only to spur the fantastic
folk who endlessly argued its details to even greater extravagances of fanciful
definition, remote analogy, empirical etymology, and wilder dialectic fury.
The Druids, they declared with many voices, were Brahmins, Egyptians,
Phoenicians, Atlanteans or Orpheans.   They were the Cabiri disguised in
British habiliments.   Their philosophy was demonstrably a provincial réchauf-
fé of Pythagoreanism.   Their powers of Magic were described as limitless,
their wisdom as profound and unfathomable.

From across the Channel were wafted the echoes of a similar altercation.
France, the "dear enemy", even during the scarlet days of the Revolution and
in the death-throes of the Napoleonic regime, poured out books and pamphlets
relating to the Druidic theory.   Druidism, French opinion maintained, was
of Gallic provenance and it was a final impertinence on the part of perfidious
Albion to claim it as a Britannic system.   As the controversy grew, and the
accents of the Scottish and Irish Celt mingled with those of Wales, London and
Cornwall, Brittany and Paris, prudent gentlemen in stocks and side-whiskers
looked askance when the name of Druid was mentioned and hastily changed
the subject.

Today the hubbub of argument has fallen to a susurrus of cryptic
muttering.   In official archaeological circles and among Welsh critics of standing it appears to be fashionable to deny that Druidism ever existed in Britain.
Another group, while grudgingly admitting its existence, describes it as the
instrument of a debased and barbarous fetishism on a parallel with that of the
Central African witch-doctor or the Tatar shaman.

Heaven forbid that I should awake once more the incandescent fires and
furious rejoinders of slumbering controversy.   But the schools of opposition, it
seems to me, err as egregiously as did the all-too-perfervid protagonists of the
Druidic hypothesis.   In his insistence in stripping the archaeological scene
of every vestige of the romance and mystery which formerly surrounded it, the
modern antiquary, suffering from the credulity of incredulity, that bane of
present-day science, has assuredly not accorded to the question of Druidism the
investigation which its importance certainly demands.   I hope in the following pages to be able to prove at least that Druidism, as practised among the
Celts, was not only a cult far removed from the abject, but one which reached
a considerably higher level of idealistic achievement than most modern authorities are willing to admit.   But before attempting to arrive at conclusions, it
will be necessary to review carefully what we know authentically concerning
Druidism, its priesthood and general circumstances within the British Isles
and elsewhere.

Even the very name of "Druid" has been the subject of obstinate contention.   Generally, and probably because of a statement of Pliny the Elder, it
has been interpreted as referring to the Greek word *drus*, "an oak".[1]   Rhys,
criticizing this, remarks that no recourse need be had to Hellenic sources, and
finds the genesis of the term in the ancient Gaulish Celtic name for that tree.[2]
George Henderson, following Thurneysen, translates the word as *dru-vid*, "very
wise", a derivation to which Canon MacCulloch accords his sanction.[3]   Mac-
Bain, a cautious etymologist, appears to accept the Greek origin of the word.[4]
Professor Donald Mackinnon approved it heartily.[5]   Camille Jullian thinks
that the possibility of it should not be excluded.   D'Arbois de Jubainville
scouted the idea bluntly enough, a criticism which Professor Anwyl regarded

as by no means conclusive.[6] Davies derived "druid" from the British *dar*, "superior" and *gwydd*, "a priest", in distinction from *gowydd* or *ovydd*, "a subordinate priest".[7] Toland thought the word *drud*, in old British, signified "a discreet or learned person".[8] In Scottish Gaelic *druidh* means "a magician, or sorcerer".[9] Herbert defines the Welsh *derwydd* as meaning "an adept of the oak tree".[10] Pezron gives the derivation from the Celtic *deru*, "oak", and *hud*, "enchantment", and states that the priests and magicians of the ancient Gauls practised divinations in oak groves. Mr. D. D. Evans follows Davies.

My own modest impression is that it is scarcely possible to divorce the word "druid" from the Old Celtic *derw*, "an oak". It should, of course, be kept in mind that the cult of the oak tree was not peculiarly a Celtic one, but was of very ancient Aryan acceptance throughout Europe. Still, I feel that the derivation of the word from *drud* or *druidh*, "wise" or "learned", has much to commend it, although it may well have been accepted from the name of the practitioners of an oak-cult. In any case, the etymological study of the term does not appear to have arrived at that stage where conclusive statement regarding it may be indulged in.

The number of writers who referred to Druidism during the "Classical" period vouches for the fact that the cult was an important one with a widespread reputation among the learned and the knowledgeable in Europe. This makes it all the more amusing that authorities on the Celtic past, and particularly that type of archaeologist who engages in practical excavation, should assume an attitude of nescience at the mere mention of Druidism. The plain truth is that the Druidic cult is very much better documented in the historical sense than are many events of vital importance to European history—than, say, the invasion of Britain by the Anglo-Saxons, concerning which we have practically no documentary evidence whatsoever, or the period of the Roman evacuation of this island, at the precise date of which we can only guess. Yet quite a small library of books has been produced on each of these subjects by official historians, while the subject of Druidism has been relegated to the tender mercies of persons for the most part innocent of historical or traditional achievement. It is beside the point that the majority of the Classical passages which deal with Druidism are generally brief and fugitive. Their number is considerably greater than the scanty historical evidences which describe the incident in which Boadicea revolted against the Romans with the loss of 150,000 lives—one of the most important interludes in early British chronicle, and an event which shook confidence in the Roman power throughout Britain and Gaul. We know rather more about Druidism than we do of the beginnings of the Christian faith in this island, yet we are invited to regard the whole question of the existence of Druidism as a hypothetical one!

"One thing at any rate is clear," remarked the late Professor Edward Anwyl, "that the Druids and their doctrines, or supposed doctrines, had made a deep impression on the writers of the ancient world. There is a reference to them in a fragment of Aristotle (which may not, however, be genuine) that is of interest as assigning them a place in express terms both among the Celts and the Galatae."[11]

I will arrange the several statements concerning Druidism by Classical writers in chronological order, for the sake of convenience. The first seemingly authentic reference to it is taken from the twenty-third book of the *Succession of Philosophers*, a work by Sotion of Alexandria, now lost, but written about the year 200 B.C., his allusion to the Druids being preserved by a passage in Diogenes Laertius. From this it is manifest that Druidism must, at that early date, have been a cult sufficiently well known to have attracted the attention of the Greeks in northern Egypt. He is made by Laertius to say that "the Celts and Galatae had seers called Druids and Semnothesi", and Laertius adds that Aristotle also alludes to these.[12]

The next allusion to the caste is recorded by Diodorus Siculus, who wrote only a few years before the Christian era and who describes the Gaulish Druids as "Saronidae", or "philosophers and divines whom they [the Gauls] held in great veneration".[13] Regarding such evidence as Julius Caesar affords us concerning the Druids, it is necessary to remark that none of it refers to the British Druids, with the exception of the single sentence in which he informs us that "this institution [Druidism] is supposed to have been devised in Britain, and to have been brought over from it into Gaul; and now those who desire to gain a more accurate knowledge of that system generally proceed thither for the purpose of studying it".[14] Unfortunately, those who have discussed this passage have frequently so delivered themselves as to make it appear that what Caesar has said elsewhere in his *Gallic War* concerning Gaulish Druidism might also refer to British Druidism. The account of Strabo (d. A.D. 24) also refers exclusively to the Druids of Gaul, while Lucan, his contemporary, likewise confines himself to a description of the Gaulish cult obviously derived from that of Caesar.

It is when we peruse the account of Tacitus concerning the military operations of Suetonius Paulinus, the Roman Governor of Britain, in the year A.D. 61, that we encounter the first definite statement respecting the British Druids. The island of Mona, or Anglesey, had, Tacitus records, become a refuge for fugitives from the Roman power, and these were fomenting rebellion among the neighbouring confederacies. Suetonius therefore attacked the island and found himself confronted by a fanatical defence. Between the intervals of the British ranks rushed wild-haired women, clad in funereal black, "like the Furies" of Roman myth, who brandished blazing torches, uttering shrill cries the while. They were accompanied by Druid priests, who hurled maledictions at the Roman interlopers, stretching their hands to heaven in tragic supplication. The legionaries, taken aback by this unwonted spectacle, remained inactive at first, probably through superstitious awe, until, encouraged by their leader, they made a concerted attack, bore down the resistance of the frantic Britons, and "enveloped them in their own flames". Suetonius cut down the Druidic groves in the island and imposed a garrison upon the conquered.[15] It has been stated that in all likelihood the settlement at Mona was one of fugitive Druid priests from Gaul, where the cult had been proscribed by the Emperor Claudius some considerable time before Suetonius' attack; but the assertion appears to be mainly of the nature of guesswork.

Pliny the Elder (d. A.D. 71) makes several interesting allusions to the Druids in general. In the sixteenth book of his *Natural History* he comments at some length upon their reverence for the mistletoe plant, an article of faith with which I have dealt elsewhere in these pages. He also speaks of their belief in the virtues of the serpent's egg, the *anguinam*, on which I have already commented. But it is evident that in some parts of his statement he is writing of the Druids of Gaul, an account of whose rites I must confine to later pages, as here I am concerned with British Druidism alone. Still, he does not altogether neglect the Britannic branch of the cultus, for, speaking of Magic and its marvels, he remarks that "Britain celebrates them today with such ceremonies that it might seem possible that she taught Magic to the Persians, and not the Persians to the Britons. . . . Why should I communicate," he adds rhetorically, "these matters concerning an art which has passed over the seas and has reached the bounds of nature?"

Plutarch, who died in the year A.D. 120, relates that the grammarian Demetrius discovered in an island near Britain "an order of Magi, reputed to be holy by the people", and he further makes mention of the Druidic tendency to human sacrifice. Of what "island" does Plutarch speak? Origen, the Christian apologist, who maintained so spirited a debate with the pagan Celsus in the middle years of the third century of our era, refers to the alleged resemblance of the Druidic ritual to that of the Jews, a statement in which his opponent concurs.[16] To the brief allusions of Valerius Maximus respecting Druidic philosophy I have already referred in the opening chapter.

This, I believe, exhausts the Classical evidence in respect of British Druidism, from which we find that only three authentic Roman references to Druidism in the land now called England and Wales actually exist, although each of these is specific enough in its terms, admitting of no question that such a cult was recognized as flourishing within that area.

Miss Eleanor Hull also points out that Nennius, in his *Historia Britonum* (edited ca. 820 A.D.) alludes to King Vortigern summoning his "Magi" for consultation, a word which in the fourteenth-century Irish version of that work is translated by the term "Druids". She regards the statement of Caesar that Druidic neophytes were in the habit of resorting to Britain for study as fairly conclusive that the order existed in what is now England and Wales.[17]

On all sides it is admitted that the Belgic tribes who had emigrated to Britain from Gaul in the century before Caesar's invasion, and who continued to settle in the south coastal parts, had no Druidical associations. These were a people of mixed Gaulish and German descent. Nor did all the Gaulish tribes accept the Druidic cultus. "It is," remarks Charles Squire, alluding to Caesar's statement on the British origins of Druidism, "curious corroboration of this alleged British origin of Druidism that the ancient Irish also believed their Druidism to have come from the sister island. Their heroes and seers are described as only gaining the highest knowledge by travelling to Alba. However this may be, we may take it that this Druidism was the accepted religion of the Celtic race."[18]

I have collected quite a number of references and traditional survivals which, I think, substantiate the theory of the existence of a former Druidic cult in what is now England and Wales. In the first instance, I may remark that the circumstance that Druidism flourished in Scotland and Ireland for some considerable time after the Romans evacuated Britain appears to argue its prior, if not its contemporary, existence in the "English" Celtic area. The survival of the word "Druid" in the Welsh or British tongue down to the present time (as in the Irish and Scots Gaelic) appears to me a powerful proof of its application to a caste which formerly flourished on Welsh and English soil. The word is found in Welsh MSS. which ultimately date to the seventh century, and its history is one of continual and proven use since the commencement of the Christian era. Pliny speaks of Druids in Gaul and of Magic in Britain within the compass of the same paragraph.

Strabo alludes to the manner in which the Druids offered up men in sacrifice to the gods by fire, as does Caesar, while the former adds that "when there is a large yield [of criminals for sacrifice] there is forthcoming a large yield from the land as well, as they think" (*Geographia*, IV. 4c., 197.4). The burning of these victims was thought to induce a heavy growth of crops. I find a striking instance of the survival of such a tradition in England in the fact that at the burning of the hapless Bishop Latimer in 1554 the onlookers were heard to remark that it was unfortunate it had not taken place earlier in the season, as then it might have saved the crops!

A stone discovered near Port St. Mary, in the parish of Rushen, in the Isle of Man, remarks Mr. Kendrick (p. 100), bears an inscription in ogham characters which has been translated as meaning "The Stone of Dovaidona, son of the Druid". It dates from the fifth or sixth century of our era, thus revealing that Druidic priests must have survived in the island until this relatively late period.

It may also be pertinently asked why, if so much of the ancient British Mythology has been handed down in the *Mabinogion*, "the Red Book of Hergest" and other Welsh manuscripts—the genuine character of which is admitted on all sides, the traditions and memory of the very caste which must have preserved it and the ideals it contained, and the recollection of its associated rites, should be thought to have perished. This is a consideration which I think has not entered into the conclusions of most writers on the subject. It is inconceivable that the myths of the Druidic caste should have survived and not the memory of their ritual and system of thought.

Apart altogether from the well-known renascence or revival of Druidism in the Wales of the twelfth century (to which I make no appeal in this place), there is an abundance of evidence that the cult of the ox, which was certainly an outstanding part of Druidic ritual, survived in what is now England and Wales. To this the Welsh bard Aneurin, who flourished in the sixth century, alludes in one of his poems, cited in Edward Davies' *The Mythology of the British Druids* (p. 574). At St. Teilo, in Wales, there is an "oxen's well", formerly kept by a family called Melchior, which, says Sir John Rhys, may indicate "a succession which seems to point unmistakeably to an ancient priesthood of a sacred spring". In Wales, says Sir Laurence Gomme, a bullock was habitually sacrificed by farmers by casting it over a precipice, when disease broke out amongst the herds. This custom continued until the year 1812. To St. Beyno, patron saint of Clynnog in Carnarvonshire, a bullock was also habitually sacrificed until at least the year 1589. In Northamptonshire such an animal was burnt, as Jacob Grimm assures us in his *Teutonic Mythology* (p. 610). Hunt, in his *Popular Romances of the West of England* (pp. 212-14) cites many instances of the same kind of sacrifice as occurring in Cornwall until comparatively recent times. "There is a tradition in Cornwall," he quotes Drew and Hitchin as saying, "which has been handed down from remote antiquity, that farmers may prevent any calamity by burning alive the finest calf they possess", and writing in 1881 he adds that he has been apprised of "two recent instances of this superstition".

At the celebration of the Godiva ceremony in the village of Southam, near Coventry, a personage was represented in the procession who wore a mask shaped like a bull's head, with horns complete, and who was known as "Old Brazenface". The name appears to be a title of the old Celtic god of the sun, whose burning visage, surrounded by lambent rays, was frequently cast in brazen discs. There is plenty of evidence for the Druidic sacrifice of white oxen, as is particularly apparent from the testimony of Pliny (*Natural History*, XVI, 249). Whence, it may be asked, were these late superstitions derived, if not from a tradition of Druidic practice? There is no other possible or imaginable source for the appearance and survival of such rites in England and Wales than the Druidic, and it seems feeble to deny or to seek to controvert the statement of their Druidic origin by an appeal to "Aryan" general practice in Europe, which, indeed, was greatly more ancient than Druidism, and which the Druidic cult must have accepted in a large degree. If it were so in Gaul, as Pliny asseverates, and in Scotland and Ireland, as I shall demonstrate later, so, surely, it must have been in the English-Celtic area.

In many parts of England and Scotland small herds of white cattle were preserved until quite recent times, and some of these still remain. That they are, or were, the fragmentary relics of Druidic herds appear to me as highly probable. The places of their maintenance in England were Chillingham; Chartley Park; Lyme Park; Neworth Castle, in Cumberland; Gisburne Park, Yorkshire; Whalley Abbey, Lancashire; Middleton Park and Hoghton Tower in the same county; Wallaton Park, Nottinghamshire; Sunerford Park, Cheshire; Woldenby Park, Northamptonshire; Leigh Court, Somersetshire; Barnard Castle and Bishop Auckland in Durham; Burton Constable in Yorkshire, and Ewelme Park in Oxfordshire. For what specific purpose were these white cattle of a primitive type so piously preserved and in so numerous herds, unless by virtue of an ancient memory handed down through the generations, that they were of a nature peculiarly sacred? The white bull was pre-eminently the beast of sacrifice associated with the Druidic cult, and I cannot conceive of any other reason why such extreme care should have been observed in English areas for the most part so closely associated with Celtic tradition to maintain these herds of white cattle unless they had anciently been derived from Druidic herds once especially retained for the purpose of sacrifice. The records associated with them reveal the extraordinary care taken for their preservation and seclusion.

In Wales, at least up to the year 1538, oxen were offered up to the idol of a "saint" or deity, Darvell Gadarn, as we learn from the contents of a letter written by Ellis Price to Thomas Cromwell, Secretary of State to Henry VIII, dated April 6th, 1538, from the diocese of St. Asaph. The people, says Price, flocked to this idol on April 5th, bringing oxen and kine. The idol was carried to Smithfield and duly burned, along with the priest who ministered to it and who bore the same name with itself. Now the name Darvell Gadarn closely resembles that of Hu Gadarn, an ancient British deity associated with the cult of the ox, and I have formed the impression that the prefix "Darvell" is a corruption of the Welsh word for a bull, *tarw*. Darvell Gadarn, I may add, has some reputation in Wales as a "saint".

I venture to think that the above instances reveal with some cumulative potency the survival in the English Celtic area of traditions anciently associated with the Druidic cult, nor do I think they will be readily disposed of in the mass. I may add that the Irish "Nennius" declares that the Druids returned to that area after the retreat of the Romans, in the reign of Vortigern, although I lay no particular stress on the authenticity of this statement.

But it is possible to derive a good deal of general information respecting the Druidic cult from those Classical statements concerning it which deal specifically with its Gallic side. It is, for example, to the Druidism of Gaul that Caesar refers exclusively, and this I wish to stress. While on his Gallic campaign he appears to have cultivated the society of the leading Druid priests, more particularly that of the Arch-Druid Divitiacus, and, doubtless, as a kind of honorary priest himself—for at the time of his campaign in Gaul he had been Pontifex Maximus of Rome for nine years—he must surely have taken more than a passing interest in the affairs and sites of an alien religion. Divitiacus was brother to Dumnorix, a chief of the Gallic tribe of the Ædui, and appears to have been a great admirer of everything Roman; and though Caesar had to converse with him through an interpreter, he probably discussed with him other things than matters merely political. Indeed, the Roman general seems to have cherished a great personal regard for the Druid Arch-priest, who not only rendered signal services to the Roman cause in Gaul, but actually travelled to Rome to interview the Senate concerning the best means of pacifying the country, but with little result .[19]   While in Rome, Divitiacus was the guest of Cicero's brother, and the great orator himself alludes to him in a strain of panegyric.   Writing to his brother, Quintus, Cicero says: "He was a guest of yours and great in your praises.   He professed to know natural philosophy, which the Greeks call 'physiology', and he used to tell, partly by augury, partly by conjecture, what was to happen in the future."

All this notwithstanding, we must exercise due caution in assessing the value of Caesar's account of Druidism.   When all is said, he must certainly have regarded it from a political viewpoint, and with the somewhat jaundiced eye of a calculating and suspicious conqueror.   He tells us that the aristocracy of the Gauls was divided into two orders, those of the Knights, or feudal chiefs, and the Druids.   These latter had the oversight of things sacred, they conducted the public sacrifices and interpreted all matters of religion.   High honours were paid to the Druids and many young men resorted to them for the purposes of instruction.   They also acted as judges in civil suits and criminal cases.   Those who did not submit to their decisions they debarred from the sacrifices, a proceeding tantamount to excommunication.   An Arch-Druid presided over the rest, and on his death the succession, if more than one distinguished leader came forward, might be contested by force of arms.   Normally, however, the Druids took no part in warlike affairs, nor did they pay tribute to the state.

Druidic training, Caesar tells us, necessitated a long and rigorous course of study.   The candidate was compelled to learn by heart a great number of verses, and his curriculum in its entirety frequently occupied as much as twenty years.   These verses must on no account be committed to writing, although in public and private transactions the Druids were wont to make use of Greek letters.   But in sacred affairs the use of the pen was regarded as derogatory to mnemonic effort, nor did they desire the people at large to acquire any knowledge of their mystical and arcane philosophy.   The Druids, he adds, did not believe that the soul perished, but that it passed after death from one body to another.   They likewise imparted to their youthful followers "many things respecting the stars and their motion, the extent of the earth, and of the power and the majesty of the immortal gods".[20]

Caesar also alludes to the nature of certain Druidic ritual customs associated with human sacrifice.   People afflicted with serious complaints or who made vows to the gods in the heat of battle or when faced with dangers of one kind or another employed the Druids to perform such sacrifices, believing that the gods would accept only a life in payment for a life.   Occasionally figures of vast size, the limbs of which were fashioned from osiers or wickerwork, were filled with living men and set on fire.   Such persons as were sacrificed were usually malefactors, and therefore more acceptable to the gods, but if thes were not forthcoming, innocent folk, probably serfs, took their places.[21]

Strabo follows Caesar for the most part in his account of the Gallic Druids, but he adds that two other castes besides were almost equally the objects of popular veneration among the Gauls.   These were the Bards and the Vates.   The Bards composed and chanted hymns.   The Vates occupied themselves with the sacrifices and the study of nature.   The Druids joined to the study of nature that of moral philosophy.   "Both these and the others (Bards and Vates) assert that the soul is indestructible and likewise the world, but that fire and water will one day have the mastery."[22]   Lucan derives his account of matters Druidic mainly from Caesar, and alludes to the dogma of the transmigration of souls held by the Gallic philosophers, a subject which I have relegated to the ninth chapter of this volume, on account of its importance as a separate topic.

The public assemblies of the Gaulish Druids were held at what is now Chartres, near the centre of Gaul, in the region of the Carnutes. Here they had consecrated a grove. In the year A.D. 68 a body of them revolted against Rome, and two years later they seem to have assembled at this spot when, with great enthusiasm, they prophesied a world-dominion for the Celtic race.[23]

Pliny states that "Gaul was overrun with magic arts even up to our own time (the sixth decade of the first century) until Tiberius Caesar did away with the Druids and this class of prophets and magicians". The passage presents a difficulty, for elsewhere in his work Pliny speaks of Druidism as still extant in Gaul. Still later, Suetonius remarks that "Claudius abolished entirely the religion of the Druids, a faith of dreadful barbarity, and forbidden only to the Roman citizens under Augustus". There is thus some dubiety as to the preci^{s}e period at which Druidism in Gaul was actually prohibited. The probability is that only the human sacrifices were abolished, and Strabo certainly gives us to believe as much. Tacitus avers that Druidic prophecies continued to be politically annoying as late as the time of Vespasian, who reigned until the year A.D. 79, eight years after the death of Pliny. After the first century of our era we find most Classical authors alluding to Druidism as a faith quite extinct. Little did they wot of what was going on in Gaul, *sub rosa*! In the fourth century Ammianus Marcellinus touches upon the history of Druidism as though it were an antiquarian subject. He tells us that when the Phocean Greeks founded Massilia, or Marseilles, the inhabitants of the hinterland became gradually civilized, and that this gave an impetus to the whole philosophy of Druidism, which began to take on a more erudite appearance, merging at last into something resembling Pythagoreanism. Pomponius Mela states that when human sacrifice was forbidden the Gaulish Druids still drew blood from the "victims" in mock sacrifice.

Naturally, French authors have taken an immense interest in the whole subject of Gallic Druidism, but here I cannot do more than summarize their views. Henri Martin in his *Etudes d'archéologie celtique* gives it as his opinion that the *Deroo* of Brittany were a caste more ancient than those Druids known to the Romans, being "primitive Druids, a sacerdotal caste of old Celts". Guenebauld, who died in 1630, published in 1621 his "*Le Reveil de Chyndonax, Prince de Vacies, Druides Celtique*, of which very rare work I have a copy. In the year 1598, he tells us, the tomb of the Druid Chyndonax was discovered at a place called Poussot, near Dijon, where under a great stone was found a cylinder containing an urn curiously shaped, of which he provides a sketch. On the tomb itself was an inscription in Greek stating that: "In this tomb in the sacred wood of the god Mithra is contained the body of the High Priest Chyndonax. May the gods guard my ashes from all harm." The burial appears to have been a comparatively late one, and the inscription reveals that by the period of the death of Chyndonax Gallic Druidism had become merged to some extent, if not altogether identified, with the Oriental cult of Mithraism—a topic to which I shall revert in a later chapter. A Roman cemetery was discovered on the site 200 years later.

Here I can only allude in passing to the interesting, if at times somewhat imaginative, writings of Baecker, Denis, Le Blanc, Leflocq, Pictet, and others of the older French school of antiquaries. In later times the works of MM. Huber, D'Arbois de Jubainville, Salomon Reinach and Camille Jullian have placed the study of Gallic Druidism on a much sounder and more philosophic footing, and to these I must refer my readers. But before departing from the subject of Druidism in Gaul I should like to quote the opinion of Professor Rhys concerning the question of its *floreat* in that region. He thinks that at the period of the Roman occupation "in the more progressive parts of southern Gaul, the neighbourhood of the Rhone and the Roman province, the palmy days of Druidism were even then over". The fall of the kingship in Gaul may have had disastrous effects upon the Druidic cult. So it was also in Ireland, he thinks. But a religious change had come over the spirit of Gaulish paganism and the Gaulish Mercury or culture-god had become its supreme figure, with results deterrent, if not destructive, to Druidic dogma.[24] As we shall see, Druidism in Ireland was bound up with the kingship in so intimate a manner that the fall of one institution dictated the cessation of the other.

Still Druidism continued to lead an underground existence in Gaul long after the introduction of Christianity. So late, indeed, as the year A.D. 658 customs and rites which can only be interpreted as the remains of Druidic worship were condemned by the Council of Nantes, and still later by the Capitularies of Charlemagne. Ausonius mentions that even in the fourth century men in Gaul were proud to boast of their Druidic descent.[25] St Beuno, in his dying hour, revealed a mingled spiritual loyalty by exclaiming: "I see the Trinity and Peter and Paul, and the Druids and the Saints!" and in the fourth century there were certainly professors at Bordeaux who could boast of a Druid ancestry.[26]

CHAPTER IV

THE PROBLEM OF DRUIDISM (*continued*)

In his *History of the Druids* John Toland suggests that when Druidism was banished from what is now England it took refuge in Scotland and Ireland. So far as Scotland is concerned, precise record fails us for the earlier centuries. One of the first allusions to Druidism in that region tells us that Drostan, the Druid of the Irish Picts, designed in war-time a magic bath of milk which healed the wounded. But these Irish-Pictish Druids, we are informed, were driven into Scotland. "From them are every spell, and every charm, and every *sreod* (sneeze), and voices of birds, and every omen"—in short, all Magic in Scotland proceeded from them.[1] I may add here that a similar magic bath of milk was resorted to by the Druid of Criomhthan, Chief of Leinster, in a war waged by the Irish and their Pictish allies with the British. The latter had poisoned their weapons, Keating informs us, but Trosdane, the Druid in question, advised the Irish leader to dig a large pit, in which the milk of 150 white-faced cows was to be poured. In this the wounded Irish and Pictish warriors were immersed, with the result that a perfect cure was effected in every case and the invading Britons were vanquished.

When St. Columba arrived in Scotland in the latter part of the sixth century he seems to have been opposed by a powerful Druidical caste, precisely as was St. Patrick in Ireland. His chief adversary was the Druid Broichan, who had great influence with the Pictish monarch Brude. Columba had won over the family of a Pictish peasant to Christianity. Some days later one of their sons died, whereupon a local Druid upbraided the parents, saying that their apostasy from his faith had brought about the lad's demise. Columba, however, restored the boy to life.[2] Such tales abound in the chronicles of Scottish Druidism. Broichan raised mists to prevent the saint from navigating the waters of Loch Ness, but Columba's vessel was, by heavenly aid, carried along against the wind. To dilate upon the magical contests of this saint with the Pictish Druids and to chronicle the sententious dialogue of both parties would occupy pages, and indeed these things are already familiar to most people.

Legend avers that Dothan, a mythical monarch of Scotland, who is said to have flourished in the first century, sent his three sons to the Isle of Man to be educated by the Druids who occupied that island, and we also read that Corbed, alleged by some to have been "the first King of Scotland", was similarly instructed by these magi. Whatever the historical value of such traditions, they at least seem to indicate the Isle of Man as having formerly been a prominent Druidic centre. Indeed, Archbishop John Spottiswood of St. Andrews, who wrote in the seventeenth century, narrates in his *History of the Church of Scotland* that the Isle of Man, for long an appanage of the Scottish Crown, was the centre of Caledonian Druidism, the affairs of which were governed by a "president" who dwelt in the island. But Cratylinth, another mythical King of Scotland, or Alba, expelled the Druids, and extirpated their superstitions, a task, adds the Archbishop, of extreme difficulty "because of the favour they had amongst the people". This view is also maintained by Sacheverell in his *Survey of the Isle of Man*, in which he contends that Druidism in the island partook of the nature of theocracy. We have already seen that at least one inscription referring to the Druids has been found on Manx soil.

St. Kentigern attracted several Druidic traditions to himself and appears to have at times acted in a Druidical manner. As I have already said, Irish tradition is fulfilled of instances in which heroes and sages betook themselves to Scotland to undergo a Druidical training, or to seek expert advice in affairs of visionary elucidation.

The proofs of the survival of Druidic rites and ideas in Scotland are manifold. Particularly was this the case so far as the sacrifice of cattle was concerned. In 1678 the Presbytery of Dingwall took action against four of the Mackenzies for sacrificing a bull in the island of St. Mourie in Loch Maree. This island was certainly an ancient Druidic centre, and the saint associated with it was as certainly the successor or legendary surrogate of a "divine king" connected with oak and well worship. The tradition casts light upon the "mistletoe" passage in Pliny, with its allusions to sacrificed oxen, as upon Frazer's theory of the "Golden Bough".[3] The cases of sacrifice at this spot appear to have been fairly numerous. Sir James Simpson put it on record that at Torphichen, only about twenty miles from Edinburgh, a cow was buried alive by a farmer as a sacrifice to the spirit of the murrain within the memory of people still living in the year 1883, while another was offered up in the same manner at Biggar, in Lanarkshire. Still another case of the same kind is recorded as happening at Dallas, in Morayshire, about the year 1850.[4] Instances of other Scottish superstitions derived from Druidic rite are alluded to in several chapters of this book in their appropriate places. I may add that nowhere did the Celtic fire-festivals survive in such primitive purity as in Scotland.

The evidence for the former existence of Druidism in Ireland is even more abundant. Certain authors, among them Mr. T. D. Kendrick, have advanced the theory that Irish Druidism was merely the "shadow" of the Gaulish system and was the preserve of a bardic caste only, who were little better than "jugglers" or "medicine men". But this view must be departed from in consideration of the proof which connects Hibernian Druidism with the cult of the divine king, with which I hope to deal more fully in the chapter on Reincarnation.

A tradition exists that Druidism was first brought to Ireland about the year 270 B.C., and this chimes to some extent with what we know of Hibernian relationships with the Continent.[5] Needless to say, however, it should not be regarded as "historical" in character. As the reader already knows, Druids are frequently referred to in the legends of the Irish "Book of Invasions" as belonging to the several immigrant tribes who settled in the island at various times. O'Beirne Crowe, on the other hand, declared that Irish Druidism was a reflection of that of Gaul, while Sir John Rhys seems to have been equally convinced that this was the case.[6] MacBain, anxious to be strictly "scientific", states bluntly that "the Druids of Irish history are mere conjurers and magicians", although he admits that they "play a most important part in Irish pagan history as chronicled by the long posterior Christian writers". But he was persuaded that Irish Druidism was "not a philosophy, nor a religion, nor a system".[7]

I have already alluded to the contests of St. Patrick with the Irish Druids. In the tripartite life of the saint we read that the Druids, on one occasion, were "celebrating an idolatrous solemnity" accompanied by "incantations and some magical inventions" along with their kings and chiefs, in Temar.[8] Of course that which was "magical invention" in the sight of the Christian missionaries was naturally "religion" in that of the Druidic officiants. At Mag-Slecht, "the Plain of Adoration", in County Cavan, was situated a stone circle at which sacrifices were made to the god Crom Cruaich. It contained "twelve idols of stone around it" and one of gold, representing the principal deity. The folk, we are told, offered up to it "one-third of their healthy offspring" in return for grain and milk. This we read of in the Books of Leinster, of Ballymote and of Lecan. What is this, indeed, but "religion", if of a primitive nature, though it must be admitted that the worship in question is not associated with Druidism in any of the accounts we have of it.

The Irish Druids were composed of two classes: the priesthood and the *Filid*, who were both bards, prophets and diviners. The latter caste long survived the former as a poetic body, retaining much of the lore of the other and more strictly religious brotherhood. Early written Irish records refer to "the Science of Goibniu", the deity of smithcraft, a master of Magic, some of whose spells are to be found in an eighth-century MS. discovered at St. Gall, in Switzerland. Mr. Kendrick, who is always scrupulously fair, lays stress upon the fact that important assemblies were held in Ireland at fixed intervals which were attended by delegates from distant parts, and remarks that "we cannot fairly assume that Irish Druidism lacked that co-ordination of its members such as obtained in Gaul". He also adds that, "It is significant that the Druids of Ireland were servants of the primitive festival-system in its Central-European form."[9]

Yet there were visible in the Irish Druid certain traces of the primeval shaman, or medicine-man. When the Druid Ciothruadh lighted "a Druidic fire" against the heroes of Munster they retaliated with a similar magical conflagration which brought down a rain of blood. The priest of the Munster host, Mogruith, called for his "dark-grey, hornless bull-hide and white-speckled bird headpiece", and flew into the air the better to dispatch his spells against the foe. Ciothruadh, observing his flight, also ascended, and the twain joined battle in the sky. Mogruith prevailed and his antagonist crashed to earth. What I wish to point out here is that in preparation for his aerial journey Mogruith dons a costume or disguise which might well be, and actually has been, worn by the shamans of at least one American Indian tribe. At the "Buffalo Dance" of the Mandan Indians, a Dakota tribe, the celebrants dressed themselves in buffalo-skins and imitated the actions of these animals, while in ancient Mexico the bird-*naualli*, or disguises, of certain gods were worn as head-dresses by the magicians. Mogruith wore the bird head-dress because he was convinced that by such means he assumed the properties of a bird, he would be identical with a bird, and should thus be able to engage in flight, while the bull-hide he wore, as we shall see in the chapter dealing with Necromancy and Divination, was closely associated with certain magical ceremonies.

George Buchanan, a Scottish historian of the sixteenth century, writing of the contemporary Irish, testifies that "many of their ancient customs yet remain; yea there is almost nothing changed of them in Ireland, but only ceremonies and rites of religion". If I do not misconceive him, he means to convey that such rites are merely empty observances, masking an underlying paganism.

That Druidism, or the indwelling spirit thereof, survived in Ireland for generations is merely the plain unvarnished fact, and those writers who make question of this survival delude not only their readers but themselves. The Catholic Church in Ireland, like the Nonconformist bodies in Wales, has very naturally done its utmost to extirpate the remains of the Druidic tradition, but with only qualified success. From the earliest Christian years the pagan spirit has been in evidence. It is strange that the late Rev. S. Baring-Gould should have written that: "under the name of Methodism, we have the old Druidic religion still alive, energetic and possibly more vigorous than it was when it exercised a spiritual supremacy over the whole of Britain". (*Curious Myths of the Middle Ages*, p. 627.) King Diarmuid MacCearbhail, who came to the throne of Ireland in A.D. 528, and who is eloquently described as "half a Druid and half a Christian", levied an army against a chief known as Guaire because he had destroyed a sacred cow.[10] Such an animal, says Owen Connelan, supplied the daily wants of nine score sacred women, who were probably Druid-esses, upon which circumstance Hackett remarks that: "The probability is that they were pagan Druidesses, and that the cows were living idols, like Apis, or in some sense considered sacred animals." Milligan, in his *Glimpses of Erin*, bears witness that he saw women in Inismurray kneeling before standing stones in an attitude of worship, while Edmund Spenser, the poet of *The Faerie Queen*, declares that he saw Irish people drinking blood in connection with certain arcane ceremonies. Mrs. Harrington, writing in 1818, found that some of the "keeners" at Irish funerals were the descendants of pagan performers. Well-worship in Ireland continues, vestigially at least, to the present day.

That the Irish Druids were in some manner associated with the tradition of the mystical Tuatha Dé Danann appears probable.[11] "They [the Druids] are represented," says Miss Eleanor Hull, an authority of standing, "as having come to Ireland with the Tuatha Dé Danann, the early magicians and kings, and to have been in the service of the Irish Cruithnigh" (or Picts). "According to tradition they must have been in Alba (Scotland) long before, for we hear that King Cormac of Tara in the third century sent for Druids from Alba to practise magic for him against the King of Munster." She adds that every Irish king had his personal Druid, as had every queen, that these priests took rank next to the king, that Druids were themselves occasionally kings, that they received large territorial grants for their services, that they married and were succeeded in office by their sons (as in the case of the early Christian priests in Scotland, up to the eleventh century), that they were genealogists, annalists and physicians.[12]

In connection with the question of Druidic system and discipline in general we find that Druid priests were thought of by some Classical authors as associated together in confraternities in accordance with the rule of Pythagoras,[13] a statement concerning which I shall have more to say in the chapter on Reincarnation.

Some writers of the type who consistently fail to provide authority for their statements have much to say concerning Druidesses and their part in rite and ceremony. Here I can supply only such information as I know to be buttressed by credible witness. Vopiscŭs alludes to a Druidess in Gaul, who was also an innkeeper, as having existed in the third century A.D. The same author tells us that the Emperor Aurelian consulted the Gaulish Druidesses concerning the question of the imperial descent.[14] In Ireland the names of some Druidesses have been preserved, as, for example, that of Geal Chossach, "the white-legged", of Inisoven, in Donegal. We also hear of Milucradh, Hag of the Waters, who transformed Fionn, or Finn, into an old man by means of water from Lake Sliabh Gullin. Eithne and Ban Draoi (whose name means "Druid Woman") were celebrated as sorceresses, and the last may be only a general type of the Druidic enchantress. I have already spoken of the religious retreats, ostensibly Christian or semi-Christian, where pagan women masqueraded as "nuns".

Strabo tells us that there was a community of women dwelling in an island at the mouth of the Loire who were devoted to a secret cult. No man was permitted to set foot on their domain.[15] Pomponius Mela, who flourished in the first century, speaks of another such island, that of Sein, or Sena, off Pont du Raz, on the western coast of Brittany, not far from Brest. Its virgin women, known as Gallicenae or Gallizenae, were nine in number, and could raise winds and storms and transform themselves into animal shapes. Strabo refers to them as "the devotees of Dionysus", which is as much as to say that they worshipped some Celtic deity with the same attributes as Bacchus. He does not call them Druidesses. They guarded the oracle of a Gaulish god, so it seems most likely that they were.[16] In the former case, that of the island in the Loire estuary, the temple of these women was unroofed by them once a year, and if any of them allowed her burden to fall to the ground during the ceremony she was instantly torn to pieces by her companions, who bore her remains round the isle in triumph. If the temple had to be unroofed annually it had once probably been roofless and was perhaps a stone circle. These two accounts have been regarded by some critics as garbled recollections of the Homeric stories concerning the sorceresses Circe and Calypso, who dwelt on magical islands. After a careful comparison of the essential factors of both traditions I can find little or nothing to support such a theory. It is an example of the kind of criticism which for so long has been directed to European myth by fanatical Classicists with a lop-sided education. There is, remarks Mr. Kendrick with his usual acumen, "nothing improbable in the stories of the islands with the holy women dwelling in them", although they may not have been Druidesses. Canon MacCulloch also points out that their rites are "paralleled from other regions".[17]

We have seen that Tacitus spoke of women clad in funereal black who accompanied the Druids of Mona when Suetonius led his attack upon that island. That these were Druidesses I find it difficult to question. I cannot well believe that the ordinary British woman of the Roman period assumed a special costume, or rushed through the ranks of the defenders brandishing a torch. Such is the attitude of the "inspired" religious fanatic. On the whole, however, I conclude that those women who are usually described as

"Druidesses" were not usually officiants or practising priestesses. All that we know of Druidism pleads against the supposition that rites of any description would be delegated to women, and I imagine that such women were rather in the position of "acolytes", or assistants, though that they frequently practised the lesser sorceries of the caste cannot be doubted.

As regards the association of the Druids with religion, quite a number of authorities have arrived at the conclusion that they had no religious status and indeed no concern with religious matters whatsoever. Professor O'Curry found "no grounds whatever for believing the Druids to have been the priests of any positive public worship" in Ireland, while Vallencey declared that in all the material he could collect regarding Irish paganism, Druidism had no part. Dr. Richey denied that the Irish Druids formed "a priesthood occupying a definite political position which the ministers of the new religion could appropriate". Ledwich and Windele were also opposed to the notion that the Irish Druids had any religious status.[18]

It will be observed that all of these writers refer to the Druidism of Ireland, and I have already adduced some proof that religious rites were practised by Irish Druids. But whether the Druids had or had not any religious standing in Ireland, those of Gaul assuredly functioned as a priesthood. The matter is clinched by the account of Caesar, who expressly states that they were "concerned with divine worship, the due performance of sacrifices, public and private, and the interpretation of ritual questions".[19] He also makes it clear that they taught the immortality of the human soul and believed that it passed into other bodies after death. Lucan declared that the Druids "knew the gods and divinities of heaven".[20] Diodorus makes it clear that "no sacrifice was in order without the assistance of a Druid".[21]

But even the Irish Druids appear to have "baptized" children, as did the Welsh.[22] Is baptism a religious rite or not? I am not here concerned with the questions of immortality and reincarnation, with which I shall deal in a separate chapter, but with the proofs associated with Druidic religious practice alone. Pomponius Mela, Lucan, Tacitus and Diodorus all remark upon the polytheistic worship of the Druids, though they do not particularize concerning its character. Caesar says that the Gauls, according to Druidic doctrine, believed themselves to be descended from the god Dis, meaning a Celtic deity having similar characteristics with that god. He mentions that the Gauls worshipped gods which appeared to him to resemble the Roman deities Mercury, Apollo, Mars, Jupiter and Minerva. Were there priests or officiants other than the Druids who served these divinities? M. D'Arbois certainly mentions a priesthood known as the Gutuatri, but it has been proved that these were merely a special caste of temple-servants attached to the Druidic body. The Gaulish religion was most unquestionably a pantheism resembling those of Greece and Rome, of which the Druids were the officiants. "The gods of the Druids," remarks Mr. Kendrick, a writer most cautious in delivering opinion, "were the familiar and multifarious deities of the Keltic pantheon".[23]

As I have mentioned elsewhere in this book, the Irish had "a god of Druidism". This deity is definitely alluded to, according to Rhys, in *The Book of the Dun Cow* and in *The Book of Leinster*, thus revealing that notwithstanding the asseveration of prominent Irish scholars, the Druids of Ireland definitely acted as the ministers of a certain deity. That the Irish Druids were also the celebrants of the Celtic solar festival-system needs no stressing. Taking the evidence as a whole, it is beyond doubt that the Gallic Druids at least officiated as a religious priesthood, while those of Ireland also appear to have held a similar status, although in this case the evidence is admittedly less definite, magical predilection appearing to have predominated in the Hibernian area over purely religious doctrine and practice.

I come now to the consideration of a question which bristles with even more thorny interrogations—that which has to do with the Druidic relationship to those famous circles composed of large and rough standing-stones with which tradition so intimately connects the Druidical brotherhood. I may say at once that practically the whole opinion of modern Archaeology is unfriendly to the supposition that the Druids were in any way associated with the circles in question. Classical writers, too, assure us that the Druids worshipped in groves, Lucan, Pliny and Tacitus making reference to the tree-encircled haunts of the brotherhood. Irish tradition also holds more than one allusion to the grove as a Druidic precinct.

Within recent years the date of the erection of Stonehenge, the last example in time of the British stone circle, has been fixed at or about the year 2000 B.C. This is at least eighteen hundred years prior to the first literary mention we possess regarding Druidism, and if we are to connect the two we must imagine a Druidism flourishing at a period considerably older than the building of Stonehenge, than which the majority of our stone circles are greatly more ancient. Mr. Kendrick makes a half-hearted plea for the more recent construction of Stonehenge in the earlier La Tène Age which extended from 500 B.C. to A.D. 100. With equal half-heartedness I find myself unable to entertain it. I admit a constitutional fondness for lost causes, but there are some pricks against which it is fruitless to kick. Nor do I think it worth print and paper to discuss a problem already disposed of, so far as such disposition is possible, by the ablest archaeologists of our time. All I care to add on this question is that it has always appeared to me as not improbable that some form of belief resembling Druidism, some early and evolutionary type of that faith, may possibly have been associated with these circles, and that the Druidic grove may have been a later development of them, or, perhaps, a return to an earlier form of them, such as we find in Woodhenge, on Salisbury Plain, where tree-trunks took the place of rough stone pillars, and which appears to have been erected, judging from the pottery discovered on its site, at much the same period as Stonehenge. But to enlarge upon the nature of the rites celebrated at such places in primitive times, even in view of the quite considerable evidence that in France and elsewhere survivals of these are not uncommon, would be foreign to my purpose here, which is to provide as trustworthy a view of Druidism as the evidence we possess makes possible.

When we come to examine the several theories which seek to account for the origin of Druidism we encounter a strange diversity of opinion. D'Arbois de Jubainville regarded the Druids as priests of the British Gaels, who succeeded in imposing their cult upon their Gaulish conquerors. The latter then imported Druidism into Gaul from Britain.[24] It seems clear that Druidism was practised by both branches of the Celts, the Gaels and the Brythons, but, frankly, we know nothing of the Gaels in the English area. Some British writers, notably Rhys and Sir G. Laurence Gomme, held that Druidism was a cultus of the pre-Celtic Iberian aborigines of Britain. Rhys thought that the Goidelic folk of Britain accepted it, but not so the Brythons, or Celts of England and Wales. Gomme believed, indeed, that the Druidic cult was the forerunner of British witchcraft, but the probable truth is that witchcraft was a broken-down system of fetishism which drew its ideas from the general reservoirs of superstition throughout the ages and which only began to take on the shape of a definite cult in our island at some time in the early Christian centuries.

Rhys distinguishes three religions in early Britain that of the Brythonic

Celts who practised an Aryan religion much the same in its type as that of Greece or Rome; that of the non-Celtic natives, who cultivated Druidism; and that of the Goidelic Celts, who combined both of these systems.[25] But, if we look facts in the face, we will realize that, although we find quite a considerable substratum of tradition in England which seems to prove the former existence of a Druidic cult within its borders, we can discover not a single literary or historical allusion to Druids acting as priests in the entire English area. We are also faced with the baffling circumstance that, while Druidism of a type somewhat different from that known in Gaul is richly documented in Ireland and has at least acceptable vouchers in Scotland, only one definite Classical statement concerning its ancient appearance in Brythonic Wales is forthcoming—that of Tacitus, when speaking of the Druidic refuge in Anglesey. For other Welsh references to Druids and Druidism we must apply to much later Welsh writings and traditions the authenticity of which is seriously challenged by critics of high standing.

Moreover, as Canon MacCulloch justly maintains, historical evidence is lacking to show that Druidism was a non-Celtic faith.[26] The Druids were not, he thinks, a pre-Celtic caste, for they practised the solar festivals of the Celts. "This," as Mr. Kendrick remarks, "is a point that goes to the very heart of the problem," for it seems incredible that a non-Celtic caste should have been able to impose itself upon its conquerors and at the same time have accepted their outstanding festivals.[27] The whole "atmosphere" of Druidism as we find it in Gaul, and even in Ireland, appears to be Aryan and Celtic; its myth is notably Celtic, its language is Celtic. The Gaulish cult, inspired by a racial pride almost unequalled in the history of peoples, was perhaps the last type of all to accept an indigenous faith.

Nor does Mr. Salomon Reinach's hypothesis that the Gaulish Celts accepted Druidism from some pre-Celtic people commend itself to me. Such a theory assumes that the Celts had no priesthood of their own; nor do we find Druids in the non-Celtic regions in Gaul. Again, the legal system associated with Druidism—for we must not forget that the Druids were law-givers and judges as well as priests—was also distinctly Aryan and Celtic in its spirit and character.

Mr. T. D. Kendrick's theory concerning the origins of Druidism deserves careful consideration. He believes that the main facts associated with it are to be found only in such records as we possess concerning its position in the Gaul of the first century B.C., an attitude with which the majority of scholars will at once agree. Druidism in Britain and Ireland, he feels, are only to be explained incidentally in respect of this governing factor. Caesar's remarks with reference to the British origin of Druidism were merely the expression of an opinion and not a statement of fact, as they have too frequently been construed. If Druidism had originated in Britain it must have taken root there at a period extremely remote. But there is no evidence in Britain of a Celtic priesthood of such power and status as that which existed in Gaul. Celtic faith in the Marne area, in Gaul, thinks Mr. Kendrick, must have been "built up on native faith" after the immigrant Gauls had occupied that area for some generations. This faith was probably carried to Britain by those Celts who had mingled with the native population of the Marne area. These newcomers would probably incorporate the native faith of Britain with their own. The racial admixture would result in "a thinning" of the Gaulish-Celtic blood and the fame of Britain as the scene of the purest non-Celtic worship would thus be established and would grow. In their ancient home in Central Europe the Celts were, in all likelihood, without priests. But in the peaceful conditions of the La Tène period the Celtic settlers in France may have developed a priestly caste, that of the Druids, at some time in the fourth or third century B.C.   Druidism in Gaul was, therefore, according to Mr. Kendrick, Celtic religion after its consolidation in the Gallic area, while Druidism in Britain presented an admixture of this Gaulish system with an aboriginal British religion which was "in itself an unaltered expression of the Continental native element in Druidism".   On the other hand, the Druids "as an organized hierarchy, were only subsequent Keltic servants of the Kelticised native faith in Gaul, a separate and accidental phenomenon of Gallic (not British) Druidism".   Druidism in Britain was, as all the evidence goes to show, in the hands of chieftains and kings.   In this island, he believes, it had no other priesthood, although a few "British elders" may have taken upon themselves the care and dissemination of its traditions. Irish Druidism, on the other hand, was "a very faint reflection" of Gaulish Druidism.[28]

The theory that Druidism was "Iberian", or non-Celtic, in its origin was, as I have indicated, strongly supported by Sir John Rhys.   In a letter which I received from him so long ago as 1901 he remarked that this hypothesis "is held to have failed".   Dr. Macbain, however, was of opinion that "it is better not to confuse their system with the ordinary Aryan religion of the Gauls", on the grounds that our information regarding the subject as a whole is "meagre".[29]   Bertrand, in his *La Religion des Gaulois*, like many another writer on this confused and tangled theme, looked towards the East for the origins of the Druidic cultus, to the Pythagorean brotherhoods, the Essenes and to Egypt.   But, as I hope to reveal in a later chapter, this is true of Egyptian influence only, and scarcely in the sense that Bertrand appears to conceive it.

But we know little of those British gods to whom the Druidic chiefs and kings in our islands officiated.   As Sir John Rhys has truly said, between Druidism and the gods of the Celts, as they are familiar to us in Welsh and Irish literature, "a great gulf is fixed".   That Irish Druids were the servants of the Goidelic gods of Ireland appears, as I have said, more than probable, but we have no evidence to show that the British Druidism of Caesar's time was definitely associated with any god whatsoever, although it is only fair to say that some of the Gaulish deities have been equated more or less successfully with those which Caesar alludes to under Latin names, and these again with British deities which are known to have existed.   We find Boadicea sacrificing Roman victims to the goddess Andate or Andraste, of whom Cassius Dio speaks, but after fully discussing this association in a recent essay on the British heroine I could find no nearer equation with the name than that of Andarta, a deity worshipped by the Vocontii of south-eastern Gaul.[30]   This goddess has been treated of by Professor Courteault and I find her alluded to by Davies, quoting Baxter's "Glossary".   It seems that her name figures in a Welsh proverb as that of a "fury", who inspired people in a transport of anger.   "Some Andrasta possesses you," runs the saw.   "Fable," Baxter proceeds, "reports that she had a *magical horse*, called *March Maten*, upon which sorcerers were wont to ride through the air."[31]   There appears to have been a lingering tradition of her, and that is all that can be said.   But links so fragile, even when connected, compose but a feeble clue by which to grope our way backward across the precipice of the centuries.

Reviewing the material contained in the last few pages, it is evident that the theories of Rhys respecting the three kinds of religion in pre-Roman Britain and that of Kendrick are not incompatible, although the conclusions of Kendrick are, on the whole, more acceptable and logical.   I feel, however, that neither has done sufficient justice to the obviously Aryan character of Druidism as it was known in Gaul.   The complete acceptance by the Druids of Gaul of a purely Aryan system of judicature and of the ritual of the Aryan solar festivals suffices to settle the question of the *racial* origins of the cultus of Druidism as known to the Romans, so far as I am concerned. Nor can I find in Druidism, so far as its dogma and ritual are known, many traces of non-Celtic belief or practice. For me, too, Gomme's hypothesis that witchcraft was derived from Druidism much more resembles a red herring than a theory. Those of us who have survived from the Gomme-Hartland era are beginning to realize how profoundly conventional and dogmatic these twin censors of late-Victorian folklore really were, and how strenuously they sought to gain a hearing for ideas which had indeed been worked out in Germany a generation before their day and found wanting. Frazer, too, certainly qualifies for mention in the same galley in more than one respect. The very fact that the Christian missionaries in Scotland and Ireland employed spells and charms of the self-same character as those of the Druids might have made it plain to Gomme and Rhys that there was little or nothing "non-Aryan" in Druidism. Were St. Patrick and St. Columba "Iberians"? Were their ideas "non-Aryan"? They happened to be Celts, and probably regarded Iberian Magic as even a shade more mischievous than Celtic sorcery. They practised the only kind of Magic they knew—Celtic Magic. If it be objected that it was "Christian Magic", I can only say that I have never heard of such a quantity.

Such religious ideas as appear to have been known to the Druids were equally familiar to the peoples of other Aryan communities—Germans, Slavs, Greeks, Romans and Hindus. Caesar, who was himself a practising pontiff and something of a stickler for facts, is not likely to have been mistaken in his general estimate of the Druidic faith in Gaul, when he not only compared its gods with certain Roman gods, but actually called them by the names of Roman deities, thus making it plain that he recognized the close resemblance betwixt these equally Aryan forms—forms which had been fixed in their essentials centuries before Roman or Celt were thought of, as the practical identity of many of their myths reveals. What Caesar beheld in Gaulish Druidism was a religion which recalled the spirit, and in some ways the letter, of his own so closely that he did not hesitate to label its deities with the titles of the Roman pantheon, precisely as much earlier Greeks gave Hellenic names to the deities of Egypt. Indeed, the writers of the Classical period and their popular contemporaries appear to have realized this underlying identity of the more outstanding figures of the several Aryan pantheons in a manner never approached by later authorities on folk-lore.

I do not mean to imply that no leaven of non-Aryan faith or Magic found its way into Druidic dogma and ritual. Such a negation would be absurd. Indeed, so many religious and magical forms are common to both Aryan and non-Aryan peoples as to make it virtually impossible to distinguish between them at times. Actually, the standards and tests by which traditionalists seek to do so are, in my view, glaringly incompetent for all practical purposes, and in face of this, I feel, it is frequently impossible to draw any hard-and-fast boundaries. At the same time, certain cultural acceptances are apparent in the pantheons of those races which it is convenient to call "Aryan" for want of a better term; these, in the case of most European races, betray their association with Aryan ideals and ways of thought, and it is roughly possible to indicate them as falling within the Aryan category. Roman, Greek, Slavonic, Teutonic and Celtic god-like forms exhibit such traits, this manner of thought, this higher idealistic outlook. The story of their struggle against non-Aryan forms is outlined in such myths as the wars of the Aryan gods against those of the non-Aryan races in the guise of Titans, giants, Fomorians and similar elder shapes, and in the Celtic mythology we discover this process as in the mythologies of Greece and Rome. It was impossible for Druidism to have accepted or developed such a pantheon unless it had been wholly at one with the ideals of Aryan intellectual progress. And here it is perhaps unnecessary to say that in employing the term "Aryan" I do not comprehend it in the outrageously possessive and exclusive manner of Teutonic racialists, but as indicative of a human type of which the German race was merely a fraction.

The earliest home of Druidism as a religious-magical system was, I believe, Gaul, where alone it exhibits all the signs of a system arrived at fruition. Its imperfect British counterpart was probably inspired by a more primitive spirit. It certainly seems to have been less highly organized on the priestly side, its functions being in all likelihood maintained almost exclusively by kings and chieftains. That the case was somewhat different in Ireland, and that there was the best of reasons for this, I shall endeavour to make plain in the chapter on Reincarnation.

But upon Druidism, as we shall find in the chapter alluded to, was to be imposed a cult which was to have the most powerful repercussions upon its general religious and magical texture. This was the cult of the divine king, the general character of which I shall demonstrate in that place. It may or may not have been an idea extraneous to Druidism; indeed, its ritual and general circumstances would appear to have been so clearly identified with what we know of Druidism that the twain cannot well be disentangled. That this cultus also appears to have been associated with other religious systems elsewhere is unquestioned. The likelihood—nay, the certainty—is that it took on a various semblance in every country to which it penetrated, mingling in all probability with the older and primitive faiths of each. But, Egyptian as it was in its remoter origin, it certainly did not supersede the Celtic element in Druidism, which absorbed it and transfused it with the Celtic spirit.

CHAPTER V

CELTIC SPELLS AND CHARMS

In Celtic Magic the spell and the charm assume certain characteristics which to some extent distinguish them from similar occult practices among other races. In the Gaelic or Irish tongue the appropriate word for spell or taboo is *geas*, derived from the word *guidh*, "to entreat",[1] so that its original mental association with the idea of prayer or supplication is self-evident. The word *orth* was also used for "spell" and *obaidh* for an incantation. But the expression *geas* is more frequently used in old Irish literature in the sense of taboo or prohibition. It was, for example, *geas*, or forbidden, to the hero Cuchullin to eat the flesh of a dog and to the bard Ossian to partake of venison. Such were mere food taboos, based, evidently, on the "totemic" belief that the animals were associated in some way with the warriors in question; for the word *cu*, "dog", appears as part of Cuchullin's name, while Ossian's mother had, before his birth, been enchanted into deer-shape. No doubt, however, an ancient notion of totemism or animal kinship lurked behind the later conception.

We find the early kings of Ireland hedged round on every side by magical taboos of this description. These rulers were regarded as reincarnations of certain of the gods, and the restrictions which thus surrounded them were ordained in order that their sacred qualities, as well as the best interests of the population, whose temporal welfare depended upon these qualities, should not suffer in any way.[2]

But Cuchullin must respect still other *geas*. He might not give his name to any other warrior, nor might he swerve a foot out of his path before engaging in single combat. It was furthermore taboo to him to decline combat or to enter a gathering without permission. The first and second are almost certainly associated with his status as a sun-god, for the sun may not swerve from its appointed orbit. The reasons for the others are by no means so apparent.[3] Such *geas* were usually laid upon a child at birth by some celebrated Druid. Cormac, son of Conchobar, was under certain *geas* of a most extraordinary kind. The horses in his chariot might not be yoked to it by a pole of ashwood. He might not hunt a stag with golden horns. It would be fraught with peril if he hearkened to the harp of Craptine.[4] By neglecting these stipulations, indeed, he finally met his doom.

The farther we penetrate into Celtic lore, the more fantastic these *geas* appear. To the British sun-god Llew Llaw Gyffes it was taboo to stand with one foot on the back of a goat and the other on the edge of a bath. Prompted to do so by his treacherous wife Blodeuwedd, he was immediately wounded by her paramour and transformed into an eagle.[5] These taboos, however, have been proved to be imported into his myth from folk-lore sources, probably of foreign origin. The High Kings of Ireland, the mortal representatives of the gods, their earthly avatars, were under the necessity of observing seven particular *geas*. Some of these were merely precautionary, others were associated with the details of the great annual religious festivals. But the more important taboos of this class were connected with the personal fate of rulers or great heroes, as is revealed by the derivation of the Welsh phrase *tyngu tynghed*— that is, to swear a man his destiny, to lay upon him predictory prohibitions which he might not break without results definitely fatal.

With the Celts, as with other peoples, the spell appears as the resultant of the exercise of a highly concentrated will-power. It was the expression of "the beautiful violent will", as it has been called by a modern writer, exerted upon the person or object it was desired to enchant or influence. It has been said that the Celtic magician, in the act of self-transformation, actually tried to assume, by mental or spiritual might, the form, character and nature of the person, animal or thing he wished to become for the nonce; or, that by some such psychic process of surpassing might he sought to transfer to any person whom he wished to transform the attributes of the man, woman or creature into whose shape he enchanted that person. According to the doctrine of the Celtic wizard, a unity existed in nature which permitted of such metamorphoses, its underlying elements were one and the same, and capable of alteration by the power of will, which could reassemble its basic factors into any shape desired. The incantations by which he verbally expressed this overriding intention were usually chanted in verse. Occasionally a Celtic wizard stood on one foot and closed one eye, as though to concentrate the whole force of his will upon the person or object he wished to bespell or transform, and of this attitude we find more than one example in Irish saga.

Among the more potent and important enchantments of the Celts was that known as *fith-fath*, or *fath-fith*. It was employed to bring about invisibility, and is still believed in to some extent in the more remote Western Isles of

Scotland, while there is also a vital tradition of its former use in Ireland. "This rite," says George Henderson, an eminent authority upon Gaelic beliefs, "under the name of *fath-fith* has existed in the Western Isles until our own day, *faeth*, or *fáth* being a kind of poem or incantation", which may be best defined in the phrase "words of magic".[6] Formerly it was thought to have been connected in some way with the tradition that certain women gifted with magical powers were capable of changing themselves into the shape of deer. It seems, however, that no grounds for this supposition exist, a false etymology having popularly confused the term with *fiadh*, the word for "deer".[7]

"*Fath-fith* and *fith-fath*," says Dr. Alexander Carmichael, "are interchangeable terms and are applied to the occult power which makes people invisible, or which transforms one object into another." He narrates the story of Fionn's sweetheart, the mother of Ossian, for whose sake Fionn had forsaken a supernatural mistress. Infuriated at his disloyalty, this sorceress placed her mortal rival under the *fith-fath* spell, so that she became a hind, and while in this shape she bore a son to Fionn, who was known as Ossian, or "little fawn".

Carmichael translates the *fith-fath* spell as follows:

> *Fath-fith*
> Will I make on thee,
> By Mary of the augury,
> By Bride of the corslet,
> From sheep, from ram,
> From goat, from buck,
> From fox, from wolf,
> From sow, from boar . . .

And so forth, through a fairly long list of other animals.[8]

Mr. W. Mackenzie quotes another rhyme in connection with *fath-fith*, which reveals a closer association with the act of rendering a person invisible:

> A magic cloud I put on thee,
> From dog, from cat,
> From cow, from horse,
> From man, from woman,
> From young man, from maiden,
> And from little child.
> Till I again return.

Which is as much as to say: "Let the person enchanted be beheld by none of these people or animals."

Mr. Mackenzie proceeds to say that *fith-fath* was a favourite charm with hunters, "for it enabled them to make physical objects invisible to the ordinary eye". As they left the forest with the prey they had hunted they were invisible to their enemies, and in this manner smugglers could render themselves unseen to the officers of the Excise.[9]

Invisibility by the aid of *fith-fath* was well known in Ireland, whence, indeed, it must originally have proceeded. It was said to have been given to the Tuatha Dé Danann by the god Manannan, whose lordship of the sea probably equipped him with power over shifting fogs and illusions. It was the especial privilege of the Irish god Angus, exercised in his Brugh of the Boyne, where he dwelt invisible to mortals.[10]

Summing up, we find that *fith-fath* was a spell ensuring invisibility. It was also possible by its aid to transform a human being into an animal. That the expression had its origin in the term *fáth*, "the poetic art", which among the Celts certainly inculcated a knowledge of that class of incantation or sarcastic and scorching verbiage which, according to Irish authorities, enabled the bard to disfigure his opponents physically by the utterance of terrific jibes alone, there can be little doubt. By extension, the ability to disfigure may possibly have come later to include both the transformation of persons into animals and the act of causing their complete disappearance. A satire of the bard Cairpre brought out blotches upon the face of Bres, while another of his lampoons caused the Fomorians to become powerless. Queen Maeve of Ulster assured a hero that if he refused combat with Cuchullin her bards would so transform him by their satires that he would perish from shame.[11] This kind of satire could scarcely have been other than magical in its essence, and incantational in its form. From this to the spell, which was thought of as bringing about transformation into animal form, is but a short step, while it will be recalled that the Celtic bards were regarded as a special class of the Druids or masters of magic.

The phrase *fith-fath* is pronounced "fee-fa", and it is not wholly impossible that it may represent the favourite ejaculation of the giants and ogres of nursery tale—"fee-fo-fum". This latter term was for long a puzzle to antiquaries of the older school, some of whom regarded it as a term surviving from the language of an aboriginal folk represented in tradition by giants and ogres. In a Breton tale a fairy changeling exclaims: "I was born in Pif and in Paf, in the country where cats are made"—that is, in the land of enchantment. Have these expressions any relationship with *fith-fath*, which George Henderson seeks to connect with Celtic words alluding to witchcraft, sorcery, or delusion?

Another spell presenting somewhat unusual features is that associated with what has come to be known as "the cow-fetters of the fairy woman", or "supernatural woman", the word *sidhe* in Gaelic implying both "fairy" and "supernatural". In the Highlands of Scotland the *burrach*, cow-fetter, or spancel, was a cord or thin rope made from horsehair, with a loop at one end and a knob of hard wood at the other for fastening it. This was placed round the feet of a restless cow at milking-time so as to hobble her and ensure that she would remain steady during the operation. The "supernatural woman", witch or fairy, was credited with having a bunch of cords made up of nine of these fetters. The ordinary spancel was for some reason associated in the Highland mind with the uncanny—*a fortiori* that of a weird wife was greatly more so. The cow-fetter was invariably hung up in a certain place in the byre, and if it were found or purloined by anyone outside of the family it was thought that this placed the *toradh*, or produce of the cattle (milk and butter), in their power.[12] Both fairies and witches were in the habit of drawing the "pith" of the milk of their neighbours magically away from the cow-house by means of a similar hair tether laid upon the grass on a dewy morning, as a woman at Dingwall was accused of doing as late as the year 1834, according to Dalyell.

The spell associated with this implement especially ensures that a person who is adjured "by the nine cow-fetters" will carry through any task imposed upon him. It is a *geas* that no one dare infringe. Should it be neglected, the person reckless enough to slight it would sooner or later encounter the dreaded weird woman who roams the countryside seeking for victims. She would strike him with her deadly cow-fetters, which she used for milking the deer. Such a blow had the effect of rendering him so "fey",or mentally confused, that the most despicable coward or fool imaginable would have the power to defeat him in single combat.

The spell or adjuration which accompanied the *geas* in question usually placed upon the hapless hero some special task or performance, and was known as "the nine fulfilments of the fairy woman"   The rhyme generally ran as follows:

> To lay thee under spells and crosses
> under (pain of being struck by) the nine
>   cow-fetters of the wildly roaming,
>   traveller-deluding fairy woman,
> So that some sorry little wight more feeble
>   and misguided than thyself
> Take thy head, thine ear and thy life's
>   career from thee.[18]

In the West Highland tale of "The Lad with the Skin Coverings" the King's daughter puts upon Ceudach and his companions "crosses and spells and the nine cow-spancels of the fairy woman, the bald tricky calf, worse than its name". The calf seems to symbolize the stupid person who will outwit the hero, but the verbiage is obscure, and it may well apply to the fairy. In the tale of "The Three Green Dogs" the malevolent sister says to her brother: "I am putting you under spells and crosses, and nine fetters of fairy wives wandering, straying, and the little calf that is weakest and feeblest, to bring your head and your ear and your life off you, if you will not go three times after other to the giants' cave and give three shouts at the door."[14] A similar incident occurs in the tale of "Young Manus, son of the King of Lochlann".

Another spell of some importance in Scotland was that known as the *frith*, which was employed to discover the situation of anyone at a distance. It was probably of Norse origin. It must be made on the first Monday of the quarter before sunrise, fasting and with bare feet. The *Frithear* walked sunwise round the house, with closed eyes, till the doorstep was reached, when he opened them, and looking through the circle made by his finger and thumb, he judged by the character of the omen revealed by the first object he beheld. If this was a sacred symbol, such as two straws crossed, all was well. A man standing was a sign of recovery. A woman in the same attitude was a bad sign. (G. Henderson, *Norse Influences in Celtic Scotland*, pp. 72-3.)

The superstition known as "the evil eye" is by no means a monopoly of the Celtic peoples, though it had a wide and peculiarly potent sanction among them. In Italy, the East and elsewhere the legend of it is still notorious, while in Lowland Scotland, a partly Celtic sphere, witches were frequently accused of possessing it. It was commonly supposed to be the result of a peculiar malignity or envy on the part of its owner, though it was perfectly possible for a person to have an evil eye and to remain unconscious of the fact. When a cow or pig was suddenly seized with sickness, or a child did not thrive, it was assumed that some visitor had cast "the evil eye" upon it, and if his or her visits coincided with distempers of the kind on more than one occasion he generally achieved a local reputation as the possessor of a magically dangerous glance. This quality was more frequently attributed to women, and especially to elderly women, than to men. In Islay it was thought that anyone whose eyes were of different colours might possess the evil eye.

The "ill e'e", as it was known in the Lowlands of Scotland, was proverbially attracted by the prettiest child or the finest cow or horse, so that it came to be regarded as unlucky to speak of these in terms of admiration. The symptoms in cattle of being "struck" or "over-looked" were loss of milk, a tendency to kick, and, as the malady progressed, a frantic wildness which usually ended in collapse. Horses afflicted by the evil eye would sweat and tremble and grow weaker daily. In the island of Lewis cows were protected from it by a charmed *burrach*, or cow-fetter, which was fixed on the animal's hind legs when she calved. A very considerable number of preventative charms were employed to ward off the evil, among them the use of rowan and juniper, horseshoes, burning cloth, tar, certain string charms, iron, and other articles which in their entirety would compose quite a lengthy list.

It was not at all essential that the possessor of the evil eye should be a witch or sorcerer, but a very definite tradition existed that certain persons had a monopoly of arcane knowledge which could nullify its powers.[15] This was, as in the case of Magic generally in the Highlands, handed down from father to daughter and from mother to son. It was not invariably necessary for the owner of the maleficent gaze to see the person or thing on which he or she desired to cast an influence, certain practitioners having the power to exercise this abhorred gift at a distance. In one case at least the appearance of the evil eye is described. An Orkney witch, Catherine Grant, who was alive and mischievous in 1623, was observed to look over her shoulder and turn up the white of her eye.[16] Others, to employ a Lowland Scottish expression, "glowered", or looked fixedly at the object of their antipathy with a lowering, smouldering expression. The effects were often instantaneous. Ale and milk could be turned sour by such a glance. In itself it does not appear to have been regarded in every case as the instrument of sorcery so much as of envy and pure malice. The Devil instructed a certain Jonet Irving, if she bore ill-will to anyone, "to look on them with open eyes and pray evil for them in his name", but this is among the few instances of purely diabolic association to be ascertained in connection with the belief.[17] A difference certainly existed between "overlooking and bewitching", but, as Glanvil remarks, how they came to be "distinguished by this hellish fraternity, I know not".[18]

The classical case of an evil eye in Irish mythology is associated with Balor, the chief god of that dark and mysterious race the gloomy Fomorians, an aboriginal people. One of his eyes was always closed because its glance slew all upon whom it fell, while some tales describe it as protected by several layers of bronze or leather. It had acquired this terrific quality because its owner had peered through the window of a house where certain sorcerers were compounding a magic potion, the poisonous fumes infecting his sight. In the day of battle the lid of this destructive member was raised with a hook, to the general confusion of the enemy. In some parts of Ireland the peasantry still call the evil eye "the eye of Balor".[19]

Anciently, among the Gaelic-speaking Celts, the word *bricht*, meaning "magical spell", was used to signify a spell or charm in the more ceremonial sense.[20] The varieties of spells or charms in use among the Celtic peoples of Britain was indeed so numerous that the chronicler of them despairs of describing them in their entirety.

Invisibility was thought to be conferred through the virtue of fern-seed, which is "supposed to become visible only on St. John's eve, and at the very moment when the Baptist was born", as Sir Walter Scott remarks.[21] Herodias, the daughter of Herod, who danced before her father so that she might be rewarded with the saint's head on a charger, was later confused with Herodias the witch or fairy queen of the Middle Ages, and through this distorted belief the seed of fern came to be associated with St. John's Day. In gathering it great perils were to be encountered from the attacks of spirits, and Richard Bovet mentions a case in point in which a gatherer of the seed was savagely treated by them.[22] Jackson was told by another seeker for the seed that it "was in the keeping of the King of Faynes", who would "doe him no harm", and added that John the Baptist was born at the very instant when the fern seed, at other times invisible, should fall, as an angel had foretold.[23]   Shakespeare alludes to the superstition (in Ist "Henry IV." ii, I) when he makes one of his characters say: "We have the receipt of fern-seed, we walk invisible."[24]

The Irish bards, who, in later times, appear to have retained much of the old Druidic magic, have left on record a passing allusion to some of the charms which were studied in the ninth year of the course stipulated by custom as essential to their complete adeptship.   Some of these refer to the manner in which thieves might be tracked, how good fortune might be secured on entering a new house, or the manner in which a journey on horseback might best be made.   Mention of these are to be found in the treatise known as *The Book of Ballymote*, written by Solomon of Droma and Manus MacDonogh about the year 1391.[25]

What was known in Ireland as "the thumb of knowledge" was associated with vision of a supernatural kind.   When the sorcerer desired "the sight", he pressed one of his teeth with his thumb.   The legend relative to the discovery of this method is to be found in the saga of Fionn, or Finn MacCoul, who on one occasion received an injury to his thumb by having it jammed in the door of a fairy knoll.   Placing it in his mouth, he sucked it, to ease the pain, whereupon he found himself possessed of supernatural sight.[26]   Another version told how Finn caught and cooked "the Salmon of Knowledge".   Laying his thumb on a blister which rose on the skin of the fish, he scalded it and applied the injured member to his mouth, whereupon foreknowledge was vouchsafed him.[27] In both cases the power was conferred through contact with a supernatural object applied indirectly to one of the organs of sense.

"The Salmon of Knowledge" alluded to in these legends occupies a somewhat important position in the Magic of the British and Irish Celts.   This mysterious fish acquired mystical lore through eating the nuts of the divine hazel-tree which conveyed to the eater knowledge of "everything that was in the world".   These nuts fell from the trees into a well situated beneath them, and were regarded as the food of the gods.   Druids and magicians sought anxiously for the *Eo Feasa*, the Salmon of Knowledge, in the hope of partaking of its flesh and thus acquiring universal wisdom.[28]

The question of counter-spells employed to dissolve those enchantments which brought about a difference in bodily appearance is, I feel, an important one, as some of the evidence has led more than one authority to assume that the process of restoration had a close affinity with certain passages in ancient initiatory rites.   By far the best illustration of a legend embracing such circumstances is that which describes the metamorphoses undergone by a hero known as Tamlane, which has long been cast into ballad shape in Scotland and which will be familiar to many readers.

The story-plot of the ballad is almost a household word, but its precise details are essential to its more attentive study.   The Young Tamlane, the son of "Randolph, Earl Murray", was taken into the household of his uncle at the age of nine, possibly to undergo the training of a page in the arts of chivalry, but on his journey thence he was cast into a deep sleep by a bitter north wind, fell from his horse, and was spirited away by the Queen of Faerie   After he had passed nearly seven years in the fairy realm he realized that the time was approaching for the traditional payment of a tribute of one of its denizens to Satan, which was yielded once in seven years.   In childhood he had been enamoured of the Lady Janet, daughter of the Earl of March, and on the eve of Hallowe'en he appeared to her when, in a romantic moment, she had betaken herself to Carterhaugh in Selkirkshire, notorious as a fairy rendezvous.   In the traditional manner of fairy lordlings, he rebukes her for pulling a rose on elfin soil and then treats her as the heroes of romance usually treat over-adventurous damsels. He reveals to her an outline of the fairy life and the magical powers it affords, but begs her to come to his aid, as he dreads the approaching day of sacrifice.

In order to free him she must repair to Miles Moss between twelve and one on the next night (that is Hallow-e'en), when the fairy court rides, bearing holy water in her hand. She must also "cast a compass", or describe a magical ring, or circle, at the spot. Three courts or bands of the elves will pass her by and she will find him in the third, mounted upon a milk-white steed, with a golden star in his crown. She must seize him, and drag him from his horse, whereupon the fairies will turn him into various shapes, which are given in the best traditional version as those of an esk, an adder, a lion and a bolt of red-hot iron. During these metamorphoses she must cling to him until he changes into "a mother-naked man", when she must cast her green mantle over him, dip him in a stand of milk and then in one of hot water. All this comes to pass and he is delivered. The only person who expresses disappointment with the result is the Fairy Queen, who exclaims that had she been aware of his attempted rescue she would have removed his eyes, replacing them by eyes of wood, and his heart, for which she would have substituted one of stone.

Themes of this kind are not unknown to Classical tale—for instance, in that told by Apollodorus of the forced marriage of Thetis to Peleus, who clung to her although she took various disguises. Mr. L. C. Wimberley, a modern American writer, has pointed out that there are no less than nine variants of the metamorphoses gone through by Tamlane, including shapes which need not detain us in the circumstances.

On the Celtic side of things we have a record of such magical changes in the story of the son of Manannan, the Irish sea-god, "who will be in the shape of every beast, both on sea and on land", a myth recalling the changeful Proteus, another sea-deity.[29] And the reader will doubtless recall the British-Celtic myth of the goddess Ceridwen and her metamorphoses into many forms in her struggle with Gwion, alluded to on a previous page.

During the process of disenchantment Janet must keep continually calling out the hero's name. Is "Tamlane" the hero's otherworld name? It has been suggested that by giving him an unearthly name the elves have cut him off from human converse, and that this resembles the initiation names adopted in savage ceremonies, as in the manhood-initiations of native Australian rites. In one version of the ballad we read:

> First they did call me Jack, he said,
>   And then they called me John,
> But since I lived in the fairy court
>   Tamlane has always been my name.

It may be so, but to my way of thinking the hypothesis seems a little over-strained. Indeed, I cannot recall any kidnapped hero or heroine in fairy legend whose name underwent a change once he became a denizen in the land of the fays. In any case the name of Tam'ane, or Tam Lin, or Thumbling, was familiar in folk-lore long before the era of the ballad.

Mr. Wimberley, in detailing the process of metamorphosis, adds: "The important magical ceremony of immersion in water or milk as a means of effecting restoration to an original shape is depicted in 'Tam Lin'."[30] He also thinks that the device of casting a compass round with holy water "may be a relic of the water or milk bath in other versions". He points out that the process occurs in Ulrich's Grail romance of "Lanzelet" in a certain Greek tale, and in an ancient version of the story of the fairy Melusine.[31] "Judging by analogy," says Professor Child, "the naked man should issue from the bath of milk or water, into which he should have gone in one of his non-human shapes."[32] But what is the value of such analogies? Do they actually, as some authorities appear to believe, descend from some well-authenticated ritual of transformation, or are they merely memories of the primitive notion that human beings could assume animal or other forms?

Child assents to the authenticity of the traditional sequence of change into esk, adder, lion, hot iron, dip into water, naked knight. He also affords us a short list of similar changes of form in Scandinavian ballads.[33] He quotes a Danish ballad which recounts the manner in which a nightingale was transformed back into human form in the sequence of lion, bear, variety of snakes, lind-worm. He says, moreover, that the dipping in milk and water has an occult and very important significance, "only very lately pointed out, and which modern reciters had completely lost knowledge of, as appears from the disorder into which the stanzas have fallen". He refers, of course, to Mannhardt's statement (in his *Weld-u Felde-kult,*" II, 64) to this effect. The illustration is associated with the story of Lanzelet, in which the serpent whom the hero kisses is not instantly turned into a woman, but must first bathe in a spring, and Mannhardt adds that the Princess in an Albanian tale plunges her dove-lover into a basin of milk to restore him to human shape.

But to what ancient and arcane ceremony of metamorphosis does Child, or Mannhardt, actually cast back? I am aware of none in the records of ancient Magic, in which I think I can with truth plead that I am not unversed. I prefer to believe that the tale of "Tamlane" and other Celtic tales which describe similar metamorphoses are merely memories, not of any explicit formula of initiatory rites, but rather reminiscences of that primitive belief which holds that people can take animal or other forms at death, the liberated soul passing into one or a series of animals. Where is the evidence that in the course of any initiation ceremony, savage or civilized, the initiate either took on the forms of several animals or was temporarily known by their names? And is it not self-evident that here we are not dealing with any such initiatory ceremony, but *with a process the very reverse*, the restoration of an enchanted man into his proper human form? It is essential to the better comprehension of Celtic Magic that the process in question should not remain in doubt as regards its general character. The theory that people taken to the Faerie were actually believed to have undergone some process analogous to death which, in a special and primitive sense, signified a transformation into animal form, and that Tamlane must naturally *reverse* this process and repass through the animal and other forms which man was thought of as assuming subsequent to his death, appears to me a much more reasonable explanation in the circumstances than that which seeks to see in his bodily changes a memory of savage initiation. In Greek myth, when the child Learchos was slain, his mother placed him in a cauldron of boiling water to restore him to life. Pelops was also restored in the same way by Klotha. In some savage initiation rites, it is true, men are supposed to become leopards, jaguars or wer-animals, and are so-called, but in no initiatory rite that I am aware of do they pass through a *series* of animal or other changes, although they certainly do according to the doctrine of metempsychosis, or reincarnation, with which the fairy change seems to have closer affinities than with initiation. I am convinced that the circumstances narrated above are those of counter-spell—or a reversal of the original spell. But, as we shall see in a later chapter, the several forms through which Tamlane passes in his disenchantment bear a rather startling resemblance to those described as having been assumed by the human soul in its evolutionary process through the abyss of Anwnn, the dim region of lowest life in Welsh-Celtic tradition. These appear to be reptilian, and perhaps also mineral, though the terms descriptive of them are obscure. It should be remembered, too, that the countryside in which the scene of "Tamlane" is set, that is Selkirkshire, is a territory formerly inhabited by Old British tribes who spoke a dialect of British or "Welsh", and who, it is maintained, conveyed many of their traditions to North Wales, where they finally settled. I may add that I believe that the bath of milk and water into which Janet plunged her lover merely denotes a final purificatory process to cleanse him from the stains of Otherworld. Milk in the Irish myths has a healing power which neutralizes poison, while water is a world-wide lustrative.

While on the subject of those charms which neutralize or destroy evil or untoward conditions it is necessary to draw particular attention to that very important belief which held that iron was a substance peculiarly dreaded by the darker powers and that by its agency it was possible to avert their disastrous intentions. Evil spirits of every kind and witches had an especial dread of all iron implements, and many students of tradition have been of opinion that this dislike or abhorrence refers to the memory of a period when the peoples of the Bronze Age encountered the men of the La Tène culture, who were equipped with iron weapons and who first flourished in the eighth century before the Christian era. This is by no means a Celtic superstition alone, but has almost a world-wide acceptance. To avert evil, iron was sewn into the clothes of children, iron pins or brooches were stuck in their caps, iron horse-shoes were nailed to the doors of stables and cow-houses to protect horses and cattle from mischievous spiritual influences. The horseshoe was particularly protective for the reason that it is roughly in the form of a crescent and has therefore a lunar significance. It should preferably be cast from the near hind leg of a grey mare, should be found accidentally and not collected haphazard, while it is essential to nail it above the door, points upward, and, if possible, with its own nails.[34] Women in childbed were safeguarded by a row of iron nails or a reaping-hook, so that evil spirits might not approach them or their infants.[35] In Islay, if butter would not "come" in the churn, the dairymaid heated a smoothing-iron until it was red-hot, and plunged it into water, repeating certain mystical words as she did so. Some of the water was then placed in the churn, "and would you believe it, the butter came back, and not only that, but with the very first churning there was a great quantity, equal to all that had been lost since things had gone wrong".[36]

In an Irish tale a charmed knife produces a similar effect.[37] In the Highland story of "The Four Hunters and the Four *Glaistigs*" one of the *glaistigs*, a peculiarly evil vampirical spirit of the waters, asks one of the hunters for a pinch of snuff. Cautiously he reached it to her on the point of his dirk. She tried to seize the hand which held the dagger, but he kept the point of the weapon towards her, prodding her with it. It was as well that he did so, for when the *glaistigs* vanished at cockcrow he found his three companions lying dead and cold, with all the blood drained from their bodies.[38]

Many spells are, of course, of the nature of invocations to spirits or supernatural powers, and these are usually couched in metre, such as "The Prayer for Long Life", which, for all its pagan associations, is said to have been written by an Irish abbot in the eighth century. It invokes "the Seven Daughters of the Sea", who act as Fates, beseeching them to grant the suppliant long life, and to destroy his "double", which probably implies that he does not wish it to appear as a presage of death—or perhaps because the tradition connected with it had a pagan origin.

The terror of the folk for the race of Faerie is expressed in the Highland spell which pleads for safeguard from the brownie and the *banshee*, from nymph and water-wraith, from troll, siren and ghoul—or their Gaelic equivalents.[39]

The usual method of composing a spell was to chew a piece of flesh and offer it up to the maker's tutelary idol. This was preparatory to falling into a trance or sleep, probably induced by hypnosis, or some narcotic drug. As he lay prostrate beside the image in slumber, the illumination of song came to the bard and he awoke with mystical verses on his lips.

Diseases of all kinds, and endemic or epidemic complaints, were personalized by the early Celts and regarded in some parts of Celtic Britain until quite recent times as demons or evil spirits who might be propitiated or kept away either by supplications or offerings. In an ancient Irish MS., the Codex St. Gall, Diancecht, the god of healing, is invoked to aid the sufferer from a growth or tumour. "I strike the disease, I vanquish . . . let this not be a chronic tumour. Let that whereon Diancecht's salve goes be whole. I put my trust in the salve which Diancecht left with his family that whole may be that whereon it goes."[40] But that many diseases were actually caused by Magic was a belief popularly entertained until at least the seventeenth century, as Alexander Drummond, a Scottish mediciner, maintained. At his trial for sorcery in 1629 he avouched that he had cured many persons of lunacy, the falling sickness, cancer, St. Anthony's fire, and those with a tendency to see apparitions, all of which he stated had been caused by sorcery. But his judges regarded him as an empiric, or worse, and he was strangled and burnt.[41]

Healing by the use of magical stones was frequently resorted to. An old woman who dwelt in Strathnaver, in the far north of Scotland, possessed a white stone which had come to her by inheritance and which was said to be capable of marvellous cures. One of the Gordons of Strathnaver resolved to possess himself of it, and as she refused to yield it up, he cast her into the neighbouring loch of Manaar, along with the amulet. The loch in question was long regarded as having acquired the healing virtues of the stone, and the halt, the lame and the mentally diseased repaired to its waters in large numbers so lately as the last quarter of the nineteenth century. It was thought that the stone had been recovered from the loch. In any case, such a pebble was in the possession of Lord Reay, who was so pestered by applications for the loan of it that at last he gave it away to a local gentleman who administered its use among the peasantry.[42] The number of miraculous stones existing, or formerly existing, in Scotland and Ireland "defies description". To cure scrofula, mare's milk should be taken from an aspen spoon and epilepsy might be held in check if a black cock were buried alive at the precise spot where the patient had the first fit.[43] But the details of cures by charm in Celtic Britain might easily occupy a portly volume.[44]

The twigs, sprays, or leaves of certain trees or herbs were regarded by the Celtic peoples as powerful charms against maleficent spirits. The rowan, or mountain-ash, in particular, was employed by them for this purpose, and its wood was either placed over the door of a dwelling or sewn into garments to ward off evil agencies. Its scarlet berries were in ancient times regarded as the food of the gods, and it was probably due to this belief that its protective powers came to be assumed.[45] The rowan, says Dalyell, is frequently to be found in the vicinity of standing stones and circles.

In Scotland and Ireland the mystical herb known as the Möan, or Mothan (either the thyme-leaved sandwort, or perhaps the bog-violet), was given to cattle as a protective charm. If anyone ate of the cheese made from the milk of a cow which had eaten this plant, he would, it was thought, be secure for ever from every species of supernatural mischief. It was said to be found on the summit of a cliff or mountain where no species of quadruped had ever fed or trod. In Lightfoot's *Flora Scotica* it is described as "*Pinguicula vulgaris, Möan, Gaulis*, Steepgrass, Earning-grass, Scotis-austral." The Möan was to be culled on a Sunday in the following manner: three small tufts of it were to be selected, and one of these was to be called by the name of the Father, another by that of the Son, the remaining tuft to be called by the name of the Holy Ghost. The finder would then pull the tufts, saying as he did so:

> I will pull the Möan,
> The herb blessed by the Domnach;
> So long as I preserve the Möan
> There lives not on earth
> One who will take my cow's milk from me.

The three tufts were then pulled, taken home, rolled up in a piece of cloth and hidden in a corner of the dairy, or milk-kist. As illustrating the virtues of the plant, it is told that a woman in the Western Isles was delivered of a son. The midwives attending her saw a shaggy little being toddle in at the door, and stand in the room as though bewildered. A voice without called to him: "Will you not bring it (the child) out?" The spirit replied: "I cannot, for the milk of the cow that ate the Möan is in his stomach." He then disappeared.[46]

The St. John's wort (*Hypericum perforatum*) was formerly carried by the people of Scotland as a charm against witches and fairies. Cameron says that a certain John Morrison, who lived in Bernera, Harris, wore this plant, known in Gaelic as *seud*, in his coat to prevent him from seeing visions, and averred that he never saw any since he had done so. St. John's wort was evidently one of those herbs which prevented the attacks of the diabolic. Scott says that he recalled a ballad in which a fiend who wished to pay his addresses to a maiden said to her:

> Gin ye wish to be leman mine,
> Lay aside the St. John's wort and the vervain.

The reddish-coloured sap of this plant was called the blood of St. John the Baptist. It is said in the Isle of Man that if you tread on the St. John's wort after sunset a fairy horse will rise from the earth and carry you about all night, leaving you only at sunrise.

Cows were protected from the influence of fairies and witches by having *bollan feaill-Eoin*, or mugwort, placed in their byres on St. John's Eve. It was made into chaplets which were worn on the heads of man and beast to protect them from malign influence.

The four-leaved clover is familiar in occult lore. A tale from Northumberland tells how a girl returning home from milking saw many fairies gambolling in the fields, which were invisible to her companions. The pad on her head which bore the weight of her milking-pail, and which was made of a wreath of grass, contained some leaves of four-leaved clover which gave one the power to see fairies. A milkmaid at Bosfrancan, in Cornwall, had a similar adventure. She beheld the piskies swarming about the cow she was milking, which for weeks had been in a fractious state. A four-leaved clover was found in the bunch of grass she had placed in her hat for convenience in carrying her milk-buckets.[47]

As regards the traditional identity of the clover, some dubiety appears to exist. The shamrock was and is regarded as a kind of trefoil, or three-leaved plant. "The plants, however, which for a long time past have been regarded by the Irish as the true shamrock, are, according to Dr. Prior, the Black Non-such or Medicago and the Dutch Clover. . . . In early writers we find that Watercress was termed Shamrock, and it is quite possible that this was the real plant, the Trefoil having usurped its place in order to meet the requirements of the St. Patrick tradition." (H. Friend, *Flowers and Flower-lore*, p. 385 f.). Objection will be made to the watercress on the ground that its leaf is not trifoliate and could not have been used by St. Patrick to illustrate the doctrine of the Trinity to which the tradition is usually referred. But this story is of modern date and is not to be found in any of the lives of the saint. The plant most usually identified in Ireland with the shamrock is the Black Nonsuch, while others regard the wood-sorrel, and still others the clover, to be that plant. Whichever plant may be the shamrock, the clover is familiar in folk-lore as a mystical plant.[49]

Spells associated with fire bulk largely and importantly in Celtic magical tradition, and I shall endeavour to explain the most outstanding as clearly as a complicated subject makes possible. These fires were religious in origin, and here I shall deal only with such magical implications as they seem to possess.

Samhain, the festival of the ancient Celts, was held on the eve of November 1st, the beginning of the Celtic winter. At Tara, in Ireland, on that night, a solemn religious sacrifice was anciently offered up to the gods. It was connected with the bringing-in of the harvest. In some parts of old Scotland it was celebrated as a kind of harvest-home, and lights were carried round the boundaries of farms to chase away evil influences. The central rite was the extinguishing and rekindling of domestic fires. The season was associated as a whole with the idea of terror and fear. November was indeed the month of death and sacrifice. The dead and their associates, the fairies, were free to wander the world on that occasion, which was thus one of peril to wayfarers, who might be spirited off by them. It was a night of mischief and confusion. The last sheaf of corn or barley was cut at *Samhain* and was dressed up in the guise of an old woman, known as "the Carlin". In the Highlands bonfires were lighted on the hills. At some of these bonfires each person present placed a white stone with his mark upon it. If he failed to find it after the fire died out he was doomed to bad luck, or worse, in the ensuing year. With the extinction of the last spark, the crowd ran helter-skelter down the hill, crying out, "May the black sow without a tail seize the hindmost". The allusion is probably to a besetting demon.

Sir James Frazer has described and discussed this festival very fully. He has made it plain that one school of traditionalists believes these fire-ceremonies to be of the nature of imitative magic "to ensure a needful supply of sunshine for men, animals and plants by kindling fires which mimic on earth the great source of light and heat in the sky", while on the other hand it has been maintained that the ceremonial fires "have no reference to the sun, but are simply purificatory"—that is, designed to destroy all harmful influences. He considered the latter view to be the more probable. In the general opinion of Celtic authorities, *Samhain* allegorically signified the failure or imprisonment of the sun-god Lugh, who at that period fell for half a year under the sway of the evil forces of winter. Certain Greek festivals which equate with *Samhain*, more or less, have a purificatory signifiance, and it seems difficult to question Frazer's explanation of the rite, which is merely a spell designed to affright evil spirits. Still, oddly enough, the distribution of the new fire in Ireland at that season seems to bring it into line with those festivals in non-Celtic lands which were allegorical of the sun's rebirth, and which were generally associated with the rites of spring.

At *Samhain* domestic hearths were quenched to symbolize the failure or sleep of the sun, and if new fires were lit, with some semblance of ritual, this does not seem to involve any mythological explanation, although traces are not wanting in Ireland that such an explanation was forthcoming in the myth of the maiden Tlachtga. This was associated with the place of that name in Meath. Tlachtga possessed a magical wheel, the *Roth Fail*, which could sail through the air, and this I have already alluded to in connection with the legend of Simon Magus. Now we know from comparison with a similar British myth that this wheel was nothing but the sun. Layamon says of the mythical King Bladud, who boasted of a similar solar airplane, that in one of his flights in that machine he "crashed" upon *the temple of Apollo* in London, and that his "'plane" was smashed—which is as much as to say that the sun-god, at the winter solstice, betook himself in confusion to the temple of Apollo, god of the Sun, his "home" or resting-place. Now Tlachtga's name is associated with the distribution of fire to the hearths of Erin at *Samhain*, so that it is pretty obvious, I think, that she and her father, Mog Ruith, a famous sorcerer, are the Icarus and Daedalus of a lost or half-forgotten Celtic myth of the "crashing" of the sun-chariot at *Samhain*—and that they are also connected with a rite which foreshadowed the regeneration of the sun, and the symbolism of the same by the distribution of the new fire, on the very day of his disaster. I venture to think, too, that the actual meaning of this rite implies that Lugh, the sun-god, was symbolically conceived by the kindling of the new fire.[49] The other seasonal fires, those of Beltane, or *Bealltainn*, and Midsummer, provide material for the discussion of the student of Comparative Religion rather than for the pages of a book devoted to the Magic Arts.

It may be added that more than one remembrance of such a fire-festival still survives in Scotland, such as "the burning of the clavie" at Burghead and other centres on the North-east coast.[50] In such cases the underlying notion seems to be simply a purificatory one, to chase away evil spirits.

As in the case of other peoples, the Celts concocted charms and potions to arouse amatory feelings in the hearts of those by whom they wished to be beloved. It is said that the river Shannon owed its source to a spring or well beneath the sea. This was the well of Connla, which was overshadowed by a wonderful hazel tree the nine nuts of which had the property of awakening love in the eater.[51] The nuts burned at Hallow-e'en to discover whether two sweethearts will remain true to one another probably owe their folk-lore origin to this tradition.

Sir John Colquhoun of Luss, in Dumbartonshire, married Lady Lilias Graham, a daughter of the Earl of Montrose, in 1633. Her younger sister, the Lady Katherine, came to reside with the married pair, and the faithless baronet conceived an unlawful affection for his sister-in-law. At first she remained cold to his advances, so he applied to a necromancer for a love-potion of a rather uncommon description. He sent a jewel of gold set with diamonds to this secret practitioner, who treated it with poisons known to arouse amatory feelings in the wearer, which so worked upon the senses of the Lady Katherine that she became infatuated with Sir John and finally eloped with him to London. Colquhoun was outlawed and his fellow-conspirator, the magician, was delated for his part in the affair, though whether he was brought to justice or not remains uncertain.[52] Lord Balmerino, a Scottish peer, died in 1612 from the effects of a love philtre administered to him by a serving-maid in his house, while the Duke of Rothes, who was beloved by Lady Ann Gordon, judged it prudent to burn the love-tokens she sent him.[53]

Certain amulets or small portable objects were frequently worn, usually to guard the wearer against misfortune or the effects of sorcery. Self-bored stones, known in England as "hag-stones" and in Scotland as "mare-stones" (i.e. spirit stones), were thought to preserve people from nightmare. The *Airne Moire,* or Virgin Mary nut, the seed of *Entada scandens*, was worn in the island of Harris as late as 1880 to counteract the pains of childbirth. These "nuts" are carried across the Atlantic by the Gulf Stream.[54] The "toad-stone" for protecting new-born children from evil spirits was dipped in rainwater, which was sprinkled over the sickly. The "cock-knee stone" is the shell of a sea-urchin, but popular tradition believed that it was to be found in the legs of an old cock. The "snail stone" was regarded as a cure for dimness of vision. The most celebrated stones of the kind in the Scottish Highlands were the stone set in a silver ring which was long preserved in the family of Campbell of Glenlyon and which was used as a cure for the complaints of cattle. Another similar amulet was in the possession of the Stewarts of Ardvorlich. But this by no means exhausts the list of amulets known to the Celtic areas of Scotland and Ireland, and it is suspected that many such charms still remain unidentified by collectors.

In this chapter I have said little concerning such spells and charms as were associated with birth, death and marriage, as most of these scarcely fall within the scope of magical practice, and in any case are connected merely with belief in popular folk-lore and therefore with sympathetic magic of the lower cultus. But a certain type of charm still current in the Highlands of Scotland is said to have reference to the practice of exorcizing or keeping away evil spirits, and for this reason brief mention should be made of it. This is met with in the rites connected with the *caisean-uchd*, the strip of skin from the heart of a sheep killed at Christmas or New Year. The fragment is oval in shape, but no knife must be used in removing it from the skin. In Lewis and South Uist it is carried round the villages, the head of the house sets fire to it, and it is given to each member of the family to smell, going sunwise round the group. It is a bad omen for the person in whose hands it ceases to burn. It is generally regarded as a charm against evil spirits.[55] In some districts the hide of a cow killed for winter use was wrapped round the head of a man, who then led a small procession, striking the hide with a switch. A similar practice was engaged in at the Roman festival of the Lupercalia (February 15th), when people in the skins of goats struck all the women who came near them with strips from the hide of these animals, the purpose being one of purification, or, as some authorities infer, the communication of new life. In the Highland instance cited the man wearing the skin seems to have been regarded as identical with the victim, precisely as was the Aztec priest who donned the skin of a sacrificed woman at the horrid festival of the god Xipe, the deity of seed-time and planting, whose life was thus, it was thought, renewed for another year.[56] I am of opinion, however, that the merely purificatory reasons assigned for the performance of this rite are scarcely satisfactory. It is obviously a reminiscence of sacrifice to spirits or other powers by burnt offering, the belief that they would be "kept away" by the odour of the smouldering skin being entirely a later and secondary one derived from a much older notion that these powers were placated by the sacrifice of the animal. That the whole conception may indeed be a remnant of ancient Druidic rite seems to me by no means improbable, as sacrifice by burnt offering is most certainly to be classed among the chief ritual practices of the Druidic cultus.

CHAPTER VI

MAGICAL BOOKS OF THE CELTS

THAT volumes especially dedicated to the purposes of the great art of Magic anciently existed among the Celtic peoples admits of no doubt. Indeed, fragments of these from the hands of more modern copyists are to be found in works and manuscripts dealing with Celtic affairs generally or in a more separate and intact form. Enough is known concerning their tendency and contents to make it certain that they must once have existed in a condition of totality and integrity. Unhappily, the efforts of modern critics appear to have been directed more to their defamation than to their appropriate description and comprehension, the motive apparently being to discredit the ideas they contain and the frequent sublimities they set forth as inimical to views more in consonance with modern self-satisfaction and scholarly assurance.

But through the pages of some of these ancient treatises there glows the light of that Celtic spirit of deathless illumination which has ever made so powerful an appeal to minds and hearts impatient of the stale and trite ideals of everyday. Be they "drenched with superstition", be they opposed in many of their tenets to the philosophy of mere worldliness, the ethics of the terrestrial and the tenets of the practically successful, they retain something of the glamour of a system of thought and belief which in its visionary enthusiasm and princely quality of imagination holds for us a brightness and majesty of conception in which most modern creeds and ethical systems are so notoriously lacking. It was not in the mood of the true Celt, imperious and somewhat contemptuous of the workaday and the inferior, either to adapt himself to conditions entirely terrestrial or to remain complacent in respect of them. His spirit soared beyond the shadow of things earthly, and while still in the mortal state he regarded himself as the potential inhabitant of a sphere of beauty and marvel—a plane the brightness of which descended not only upon his dreams but coloured his daily musings with intimations of a more kingly and splendid existence. Not for him the tardy and humble progress towards the divine of the Buddhist or the self-denying ordinances of the pious Christian. He envisaged entrance to his paradise not only as a free and unfettered individual, but as a prince, inheriting a new and glorious kingdom where he would live surrounded by that magnificence of remote beauty of which he had dreamed while still on earth.

Several Christian writers allude to the existence of a Druidic literature in ancient Ireland. We are told that St. Patrick, in his religious zeal, burnt one hundred and eighty books belonging to the Irish Druids, a holocaust surely as ignorantly vindictive as that of the Islamic destruction of the great Library of Alexandria, or the incineration of the native manuscripts of Mexico by the fanatical Spanish clergy. Gilla Isa Mor MacFirbis, compiler of *The Great Book of Lecain* in the year 1416, alluding to this senseless destruction, says that "such an example set the converted Christians to work in all parts, until in the end all the remains of the Druidic superstition were utterly destroyed", and other writers make mention of the occurrence.

So far as Britain is concerned, the Hon. Algernon Herbert has given it as his opinion that the cult of Arthur set down its doctrines and secrets upon certain tablets of stone known as the "stones of Gwyddon", upon which all human knowledge was inscribed. Of these inscriptions I can find no reference in

British writings or traditions, and indeed the statement appears to rest solely upon the surmise of that learned though eccentric author, whose attitude to the entire Druidic tradition was certainly tinged by a curious hostility.[1]

The remains of a work which recounts the famous "Battle of the Trees" is to be found in the *Book of Taliesin*, edited by Skene.[2]   In it the British gods Gwydion and Amaethon wage war against Arawn, King of Achren, or Hades, in order to wrest from him three boons greatly to the behoof of humanity—the dog, the deer and a bird, the name of which is usually translated "lapwing". Arawn on his side had the assistance of Bran.   But the Magic of Gwydion, that enchanter of might, "changed the forms of the elementary trees and sedges", so that they acted as warriors.   The front of the battle-host was led by the alder trees, the elm was a tower of strength, so firmly he stood, but the willows lingered in joining the array.   The oak with his stout sides, and the holly, naturally armoured, proved doughty champions indeed.   Arawn, on his side, had more than one weird ally.   A great monster with a hundred heads bore an entire company of warriors beneath its tongue, and another evidently at the nape of its neck, while a hideous and gigantic serpent carried within its vitals five score lost souls continually in torment, whose agonies urged it to furious and vindictive wrath.

But one of the host of Arawn might not be vanquished unless the foeman with whom he engaged could guess his name.   That name endowed him with an access of magical power which rendered him invincible.   This was Bran, famous among the elder gods of Britain, whose severed head on its trencher recalls so intimately certain passages in the Grail legend, and who became in later Christian tradition the sainted Brons, the guardian of the holy vessel. Gwydion guessed the name, Bran and his colleagues gave way before him, and the day was won by the gods of light—although what the beneficent Bran was doing in the plutonic galley it would be difficult to say, except that, as he was one of the gods of the older stratum of British belief, he may have come to be bracketed with the denizens of Hades.   The gods of an elder and defeated race are almost invariably the devils of its successors and conquerors, be they good or bad.   The entire spirit of "The Battle of the Trees" breathes an atmosphere of Magic and may be classed as having formerly belonged to an occult disquisition of early origin.

In certain ancient Welsh poems allusions are made to "leaves" and "trees" which can only be construed as meaning that these were of the nature of occult volumes.   Do we not still speak of the "leaves" of a book?   I should like to indicate that in the ancient poem entitled the "Avallenau", or "Apple-trees", an orchard is referred to which contains no fewer than one hundred and forty-seven apple trees which had been secretly revealed by the bard Merlin, the reputed author of the poem, to his lord Gwendoleŭ.   This orchard, the poem tells us, is borne from place to place by the enchanter in all his journeyings. That the word "orchard" is here used as a rhetorical figure by Merlin is, I think with Kenealy, more than probable.   The ignorant must not partake of its inspiring fruit.   "Rustics in raven hue must not ascend its branches." That it refers to some British Kabbala which has been swallowed by the grave of the centuries one feels convinced.   What, indeed, have we Britons not lost in our quest for alien Magics and the neglect of our own native traditions! But I will refer once more to this particular passage in our arcane history when I come to write of British mystical matters at greater length.

The Welsh *Black Book of Caermarthen*, which dates from the third quarter of the twelfth century, makes numerous references to Magic.   The dialogue it contains between Merlin and Taliesin will be found in Skene's *Four Ancient*

Books of Wales. Concerning the collection of British mystical writings made by Iolo Morganwg and generally entitled *Barddas,* I have written at length in a former volume, and though I am assured by Welsh authorities of high standing that it is suspect in the highest degree as "a bundle of pure forgeries", I still believe that it contains, at second, or perhaps at third, hand, a leaven of the ancient wisdom conveyed by a man deeply versed in Brythonic lore and steeped in its ancient tradition if careless almost to criminality in the slipshod and sometimes grossly inventive method he employed in demonstrating it.[3]

The Prophecies of Merlin, which appear in the seventh book of Geoffrey of Monmouth's *Historia Britonum,* ostensibly date from the reign of Vortigern in the fifth century and in all likelihood were separately issued by Geoffrey before he penned his history. In any case two tracts from his pen concerning them are known, apart from the publication of the prophecies in his *Historia.* These are "Merlini Prophetia" and "Merlini Prophetia Continuatio" (see Lefèvre-Pontalis, *Chronique d'Antonio Morosini,* Appendix IX, vol iv., pp. 316-327). Their obscurity is the chief attribute of these prophecies. That some body of prophecy traditionally associated with Merlin was current in or before Geoffrey's day, the twelfth century, is obvious enough from the circumstance that he remarks that many men in authority had entreated him to give these vaticinations publicity, and he adds that he had "translated them out of the British"—presumably the old Welsh. It seems not improbable that they may contain a certain amount of actual traditional material. We know that in recent years well-founded pleas have been made for the authenticity, or at least the good faith, of Geoffrey's work as a whole, more particularly by Mr. Acton Griscom, who to the controversy concerning Geoffrey's *bona fides* has introduced so many new factors of debate as almost to revolutionize the entire discussion and to call for a fundamental reconsideration of Geoffrey's position as a historian.[4] "Geoffrey," thinks Mr. E. H. Chambers, "is probably letting his imagination revel," but he honestly admits that "the Prophecies must originally have become known in an independent form," as Ordericus Vitalis made use of them in his *Historia Ecclesiastica,* referring to other sources than Geoffrey.[5] As Ordericus' book was first published in the year 1134 it seems unlikely, I think, that he could have referred to that of Geoffrey, which did not make its appearance until the year 1135 or thereabouts. All of which seems to show that the "Prophecies" had an independent origin apart from Geoffrey's account, although I admit that the point is a nice one, considering the close original appearance of the two works mentioned. Whether the two tracts alluded to above had appeared before Ordericus wrote is not known. Yet Ordericus refers in his work to a "lectiuncula", "de Merlini libello"—that is, "a short illustration" in "a little book concerning Merlin", and this seems to fortify the assumption that such a work existed separately from that of Geoffrey's interpolation on the Prophecies in his *Historia* and had been among those sources of which the British writer availed himself. Indeed, it was probably one of the tracts mentioned above.

Regarding the "Prophecies" themselves, or their accuracy as forecasts, I do not think that even the most adventurous writer would choose to commit himself to any definite conclusion respecting the whole.

I may, however, quote an example of one of these prophecies, which has reference to ancient London: "Then shall the calamity of the White (dragon) be hastened and that which is builded in his little garden shall be overthrown. Seven sceptre-bearers shall be slain and one thereof shall be canonized a saint. Children shall perish in the wombs of their mothers and dread shall be the torments of men that thereby may they that were born in the land be restored unto their own. He that shall do these things shall clothe him in the brazen man, and sitting through many ages, shall keep guard over the gates of London, sitting upon a brazen horse."

This prophecy seems to me to refer to the British hero Cadwallo, who waged a dreadful war against the Saxons for forty years and whose ashes were said to have been placed in an image of him mounted upon a horse of brass at the West Gate of London—that is Ludgate. Such a method of placing the remains of national heroes at points of vantage where their presence as fetishes might have the effect of retarding invasion is very frequently encountered in that kind of British history which shades into myth. The head of the god Bran, for example, after being carried in pilgrimage by his companions for more than eighty years, was borne to London and buried beneath the Tower, as a Welsh. triad assures us, with the face towards France. But Arthur, at a later time, proudly disinterred the head, preferring to hold the island by his own strength alone, and not by Magic—an act which is recorded as one of the "fatal disclosures of Britain", as it left the way open to the invading Saxons. The ashes of Belinus were enclosed in a golden urn and placed upon the tower of Billingsgate. Vortimer, the patriotic son of the traitorous Vortigern, desired that his ashes should be gathered into a statue of copper and set "at the port where foreigners landed [probably Rutupiae, or Richborough], for that whilst they should see there an image of himself, they would never venture to approach it" But no regard was had to his last wishes, as he was buried at London, or, as some old writers say, at Lincoln.

Although it somewhat interrupts the train of this chapter, I may perhaps be allowed to interpolate a few words here on the subject of this curious magical device, the tradition of which must surely have been derived from a former actual practice. The interment of a famous hero at the entrance to a city or on the seaboard was evidently thought to have the effect of magically rebutting foreign invasion. In all likelihood the ashes of Vortimer were interred at London instead of on the coast for the reason that the Saxons had already a footing in the island, while the capital was not yet at their mercy. But Nennius, one of the early historians of Britain, who flourished at the beginning of the ninth century, regards his burial at a distance from the coast as "imprudent", adding that Vortimer, speaking of the Saxons, had remarked upon his deathbed that "even though they inhabit other parts of Britain, yet, if you follow my commands, they will never remain in this island". "The Brut of England" and Matthew of Westminster are at one in alleging that he was buried at London.

It was with the same intention that the Greeks were in the habit of placing statues of their gods on the headlands of their coasts, and that the great carven heads on the beaches of Easter Island, in the Pacific, were set up in the belief that they would either scare away invaders or that the innate power or "virtue" of those whom they represented would repel a landing. We discover a similar train of reasoning in the placing of images of guardian spirits at the entrance to pagan temples—to ward off evil influences or to affright the impious.

The Hon. Algernon Herbert, a writer who, according to the lights of his time, had a profoundly curious, if not very precise, knowledge of Celtic mysticism, described what he called "the Book of the Saint Greal" as associated with the darker side of mysticism. "It is," he wrote, "no romance but a blasphemous imposture, more extravagant and daring than any other on record, in which it is endeavoured to pass off the mysteries of Bardism for the direct inspiration of the Holy Ghost." To which work on the Grail he alludes is by no means clear, though he observes it was translated into Latin by Walter Map, but was first composed in Welsh in the year 717. Anything respecting the Grail in Welsh, and in the form of a romance, is known to be late—of the early thirteenth century at least, and a borrowing from Norman-French at that, and to do Herbert justice he admits that "some doubt exists with respect to the translations of it". He was convinced that one Tysilio wrote the Grail Book. Tysilio, the bard, flourished in the late seventh and early eighth centuries. In its pages, Herbert thought, Tysilio unfolded bardic secrets which he should not have divulged, and those of the Round Table to boot. The bard Cynddelw, who lived and sang five centuries later than Tysilio, certainly states that

> Tysilio, beyond all controversy,
> Touching my sanctuary, declares far too much,

and others have also reviled him for this. The legend of Lancelot du Lac also draws down Herbert's disapprobation as a pagan deliverance. "Its authors knew more than they should." It seems surprising today that a romance, the erratic interpolation of which into Arthurian literature almost as of a foreign quantity, and whose origins still distract students of the Arthurian corpus, should have been selected for Herbert's disapprobation. But I merely allude to these works in a catalogue of magical or supposedly magical books for the sake of completeness and will return to the topic of their authenticity in the chapter which deals with "The Cult and Mysteries of Arthur" and that on "The Mystery of the Grail".

The Book of Ballymote, written in that place about the year 1391 by Solomon of Droma and Manus Tomaltach, or MacDonogh, contains some information concerning the curriculum for study in the higher grades of the Bardic colleges of Ireland, and I have quoted from it in the chapter dealing with "Celtic Spells and Charms". It is chiefly valuable to the student of Magic in that it contains allusions to such incantations as were studied during the ninth year of the bardic course.[6] Numerous magical and mystical references are also to be encountered in *The Book of the Four Masters*, compiled in the seventeenth century by a quartette of Irish scholars of the day, and derived from ancient sources. It has been edited by Dr. J. O'Donovan. In British lore we have the skilful and authoritative work of W. F. Skene, *The Four Ancient Books of Wales*, which contains translations of numerous ancient Welsh poems and triads abounding in mystical references, though these are sadly obscure. But the renderings of some of these certainly do not satisfy the requirements of modern Welsh critics. *The Myfyrian Archaiology* unfortunately still remains without a translation. The Welsh *Mabinogion*, translated by Lady Charlotte Guest, abounds in magical material, some of the more outstanding passages of which are referred to in this book. Professor W. J. Gruffydd has revealed some of its secrets in his *Math vab Mathonwy* in the most surprising manner.

Other Celtic magical works of which little more than floating legends remain may be added to our catalogue because of their traditional value. From Argyllshire come tales of a mysterious volume known as *The Red Book of Appin*. People whose cows stopped yielding milk actually repaired to Appin in considerable numbers to consult "the man of the Red Book". This tome was acquired, it is said, by a person living at Appin under somewhat marvellous circumstances. He had adopted an orphan boy who, when he grew up, was sent to the pastures to herd cattle. While so engaged, he fell in with "a fine gentleman" who offered to take him into service at high wages. But the lad refused to accept the offer until he had first consulted his master. The gentleman thereupon requested him to sign his name in a large red book which he carried under his arm.   The young herdsman, however, bluntly declined to do so.   The gentleman then suggested a rendezvous at sunset the next evening, to which the lad assented.

On returning home, he acquainted his master with what had befallen, who advised him to proceed with the greatest caution.   He provided him with a trusty sword and instructed him, before he forgathered with the specious "gentleman", to draw with its point a circle round himself in the name of the Trinity, and to outline a cross in the centre of it, upon which he must stand. To leave the confines of the circle, his master added, would be fatal.   The stranger would ask him once more to sign his name in the book, but the lad was to request him to hand it across for signature.   All this took place.   The strange gentleman duly appeared and made every effort to induce the young man to leave the secure position he had taken up.   At length, desisting from his cajolery, he stretched forth the book, which at once fell from his hand inside the charmed circle.   When the stranger perceived that the boy had no intention of returning the volume, he flew into a towering passion and assumed numerous alarming shapes, blowing fire and brimstone from his mouth and nostrils, and transforming himself in turn into a horse, a great cat, and lastly a terrific monster, ravening round the circle and howling dismally the while. At length day broke, and taking the shape of a large raven, the mysterious fiend flew away, giving vent to an appalling shriek.   The sun was now up, so, making his way home, the herd gave the Red Book to his master, and it appears to have remained in his family for some generations.[7]

The Red Book of Appin was in manuscript, and is known to have been in existence within the last century.   Its contents dealt chiefly with the cure of diseased cattle, the increase of flocks and herds and the theme of agricultural fertility, for all of which it supplied spells and incantations of potency.   When last heard of, it seems to have been in the possession of the now extinct family of the Stewarts of Invernahyle.   The volume appears to have conferred powers of secondary sight or prevision on its owner, who knew intuitively what questions were to be put to him.   When in the act of consulting it, so potent were its emanations, it was necessary to wear a circlet of iron on the head to neutralize these occult influences.[8]

In the year 1628 a woman who appeared before the Presbytery of Perth on a charge of witchcraft declared that she was the possessor of a magical book from which she obtained all her cures and charms.   It was "her goodsire's" (grandfather's), and was, she averred, "a thousand years old".   She was unaware "what book it was", but her son, Adam Bell, read it to her.   In all likelihood it was a volume of the same character as *The Red Book of Appin*.[9]

The notable wizard Michael Scot, who flourished during the thirteenth century, and whose occult studies carried him as far afield as Spain and Italy, is reputed in both the Lowland and Highland lore of Scotland to have been the possessor of a magical volume.   This, says tradition, was interred along with him in Melrose Abbey.   An old rhymer of doggerel verse, one Satchells, says that in 1629 he chanced to be at the village of Burgh-under-Bowness, in Cumberland, where a person named Lancelot Scott revealed to him an extract from the writings of Michael Scot, in which no man dare read, along with his pen, which appeared to be made of steel, or some equally hard metal.[10]

Lastly, we may mention a modern book of Celtic Magic, the admirable *Carmina Gadelica*, compiled by the late Dr. Alexander Carmichael, which contains, besides songs and hymns collected by that Highland genius, numerous examples of Scottish Gaelic rhymed spells and charms.   But if it is couched in a modern and scholarly vein, its contents are, for the most part, as ancient as anything known to the traditions of Alba.

CHAPTER VII

THE CELTIC SPIRIT WORLD

As might be expected of a strain in whom the mystical preponderates, the Celt believed himself to be surrounded by numbers of viewless beings of varied type and character, some beneficent, others the reverse. His ideas concerning these naturally differed considerably throughout the centuries and according to local circumstances, but it has often been remarked that the Celtic attitude towards the phantom world is distinguished by a certain gruesome relish and appreciation seldom to be met with in other races. As a Scotsman I have frequently had occasion to note this extraordinary predilection for the gloomy and the weirdly repulsive. The primitive nature of many of our ghost-forms is self-evident. Our ballad literature is replete with instances in which the dividing line between dead and living is imperfectly conceived. In such cases the ghost is usually a body rather than a spirit, thus resembling the vampire of the Balkans and other areas. The lover returns to his mistress at midnight, in the same form as he assumed before death, yet bearing all the signs of mortality.

To the Celts, as to many other primitive folk, the inhabitants of the supernatural world were regarded as one in essence, merely varying forms of spiritual life. They did not distinguish very clearly between spirits of men, animals or birds. To them, indeed, spirit appears to have been of human origin alone, and might for a season attach itself to a body and then leave it —to take up residence in a tree, a rock or a watercourse. As the centuries passed this crude original notion was greatly modified, but almost to the day before yesterday we find instances of its acceptance. The writer's maternal grandmother, who would have been regarded in educated circles as a woman of culture, assured him on her death at the age of eighty that she would return in the shape of a bird and would peck at his window. Her mother was gifted with the second sight, and the occult experiences of both were of so continuous and complicated a nature as to be accepted by the remainder of the family— hard-bitten shipbuilders, naval surgeons and the managers of large industrial concerns—as the common coinage of everyday occurrence. Nor are such cases rare in Scotland, Ireland and Wales, as thousands are aware.

This sentiment of fellowhip with the supernatural, the sense of living on the edge of it, or in constant communion with it, has naturally conferred upon the Celtic ghost qualities not usually discovered in the *larvae* of other races. He (or she) is horrible, frequently repulsive, yet it is understood that so he should be. If he were not it would indeed be quite out of keeping. It is expected of him that he should be as ghastly as possible, as if otherwise, his reputation would rapidly deteriorate. For something happens to the Celtic person after death; he assumes by enchantment a certain property of untouchableness, of separateness from the terrestrial sphere which renders it risky in the extreme to have dealings with him. This particular condition is expressly conveyed by many passages in the ancient Irish sagas. Even a journey to the home of the gods will bring about such a state of things in the case of a living man. We are told, for example, in *The Book of Leinster*, that when Loegaire, son of the King of Connaught, returned from the home of the gods, he was advised by his hosts that he and his comrades should not dismount from their horses when they reached earthly soil.[1] To do so would have brought about their instant transformation to dust. The dwarf ruler who entertained the British King Herla in the Otherworld issued a similar warning to his guest and his followers, but in some cases it went unheeded, so that the neglectful crumbled into dust when they dismounted in their own country.[2] This species of enchantment is alluded to by Malory in speaking of King Arthur. Some men, he remarks, aver that the king is not dead but still survives. "I will not say that it shall bee so," adds Sir Thomas, "but rather I will say that heere in this world *hee changed his life*."[3]

This belief undoubtedly arises from the primitive idea that death was an unnatural contingency, a calamity caused by the spells or malevolent magical devices of supernatural beings, ancestral spirits, or wizards. Once the Celt crosses the borderline which separates the living from the dead his general nature undergoes an entire alteration, he assumes the magical character and abilities of the inhabitants of the Land of the Dead. He is the creature of another element. He is surrounded by a set of taboos which bear no relationship to existence in the earth-life.

All this differentiates the Celtic idea of death very markedly from that as understood by other races. When mortals of other than Celtic stock return from the Land of the Gods or the Land of the Dead they usually do so as heroes, bearing with them gifts of usefulness to humanity, framing new legal codes, bringing knowledge to men. But the Celtic visitor to the Land of the Dead lingers on earth miserably for a space, until, with the echoes of the divine place where he has sojourned ringing in his ears, he once more seeks its peace and is not again seen in the haunts of men.

That the spirit of man could function as a "ghost" even while he was still alive appears to have been a doctrine acceptable to the Celts, and this associates it in a measure with the belief in the vampire. The Celtic belief in a species of "döppel-ganger", or astral counterpart, is revealed in the writings of the mystical Robert Kirk, the minister of Aberfoyle, towards the end of the seventeenth century (a secret Rosicrucian, if I mistake not), for he speaks of a "Reflex man, a Co-walker, every way like the Man, as a Twin-brother and companion, haunting him as his shadow, as is oft seen and known among Men (resembling the Originall), *both before and after the Originall is dead*".[4] This appears to be much the same as the Irish "fetch", whose name seems to me to be a corruption of the Irish Gaelic *taidhbhse* (pron. "taish"), meaning "ghost". Should one see the fetch of a person in the morning, the incident has no doomful significance. To see the double at night implies the death of the person seen. Mrs. B——, the wife of a doctor in an Irish town, beheld the fetch of her husband standing near the window while he slept by her side. Later, the doctor confessed that he himself had seen the apparition. On the following night Dr. B—— rose from his sleep, calling for help, but shortly expired.[5]

It is believed in Ireland and some parts of Scotland that when the spirit leaves the body "it will travel all the ground travelled over while alive, and during this time it is visible". It is also held that "the spirit of the person who has been last interred must watch the churchyard until the next funeral takes place or for a year after interment". "The belief that the soul takes the form of animals is almost universal, and there are many examples of it in the British Isles." Seagulls are frequently regarded as the souls of the dead on the Scottish coasts.[6] The writer recalls a humorous incident of a fight arising between two fishermen at Granton, near Edinburgh, because one of them had alluded to his dead father as "a —— seagull".

A ghost, an ancestral ghost, yet something more, the banshee has a name which may be translated "supernatural woman" and, perhaps in view of her especial characteristics, "dead woman". Indeed, she has many of the attributes of mortality, for her nose is sunken, or not apparent, and her eye-sockets are large and hollow. Occasionally she is decked out in green silk and gold ornaments, and such cases may be associated with those tales as speak of her as the ancestress of a great family.

In some parts of Scotland, particularly in Argyllshire, the contiguous islands and Skye, the banshee is known as the cointeach, or "keener", from her habit of indulging in outbursts of dismal wailing. In these regions she is found attached to the families of the Macmillans, the Mathisons, Kellys, Mackays, Macfarlanes, Shaws and Curries. Sometimes she is described as having the appearance of a small child; at others as "a small or very little woman in a short green gown and petticoat, with a high-crowned white cap". One local traditionalist speaks of the cointeach as "a little white thing, soft as wool", and without flesh, blood or bones—clearly a popular rendering of a very primitive idea of the rather amorphous appearance and condition in which the soul was supposed to exist in its separate state. In its more human shape it haunted the backs of houses, wailing and prophesying death. When a fatal event impended in the family of the clan Mackay, the cointeach, attired in a green shawl, was wont to warn them by squatting outside the sick man's door, raising her mournful keening.

I cannot hope to review the evidence relating to the banshee in Ireland in its entirety, but must follow its main directions only. "The popular belief in Clare," wrote the late Mr. T. T. Westropp, a major authority, "is that each leading Irish race had a banshee, Eevul, the banshee of the royal O'Briens, ruling over twenty-five other banshees, always attendant upon her progresses".[7] Elsewhere he says : "The banshee appears in Mayo as a dark-cloaked grey-haired woman sitting on a rock or fence moaning or crying, more frequently heard than seen. In Connemara she wears a red cloak, and sings before a death; her voice travels with the gust of wind."[8] Another of these hags, he tells us, was Bronach, "the Sorrowful one of the Black Head", who is described as crooked, thatched with elf-locks, foxy-grey and rough like heather, with wrinkled brow, bleared eyes and a flattened blue nose. When seen, she was usually engaged in washing blood-stained garments.[9]

The Irish banshee uttered her warning only in the case of ancient and noble families. When she did so, according to Crofton Croker, she walked beside those who met her on some lonely road, keening and clapping her hands, her long white hair falling about her shoulders, repeating the name of the person who was about to die.[10] Elsewhere he describes her as "a tall, thin woman, with uncovered head and long hair that floated round her shoulders attired in something that seemed either a loose white cloak or a sheet thrown hastily about her".[11]

In The Wars of the Gaedhil with the Gaill it is told how Brian, the King of Ireland, was warned of his coming death by the banshee Aibhill (pron. Eevul) of Crag Laith. In 1318 the Normans, under Richard de Clare, were marching to engage the O'Deas of Dysert, when they beheld a hag washing armour and clothes. She said to them: "I am the Water Doleful One. I lodge in the green mounds. Thither I invite you. Soon we shall be dwellers in one country."[12]

In ancient Ireland a series of war-goddesses, somewhat resembling the Norse Valkyries, seem to have been the objects of particular fear and reverence. These warlike goddesses were five in number, and they were presided over by the Morrigan, or "Great Queen", whose favourite disguise was that of a carrion crow. All of these were collectively described by the name of *badb* (pron. bive, or bibe). After battle these furies revelled among the bodies of the slain, and their memory still survives in the superstitious aversion of the Celtic peasant for their folk-lore descendant, the "hoodie" crow.

Everything points to the conclusion that the *banshee* was in one sense a modern expression of the *badb* or "royston" crow, which appears to have been associated with the goddess of battle in ancient Irish mythology, presiding over death and slaughter. J. G. Campbell gives it as his opinion that ":*baobh*", as used in Scotland, is a term which commonly expresses "an evil woman, hence is a common name applied to witches", although in some cases it is employed as indicating that a woman "was not of mortal race".[13]

"The name *badb*," says Wood-Martin, "meaning 'rage, fury or violence', came to be applied to a witch, fairy or goddess, represented by the scare-, scald-, or royston-crow. Her sisters were Neman, Machan and Morrigan. '*Badb*' would seem to have been the generic title of beings ruling over battle or carnage. Neman brought madness, Morrigan incited to deeds of valour, Machan revelled among the bodies of the slain. All three are described as the wives of Neit, the god of battle."[14] A raven flapped against the windows of the Ross Lewins of Clare as a symbol of approaching death, and this seems to indicate that it was the family banshee in *badb* or raven form.[15]

Elsewhere we are told that crows or ravens were the birds announcing the presence of the Fomorians, the Irish gods of death and night. The wife of Tethra, chief of the Fomorians, was the female of the crow or raven, who flew over the battlefield in the hour of carnage. A late eleventh-century manuscript has preserved for us a quatrain written by a poet of the ninth century on this subject:

> The wife of Tethra's longing is for the fire of combat:
> The warriors' sides slashed open,
> Blood, bodies heaped upon bodies:
> Eyes without life, sundered heads, these are pleasing words to her.

An old Irish grammarian who flourished about the end of the eleventh century, glossing the obscurities of this quatrain, explains "wife of Tethra", or Teathur, as "crow" or "raven".[16] Indeed, all the warrior-goddesses of Ireland appear to have been generally known as *badb*, or "crow".

It seems to me not improbable that the *banshee* may have been regarded anciently as a tutelary guardian of the royal house of Stuart. My reasons for entertaining this belief are that the coronation stone of Scone, now the basis of the royal throne of the British Empire, in Westminster Abbey (which must not be confused with the Lia Fail of Ireland), is said by at least one old English writer to have been the dwelling-place of a tutelary spirit. It seems not unlikely that it may have been partly for this reason that the highly romantic and superstitious King Edward I. had the stone removed to Westminster. In an English account of the assassination of King James I. of Scotland at Perth in 1437 entitled *The Dethe and False Murdure of James Stewarde, Kyng of Scotys*, written about 1440, by John Shirley of London, or rather translated by him from the Latin text of what was probably an official Scottish account of the affair, he tells us that as the King rode to Perth, to hold Christmastide there, and came to the Water of Leith, a woman of Ireland (that is, of the Highlands) who called herself a soothsayer rose in the midst of the way, and cried with a loud voice: "My lord Kyng, an ye passe this water, ye shall never return agane on lyve". On being asked how she could so prophesy, she said that "Huthart told her so".[17]

The spirit Huthart may almost certainly be associated with the Scottish term "Huddy", employed for the hooded crow, which is connected with the *banshee* in Ireland. "Huthart " seems to be the same as that "Ethart" who is mentioned by the Rev. Robert Knox in a letter to the Rev. Mr. Wyllie (1677) as the familiar of a lady who dwelt in "the West marches" of Scotland, who accompanied her on her journeys.[18] It is not impossible otherwise that the name Huthart may be a corruption of the Irish Gaelic Teathur, or Tethra, who, as we have seen, was associated with the scald or royston crow in Ireland in her form of the *badb*, the bird whose shape the *banshee* occasionally took. This Teathur, who, in human shape, was one of a trio of mythical kings of Ireland, was one of the mysterious Tuatha Dé Danann. The name seems comparable with that of Arthur, who according to English mediaeval superstition took the shape of a crow, a passage in Cervantes' *Don Quixote* having it "that no Englishman would shoot a crow for Arthur's sake", a statement supported by Cornish tradition.[19] Morgan La Fée, Arthur's sister, also took crow or raven shape on occasion, and she has been connected mythologically with the Irish Morrigan, or crow-goddess of war.

We have thus good reason to associate "the woman of Ireland", who warned King James, with the *banshee*. That she made a further effort to interview the King at Perth on the eve of his murder, but without effect, is on record.[20] The whole passage, indeed, gives me to think that a legend existed which more or less definitely associated the Stuart line with a *banshee*, and that this spirit, in the contemporary accounts of James I.'s assassination, became "euhemerized", or humanized, into a Gaelic soothsayer or wise woman, whereas the current popular version of this part of the affair might have been susceptible of a more mystical interpretation, associated with an ancestral familiar of the ancient Celtic line of Stuart.

Welsh tradition preserves the belief in more than one spirit of the *banshee* type. The *cyhiraeth* comes in a dark mist to the window of a person about to die, flapping her wings against the glass, whilst repeating his or her name. In appearance she is even more repellent than the *banshee* herself. Her locks are tangled and knotted, her teeth are long and black, she displays shrivelled arms. Sir John Rhys believed her to be an ancestral spirit.[21] Like the *banshee*, she gives forth a dreadful noise in the night before a death or burial. "Its first cry is strong, its second lower, its third still lower and soft. If one hears the *cyhiraeth* and then proceeds to the death-bed he will hear the dying man's moans precisely like those he heard from the *cyhiraeth*." This spirit especially infested the twelve parishes in the hundred of Inis Cenin, which lies on the south-east side of the River Towy on the sea-coast of Glamorganshire. Her moaning, accompanied by lights, precedes a wreck. Occasionally she passes through a village by night, groaning and rattling the windowshutters. She invariably appears before the visitation of an epidemic.[22]

Another Welsh spirit of the *banshee* kind is the *gwrach y rhibyn*, or "hag of the dribble". Her appearance is almost similar to that of the *cyhiraeth*, and like her she utters a dreadful keening. Occasionally she appears in the mist of a mountainside, or at cross-roads, or near a sheet of water, which she splashes with her hands. Sometimes this spirit appears as a male. A man who had seen it at Llandaff told Mr. Wirt Sikes, the United States Consul at Cardiff in 1878, that it looked like a horrible old woman, with long red hair, a face like chalk and great tusk-like teeth. He said: "It's not these new families that the *gwrach y rhibyn* ever troubles, sir, it's the old stock."[23] The "hag" is said to be the wife of the mythical power *Avagddu*, a word which implies lordship over death, and so she may justly be equated with the *badb* wife of Teathur, the Irish death-god. She has also been described as rising out of swamps and creeks, and haunting ruined castles, as "a *banshee*, an ancestral spectre". That birds are also associated with "warnings" in Wales, as is the crow or raven in Scotland and Ireland, is revealed by the tradition concerning the *aderyn y corph*, which chirps at the doors of persons fated to die.

Equally revolting to modern susceptibilities, but revealing much of that gruesome quality which seems inherent in the mentality of the race to which the writer is privileged to belong, is the notion of the *glaistig*, a female Scottish ghost who is described as "a woman of human race, who has been put under enchantments", and to whom a supernatural character has thus been given. She was usually regarded as "a woman of honourable position, a former mistress of the house, the interests of the tenants of which she now attended to".[24] Like the *banshee*, she has a peculiarly dolorous tone of voice, and her dreadful keening can at times be heard along the whole black length of a nightbound glen.

Her most intimate task appears to lie in the entertainment of visitors, upon whom, however, she occasionally plays ghostly pranks. Some *glaistigs*, like that of the Macleans of Breachacha Castle, in the Island of Coll, made life rather difficult for occasional guests, while others, such as that of the Mac-Dougalls of Dunollie, acted as amateur laundresses, washing the family linen. But other *glaistigs* are more fiendishly inspired and plague the hunter or crofter. Some spirits of this species insist upon a cogue of milk being set out for them at nights, and if this offering be neglected the cattle are almost certain to suffer. If one could capture a *glaistig* he might exact from her the gift of particular skill in handicraft for his descendants. One could keep a *glaistig* at arm's length with a drawn dirk, but if permitted to come to close quarters she might assume the attributes of the vampire and suck his veins dry. The *glaistig* occasionally took the form of a man's sweetheart, and in this form might absorb his heart's blood. That she was substantially an ancestral spirit is clear enough. Libations of milk were made to her in a hollow stone, and at one farm, Sron-charmaig, on the side of Loch Fascan, in Lorn, this custom was upheld so lately as the nineties of last century.[25]

The *bean-nighe* is "the washing-woman", whose legend has been immortalized by Fiona MacLeod, that occasionally brilliant if somewhat theatrical master of the pseudo-Celtic, in his gruesome tale *The Washer at the Ford*. She is common to both Scotland and Ireland. Tradition avers that she is to be seen after nightfall in desolate places near a water's edge, or at a ford, washing the shrouds of those who are about to die. In the main, she is confined to the larger islands of Scotland—Lewis, Harris, Uist and Coll—where her appearance is regarded as a warning of death. But her presence is not unrecorded elsewhere, although her name varies with the region. Thus in Islay the *coin-teach* and the *bean-nighe* seem to be one and the same. The *cointeach* of Islay is said to be particularly vindictive to those who disturb her at her dreadful business, and she punishes them by striking them on the legs with the shroud she is washing—a blow which may possibly amputate these members.

In the Hebrides the *bean-nighe* is not attached to particular families. She is said to resemble a woman of small size, and some emphasis is laid on the fact that her feet are red and webbed like a duck's. Like the *banshee*, she sometimes sports green attire. The usual seasons for her appearance are after dark and in the early morning. The noise she makes at her work is described as like "the clapping of hands" and the splashing of water. Though evil follows upon the sight of her, that, we are told, is no fault of hers. If one can get between her and the water she is bound to grant any request or boon he may ask.

In Perthshire the washing-woman is described as small of stature and rotund, and clad in a muslin-like green garment. In Skye she is squat and resembles a shrunken, rather miserable-looking child. If caught while at her labours she is bound to reveal the circumstances of her captor's fate, so long as he truthfully responds to her questions in turn.[26]

In Ross-shire and Sutherlandshire the *bean-nighe* is locally known as the *vow*. Her favourite locality is the River Carron. Those who seek to cross the waters which she haunts do so at the risk of their lives. She washes clothes in the same manner as the *bean-nighe*, and is sometimes identified with the kelpie. But, as the *vow*, she is not a Lowland equivalent of the *bean-nighe*, as has been stated. "In Carradale, in Kintyre, is a point called Sroin na h-Eannachair, the haunt of a supernatural being who makes an outcry on the death of any of the clan MacMillan. *Cannachan* is the local name for the *cointeach* of the MacMillans. The word seems to be associated with ponds or water."

Such a creature haunted a loch in the Alvie district of Inverness-shire, but could be seen only by those about to die. The local belief concerning her was that she represented the phantom of a mother who had died in childbed, and whose garments had not been washed at the time of her burial. Accordingly she seems to have been doomed to wash the shifts of all those about to die, or to be slain in battle between the date of her actual death and that on which she would naturally have died, death at childbirth being deemed unnatural.

It is dangerous to the traveller by night if the *bean-nighe* observes him before he has set eyes on her. If he espies her first she cannot stir until she is caught and spoken to. A Lewis legend recounts that a certain John Smith of South Shawbost saw her washing at Lochandubh-na-beinne. He enquired what she was about and she replied that she was washing the clothes of those who were to be drowned that year in the loch, adding, "But as I have been caught, I shall not be seen any more here. Let me go, and I shall give you any of three gifts you may choose." The interloper asked for wealth and received the boon, but was informed that he would have no sons.[27]

The *bean-nighe*, or washer, is even more commonly to be met with in Ireland than in Scotland. In the events which preceded the death of the great Irish hero Cuchullin, the Druid Cathbad points out such a washer to the hero. She is the daughter of the *badb*. She is slender and white of body and yellow of hair. On the ford's bank she washed and wrung crimson and bloody spoils.[28] Oscar, grandson of Fionn, and son of Ossian, on his way to the battle of Gavra encountered such a supernatural woman, and thus addressed her:

> Weird woman that washest the garments,
> Make for us the self-same prophecy.
> Will any one of them fall by us,
> Or shall we all go to nothingness?

The reply of the *bean-nighe* was:

> There will be slain by thee nine hundred,
> And the King himself be wounded to death by thee.[29]

In the long ago, we read, Ireland was better adapted to the chase than Albainn, or Scotland, and many Scots went there for that purpose. When the Feinne, the band of Finn MacCoul, went to hunt in Ireland they appear to have encountered several *bean-nighean*. One of these prophesied that Finn should be slain in battle, and this duly came to pass.

In his *Folk-lore de France* M. Paul Sebillot remarks that the idea of the washer of the night is familiar to Brittany. There she is known as *Eur-cunnerez-noz* (the plural form). She appears on the banks of streams, and calls to passers-by to aid her to wash the linen of the dead. If any refuse, he is dragged into the water and has his arms broken. The legend of the super-natural washerwoman is also widespread in the Slovene districts of Jugo-Slavia.[30]

The fairies bulk so largely in Celtic tradition and Magic that the prob-lems associated with them cannot be ignored in such a work as this. In Wales they are known as the *Tylwyth Teg*, or "the fair family", and are ruled by Gwyn ap Nud, formerly a British god, who is also regarded as lord of the dead. In Ireland they are the remains of the Tuatha Dé Danann, once the gods of Ire-land before the invasion of the Milesian race. The Tuatha Dé Danann, or gods, were thought of as being reincarnated in the kings and chiefs of Ireland, as all authorities agree, and this has a direct bearing upon the fairy problem, as we shall see.[31] In Scotland there is no evidence that they were derived from these gods. Three main theories seek to account for the origin of fairies. These have been set forth by Professor Krappe as follows: "According to one (school) they are the dead; according to another they are elementary spirits; and according to the third they are due to reminiscences of former inhabi-tants, crowded out by the newcomers and compelled to retire to the moun-tains or near the sea-shore. Let us say at once that a good many story-types are in accord with the first theory—in fact, probably a majority—that certain features are better explained by the second, and that there is no solid basis of fact behind the third."[32]

Most students of tradition would, I think, agree with Professor Krappe's statement of the problem, which he proceeds to elaborate in brief compass. He shows that both Teutonic dwarfs and Celtic fairies possess characteristics which appear to identify them with the dead, dwelling as they do underground, and luring the living to their subterranean abodes. Moreover, they appear in the guise of ancestral spirits possessing superhuman wisdom and are associated with certain localities and families. Also they receive gifts or oblations of food, and thus seem to be the governing spirits of a definite cultus, as ancestral forms are everywhere. They preside over the growth of the crops, as do the dead ancestors, and they haunt barrows and stone circles known to be places of ancient sepulture.

But Professor Krappe warns us that we must not draw any hard and fast line between the ancestral cult and the worship of elementary or nature-spirits. In saying as much, he is at one with the leading exponents of modern folk-lore. As the late Mr. Sidney Hartland laid it down in his *Science of Fairy Tales*, no very clear division can be made between the fairy and the ghost, in the folk-lore sense. They have the same traits, the same taboos are exercised against both, the same stock legends and stories are common to both. As to the third theory to which Professor Krappe alludes, that which embraces the idea that Faerie may be due to reminiscences of the former inhabitants of a country, and especially to small and undersized races, it is evident that he denies this *in toto*. I believe that the *main* element in the tradition is that which regards the fairy belief as associated with the spirits of the dead.

As regards the actual proof of the theory that fairies are no other than the dead in the belief of primitive man, past and present, that is of a nature so extensive that I despair of being able to place it adequately before the reader in the compass of a few paragraphs. Here I can deal only with its main outlines and superscriptions, but I can assure my readers that it has received the overwhelming acceptance of many folk-lorists of standing. Primitive man did not and does not believe, as we do, that death is a thing inevitable. He regarded it, and regards it, as brought about by magical means of some kind, and out of this idea has arisen that description of story which tells how people might be rescued and regained from the Land of the Dead.

Let us glance at some of the instances of that body of proof which serves to maintain the theory that the fairies were in the main the spirits of the departed. In Wales, for example, as Wirt Sikes tells us in his interesting study, *British Goblins*, "the popular theory of the fairies is that they are the souls of dead mortals, not bad enough for hell, nor good enough for heaven".

"We are confronted," writes Mr. L. C. Wimberley, in his *Folk-lore of the English and Scottish Ballads*, "with striking resemblances between the ballad ghost and the ballad fairy", and he proceeds to illustrate the theory by a wealth of instances culled from British popular lays.[33] "When analysed," says Wentz, "our evidence (culled from Celtic lands) shows that in the majority of cases witnesses have regarded fairies either as non-human nature-spirits, or else as spirits of the dead . . . the striking likenesses constantly appearing in our evidence between the ordinary apparitional fairies and the ghosts of the dead show that there is often no essential or sometimes no distinguishable difference between these two orders of beings, nor between the world of the dead and fairyland. . . . The old people in County Armagh seriously believe that the fairies are the spirits of the dead, and they say that if you have many friends deceased you may have many friendly fairies." Steven Ruan, a piper of Galway, told Wentz that "there is one class of fairies who are nobody else than the spirits of men and women who once lived on earth".

The Scottish evidence for this widespread belief is equally definite. Dalyell tells us that a witch of Orkney beheld the fairies "rise out of the kirkyard of Hildiswick", and in the witch trials of the sixteenth and seventeenth centuries numerous Scottish witches bore witness that they encountered dead friends and relations in Fairyland, whither they themselves had been spirited away. Canon MacCulloch, in the article on "Fairies" in *The Encyclopedia of Religion and Ethics*, remarks that "fairies have many things in common with ghosts and are repulsed by the same taboos". They have in some cases succeeded ghostly tenants of tumuli or barrows, or have become merged with them.

Bessie Dunlop, of Dalry, in Ayrshire, an associate of the witches, at some time about 1573 encountered "a fairy man", one Thome Reid, who had been slain at the battle of Pinkie in 1547. At her trial she actually claimed to have seen this person walking in the High Street in Edinburgh, but, as fairies must not be addressed in public, she refrained from recognizing him. Says Andrew Lang, "there are excellent proofs that Fairyland was a kind of Hades, or home of the dead". To Robert Kirk, the good pastor of Aberfoyle, the fairies were "an abstruse people", the human doubles or astral bodies of the living. At the death of the man they represent, these "co-walkers" return "to their own herd", that is to a separate existence in some appropriate limbo. He tells us that the folk on the Highland line in his day (*circa* 1660-90) believed that the souls of their predecessors dwelt in the fairy hills. "And for that end, say they, a Mote or Mount was dedicate beside every Churchyard, to receive the souls till their adjacent bodies arise, so became as a fairy hill."[34] That is, there was a separate sepulchre or dwelling for the "fairy", or human, soul. Reading this, we may understand how the Orkney witch came to behold the fairies "rise from the kirkyard of Hildiswick". Kirk, who, I have always believed, was a Rosicrucian, perhaps imposed upon his own local folk-lore something of the doctrine of spirits as he found it in Paracelsus and in the writings of Fludd and Vaughan.

In the Western Isles of Scotland the *Sluagh*, or fairy host, was regarded as composed of the souls of the dead flying through the air, and the feast of the dead at Hallowe'en was likewise the festival of the fairies. The testimony of Lady Gregory and the late Mr. W. B. Yeats, as great a mystic as he was a poet, who jointly collected much Irish folk-lore, reveals that the majority of the people whom they examined believed that Fairyland was a region to which the souls of living folk might be spirited away while their bodies remained upon earth. "The dead," wrote the great Jacob Grimm, "were known to the Norsemen as elves."

The resemblance of the subterranean fairy world to the pre-Christian Hades helps to make plain the likeness of the whole fairy economy and background to those of the dead. Pluto and Proserpine, the Classical monarchs of the departed, were in early mediaeval times identified with the King and Queen of Faerie. In the early English poem of "Orfeo and Heurodys", which localizes the story of the myth of Orpheus and Eurydice in England, Hades is called "Faerie". But we must not confuse this idea with that of the Celtic insular otherworld, which was at first assuredly a Land of the Gods, and which later became confused with the conception of Fairyland. In the ancient Scots-English romance of "Thomas of Erceldoune" (Thomas the Rhymer) the background is that of the mediaeval Hades, fused with that of the Celtic paradise, the apples on its fruit trees must not be eaten, and "the fiend of hell" comes once in seven years to claim a victim from among its inhabitants.

The germ of the primitive and prehistoric view of Faerie was indeed the idea of that subterranean mode of existence or "dead-aliveness" which early man conceived as going on in the mounds and tumuli in which he buried his dead. By poets and scholars it was confused with the Classical Hades, and later, by the churchmen who copied the old Irish sagas, with that of Purgatory.

And if I find difficulty in appropriately presenting in brief compass the evidence that the fairies are one and the same with the dead, what shall I say of that even greater body of proof which reveals their association with ancient places of sepulture, barrows, tumuli and stone circles? This part of the evidence has been almost entirely neglected in our country, although the pioneer labours of Mr. L. V. Grinsell in his *Ancient Burial Mounds of England*, and elsewhere, has done much to redeem the reproach. In France the work of MM. Saintyves, Le Rouzic and Professor Salomon Reinach has proved beyond question that standing stones in Brittany and other parts of that country are associated with fairies, who are thought of as inhabiting or "ensouling" them. That these fays represent the spirits of dead chieftains once worshipped ancestrally admits of no doubt.

But we must regard the fairies as the dead in an especial sense, for they were *the spirits of the departed who awaited rebirth or reincarnation.* Good evidence exists, and is multiplying, that savage people in a low condition of culture in Australia, Borneo and elsewhere believed that the spirits of the dead gather in communities in wild and deserted places, in hills, forests and lakes, and that when the period for their reincarnation comes round they take up a position of vantage in some isolated rock, tree or pond, from which it is thought they spring out upon a passing woman and enter the body of her yet unborn infant. Such spirits possess fairy-like traits and habits and are regarded by savages precisely as the ancient peoples of Europe regarded fairies.[35] In Scotland, Ireland and Wales, numerous woods and copses, stones and rocks, lakes and lochs were formerly regarded either as the dwelling-places of the fairies or of the dead, and this reveals that such a belief as presently obtains among peoples of low culture today formerly flourished in Britain. Moreover, the idea associated with fairy changelings was certainly associated with that of reincarnation—the changeling, when unmasked, being invariably the spirit of an ancient man, or ancestor.

This theory not only accounts for the origin of fairy spirits, but it also explains and absorbs the remaining theories that fairies are either elementary spirits of nature or that they are a memory of vanished aboriginal races. Their residence in trees, stones and watercourses while awaiting reincarnation may make them appear as nature-spirits, but *per se* they are nothing of the kind. As Ridgeway says, all nature-spirits are regarded as having once been human beings. In early times the human dead were thought of as seeking an abode in desert places far from the dwellings of men. The theory that they were exclusively vanished races naturally also falls to the ground when we come to regard them as the ghosts of aboriginal folk of the Stone and Bronze Ages, which, in the first instance, they most certainly were, a tradition which appears to have survived throughout the ages.

There are several instances on record of what would appear to be a relationship between Druidism and the fairy folk, although, to judge from at least one passage in Irish myth, no love seems to have been lost between the disciples of the two cults—if as separate cults they may be described. That a secret fairy cultus did actually exist until late times, having its own priesthood and initiates, I hope to be able to prove, but whether it was associated with Druidism or not it would be difficult, if indeed at all possible, to ascertain.

We read in Welsh folk-lore that fairies are the souls of good Druids who died before the introduction of Christianity, and who were "not good enough for heaven and not bad enough for hell".[36] It was also conjectured by Maury that the functions of prophetic Gaulish Druidesses were confused with those of the fairies.[37] Wirt Sikes observes that some Welsh traditions exist which relate that the fairies were merely the Druids in hiding from their enemies.[38] This, of course, is to confound the priests or worshippers with that which was worshipped. The same belief exists in Cornwall, the fairies there being regarded as Druids who had shrunk in size "because they would not give up their idolatries"![39] The self-same notion, almost, was put forward by the Rev. P. Graham in his *Sketches of Perthshire*, in which he explained the superstition regarding fairy changelings as a species of kidnapping by which the Druids, harassed by the priesthood of the new Christian faith, "procured the necessary supply of members for their order".[40] But a tradition actually appears to exist that the Druids had a close association with the fairy sphere. "The Druids," says Joyce, "were the intermediaries with the fairies and with the invisible world in general for good or evil, and they could protect people from the malice of evil-disposed spirits of every kind."[41] In Irish lore we are informed that the Druids reverenced the well of Slan and "offered gifts to it as if it were a god". As Whitley Stokes indicates, this is the only passage connecting the Druids with well-worship, and Wentz remarks upon its importance, because it establishes the relation between the Druids and their control of spirits like fairies, who were thought of as haunting or inhabiting such wells.[42] In one passage in Irish tale we read of a "fairy Druid" (*sighe-draoi*), named Lassa Buaicht, which seems to infer a close connection between the fairy and Druid beliefs or cults.[43]

Is it probable that the fairy faith constituted a cultus in any way associated with or descended from Druidism? The Scottish evidence at least appears to be in favour of such a theory. That many people, especially witches, entered fairy mounds for the purposes of initiation seems apparent. Indeed, I would differentiate between the terms "fairy" and "fairy folk", the last so commonly encountered in the accounts of witch-trials in Scotland, as applying in the first case to the fairy spirits and in the latter as signifying the priests and worshippers of the fairy cult. Such places of initiation were, of course, frequently confounded with the Land of Faerie itself, which appears a not unnatural error in the circumstances. But that they were the seats of a faith associated with the belief in Faerie, a fairy cultus, seems obvious enough to me, and that the people who inhabited them were the initiates, hierophants, and mystae of that faith seems an equally reasonable surmise, judging from the numerous tales of the all-too-human character of these mound-dwellers. The hillock of Cnocnam Bocan, or the Knowe of the Goblins, in Menteith, is spoken of as formerly "the headquarters of the faries of the whole district of Menteith", who were granted by the Earl of Menteith the Cui-n'an-Uriskin, or Cave of the Faries in Ben Venue, at which, says Dr. Graham in his *Sketches of the Picturesque Scenery of Perthshire*, "*the solemn stated meetings of the order were regularly held*". Great nobles do not confer messuages either on hill or in dale upon airy spirits, nor do the "orders" of the same meet on earth. Indeed, the Earl in question was spoken of as "overlord of the faery folk". The "folk" in question were probably initiates of the fairy cult, and thus real enough.

Also it must be clear that the very large number of fairy knowes or hills in Scotland and elsewhere have some association with such a condition of things. The knowe at Aberfoyle, a very extensive one, to which the Rev. Robert Kirk was eventually spirited away, as legend avers, the Eildon Hill, the Brogh of the Boyne in Ireland, the Calton Hill at Edinburgh—all such places seem to have been centres at which a process of initiation in the fairy cult could formerly be gone through. Such a spot was the knowe at Aberfoyle; the Maes-howe in Orkney; Coldach broch, Perthshire, and many others. Such places have usually a long passage leading to a chamber with cells on either side, such as are typical of ancient centres of initiation.

Returning to the consideration of other classes of spirits, we find considerable dubiety existing concerning the precise nature of the *gruagach*, so frequently encountered in Irish and Scottish lore. The name means "the long-haired one", and there is abundance of evidence that this spirit was until quite recent times placated in the Western Isles of Scotland by oblations of milk, which were poured into a hollow stone known as "the *gruagach's* stone". That he was a godling or spirit who acted as a guardian of the cattle is not in doubt. But in folk-tale he appears as a valiant warrior and sorcerer. J. F. Campbell was of opinion that he represented a folk-memory of members of the Druidic caste. The *gruagach's* acts of sorcery in folk-tale are numerous, but I adhere to the view that he is a broken-down form of the sun-god, as his streaming hair, prowess in arms and generally gorgeous appearance in folk-tale, as well as his patronage of cattle, would seem to indicate.[44]

The *urisk* is a shaggy, satyr-like spirit which appears to haunt lonely, desert places in the Highlands, and more particularly waterfalls. He closely resembles the Irish *phooka*, which has also a goat-like appearance, and the Manx *phynoderee*, who partakes of the same attributes. But he has also the traits of the brownie, as he assists the farmer in his agricultural tasks. Brownie so closely recalls the *lar*, or spirit of the dead ancestor, formerly worshipped in Rome, that I believe him to have had a common origin with that species of spirit at a remote time. He is the spirit-ancestor of the farmhouse, as is the *banshee* of the castle.

A particularly militant spirit is the *ly erg*, which frequented Glen. More. He appears, says Sibbald in his MS. collections, in the habit of a soldier with a red hand, challenging wayfarers, and should anyone engage him in combat he is certain to die soon thereafter. Certain Celtic spirits are of so fantastic and repellent a type as to inspire the feeling that they must have sprung from the imagination of an exceedingly primitive race which preceded the civilized Celts in Ireland and Scotland. Of the terrible *fachan* we read that he "had one hand out of his chest, one leg out of his haunch, and one eye in the front of his face. He wore a mantle of twisted feathers and his head was crowned by a tuft. Another and similar horror was the *bocan*, which leapt upon unwary travellers in the Isle of Skye and slew them, mutilating their bodies terribly."[45] The *fuath* is a water-spirit resembling the *bean-nighe*, with webbed feet, yellow hair, a tail, a mane and no nose—yet she dresses in a green kirtle! But the name of such creatures is indeed legion. They have on the whole a close affinity with the water-kelpie.

Perhaps no Scottish spirit has been so frequently described as the water-kelpie, a river goblin which usually appears in the form of a horse, but which on occasion takes the form of a handsome young man. The kelpie haunts fords and pools, and seeks to lure unwary travellers to their doom. The wayfarer may see a horse browsing by the waterside and seek to gain the opposite bank by mounting it. But once in the middle of the stream, the kelpie throws his rider, leaving him to perish in the flood. His general appearance was that of a black horse with wild and staring eyes. Countless tales are told of the demon-animal and nearly every stream of any size in Scotland at one time could boast of its kelpie.

In his human form the kelpie might appear as a goodly youth and sometimes the maiden on whom he had set his affections became timeously aware of his supernatural character by observing a fragment of water-weed or rush in his hair. If caught in his equine form, he could be yoked to heavy work, the best means of capturing him being to cast over his head a bridle on which the sign of the cross had been made. But once in harness, he could be forced to carry stones to build a mill or steading, though in the end he usually contrived to make himself scarce.

In the Island of Lewis a sacrifice to a sea-god known as Shoney, to secure good fishing and plenty of sea-ware, was celebrated at Hallow-tide or Hallow-e'en, and was discontinued only about the year 1660. At nightfall the fisher-folk went down to the sea, and having knelt and repeated the Paternoster at a spot some four miles distant from the chapel of St. Malvey, a representative of the community carrying a vessel brimming with ale, waded waist-high into the water, crying: "Shoney, I give you this cup of ale, hoping that you'll be so kind as to send us plenty of sea-ware for enriching our ground the ensuing year." He then poured the ale as a libation into the sea, after which the company repaired to the chapel for a space, whence, after a brief season of silence, they finally betook themselves to the fields, where they spent the rest of the night drinking and dancing. These folk, it may be remarked, were almost exclusively Protestants.[46] Shoney of the Lews is almost certainly the same as the "Davy Jones" of maritime proverb—that is "the old John", or fiend, of the sea, in whose "locker" drowned seamen are retained—a memory of the belief that the drowned mariner was once regarded as a sacrifice to the demon or deity of the sea.

The *muireartach*, or "hag of the sea", whose legend has spread all over the

Highlands from Caithness and Lewis to the Southern Hebrides, is bald and ruddy-haired, with a dark blue-grey face the colour of coal, and protruding jagged teeth. In her forehead gleams one goggle-eye. She is the Carlin of the storm which beats upon our western and northern coasts, the mother of the king of Lochlann, the under-water realm of Celtic myth.[47]

"The Blue Men of the Minch", who haunt the narrow channel between Lewis and the Shiant Islands, are described as blue in colour, with long grey faces, floating from the waist out of the water and following in the track of boats and ships to lure their occupants to destruction. One of these Blue Men was captured by the crew of a ship and was bound hand and foot. But his companions followed and, hearing their voices, the captive, by a mighty effort, burst his bonds and regained his freedom. It is scarcely necessary to add that these "Blue Men" are merely personalizations of the waves.[48]

As regards the spirit who presides over the Clyde, the late Professor Rhys was of opinion that she enjoyed a reputation rich in literary tradition. He equated the "Shalott" of late Arthurian romance with Dumbarton, and the famous Elaine of Astolat with the patron spirit of Clutha's stream. "The original of the name (Dumbarton) which variously appears as Shalott, Escalot and other forms," he wrote, "was probably Alclut, the old Welsh name of the rock of Dumbarton on the Clyde", while Elaine was, like Undine, Fand or Vivien, "a woman of the lake-lady type", and her magic mirror, which cracked when the famous Tennysonian curse came upon her, was a symbol of the water which surrounded her rock-built castle. This, of course, is mythological interpretation with a vengeance and very much according to the methods of the day-before-yesterday. Dumbarton is certainly one and the same with Alclut, a name which became Normanized into Shalott or Astolat, but I can find no sufficient reason for identifying Elaine, "the lily maid", with a river deity, while the notion that her magic mirror typifies the Clyde seems unsound in view of what we know of scrying-glasses or other visionary surfaces, rivers never being employed for the purposes of divination, so far as I am aware. "Elaine" is merely a form invented by Sir Thomas Malory from older Welsh myth, and her original is that "Eleu" who was the wife of Merlin, and a British goddess of the dawn. She it was who built the glass castle which imprisoned him, and the cracking of her mirror is an allegory of the breaking of the morning mists symbolized by the house of glass, at the approach of the rising sun.[49]

Ireland knows of yet other spirits than the *banshee* and the *bean-nighe*. The *cluricane* or *luricane*, sometimes called the *leprecaun*, is a kind of supernatural cobbler of very diminutive proportions, who dwells in caves and nooks, where he makes tiny footgear. The name has a suspicious resemblance to the old English "lubberkin", a word used of a goblin. The *fir larrig*, or "red man", is a spirit garbed in a sugar-loaf hat, a scarlet coat, corduroy breeches and woollen stockings. He had a long, yellow face and streaming grey hair. He usually announced his presence to the families he was in the habit of visiting by thrusting his arm through the keyhole of the cabin door. If it were not opened to him, mischief would befall the cattle.[50]

Wales has also her own complement of spirits other than the *Tylwyth Teg*, or fairies. The *bwbach*, or *boobach*, closely resembles the brownie, and undertakes domestic work in exchange for provender. Like him, too, it had a tricksy side and was fond of practical jokes and horseplay of the rougher sort, pulling stools from under folk and jangling the fire-irons on the hearth—a species of poltergeist, indeed.[51]

Gwyn ap Nudd, the Lord of the Dead, and an ancient British god, remains in Welsh and English tradition as the Wild Huntsman who leads the *Cwn*

Annwn, or the hounds of Hades, over the waste lands at night. They are thought of as bearing away the souls of the dying. In Devonshire, a predominantly Celtic province, they are known as "the Wisht Hounds", who career through the midnight spaces of Dartmoor, and in Durham and Yorkshire, where a good deal of Celtic blood remains, they still flourish as "Gabriel Hounds", a pack which foretells death or disaster. The clamour they make is sometimes attributed to the "gaggles", or flocks, of bean-geese, which fly southward from Scandinavia on the approach of winter. The superstition has many analogies in other countries, especially in Germany, where it is known as "the Hunt of Woden" or Odin. [52]

From what has been said of British Celtic spirits as a whole it must be obvious that a large proportion of them, judging from their wild and frequently superhideous appearance and traits, must have been the imaginative generation of a fancy greatly more barbarous than any which might have issued from the comparatively civilized Celtic mentality. That they were the product of the imagination of peoples relatively aboriginal to the Celts is scarcely to be questioned. At the same time a few of them at least appear to be found among the Celtic gods in a decayed and "broken-down" stage, the memory of whom has remained among the Celtic peoples and whose traits have been exaggerated into modern and sometimes grotesque forms by the fears or the superstitions of a peasantry prone to the fantastic.

A host of mythical or magical animals, birds and monsters were regarded as haunting the Celtic peoples. In England the memory of these has either perished or is remembered only in legends of local dragons or serpents. In Wales the chief representative of this class is the *avanc*, a monstrous creature which dwells at the bottom of a lake, and the capture of which appears to have been one of the outstanding duties or adventures of British deities and heroes. Nor can Ireland boast of many mythic beasts, save the *phooka*, which is as frequently a goat, or a horse, as one of the manifestations of a Puck-like spirit. Celtic Scotland, on the other hand, is a veritable mine of grisly monsters which possess a most complete occult zoology of their own, and until recently these bulked largely in the rural imagination.

The *lavellan*, says Sibbald, is an animal peculiar to Caithness, living in the waters or marshes of this northern shire. It has the head of a rat or mouse, and is of the same colour as those rodents. It was believed to have the power of inflicting injuries upon cattle from a distance of more than a hundred feet. When in Ausdale, in Caithness, Pennant made inquiries about the *lavellan*, and suspected it to be the water shrew-mouse, or water-vole. The country people, he added, believed it to be noxious to cattle. They preserved the skin, and, as a cure for their sick beasts, gave them the water in which it had been dipped—an instance of the supposed curative power of sympathetic magic. It is mentioned by Robb Donn, the famous Sutherland bard, in a satirical song, in which he warns the subject of his scorn not to leave the clachan or go to moss or wood, "lest the *lavellan* come and smite him".

The *uilebheist* is a sea-monster with several heads, frequently mentioned in Highland story. It is sometimes called the *draygan*, and this would seem to give it a community of origin with the Norse sea-serpent or "drake". A gigantic waterbird known as the *boobrie* was supposed to haunt the fresh-water and sea-lochs of Argyllshire. His appetite matched his bulk, and he devoured sheep and even cows wholesale. One who claimed to have seen him described him as resembling the bird known as the great northern diver in form and colour, with the exception of white patches on the neck and breast. The neck was long and the beak hooked at the extremity like an eagle's. The feet were webbed, with tremendous claws.   The footprints of the *boobrie* covered a space equal to that contained within the span of a pair of large antlers, and its voice was "like the roar of an angry bull".   That this creature had at least an existence in the popular mind less than a century ago is proved by the number of local stories concerning it.

Many travellers in old Scotland allude to the barnacle goose, and even some of those who visited our Western coasts in the eighteenth century did not scruple to include it in their list of Caledonian marvels.   Some believed it to grow upon trees, and to take final bird-shape on dropping from their branches into the water.   But the most common tradition referred the origin of the *cadhan*, as it was called in the Hebrides, to the worm which attaches itself as a parasite to floating wood that has been some time in the water, often covering it so thickly as to conceal the surface of the log.   The superstition is akin to that once current in the Highlands that eels grow from horsehairs.   Those who partook of their flesh would, it was said, become violently insane.   An associated idea was that porpoises were developed from dog-fish.   But the barnacle goose was in no sense peculiar to Scotland, and was known in Wales and parts of Europe.

Reminiscent of the hound of the Baskervilles is the *Cù sith*, or fairy hound, which the Western islanders describe as being as large as a two-year-old cow, and of a dark green colour, with ears of still deeper green.   Its long tail was rolled up in a coil on its back, but was sometimes "plaited like the straw rug of a pack-saddle".   It was usually kept in the fairy knowe or brugh as a watch-dog by the elfin folk who dwelt there, but at times roamed about loose, making its lair in the clefts of the rocks.   The tracks made by its feet were as large as the spread of the human hand, and the noise made by its passing was like that of a horse galloping.   Thrice only does it bark or bay, in short, sharp growls, and at the third bark the terrified traveller is overtaken and pulled down.

The fairy cat is as large as a dog, and is pure black, save for a splash of white on the breast.   There is a good deal of evidence either that the cat was formerly worshipped in certain parts of the Highlands, or that it possessed some totemic significance in these regions, if the number of clan- and place-names derived from it are any criterion.

Monsters of a nebulous character, difficult to describe because of the very obscure terms in which they are spoken of by old writers, abounded in various districts in Scotland.   The Ettrick Shepherd writes of a creature called *falm*, which haunted a mountain at Glen Aven.   "He appears," writes Hogg, "to be no native of this world, but an occasional visitant, whose intentions are evil and dangerous.   He is only seen about the break of day, and on the highest verge of the mountain.   His head is twice as large as his body, and if any living creature cross the track over which he has passed before the sun shine on it, certain death is the consequence."

The water-horse of the Western Highlands (*each uisge*) must be differentiated from the kelpie, to which, indeed, it has only a general resemblance.   In shape and colour it resembled an ordinary horse, and, indeed, frequently mixed with horses when placed out to graze.   But should anyone mount it, it galloped off with him to the nearest loch or inlet, and plunged into the depths, where it devoured its rider.   It had the power of transforming its shape, and could appear as a young man or a boy, or even at times as an inanimate object.

He who could place a cow-shackle about its neck or a cap on its head com-pletely subdued it, and, so long as these were kept in place, it would do the work of an ordinary farm-horse.   In Skye it is credited with a sharp bill or snout of a brown hue, but its body-colour was either grey, or black with a white blaze

BAS-RELIEF OF THE GOD CERNUNNOS, DISCOVERED ON THE SITE OF NOTRE DAME, PARIS

BAS-RELIEF OF THE BRITISH SUN-GOD AT THE ROMAN BATH AT BATH

on the forehead. When taking man's shape it could not divest itself of its hoofs, which usually betrayed it. Those farmers who were foolish enough to use it as a beast of burden were sooner or later involved in ruinous loss. When killed, the water-horse proved to be "nothing but turf and a soft mass like jelly-fish". It could be shot only with a silver bullet, excellent proof of its supernatural character.

The water-bull was supposed to dwell in lonely moorland lochs, whence it issued only at night. It frequently mated with ordinary cattle, and, as it had no ears, calves having short or rudimentary ears were thought to be its progeny. It had a strange, unnatural bellow, something like the crowing of a cock, and is described as being "a small, ugly, very black animal, bull-shaped, soft, and slippery", its aqueous origin doubtless dictating the latter qualities.

A much more formidable mythical beast was the *biasd na srogaig*, or "beast of the lowering horn", which seems to have been peculiar to Skye. Indeed, from all accounts it closely resembled a unicorn, with a single horn on its forehead, and dwelt in lochans and small sheets of water. It was a bulky, clumsy animal, with long, ungainly legs. More terrible still was "the big beast of Lochawe", which had twelve legs, and could be heard in winter floundering among the ice. Accounts of its appearance varied, some giving it equine form, while others described it as resembling a large eel or serpent.

Scottish folk-lore has many accounts of a strange white serpent which is certainly mythical, and whose flesh or skin possessed a valuable medicinal virtue. The legend of the Ramsays of Bamff recounts how an ancestor of the line gained fame and fortune as a physician by catching the snake and eating its flesh, which permitted him to cure the King of Scotland of a serious complaint by the simple expedient of looking through him, the reptile's virtue of clair-voyance being passed on to the practitioner—surely the earliest example of X-rays!

An insect with an amusing as well as a fabulous name and existence is the Gigelorum, or *giol-daoram*, said to be the most microscopic of all created things. It is supposed to make its nest in the mite's ear, and thus can never have been seen by the naked eye. The *burach-bhaoi*, that is "the wizard's shackle", was a mythical creature of the eel or leech species which abounded at fords in the Western Highlands, and which twined itself like a band around the feet of passing horses, so that they fell into the water and were drowned, when it sucked their blood. It had nine eyes in its head and back, all of which squinted. In Skye it was believed that this animal was to be found in Badenoch, and it was thought to haunt especially the dark waters of Loch Tummel, in Perthshire, and certain streams in Argyll.

There was formerly a popular saying in the Western Highlands that "seals and swans are kings' children under enchantment"—a reminiscence probably of the well-known Celtic myth of the "Children of Lir". They have been seen by men in lonely places to divest themselves of their covering of feathers or fur, and to take the shape of handsome princes and princesses. Myths and legends of such enchanted animals are legion. Seals, which abound in the Shetland Islands, were formerly believed to be Finn men and women in dis-guise who had swum to the islands in seal-shape. Could one seize them when they had cast off the skin which gave them animal form, he could retain them as prisoners at his pleasure, unless they succeeded in recovering the pelt, when they plunged into the sea and escaped. There was formerly a sept in North Uist known as "the MacCodrums of the Seals", who, tradition avers, were descended from these enchanted animals.

In many of the holy wells of Scotland a pair of mystical fishes were said to have their abode.   In such a well near the Church of Kilmore, in Lorne, two black fishes were still to be seen in the seventeenth century, and were said to have existed there for generations. The natives called them *easg saint*, or "holy fishes".   The superstition surrounding such mysterious fishes can perhaps be attributed to a Druidical origin.   The wells they inhabited were usually situated beneath a hazel tree, the sacred red nuts of which were supposed to fall into the well and afford them sustenance, as they seem to have done in the case of the "salmon of knowledge", the red spots on whose skin were thought to be due to the same cause.   The fishes in question were believed to be the presiding spirits of the well, and seem to have had a certain oracular character, gained from the magical nuts on which they fed.   To kill or eat them was regarded as a crime certain to bring down celestial punishment upon the perpetrator.

CHAPTER VIII

NECROMANCY, PROPHECY AND DIVINATION

THE great art of foretelling and prevision in all its branches was as second nature to the Celtic peoples, who, from the earliest recorded times in their history, almost until the present, have been regarded by their neighbours as prophets and diviners *par excellence*.   It is noticeable that in Celtic vaticination there is little or no resort to outside agencies, no recourse to heighten "with euphrasy and rue the visual nerve", or to employ narcotic draughts to quicken the native gift of prophetic sight, as in Oriental Magic.   In this chapter I shall divide the evidence for Celtic prevision into its necromantic, prophetic and divinatory aspects, leaving the question of Second Sight for a separate and later chapter.

The term Necromancy, strictly speaking, signifies divination by the aid of the spirits of the dead, but it is frequently applied to divination through spirits of any kind.   It is in the latter sense almost exclusively that I will employ it here, as the raising of the spirits of the dead by Celtic magicians seems to have been a matter of rare occurrence only.   By far the most celebrated and usual method of employing the necromantic faculty was by what is known as *taghairm*, a word which signifies "an echo"—that is, a response as from a distance, a spiritual reply.   Perhaps it may most fittingly be Englished as "the spirit call".

The awful and mysterious—and frequently repellent—rites of *taghairm* were certainly not of one particular kind, but appear to have been multiform. In its modern form it appears to have been confined exclusively to Scotland. The less obnoxious examples of it were associated with the wrapping of the seer in the hide of a newly-slaughtered bull, much after the manner in which the priests of Egypt and those of the Jews and the Babylonians donned the fleece of a ram when engaged in certain magical or divinatory acts.   Thus attired, he stretched himself beside a waterfall, or at the foot of some wild precipice reputed to be haunted by spirits, and awaited their coming.   Whatever the seer desired to know, the fate of a family or the outcome of a battle, was duly communicated to him by agencies who may have been demons or nature-spirits.

Martin, in his *Description of the Western Isles*, provides a startling picture of this mystical proceeding.   The seer, he tells us, who was frequently chosen by lot, was left by his companions beside some stream which marked the boundaries of two villages.   When he had closed his eyes, four of the company laid hold of him and, rocking him to and fro, struck his hips forcibly against the bank of the rivulet.   One of them then exclaimed as though in question, "What have you there?" to which another replied: "A log of birchwood."   The intention seems to have been to delude the spirits into the belief that the seer was one of these logs or rude images which fairies and other spirits were in the habit of placing in children's cradles when they kidnapped the infants, or which they employed as magical substitutes for grown-up persons whom they had spirited away.

This part of the rite must indeed have been a relic of more ancient and primitive practice.   The first speaker then cried: "Let his invisible friends appear from all quarters and relieve him by giving an answer to our questions." At this a swarm of diminutive spirits rose from the sea some distance away, replied to the man's queries more or less satisfactorily, and as suddenly disappeared.   The seer was then liberated and the company returned home, bearing with them the appropriate, if ambiguously oracular, rejoinder of the spirit host.

"Mr. Alexander Cooper," adds Martin, "present minister of North Uise, told me that one John Erach, in the Isle of Lewis, assured him it was his fatt to have been led by his curiosity with some who consulted this oracle and that he was a night within the hide as above mentioned; during which time he felt and heard such terrible things that he could not express them."   The impression was ineradicable, and "he would not for a thousand worlds be concerned in a like performance".[1]   A second method, says Martin, was to leave the seer in the hide at a remote place throughout the night, and it was obviously this to which the case just alluded to applies.   That this description of *taghairm* was practised in Wales is clear from a statement in the tale known as "The Vision of Rhonabwy", in which Rhonabwy, a warrior of Powys, beheld a vision of the Court of King Arthur while sleeping on the skin of a yellow heifer, as we read in the *Mabinogion*.

Still a third and much more cruel and barbarous magical device went by the name of *taghairm*.   This was known in tradition as "giving his supper to the devil", and at least three instances of it are recorded in Highland lore. The most celebrated case is that in which one Lachlan Oer and a companion, Allan, the son of Hector, shut themselves up in a barn near the Sound of Mull, and, impaling black cats on spits, roasted them alive by a blazing fire.   Other cats entered the building, setting up an infernal caterwauling, which wellnigh daunted the men, but they remained inexorable until a greater cat of ferocious appearance entered and remonstrated with them, threatening them that if they did not desist from their horrid employment they would never see the face of the Trinity.   Lachlan struck the hideous animal on the head with the hilt of his sword, whereupon the devil, for he it was, assumed his appropriate shape and asked the pair what it was they wanted of him.   They replied that they craved prosperity and a long life to enjoy it.   This was granted, and it is said that Lachlan, for his part, never relented of the dreadful act, even upon his deathbed.[2]

Although it might seem that these two rites of *taghairm* differ in their origin, the underlying intention is the same in both cases—to compel supernatural beings to rescue one or more of their kind or species who are in the power of mortals by agreeing to some bargain which will be to the lasting benefit of those mortals. Those who bore the man wrapped up in a bull-hide, as related in the first instance, pretended that he was a fairy changeling whom they were maltreating by striking his body against the river bank, and they then called upon "his invisible friends" to rescue him. In the case in which cats were tortured the same idea prevails, except that the cat—believed to be a diabolical creature—was actually maltreated in the hope that its satanic master would come to its aid. The other description of *taghairm*, described by Martin, was obviously of a different nature. In carrying it out, the seer was wrapped up in a bull-hide in the hope that the spirits of the deserted locality where he was placed would be tempted to approach him by the odour proceeding from the hide, and that he would learn of some coming event from their conversation.

It is said that Cameron of Lochiel received at a *taghairm* a small silver shoe, which, if placed on the foot of a new-born son of his family, would endow the child with courage and fortitude. One baby, however, had, at his birth, a foot too large for the shoe, a defect inherited from his mother, who was not of Cameron origin. His lack of the magically bestowed courage was apparent at the battle of Sheriffmuir, where he fled before the enemy.

Another divinatory rite in which the bull figured—in this case a white bull—was associated with the election of an Irish king and was known as *Imbas-forosnai*, or "divination by holding the cheeks". The flesh of a white bull was partaken of by a man, who then went to sleep, holding his cheeks in his hands, four Druids chanting over him "to render his witness truthful". He then saw in a vision the person who should be elected king and what he was doing at the moment. Probably hypnotic influence entered into the rite. Sometimes a piece of pig's, dog's or cat's flesh was chewed instead, and then offered to an idol of the god in cases where the divination had no connection with royalty. Canon MacCulloch alludes to this method of divination in his *Religion of the Ancient Celts* (p. 248).

Giraldus Cambrensis, in the sixteenth chapter of his *Itinerary Through Wales*, alludes to a certain class of persons there whom he calls Awenydhyon, or people inspired. When consulted as to the future, they were in the habit of roaring violently, seeming to become possessed of a spirit. They did not deliver the answer to any question put them in a rational or connected manner, and the gist of their replies usually had to be disentangled from incoherent speeches. That these were the remaining practitioners of a Druidic tradition can scarcely be questioned when the resemblance of their procedure to the rite of *Imbas-forosnai* is considered.

Prophecy may be defined as ecstatic utterance concerning future events delivered under great spiritual and mental stress. It has no artificial or outward aids, as has divination or auspices, and, if truly inspired, is usually regarded as divine utterance voiced through a human mouthpiece. In Celtic lore the Druids are generally associated with the prophetic afflatus. It was an Irish Druid who revealed to the Fomorian god Balor that he would meet his death at the hands of his grandson. Determined to render the prediction vain, Balor imprisoned his daughter Ethnea in an impregnable tower built on the summit of an almost inaccessible rock at the eastern extremity of Tory Island, at the same time directing a company of twelve matrons to guard her. But the hero Mackineely, by the aid of another Druid, gained access to her and she gave birth to three sons, whom Balor cast into a whirlpool. One of them escaped, however, and later slew the darksome god, as had been predicted.[3]

When the Tuatha Dé Danann were challenged by the Milesians to yield the soil of Ireland to them they consulted the bard Amairgen, who predicted that the Milesians would temporarily abandon the island to the Tuatha Dé so far as "the distance of nine waves"—a typically oracular saying, for, after taking ship, the Milesians landed again elsewhere![4]

In his *General History of Ireland* Keating relates that in an ancient book known as *The Etymology of Names* he discovered a passage which narrated how a certain Druid, who had the gift of prophecy, foretold to Daire, an Irish monarch, that he should have a son whose name should be Lugaidh, and that, to give the prophecy the fullest force, he must call all his sons by that name. The Druid had added that this particular son should sit upon the throne of Ireland. When his sons arrived at man's estate, King Daire enquired of the prophet which of them should succeed to the throne. The Druid advised him to take all five of the young men to Tailtenn, at which place a meeting of the nobility was to be held, when a fawn would appear before the gathering. This animal was to be pursued by the five lads, and that one who overtook and killed it should be his father's heir. The advice was accepted, the fawn was duly chased, a magic mist enveloped it, but the genuine Lugaidh succeeded in running it to earth and dispatching it.

On another occasion, by the prophecy of a Druid, three brothers of the family of Colla, says Keating, were saved from execution. They had rebelled against the King of Ulster, but when the Druid Dubhchomair predicted that the crown of Ireland would not descend to the dynasty which then enjoyed it, should they be slain, their lives were preserved. Later they fled to Scotland, but learning that, should they die by order of the Irish monarch their heirs should succeed to the throne, they returned to Ireland, gave battle to the royal forces, were victorious, and divided the land between them. It would seem, therefore, that the prophecy does not appear to have been accurately forecast or fulfilled.

But the most outstanding topic in Celtic prophecy is that of the Lia Fail, the ancient coronation stone of the Irish Kings, a prophetic stone indeed, and, as its importance demands, we must make a very real endeavour to come to conclusions concerning the origin of this ancient relic, the legend of which is bound up with the destinies of the British race. I have already alluded to the Irish legend of the Lia Fail in the second chapter of this book. The Tuatha Dé Danann, it is said, conveyed it from the mythical isle of Fal (Destiny) or from the "city of Falias" to Ireland, where it became the test-seat of the Kings of Ireland, crying out when the genuine heir to the crown of Eire placed his feet upon it.

Now we find that a stone of a similar kind existed at Scone, the later metropolis of the old Celtic Kings of Scotland. "Legend," says William Skene, "has much to tell of how it was brought from the East to Scotland, but history knows of it only at Scone."[5] The great majority of Britons still credit the ancient tradition that the Coronation Stone at Westminster Abbey is ultimately of Irish origin, that it is actually the "Lia Fail", or Stone of Destiny, spoken of in Irish legend which was brought to these shores by the conquering Irish Scots from the Hill of Tara. Are there any grounds for assuming the credibility of this time-honoured notion?

There are not. The Coronation Stone, as we know it, can most definitely be proved to have been situated in the royal Scottish demesne at Scone in the thirteenth century, being housed, in all probability, at the Abbey there, and not in the open, as some authorities have stated, until it was removed by Edward I to Westminster in the year 1296. In all likelihood it had been at Scone from much earlier times. But what is the basis for the belief in its transportation from Ireland?

The very earliest Scottish "edition" of the legend of the Stone known to us is the statement of Baldred Bisset, one of the Scots Commissioners sent to Rome in 1301 to plead the cause of Scottish independence before the Pope. In quite a few words he tells us that the Stone was brought to Ireland by the Princess Scota, "the daughter of Pharaoh". Later she came to Scotland, carrying the relic with her, conquered the Picts and gave the country its present name. The Scottish Government of the time did not, however, substantiate Baldred's story, and in a separate report made no mention of it or of the Stone whatsoever, although in a famous communication to Rome, dated from Arbroath in 1321, and outlining the reasons for the separate existence of Scotland as a nation, it received passing mention.

If we follow the course of the legend, we find the next allusion to it in an English manuscript, the *Scalachronica*, written about 1355, which, relates that one Simon Breac, a son of the King of Spain, sailed to Ireland, taking with him a stone on which the monarchs of Spain were accustomed to be crowned. This, of course, is merely a version of the Irish myth as given in the *Book of Invasions*. The royal seat, we are informed, was later carried to Scone by a certain chieftain, Fergus, son of Ferchar.

The Scottish historian Fordun, writing a little later, associated this account with that which refers to the Princess Scota, whom he made the ancestress of Simon Breac. But he adds an alternative tale that the Stone was fished up out of the sea off the coast of Ireland by the anchor of one of Simon's ships. Fergus, son of Farquhar, he states, later brought the stone from Ireland to Scotland. Andrew of Wyntoun, writing about 1424, accepted this version, but preferred to assume a more historical and much later Fergus as he who brought the Stone to Scottish soil. This chieftain, he assures us, set up the relic in Iona. Blind Harry, the Minstrel, a Scottish poet, followed this account in part and averred that the Stone was brought to Scone from Iona by King Malcolm Canmore.

In the somewhat mendacious history of Hector Boece we have the legend in its latest and fullest form. The Egyptian Princess Scota and her husband Gathelus, he tells us, fled to Portugal after the disaster to the Egyptians in the Red Sea and reigned in that country. Their descendant, Simon Breac, brought the Stone to Ireland, whence it was carried to Dunstaffnage in Argyll by Fergus, son of Ferchar, the first King of the Scots to reign in Scotland. Later, the second Fergus placed it in Iona, but Kenneth MacAlpine, after he had conquered the Picts, brought it to Scone. The story is so explanatory in its circumstances as to render its hypothetical character apparent.

The belief that the Stone had once been situated at Dunstaffnage Castle rests upon the authority of Boece alone. In the nineteenth century, McCulloch, in his *Western Isles of Scotland*, remarked that the Coronation Stone bore a strong resemblance to that which crowned the doorway of Dunstaffnage Castle. Almost at once a rumour arose that it had actually been removed from that building, and the very space from which it had been taken was solemnly pointed out!

But long before McCulloch's day a popular notion seems to have been in circulation that a missing stone at Dunstaffnage was none other than the famous Lia Fail, or Stone of Destiny, which, said the Irish "Leabhar Gabhala" or *Book of Invasions*, had been brought from "the city of Falias" to Ireland by way of Scotland. The stone was associated with a prophecy which averred that wherever it was situated "the Scottish race should rulers be". This, all Scotland devoutly believed, was the stone which had been carried from Ireland to Argyll and thence to Scone. But Irish antiquaries have proved conclusively that the stone believed to be identified with the Lia Fail, and which was situated on the Hill of Tara, *is still there*.

Petrie, in his *Antiquities of Tara Hill*, says that in 1798 it stood near the hill known as "the Mound of Hostages", when "it was removed to its present position in the Rath near the Forradh, to mark the grave of the rebels slain in the insurrection of that year". That this stone still remains there is indeed common knowledge among Irish antiquaries. It is a pillar, and by no means an easily portable one, and does not at all resemble the Coronation Stone at Westminster. Petrie quotes a tenth-century Irish poem which reveals that the Lia Fail remained in Ireland. Indeed, Skene has made it particularly plain in his monograph on the Stone that it had no association with its Irish equivalent, which, he assures us, never left Ireland, and was there in the eleventh century.

The Scottish Stone, now at Westminster, was not situated in Argyll during the early times of the Scots dynasty there, the ancient historians of that province, Adamnan and Cumine, making no mention of it in their accounts of contemporary coronations. The tale that it was carried from Dunstaffnage to Scone is frankly mythical, a mere political legend, devised to give it an antiquity to which it can lay no claim.

Geologists who have examined the Stone are in substantial agreement that it was quarried at or near Scone. The late Professor Geikie wrote: "I do not see any evidence in the Stone itself why it may not have been taken from the neighbourhood of Scone; indeed, it perfectly resembles the sandstone of that district." Professor A. C. Ramsay arrived at much the same conclusion, though he indicated that it might have come from any part of Scotland where red sandstone abounds.

The even more absurd story that it was the stone on which Jacob pillowed his head while sojourning in the desert was the invention of one Rishanger, an English chronicler of the thirteenth century. St. Columba's pillow of stone at Iona, mentioned by Adamnan and Cumine, has also been confused with the Coronation Stone, but the former writer states most distinctly that the stone associated with the Saint was placed on his grave.

The Celtic peoples almost invariably employed stones of the kind in connection with the ceremonies of a royal inauguration, and I cannot doubt that when the Scottish monarchy first selected Scone as its capital in the ninth century it had such a stone quarried in the neighbourhood for that specific purpose. But where did the stories of its Irish and Egyptian origin spring from? The first was evidently a garbled version of the Hibernian myth respecting the Lia Fail applied to the Scottish Stone, the *sedes*, or throne-seat of a dynasty originally hailing from Ireland. The latter story may be a distant recollection of the myth of the divine kingship, which had its rise in ancient Egypt. If the whole cult and circumstances, ritual and legend, of the divine king could make its way from Egypt to Ireland, as I have, I think, made plain that it did in the twelfth chapter of this book, I see no reason why the story of the Princess Scota, obviously a myth intended to explain its introduction, could not have accompanied it. Indeed, such myths, explanatory not only of the divine kingship but of many other institutions, invariably accompany the cultus which they seek to elucidate, as the whole history of mythic development reveals.

But Edward the First of England, that highly romantic and superstitious monarch, had at least the best of occult reasons for carrying off the stone from Scone to Westminster, for he believed it to be the habitation of an oracular spirit which advised the Scots both politically and in a military sense. This is clear enough from the terms of a poem in doggerel Latin which is to be found in the Bodleian Library, and a rough translation of which avers that:

> In Egypt, Moses preached to the people saying
> That Scota, the fairy maiden, who is the stone,
> Told of the strange manner in which the land should be conquered.

These words seem to imply that the spirit of Scota inhabited the stone and prophesied therefrom, and parallels the tradition in the Irish *Book of Invasions* that such royal monuments were haunted by a "demon", who exclaimed in recognition when the rightful monarch of Ireland took his seat upon it. So that we find Scota, the mythic representative of the divine kingship in its Celtic form, acting as the Egeria, or advisory and prophetic nymph, to her royal descendants and employing the stone of hereditary regality as her shrine. It follows that if the Scottish royal stone, which is known as the Coronation Stone, is not the genuine Lia Fail, she must have been thought of as inhabiting it in a complimentary sense only, as an Irish *banshee* might have been inherited by a younger branch of a family betaking itself to Scotland. And I think, as I have mentioned in my remarks on the subject of the *banshee*, to be found elsewhere in this book, the royal family of Scotland were favoured by the patronage of a spirit of that class. The whole legend is mnemonic of the ancient belief that the royal race of Ireland, and thus of Scotland and consequently of Britain, were, in their successive kings, the avatars or reincarnations of the Celtic sun-gods. It follows that, according to this belief, our present King George VI. is, in the mythical sense at least, as certainly the living representative of the Celtic solar deity as the Emperor of Japan is of the sun-goddess Ama-Terasu. I may add that I have devoted so much space to this topic for the excellent reason that so much confusion prevails concerning it—a confusion which, as it affects the authenticity of the most ancient royal and prophetic relic in our islands, should surely be dispelled.

The occult science of augury or divination does not appear to have taken any form among the Celts unknown to the arcane practice of other races. Among the Celtic races we observe divination, or forecasting the future, by means of omens and auspices, through the media of the flight and motions of birds, by the casting of bones, or omen-sticks, the movements and direction taken by animals, by dreams and crystal-gazing, almost precisely as we find these several methods employed by many other races. Yet there were one or two forms of divining which may have been either exclusively of Celtic provenance or more particularly in use among the Celtic tribes, and these I will indicate when dealing with their circumstances.

Diodorus Siculus expressly states that the Druids predicted the future from the flight of birds.[6] Diodorus was a Sicilian Greek and a contemporary of Julius Caesar and Augustus, and if he did not penetrate to Britain, he is known to have exercised the greatest care in sifting his information. Indeed, his statement is fortified by quite a number of instances of omens drawn from bird-flight which appear in Scottish and Irish folk-tales. In a well-known Gaelic poem attributed to St. Columba, the saint is made to say that he pays no heed to "the voices of birds", which seems to imply that the Druids to whom he alludes in these strophes, divined the future from bird-song, or flight, as did the augurs of ancient Rome.[7] We have no "official" statement of the manner in which the Druids divined coming events by this means, but it seems probable that they effected it in a manner similar to that practised by the Roman augurs—that is, by marking out a given space and judging from the species of birds, lucky or otherwise, which alighted there or passed over it the nature of their flight and their cries, whether such and such a question was answered in the affirmative or negative. It is remarked that it was from Pictish settlers in Ireland that the Irish derived "every spell, every charm, every augury by sneezing, voices of birds, and every omen". The Irish would seem to have domesticated the wren and the raven for the purposes of divination. If a raven cried from above the bed in a house a distinguished grey-haired guest would visit it. If it called *bach*, the visitor would be a monk; if *gradh, gradh*, twice, it would be one of the clergy. If it called from the north-east end of the dwelling, robbers would raid the place; if it called from the door, strangers or soldiers. If it spoke with "a small voice", chirping *err, err*, sickness would come upon the inhabitants. Each sound, position and movement of the tame bird had its own significance. The subject has been closely examined by Mr. R. I. Best, the translator of D'Arbois de Jubainville's work on the Irish Mythological cycle, in *Eriu*, the journal of Irish studies (Vol. VIII.)

"I heard the cuckoo while fasting, and I knew the year would not go well with me," exclaimed a Scottish Gael. It is unlucky in the Scottish Highlands to hear the first cuckoo of the season ere one has broken bread.[8] When the minister of the parish of Dornoch, in 1816, was ill, a large cormorant settled on the steeple of the parish church, and the minister's death a few days later was regarded as a fulfilment of the fatal omen. When, thirty-five years later, a similar appearance occurred and the incumbent also died, the people regarded their predictions as amply justified. "Raven-knowledge" or wisdom was also a well-known portent in the Highlands, and especially in the remote isle of St. Kilda.[9] It is referred to in a poem entitled "The Massacre of the Rosses", and is amply documented by Toland in his *History of the Druids*. When at the village of Finglass, near Dublin, in 1697, he tells us, he struck up an acquaintance with two gentlemen "of the old Irish stock", who were on private business, and says that these were assured that the affair they were concerned in would proceed fortunately because of the appearance on the road of a raven which had some white feathers in its plumage. They refused to stir until they saw in which direction the bird would fly, and when it disappeared southwards their certainty regarding the success of their mission was confirmed. They assured the Celtic sage that a raven so marked, and flying on the right hand of any person, croaking the while, "was an infallible presage of good luck", and he, for his part, recalled that Pompeius Trogus, a Roman historian of the first century, had laid it down that "the Gauls excel all others in the skill of augury".[10] Cicero, however, was of opinion that Druidic predictions were as much grounded on conjecture as on the accepted rules of augury.[11] He was probably thinking of the hard-and-fast Roman code as contained in the *Libri Augurales*, or "Book of Auguries".

A belief seems to have lingered in Lancashire that the cuckoo was able to predict how long one was to live—a reminiscence, perhaps, of Celtic augury by bird-call.[12] In the north-east of Scotland a crow alighting on the roof of a house indicated that death was hovering over it. If rooks flew up and down in a tumbling fashion it was held to be ominous of windy conditions. To meet a magpie in the morning, in the same area, was unlucky. To scratch a magpie's tongue and insert in the wound a drop of blood from a human tongue was thought to endow the bird with human speech. A dove flying round a person's head was considered a sign of approaching mortality.[13] Leyden remarks how unlucky this bird is in Scottish eyes.

In Wales the eagle was a bird of divination. "The descendants of a person who had eaten eagle's flesh to the ninth generation possessed the gift of second sight."[14] In the time of Henry I., Gruffyd ap Rhys ap Tudor, the rightful Prince of Wales, according to native genealogies, was informed by Milo, Earl of Hereford, when they were riding past Llangorse Lake in Brecknockshire, that a tradition existed which averred that if the natural Prince of Wales commanded the waterfowl upon this lake to sing they would obey him. The Norman, who bore the minor title of Lord of Brecknock, himself tried the experiment, but without result. Gruffydd, dismounting from his horse, prayed earnestly that the Lord would justify his claim to the principality of Wales by causing the birds to sing, whereupon they rose into the air and chorused vociferously. When the incident was reported to the King he generously admitted the Welsh prince's hereditary claim, though he was careful to take no steps to enforce it.[15]

The wren is also a bird of augury, as the Latin *Life of St. Moliny* avers. "The Pseudo-Cormac Glossary," says George Henderson, "explains it as *drui-en*, a Druid bird." In Welsh the wren's name is *dryw*, an etymological resemblance of significance.[16] O'Curry remarks that the Druids divined the course of events from the chirping of tame wrens. Duncan Campbell, in his *Memoirs*, mentions that "some will defer going abroad, tho' called by business of the greatest consequence if, happening to look out of the window, they see a single crow." It will, of course, be understood that here I am concerned only with such beliefs as may properly be regarded as Celtic in origin and ominous in their nature, and not with the British folk-lore of birds in general, although I cannot claim that the above enumeration of such instances is in any way exhaustive.

Omens from the habits or movements of animals were certainly drawn by the Celts. Before going into battle against the Romans, Boadicea, the courageous Queen of the Iceni, a British tribe dwelling in Norfolk and Suffolk, drew a hare from her bosom, "and," says Cassius Dio, "since it ran on what they considered the auspicious side the whole multitude shouted with pleasure", seeing victory within their grasp.[17] "The hare," says Rhys, "was regarded as an animal sacred to the Celtic Zeus or to his associate."[18] Superstitions still cling to the hare in Wales. Sir Laurence Gomme thought that the above occurrence was an instance of the totemic animal serving as an omen to its clansmen.[19] The head of a black bull was ominous of evil throughout Scotland—wherefore is unknown—but the appearance of such a trophy at the "Black Dinner" given to Earl Douglas and his brother at Edinburgh Castle by the supporters of James II. was the signal for the massacre of the unhappy guests.

In Celtic Devonshire, if a swarm of bees alights on a dead tree it is believed that there will be a death in the owner's house within the year. A strange swarm settling in one's garden implies an access of prosperity.[20] Divination by worms was also formerly practised in Scotland. If a certain worm in a medicinal spring on the top of a hill in the parish of Strathdon were found alive it augured the survival of a patient, and in a well at Ardnacloich, in Appin, the questing invalid, "if he bee to dye, shall find a dead worm therein, or a quick one, if health be to follow".[21] A witch, arraigned for sorcery, was charged with having described a circle in a field and making a hole in the midst of it, from which issued a great worm, followed by a smaller one, and a third, which died because it could not crawl out of the circle as the others had done. She informed those who had sought her advice that the first worm represented the head of the household, who should live, that the second and smaller worm was an infant, still unborn to his wife, and that it should survive, and that the last stood for the woman herself, who should die—"all of which came to pass".[22]

I see nothing unreasonable in the theory that these ominous beliefs concerning birds, animals and insects represent the survivals or reminiscences of an older Druidic system of augury, from which they have descended. They are in no wise associated as regards their origin with witchcraft, or later arcane practice, which appears to have merely adopted them, and they seem to me to be associated with a much more definite and well-digested system of augury than any which the looser and less intelligent sorcery of a mediaeval peasantry could have devised.   Indeed, the evidence for the existence of such a divinatory system in Druidic times is much too strong to admit of the theory of a more modern origin.

Omens were frequently drawn from the direction taken by the smoke and flames of sacred fires and from the appearance of the clouds.   The Irish *file* or Druid bard discovered auspices by the practice of what was known as the *Teinm Laegha*, or the "Analysis of Song".   He composed verses and sang them over any person or object respecting which he sought information, or placed his magical staff over a man or woman to secure the arcane information he sought respecting them.   The Irish diviners forecast the appropriate time for building a house by the stars.   If an Irish Druid wished to get on the track of stolen goods, he sang an incantation through his half-open fist, using it as a trumpet. If this did not serve, he went to sleep and traced the stolen property through a dream, or trance.   What was known as "illumination by rhymes" was brought about in a heavy sleep by a professional seer, who, after roaring violently, became lucid and gave the information required.

It was in a dream, too, that the beautiful Eachtach, the favourite of Art, son of Conn of the Hundred Battles, beheld a terrible vision, in which she saw her head slashed from her shoulders and a tree growing out of her neck, whose branches overspread the whole kingdom of Ireland, as Keating tells us.   But the sea rose and destroyed the tree, and when a second sprang up in its place it, too, was blasted by a west wind and perished.   This dream Art interpreted as signifying that he himself would be slain in an impending battle, and that their son, still unborn, should sit upon the throne of Ireland, but would die from a fishbone sticking in his throat.   The second tree symbolized this prince's son, who would perish in strife with the Fianna Eirionn, or Militia of Ireland, who would rise in arms against him and who were represented by the western tempest.   All these happenings came to pass, as the lady's dream foretold.

What was known in the Scottish Highlands as *slinneineachd*, and in occult practice generally as *scapulimancy*, or divining by means of the shoulder-blades of animals, was formerly engaged in by certain people as a definite profession.   Important events were foretold in the life of the owner of a slaughtered animal from the marks on its shoulder- or blade-bones.   The right blade-bone of a black pig or sheep was considered the most suitable for this purpose.   It was thoroughly boiled so that not a particle of flesh adhered to it, but great care had to be exercised to ensure that it was not scratched or marked in any way.   The bone was then divided into areas corresponding to the natural features of the district in which the divination was to be made.   "Certain marks indicated a crowd of people, met at a funeral, fight, sale, etc."   The largest hole or indentation symbolized the grave of the beast's owner, and from its position the problem of whether he should survive the current year, or otherwise, was resolved.   If it lay near the side of the bone, the omen was fatal, but if in its centre, prosperity was indicated.

A celebrated bone-reader in Barra, says J. G. Campbell, was present at the festivities connected with the completion of the Castle of the MacNeills and was pressed to divine its fate.   He foretold that it would become an abode of thrushes, and that this would happen "when the Rattle stone was found", when people worked at gathering seaweed in a village then far from the sea, and when deer swam across to Barra from Uist.   "All this happened and the castle is now in ruins." On the night of the treacherous massacre of Glencoe, a party of MacDonalds were amusing themselves by examining the shoulder-blade of a beast that had been slaughtered to provide food for the Government troops who had been billeted upon them, and who subsequently attacked them. Suddenly one of them exclaimed, "There is a shedding of blood in the glen," and sensing that treason of some kind was afoot, they made a hasty departure and were among the few who escaped from butchery on that terrible night,when Highlander slew Highlander without mercy.[23] Numerous references to divination by shoulder-blade are made in the Old Testament, and the right shoulder of a sacrificed animal was the especial perquisite of the priest. On one occasion Samuel set before Saul "the shoulder and that which was upon it", to elucidate a divinatory act (Samuel ix, 24). Dalyell states that "the humbler class of Scottish seers" turned towards the east "when divining futurity from the lines, shades or transparence disclosed by its inequalities".[24] And MacLeod ("Theophilus Insulanus"), in his book *On the Second Sight*, alludes to it as "another kind of divination, whereby, on looking into the shoulder-blade of a sheep, goat, etc., as in a book, some skilful in that occult science pretend to read future events".[25]

John of Salisbury speaks of this practice as being common in England in the twelfth century,[26] and Giraldus Cambrensis writes of it as a familiar proceeding in the Wales of the early thirteenth century. He mentions that the bone usually employed was the right shoulder-blade of a ram, boiled, not roasted, and he provides specific instances in which this method was resorted to. That it was also customarily an Irish usage is clear from an allusion by Camden.[27] The practice had, indeed, a wide acceptance among peoples in many parts of the world.

What were known as *coelbreni*, or "omen-sticks", were, it is alleged, employed by the Druids for casting lots.[28] As the sticks fell, so the diviner interpreted the fates. On All Saints Eve (October 31st), in Wales, it was formerly customary to build a great fire known as *coel coeth*, and when it was almost extinguished, to mark a white stone for each member of the household and throw the same into the ashes. In the morning these were sought for, and if any were missing, the person who cast it in, it was believed, "would not see another All Saints Eve".[29] This custom was also maintained in Scotland on the same date.[30]

That divination by crystal-gazing was familiar to the Celtic peoples is evident. When prophesying to Queen Maeve of Ulster before the Cattle Raid of Cooley concerning its probable results, the mystic maiden Fedelm appears to have gazed into a glass or crystal, "seeing all red".[31] To eat of a roasted egg for three Sundays in succession and then with unwashed hands to wash one's eyes was regarded in the Highlands as imparting mystical knowledge of all things.[32] To divine the presence of the distemper known as *esane*, ascribed to fairy influence (probably the "fairy stroke"), Irish necromancers put some burning coals into a cup of clear water and called upon the elves from the four parts of the compass.[33]

A strange method of divination practised in the North of Scotland was "the swimming of names in water". It was resorted to in cases of theft, in order to discover the guilty person. The names of those suspected were written upon slips of paper and cast into water, and that which sank was regarded as belonging to the miscreant. In the same area, the seat of a disease was divined by taking three stones representing the head, the heart and the body, and placing them overnight in the hot ashes of the hearth. In the morning they were dropped into a basin of water, and that which made the loudest sound when it came in contact with the water revealed the part chiefly affected.

In Scotland dumb people were frequently regarded as diviners and even as necromancers. Dalyell cites several such cases in his *Darker Superstitions of Scotland*. "Jonka Dyneis, being questioned after a vision, 'could not give answer, bot stude as if bereft of hir senssis' ", and after a vision, or some spectral illusion, one Elspeth Reoch "had na power of hir toung, nor could not speik". Penance was imposed on several persons for consulting a dumb woman regarding a theft, while a man was fined for letting a house to Margaret Rannald and her two dumb daughters. For being acquainted with "the signs" of a dumb woman, two people in Edinburgh were cited to appear before the Kirk Session there in the year 1596. Dumb folk alleged to be sorcerers appear to have abounded in the Scotland of the sixteenth century, and it is plain from the circumstances of their trials that quite a fair proportion of these merely simulated speechlessness. The mere fact that a sorcerer was dumb appears to have attracted scores of people to seek his advice. In any case the dumb were thought to possess second sight and an uncanny prescience of future events. Probably the strange sounds they emitted and the curious gestures they made heightened the popular belief in their arcane or diabolic associations.

Gregor, in his *Folk-lore of the North-East of Scotland*, tells of a weird method of divination by which it was thought possible to discover whether a case of illness would end in death. Two holes were dug, one being described as "the living grave" and the other as "the dead grave". The sick person was laid between them, without being told which was which. If he turned with the face to the "living grave" he would recover; if the reverse happened he would perish. For engaging in this practice a woman named Marjorie Pulmer, who had an ailing child, was debarred from the Sacrament by the Presbytery of Cullen, in Banffshire, in the year 1649.

Elsewhere in this book I have dealt with the subject of human sacrifice by the Druids and the divinatory methods resorted to by them on such occasions. They also appear to have used for the purpose of divining a species of frame, known as *peithynen*, or "the Elucidator". This object has sometimes been described as "the Druids' wheel". Sir John Daniel (who illustrates the apparatus on page 136 of his book) says of this machine: "The Elucidator consisted of several staves called faith-sticks or lots, on which the judicial maxims were cut, and which, being put into a frame, were turned at pleasure, so that each staff or bar, when formed with three flat sides, represented a triplet; when squared or made with four flat sides, a stanza (in verse). The frame itself was an oblong, with right angles.' [34]

It has been said that the Druids also divined from the appearance of the roots of trees and from the howling of dogs, as from the manner in which smoke arose from a fire.[35] Divination by sticks is alluded to frequently in the mystic Welsh poems. Thus Taliesin exclaims:

> I am Taliesin,,
> Chief of the Bards of the West,
> I am acquainted with every sprig
> In the cave of the Arch-diviner,[36]

and Llywarch Hen alludes very freely to the "Elucidator" in one of his poems.[37] Davies also informs us that the Druids of Ireland employed "an alphabet of their own which, in all its essential points, agrees to that of the Bards in Britain". It was, he says, "a magical alphabet", and was used by them in their divinations.[38] There were, however, three such alphabets in Ireland, he adds, and these have been described by O'Flaherty in his *Ogygia*, and by the present writer in his work *The Mysteries of Britain*.

The Scottish expression "fey", used of a person who appears to be fated or doomed, or raised to a pitch of supernatural excitement, is usually associated with a condition of mind in which the sufferer becomes ecstatic or prophetic. It appears to be derived from the Old English "fay", signifying "enchanted". Those who were afflicted with it, says Kirk, were supposed to have been wounded by fairy weapons, or were "fairy-struck", "which makes them do somewhat verie unlike their former Practice". Dalyell says that the persons who lost their white stones in the Bealltainn fire were regarded as fey, or "devoted". But the term appears to have also had a magical meaning in Old Irish. According to Cormac's "Glossary" the *Fé*, or magic wand, was so called, while the expression *Fá* seems to have been associated with the Lia Fail, or Stone of Royal Destiny, and with the spell of *fith-fath* (pronounced "*fee-fa*".).

I must not conclude this chapter without some remarks upon the weird women whom Shakespeare introduced into the greatest of his tragedies. Do the "witches" in *Macbeth* actually reflect the Celtic idea of prophetic sibyls? Are they merely ordinary Highland sorceresses, or a memory of Caledonian Druidesses? The question is not unimportant, as the very frequent presentation of the great work alluded to may well inspire erroneous ideas concerning the nature of Celtic sibylline characteristics in the minds of thousands.

The whole passage, so far as criticism is concerned, has produced an extraordinary tangle of Gordian knots. Nor is this surprising, for when the man of letters approaches mythical or occult problems he is, as a rule, much in the same category with the blacksmith who claims to be an authority upon motor engines. Neither the old criticism nor the new has uttered anything definitive concerning the weird sisters who so sedulously haunted the Celtic monarch nor have the oracles of folk-lore been other than equivocal regarding them.

The early nineteenth century saw in Shakespeare's weird women "typical Scotch witches", and the prints which illustrated its contemporary theatre displayed them as attired in voluminous swathings of tartan. Critics wrangled as to whether they were terrestrial or spiritual in origin, but as the main facts concerning witchcraft were still obscure, the conclusions they arrived at were more or less negative. Indeed, Shakespeare himself left the question of their actual affinities very much an open one. In one scene he gave them the prophetic character of Norns or Fates, while in the next they appear as very ordinary Elizabethan witches who might have haunted the purlieus of Wapping or the Burgh. In the first of these capacities they foretell events and unroll the flying scroll of visionary prophecy in a manner no self-respecting British witch would ever have thought of doing, while in the second they definitely reveal themselves as the creatures of literary reflection, the hag-shapes of a popular belief in sorcery.

That Shakespeare made his fatal trio speak their lines in the Sibylline metre of accepted magical utterance seems to show that he must have gone to ancient Rome or to Scandinavia for hints as to the speech of the sisterhood of sorcery, even though the language he puts into the mouths of his crones is by no means exclusively classical or Scanian. The opening scene has been strangely neglected by generations of critics, although it strikes the keynote of the tragedy to come. It gives the impression that the weird women have been flying over the field of battle, where King Duncan is contending with the Norsemen, much as the Scandinavian Valkyries or the Morrigans of Irish myth were wont to hover above the plains of conflict. Yet this rather obvious clue remains so far unnoticed both by critic and theatrical producer. In the same breath, however, in which the witches chant of battle, they call upon their familiars Paddock and Grimalkin, as any beldame from Suffolk or Essex might have done, for the familiar was certainly not a ubiquitous figure in British witch-craft, being confined almost entirely to the south-east of England and nearly unknown to Scotland.

It is in the third scene of Act I, however, that the weird sisters appear in what most critics believe to be their truly Jacobean or Elizabethan guise as genuine English witches. Yet in this passage practically every expression they employ, every allusion they make, if we except the First Witch's lines descriptive of her meeting with the "rump-fed ronyon" munching her chestnuts, proves the opposite. Even here the local colour disappears, for the allusion to the witch sailing in a sieve is Scythian, and has only two definitely British analogies, the best known of which is that of the North Berwick and Edin-burgh covens who had conspired to shipwreck James VI. on his return from his honeymoon at Oslo. These are said to have put to sea for that purpose in their "riddles or cives". Had Shakespeare read *Newes from Scotland*, the descrip-tion of a contemporary English journalist of that dingily picturesque incident? The raising of winds mentioned in this scene is more in keeping with the witches' character as Scottish beldames of the more ancient world, derived as it is from Finnish magical practice current in the Orkneys and the Western Isles.

The sisters predict the destinies of Macbeth and Banquo as might the Greek Moirai or the Norns of Scandinavia. I cannot recall a single instance in the history of native English or Scottish witchcraft racy of prophecy in the grand manner. But that prophecy was practised by Druidesses we have already seen. It is when we find them calling themselves the "weird sisters", however, that we receive the first clue to their actual character and position.

For the expression "weird" carries us back to the Scandinavian Norns. That it was in common use in the older Scotland as a word expressive of pro-phetic foresight is clear from several instances, as, for example, that in Gawain Douglas's translation of Vergil, and in the *Complaynt of Scotland*, where, among the titles of popular tales, some now entirely lost to us so far as their content is concerned, is to be found that of "The Thrie Weird Systers", which, in all likelihood, had reference to the occult passages in the history of Macbeth, and may have been taken from a more ancient Celtic or Norse original. The three Scandinavian Norns were Urdhr, Verdandi and Skuld, the Present, the Past and the Future, and the name of the first was used to describe generically all three of them as dispensers of destiny. From this is derived the word "weird" as implying the prophetic quality, which came in time, and by popular accept-ance, to describe the uncanny or the occult.

The Norns were thought of as prophetic concerning the destiny of children at their birth, but they were also gifted with powers to predict the future at any period of life, as the "Nornagests Saga" makes plain when it tells us that they "travelled about the land, foretelling their fate to men". In like manner the old Roman Fatae, or Fates, became in the Romance-speaking lands of France, Spain and Italy the Fée, the Fatua and the Hada, travelling sisters who foretold men's futures from the cradle to the grave. In the older Scotland a similar trio of supernatural spaewives seem to have "dreed their weird" to all and sundry. Indeed, Norns, Fates and the Greek Moirai would appear to have had a common origin in a primitive Pan-European mythology.

It is, however, in the cavern scene, where they are discovered at their nefarious rites with the bubbling cauldron, that the three sisters depart more than ever from British witch-practice. For the cauldron is Scythian, Scandi-navian, Finnish, and still more remotely Hellenic in its Folk-lore symbolism. Nor do the ingredients of the seething pot, as "listed" by Shakespeare, bear any resemblance to the components of any known system of witchcraft or sorcery, with the exception of the toad and the "witches' mummy", the desiccated corpse-flesh familiar to Scottish witch-lore and known to some English witches of Shakespeare's time. But the cauldron, as we have seen, is also Celtic, though in the Celtic version of it its components were not of a deadly nature.

The phantasmagoria revealed to Macbeth in this scene, the crowned figures and blood-boltered babes, are also utterly alien to the humilities of British native sorcery, and are reminiscent of the more highly coloured necromantic spectacles of mediaeval and classical magic. These visions were, of course, designed out of compliment to James VI. and I., the new King of Great Britain, and were prophetic, in the poetic sense, of a presumed illustrious survival of his house, as well, perhaps, as sympathetic to his notorious personal interest in witchcraft —though the revelation of a glorious descent through the agency of those very arcane forces which the royal James had so persistently sought to destroy appears as scarcely tactful in the circumstances!

Shakespeare's witches are therefore a mingling of the Elizabethan English witch, of the Scandinavian Norns and the classical Fates, while the ritual they employ is mainly Scythian, Finnish or Scandinavian. That the weird sisters in the lost Scottish legend concerning them—that alluded to in the *Complaynt of Scotland*—were a later conception of the three Scandinavian Norns is scarcely to be doubted, and that the idea of these prophetesses was imported from Norway to the north of Scotland, which, in Macbeth's time, was occupied by people of Scandinavian origin, seems highly probable. That these circumstances were reflected in Holinshed's *Chronicle*, from which Shakespeare certainly derived the plot of *Macbeth*, and that links between Holinshed's account and an older Celtic-Scandinavian narrative are visible in more than one of the more venerable Scottish historians, is scarcely to be gainsaid. Of course it is just possible that the weird sisters may have been derived from the Irish *Badbhs*, or *Morrigans*, the Valkyrie women of Irish myth. In a word, Shakespeare's witches are not "Scotch", as most authorities have believed them to be. But that they possess certain Druidic traits—the gift of prevision and the use of a cauldron seemingly associated with the gift of prophecy—cannot be denied.

CHAPTER IX

THE CELTIC BELIEF IN REINCARNATION

FEW beliefs have excited more universal interest than that in reincarnation. Down through the centuries the idea that after the death of his body the soul of man inhabits another is credited by thousands in both the Eastern and Western hemispheres, while in the distant past it seems to have been as definitely a part of the religious creed of British man as it is today that of the dwellers on the banks of Ganges or Irrawaddy. In answer to the question: did our ancestors actually believe in the passage of spirit from one body to another after death? it may at once be asserted that the evidence for such a belief is unquestioned. If, again, it be asked whether the Celtic idea of reincarnation is in any way derived from Pythagorean doctrine or dogma, it is safe to say that few grounds exist for such a hypothesis.

ANOTHER VIEW OF THE BAS-RELIEF OF THE BRITISH SUN-GOD AT THE ROMAN BATHS AT BATH

THE GRAIL APPEARING ON THE ROUND TABLE
(From a MS. of the XVth century)

The first clue to the former existence of a belief in reincarnation among the Celtic peoples is naturally to be discovered in the writings of those authors of the Classical period who were attracted to the discussion of Celtic affairs by a strangeness in mental attitude unknown to the practical Roman or the cynical Greek. Diodorus Siculus, writing in the first century B.C., states that: "The Gauls believe that the souls of men are immortal and come to life again after a certain term of years, entering other bodies." We get another hint of this doctrine from Clement of Alexandria, who testifies that "Pythagoras was a disciple of the Galatae (or Celts) and the Brahmins." [1] Valerius Maximus, too, declared in the early part of the first century of our era that the Gauls lent sums of money to each other which were repayable in the next world, so trenchant was their belief that the souls of men are immortal. He adds that one might smile at the custom were it not for the fact that what was the conviction of these "trousered barbarians" was also the dictum of the Greek Pythagoras himself. [2]

The poet Lucan also alludes to this persuasion of the Celts. Apostrophizing the Druids in the lofty manner habitual to the Roman devotees of the Muses, he concludes his strophes with the words: "You it is who declare that the spirits of the departed seek not the silent land of Erebus and the pale halls of Pluto; rather you assert that the same spirit takes a body again elsewhere and that death, if what you sing be true, is but the midst of an extended life." [3]

Hippolytus, an early Christian father who flourished in the third century A.D., also comments upon the Druidic belief in reincarnation, telling us that the Celtic Druids had been initiated into the Pythagorean philosophy by Zamolxis, a Thracian, the slave of Pythagoras, who, after the death of his master, dwelt among the Celts. Origen also alludes to this story. The Druids, adds Hippolytus, foretell events by the Pythagorean reckonings and calculations. Some writers, he mentions, have presumed to see distinct schools of philosophy among the Celts. [4]

As I will have occasion to refer to the philosophic ideas of Pythagoras in more than one place in this book, it will be necessary here to provide some brief description of that thinker's attitude to the problem of reincarnation. Pythagoras, who lived in the sixth century before the Christian era, was a native of the isle of Samos in the Ægean Sea, whence he went to Croton, a small Greek city in southern Italy. There he established a school of religious thought, the principles governing which were probably derived in the first instance from the teaching of the Orphic Mysteries. Regarding his general attitude to eternal things, it may be said succinctly that it is based upon the Orphic dogma of moral dualism, in which the soul is regarded as in opposition to the material body. But in his particular code this idea is combined with the doctrine that the substance of the universe is unlimited in principle, and that this quality of limitlessness is only corrected and rendered practical and harmonious by the application to it of the quality of the limited, or determinative, the two, when balanced, producing the normal, or usual. This balance, he thought, issued in what we call morality. So far as reincarnation is concerned, he appears to have believed that men's souls at death entered new bodies, either human or animal, in this world and as an expiation for their shortcomings.

There is no proof whatsoever that Pythagoras ever came in contact with the Celtic world, nor that his servant Zamolxis did so. [5] It is more probable that the establishment of Marseilles, or Massilia, as a Greek city on Celtic soil may have brought about the acceptance of the ideas of Hellenic philosophy among the neighbouring Gauls, and we know that a celebrated Druidic grove, or place of ritual and worship, existed not far from Massilia.

At the same time, the spread of the Pythagorean doctrines appears to have been confined to the Greek world alone, and it is known that entrance to its arcane brotherhood was decidedly limited and exclusive. Nor, in its original sense, was it a cult of long existence.[6]

Nor are the resemblances betwixt the Pythagorean and Celtic ideas of reincarnation so remarkable as to invite any theory of the origin of the second from the first. The notion of repaying debts after death, or that associated with the burning or burying of articles of personal use at a funeral, which Pomponius Mela tells us the Gauls entertained, are not in unison with the Pythagorean idea of reincarnation. These Gaulish customs are eloquent of a belief in the immortality of the individual, and his continued identity, whereas Pythagoreanism posits a change into a different body, human or animal. The thought of a secondary existence of expiation did not enter into the Gaulish belief, though it may have done so in other parts of the Celtic world at a much later time, as I will indicate in another place. The theory that Pythagoras received his ideas of reincarnation from Celtic sources is even more fantastic. In short, the Romans would appear to have "combined their information" concerning Hellenic and Celtic notions of rebirth. The conception of reincarnation was novel to them, it was credited by both Greeks and Celts, *ergo* the beliefs of Greeks and Celts regarding it must "naturally" have had a common origin!

In his erudite essay upon "The Celtic Doctrine of Rebirth", to be found in his remarkable work, *The Voyage of Bran*, the late Alfred Nutt powerfully argued the possibility of early Celtic, and particularly Irish Celtic, borrowings from Greek religious and philosophical ideas. Here I cannot describe or even hope to summarize his arguments, but I may say in respect of this most scholarly, if rather operose, performance that it is among the very few deliverances of a masterly mind with which I have found myself in general disagreement. That Pythagorean or Orphic ideas found their way to early Ireland at one time or another can scarcely be questioned. That they were received there in any manner implying an intellectual acceptance or indeed with anything but the most confused mental recognition I cannot credit. To my way of thinking, the whole hypothesis is too laboured, too complicated in its suggestion of possibilities, for logical acceptance or appreciation. But I believe it not improbable that other influences more readily acceptable by a semi-barbarous folk may have found their way to the Irish area, as I shall presently attempt to make plain.

Indeed, it appears to me as more practical to appeal to the Celts themselves. "Irish literature," said Sir John Rhys, a Celt of the Celts, "preserves traces of a belief in the reappearance of an ancestor in the person of a descendant: in other words, the same person or soul might be expected to appear successively in different bodies."[7] Wentz remarks that "there was also a belief, probably widespread, among the ancient Irish that divine personages, national heroes who are members of the Tuatha Dé Danann, or *sidhe* race, and great men, can be reincarnated; that is to say, can descend to this plane of existence and be as mortals more than once."[8] The same conclusion was reached by Miss Eleanor Hull, who, writing on the Cuchullin cycle of Irish literature, stated that: "There is no doubt that all the chief personages of this cycle were regarded as the direct descendants, or, it would be more correct to say, as avatars or reincarnations of the early gods . . . there are indications in the birth-stories of nearly all the principal personages that they are looked upon simply as divine beings reborn on the human plane of life."

Dr. Douglas Hyde, another authority of standing on the subject of Celtic belief, has given it as his opinion that there is abundance of evidence to show that the doctrine of Reincarnation was familiar to the pagan Irish. But he holds that there is no literary testimony that the belief was ever "elevated into a philosophical doctrine of general acceptance, applicable to everyone", and that there was "no ethical stress laid on the belief in rebirth"—that is it was not regarded as an expiation of one's sins, as in the case of the Pythagorean system of belief. As it has come down to us, thinks Dr. Hyde, we find that the pagan Irish believed that supernatural beings could become clothed in flesh and blood, could enter into women and be born again, could take various shapes and pass through different stages of existence as birds, animals or men.[9]

Sir John Rhys and George Henderson indicate that vestiges of this belief survive in Wales and Scotland, particularly as regards the importance of the custom of calling a child after some deceased ancestor. This, in the Highlands, was known as *togail an ainm*, or "raising the name". My own experience leads me to believe that throughout Scotland it is regarded as customary to call children by the names of their grandparents, though the habit of baptizing them by fashionable and romantic names has crept in more recently.

But the belief in the transmigration of souls is by no means exclusively Celtic. As Hartland says: "Among many savage peoples the son is regarded as identical with his father, in a sense at least. . . . And traces that the child is the reappearance of an ancestor are to be found all over the world." He cites numerous instances of this idea among barbarous races.[10]

Celtic legend, Irish and British, is eloquent of such cases of the transmigration of souls. One of the most striking of these is the story of Tuan Mac Carell, a man of Ulster, with whom St. Finnen is said to have forgathered about the middle of the sixth century. The ancient warrior unfolded to the saint the tale of his many previous existences. He spoke of the five invasions of Ireland, of how he had, as a man, been saved from the plague which had attacked the primitive tribe of which Partholan was the leader. In that stage of existence he reached extreme old age, dwelling in waste places and growing almost bestial in appearance. He beheld the Nemedians take possession of the island, but kept away from them. One evening he fell asleep as usual and awakened in the form of a stag, in which shape he was the leader of the herds of Ireland. When the Nemedians perished in their turn, he became a wild boar. Some time after the settlement of Semion and his folk, the progenitors of the Firbolgs, Tuan was metamorphosed into a vulture or eagle—he does not appear to be quite certain which—and during the regime of Beothach, the remote ancestor of the Tuatha Dé Danann, he retained that form. The Milesian Celts then entered the island and during this epoch Tuan became a salmon. After avoiding the nets of fishermen for many days, he was at last caught and taken to the wife of Carell, the Queen of Ireland, who ate him whole. She conceived him as a child and he was reborn of her in the body in which he encountered St. Finnen.[11]

Somewhat different was the process by which the hero Cuchullin, who is obviously the son of the sun-god, and therefore a later avatar of that deity, reached the terrestrial sphere. His mother, Dechtire, was about to be wed to the chieftain Sualtam, and was seated at the wedding feast when a fly fell into her wine-cup. She swallowed the insect at the next draught, and shortly afterwards fell into a profound sleep, in which the sun-god Lugh appeared to her and informed her that it was he whom she had swallowed. He then transformed her, along with fifty of her maidens, into bird-shape. Later her infant was revealed to the men of Dechtire's brother Conchobar and was taken to Ulster.[12]

But before parting with Cuchullin I must mention that we discover another reference to that hero which is concerned with the belief in reincarnation. We are told that when he had reached manhood he was yet unmarried. The warriors of Ulster, anxious that he should have an heir, urged him to take a wife, assuring him "that his rebirth would be of himself"—that is, that the son of his body would be in a sense his own reincarnation.[13]

Mongan, King of Ulster, who seems to have been an historical personage, was believed to be the avatar of a god. The Irish annals speak of him as having been slain by a Briton named Arthur, son of Bicur, in the year 625. He was regarded as a reincarnation of the ancient hero Finn Mac Coul, the chief figure of the Ossianic cycle of legend, who is said to have flourished in the third century. But Mongan was also identified in the same manner with the hero Find, who had been slain about the end of that century. Confusion may have crept in here, or perhaps two separate rebirths were credited.[14]

We learn, too, in the tale of "The Generation of the Two Swineherds", that the bulls alluded to in the great saga of "The Cattle Raid of Cooley", which brought such disastrous consequences to Ireland, had formerly been swineherds respectively belonging to Bodh, King of the *sidhe*, or gods of Munster, and Ochall, King of the *sidhe* of Connaught. They had successively taken the shapes of two ravens, two sea-monsters, two warriors, two demons, two worms, and finally two bulls.[15]

Etain, the surpassingly beautiful wife of Mider, a god of the Irish Otherworld, was also the subject of a tale of reincarnation. Carried off by Angus, the divinity of Love and Youth, from her husband, she was imprisoned in a magical bower of glass, but was freed by a rival lady, who, out of spite, changed her into a fly, in which form she fell into the golden ale-cup of the wife of Etair, one of the vassals of Conchobar, and was reborn as her daughter. But Mider was resolved upon her restoration, and by beating Etain's husband Eochaid at chess regained her for himself.[16]

If we turn to the legends of Wales for instances of reincarnation we certainly do not find them so much in evidence, yet they are none the less enlightening. In the first chapter I briefly recounted the manner in which the bard Taliesin was reborn of the goddess Ceridwen. In the tale which refers to him in the *Mabinogion*, Taliesin sings of his adventures in answer to King Maelgwn, who asks him who or what he is. His original country, he says, is the region of the summer stars. Idno and Heinin called him Merddin. "At length every king will call me Taliesin." He was with his lord in the highest sphere, on the fall of Lucifer into hell. He had borne a banner under Alexander of Macedon. He was in the Galaxy at the throne of the Distributor. He conveyed the divine Spirit to the level of the Vale of Hebron. He had been at the Tower of Babel, and with Noah in the Ark, with Moses, Mary, and other celebrities of Christian story. He was Gwion Bach, bard to Lleon of Lochlin, at the court of Cynvelyn, and would be in the world until the day of doom. It was not known whether his body was flesh or fish.[17]

Other shapes assumed by him included a sword-blade, a drop in the air, a star, a word in a book, a bridge, an eagle, a boat on the sea, the string of a harp, the foam of water. "There is nothing in which I have not been," he finally exclaimed.

Let us try to identify the types of the several Celtic reincarnation stories we have just perused. The first, that of Tuan Mac Carell, is an account of simple transmigration from a human body through stages of brute form into human shape once mre. Etain and Cuchullin, again, assume insect form and are then reborn, and much the same may be said of Taliesin, whose metamorphoses through animal shapes in his flight from Ceridwen resemble the transformations of magical shape-shifting rather than the "avatars" of a soul taking up its residence in a series of bodies. I may add that this particular passage recalls the circumstances of the ballad of Tamlane, which I have criticized elsewhere in this book. I should also indicate that the fly-shape assumed by Etain and Cuchullin is a well-known form frequently taken by the soul in folklore, more especially in the Balkans and in the case of vampires.

But in the allusion to Cuchullin's marriage we seem to have a direct reference to the belief that the son of a god or supernatural hero was actually none other than that hero in a secondary form, a distinct projection of him, and that it was thought possible that the son of a god could assume a form identical with that of his father and function in the same manner. Indeed, in Irish myth we discover so many instances of this process, particularly in the case of the sun-god, that it has frequently puzzled students of mythology to account for a plurality of sun-gods—a phenomenon with which we meet also in Greek myth and other religious systems. The story of Mongan, again, is one where transmigration appears to take place after the lapse of centuries. The second story of Taliesin's various transmigrations is almost certainly of late origin and reveals alien and imported ideas.

Now as regards these metamorphoses, some are assumed by a well-known folk-lore process of change; that is, first into animal and then again into human shape, while others presume the projection of a sun-god, through the process of birth, of a filial image of himself. In these myths we encounter both a tradition associated with the lower cultus and a belief connected with the cult of a solar divinity. But be it especially remarked that *all* are narrated of personages who in one way or another are connected with a solar cult and are, moreover, of royal race—if we except the egregious instance of the swineherds of the rival *sidhe* rulers, who, after all, have a royal association, if it be a remote one.

It is in this royal association, however, that we discover a factor which cannot be neglected in any effort to explain the Celtic doctrine of reincarnation. If we wish to attempt such an explanation we are forced back upon a theory which, in the last forty years or so, has compelled the attention of the foremost British authorities on tradition. This theory, which has come to be known as that of "the divine kingship", has been quite elaborately discussed by Sir James Frazer, Sir Grafton Elliot Smith, Mr. W. J. Perry, Professor Hocart, Professor Hooke, and, as regards its Irish associations, by Miss Eleanor Hull and Professor Macalister among others.

Here, however, I must deal with it in summary fashion only. In ancient Egypt, it is now realized, the Pharaoh was regarded not only as the son of the sun-god Ra, Osiris, or Ra-Osiris, but as being actually that deity in his earthly form. The establishment of this doctrine appears to have taken place about the year 2750 B.C., when a dynasty connected with Heliopolis and its solar cult gained possession of the throne of Egypt.[18] "When the god procreated a king," says Mr. Perry, "he gave him the gift of life, strength, and duration in the form of a magnetic fluid, so that in his veins ran 'the liquid of Ra, the gold of the gods and goddesses, the luminous fluid from the sun, source of all life, strength and persistence'. This fluid the King transmitted to the Crown Prince, who was associated with him." The King was the master of all Magic. He could bring on rain or make sunshine. Prior to that a phase had existed in which the King was regarded as a power associated with the water supply, the growth of vegetation and all fertility. But the solar idea superseded this, although I believe the older notion continued to exert considerable influence. The entire business in life of the divine king was thus the prosperity of his land and people, the fertilization of the soil, the flocks and the folk, in a manner suggested by the fertilizing power of the sun itself. The punctual appearance of the Nile floods which fertilized the land, the fertility of women and animals, were all due to his personal vigour and virtue as the surrogate of the sun on earth.

So immense was thought to be the drain upon this vigour that it is not surprising to find that the impression shortly prevailed that the strength of the solar king must rapidly deteriorate and doubtless this was suggested by the appearance of lean years or a "run" of inauspicious weather. In such a contingency the national well-being dictated the sacrifice of the monarch and his substitution by his son, whose strength was unimpaired. At first such a sacrifice may have been carried out annually, to ensure a perfect continuance of the royal functions, but at a later stage this would appear to have been departed from in favour of a change of monarchs every seven or eight years.[19]

This doctrine, it is claimed, came by degrees to find acceptance over a very wide area, and the evidence for its dissemination in Europe is to be discerned in lands so distant from that of its original inception as Scandinavia, Greece, Italy and Ireland. Here I cannot attempt to display the evidence for its passage from one area to another, but that evidence I sincerely believe to be at least "respectable". The main point is that we certainly find it in Ireland, and probably in Britain itself, and I think that it explains much in Druidic history which would otherwise have been vague and unsatisfactory.

Miss Eleanor Hull summarizes the evidence for such a condition of things in Ireland with neatness and lucidity. Tara, she tells us, "was the centre of the pagan cult and high-place of Druidic manifestations. The whole ceremony and choice of kings shows that it was not only his admission to the sovereignty of Ireland, but his reception into a higher sphere of action as a divine being endowed with superhuman qualities and capabilities. The high Kings of Ireland were guided to the choice of Tara as a capital by its religious traditions, which they were held to impersonate and continue, *for the benefit of their people*" (italics mine). To their subjects, they, too, became semi-divine beings, endowed with superhuman influences and powers. A study of the taboos imposed on these kings strengthens this view. "They were subjected to special and harassing restrictions lest the powers that were incarnated in them, and in whose preservation the well-being of the people was involved, should suffer injury." Miss Hull adds that they exercised a priestly as well as a kingly office, and that they showed every sign of being a succession of priest-kings, such as we find in other early dynasties. "The secular and priestly offices may at first have been united."[20] We read that there was a Druid-King of Munster, Ailill Aulomon, in the first century, while three Druid-kings reigned in "the Isle of Thule", and these were not the only instances of royal Druids in Ireland.

Mr. W. Y. Evans Wentz, commenting upon the circumstances of the Irish Kingship, contends that it was associated with "a cult of royal or famous ancestral spirits identified with the god-race of Tuatha Dé Danann, who, as we know, being reborn as mortals, ruled Ireland".[21] We find that the "pledges" or hostages given by the three Kings of Emania, in Ulster, that they should rule by rotation, were seven chiefs who were liable to be burned if the king for whom they were security did not resign at the end of his term of seven years.[22] The term of seven years is significant, as is the rotation of these kings, implying as it does a seasonal renewal of the royal vigour. The burning of the hostages, too, may have been a relic of the sacrifice of kings, a substitution of less important lives for the royal person. It is also significant that a tradition remained that Eochaid, Prince of Leinster, desired to keep his court at Tara, but that "a Druid of principal note" informed him that by doing so he had violated the custom of the place, which enjoined that no person might do so unless he had first been admitted into the order of knighthood, whereupon he withdrew from the religious capital.[23] This allusion to a Druidic caveat would make it appear that a definitely religious custom had been infringed, a custom, too, associated in some manner with an initiatory rite connected with the cultus of kingship.

Dion Chrysostom states that the Druids were closely associated with the kingship. "Without their advice," he says, "even kings dared not resolve upon nor execute any plan, so that in truth it was they who ruled, while the kings who sat on golden thrones and fared sumptuously in their palaces became mere ministers of the Druids' will."[24] This may well have been the case in Ireland (always discounting the golden thrones), where the priesthood was regarded as being very powerful in a magical sense, and indeed a king whose very life depended upon his conduct may frequently have been sensitive about taking any step without consulting his ghostly advisers. In any case, Irish literature is eloquent of this very close collaboration between the kings and the Druids, as countless passages in it proclaim. In *Tain Bo Cuailnge* we read that "the men of Ulster must not speak before the King, the King must not speak before his Druid". In the Irish Druidic claim, too, that the brotherhood had actually "created the universe", we seem to find a suggestion that a caste associated with the great solar power believed its predecessors responsible for this act because of its connection with the sun, which in its eyes was the ultimate life-giving power.[25]

In that period of Irish history when the vassal clans rose and slaughtered the free clans by treachery, "the earth would not yield its fruit to the vassals, and famine ensued". They consulted their Druids, who assured them that this failure of crops was due to the manner in which they had entreated the king and the free clans, and that the land would not yield until a descendant of the rightful sovereign was placed on the throne.[26] In the reign of Cairbre, a bad king, "there was not one grain in the ear, one acorn oh the oak, or one nut on the hazel", the earth withholding her fruits during five years of his unrighteous tenure. In the days of the good King Conaire, on the other hand, the fish were plentiful in the rivers, there was abundance of everything and fair weather prevailed.

But a king must be free of all bodily blemish, or his reign would be marred. He must also be wed to a virtuous wife. Conn, King of Tara, had so good a wife in Eithne, his queen, that, as a consequence, three harvests of corn were reaped every year. When she died, Conn married a fairy wife, with lamentable results, for during the year they dwelt together there was neither corn nor milk in Ireland. The Druids sought for "the son of a sinless couple" whose blood might be mingled with the blighted earth and the withered trees, in order that these might be magically refreshed by it. But when this was about to be done. a mysterious woman appeared with a cow and offered it in the youth's place, This "weird wife", as she seems to have been, suggested the removal of Conn's obnoxious queen, as so long as she remained as royal consort corn and milk would be lacking in Ireland. It is sad to find that the narrow "piety" of some early Christian copyist has added to the account that this prophetess also proposed that the Druids should be put to death! [27]

I should add here that in the tradition of the divine kingship the consort of the monarch is of practically equal importance with her husband, and that she was carefully selected for her virtues. As for the King, that unfortunate man was surrounded by taboos so grievous and restricted that he certainly could not call his life his own. We find it said of the highly virtuous Conchobar,

King of Ulster, that "there was not on earth a creature wiser than he", yet his advice on any matter of importance was not sought, in order that he might not deliver a false judgment, "so that his crops might not be the worse thereof". He was a mighty warrior, yet he must not risk his life in battle "in order to guard the King's son". This latter clause seems to have reference to the sympathetic magic which existed between the King and his son, who was regarded as the King himself in another form. When Conchobar was severely wounded by a ball made from the hardened brains of a sub-king of Leinster which lodged in his head, the people said, "It is a small thing for us compared with his death," which would have brought about a lack of fertility. After this incident he lived for the "statutory" term of seven years.[28]

In his masterly and comprehensive treatise on *The European Sky-God*, Mr. A. B. Cook furnishes many instances of Celtic divine kings, as does Sir James Frazer in his *Kingship*, and to these works I would refer my readers, as to the equally informative essay on "Tara" of Professor R. A. S. Macalister, a performance of rare ability. King Conchobar is alluded to in one text as "a terrestrial god". As Canon MacCulloch indicates, kings were probably slain before they grew too old and frail to lose their magical powers of fertility, and this may account for the wistful exclamation of King Ailill: "If I am slain, it will be the redemption of many." There would seem to be evidence, too, that criminals were slain as the divine king's substitute,[29] and this may account for the holocausts of such malefactors who were burnt wholesale in great wicker-work cages in Gaul.

Annually, on August 1st, the feast of the sun-god Lugh, the *Lugnassad*, was celebrated in ancient Ireland. It was chiefly held in honour of the dead ancestors, but here I wish to reveal a certain association which it had with the god's ritual marriage. It is indeed described as "the wedding of the kingship", and the word *"nassad"*, as Rhys infers, seems to hold the meaning of "tying, or binding together", as understood by the marriage rite. It is, in my view, a recollection of the ritual nuptials of the "sky-father", or sun-god, with the "earth-mother". Human marriages were also made on that day, and at the fair which survived at Tailltenn into Christian times, and indeed until a comparatively recent period. From *The Book of the Dun Cow* we learn that the reward to the people of Leinster for celebrating this festival of the *Lugnassad* was "plenty of corn, fruit and milk, abundance of fish in their rivers, and domestic prosperity".

If we refer to a certain class of Irish legends we shall find the best of reasons for believing that this ritual marriage between the sun-god and the soil was actually carried out in the person of the King, as it was in ancient Egypt and in Rome. That this ritual marriage betwixt sky and earth was associated with the Roman and Egyptian idea of the divine king and queen as its prototypal myth cannot be questioned, and that we find it in Ireland is equally certain.

One ancient story describes how five royal brothers, while hunting, encounter a hag who offers them shelter if one of them will share her couch. Four of them scornfully reject her advances, but the fifth, out of courtesy, agrees. At once she is transformed into a marvellous beauty, and assures her lover that "I am Sovranty, and thou shalt obtain the sovranty of Erin".[30] The same thing happens to Niall, afterwards King of Ireland.[31]

The hag represents the sovereignty of Erin, that is the soil of the country. According to *The Book of Invasions* the goddess Eire, or Erin, the personification of Ireland, has the disposal of its sovereignty, and that the hag represents her I cannot doubt.[32] In these stories it is plain that the spirit of Ireland, an ancient goddess, puts her lover to certain tests not only with the object of discovering whether he be in the true hereditary line to the crown, but also to ascertain whether his character is of a royal and generous nature such as will fit him for such a career. The theme appears to contain a memory of a ritual marriage between the King of Ireland, or a part of it, with the goddess of the soil. By marriage with this goddess he becomes the only fitting ruler of the land. Egeria, a goddess of fertility, who was the wife or mistress of the wise King Numa of Rome, and who counselled him on occasions of difficulty, is a similar figure. Frazer believed that a ceremonial marriage between the ancient Kings of Rome and the nymph Egeria was periodically performed. The resemblance between the stories of Numa and Egeria and Thomas the Rhymer and the Faerie Queen has more than once been indicated, and the amour betwixt the two last personages may, indeed, be a late reminiscence of a ritual marriage between an ancient Celtic king and the goddess of the soil. Egeria, I may add, was merely a surrogate of Diana, the goddess of the woods and of vegetation.

We know from the myth of Conn, King of Ireland, that when he entered a mysterious rath he beheld the sun-god Lugh and a princess of great beauty, who was known as "The Sovereignty of Erinn till the day of doom", who typified the kingdom of Ireland. She was the bride of Lugh, and was married to him ritually at the annual festival of the *Lugnassad*, the re-arisen sun. It seems clear, therefore, that the High Kings of Ireland, who were regarded as the earthly representatives of Lugh, may have been ritually wedded to this goddess upon their coronation, as was evidently the custom in ancient Rome, and we can scarcely doubt that on such an occasion ritual tests were put to ensure their capability for such a position. Indeed, that tests of some kind were applied I will make clear. The legend found its way into later mediaeval romance as the tale of "The Loathly Lady".

An Irish King had to subject himself to certain magical tests of his fitness before coronation. Two flagstones were situated at Tara. These were known as "Blocc" and "Bluigne", and the aspirant to royal honours must be able to ride his chariot between them. If the stones recognized him as the rightful sovereign of Ireland they would open to let his chariot pass through. These stones were named after certain Druids who had officiated at the Court of King Conn, "the Hundred Fighter", who is said to have come to the throne in A.D. 177. But should the candidate be otherwise than acceptable they would close, thus blocking his path. The chariot which he mounted was also a test-piece, for, were he not the legitimate monarch of Eire, it would throw him off the footboard, while the horses which drew it would attack him. If he passed these tests he must then drive up to the Stone Fal (the Stone of Destiny), which would hail him with a resounding cry of welcome as the wheel of his chariot passed over it.[33]

When a high king of Ireland was chosen, a rite known as *Imbas-forosnai* (the illumination between the hands) was celebrated. A white bull was slaughtered and its flesh was partaken of by a priest, who lay down to sleep, holding his face between his hands, while four Druids chanted over him "to render his witness truthful". He then beheld in a dream or vision the man who should be chosen King and what he was engaged in at the moment—an important piece of testimony.[34]

We have already seen that the belief in reincarnation was associated with the idea that the spirits of deceased folk inhabited trees, rocks and other natural objects. In the same manner they were regarded as the seats of divine beings. This was so in ancient Egypt, where we find the tree as the abode of the sun-god in Heliopolis, where in "the Great Hall" a sacred tree stood, on the leaves of which the god Thoth and the goddess Sufekht wrote the name of the monarch, who was thus endowed with immortality.[35] Spirits dwelling in such trees are still regarded as having the power to make the crops grow.[36] Thus the sacred tree is also known in Ireland in connection with the divine kingship as it was in ancient Rome, not far distant from which stood the tree which bore "the Golden Bough" in the grove at Nemi, as Frazer has so elaborately recorded. Certain Irish trees were said to be divine, such as that yew which is described as "a firm, strong god", on rods made of which divinations were written in the Ogham character. The lives of kings were associated with trees of the kind, thus implying their connection with the idea of fertility.[37]

Miss Eleanor Hull criticizes the view of Professor Macalister that such trees in Ireland correspond in their nature with that at Nemi on the ground that the royal lists on which Macalister relies are not authentic. There is, however, express reason to believe that his main conclusion is a correct one. We find, for instance, that the famous tree and well at Eilean Maree, stiuated in Loch Maree, in Scotland, are not called after a certain "St. Mourie", as had been thought, but that the name is a corruption of *"Eilean mo Righ"*—that is, "the island of my king", or, perhaps, *"Eilean a Mhor Righ"*, "the island of the Great King",[38] thus revealing the association of the tree in question with the royal tradition. Davies, quoting an ancient Welsh poem, tells how the bard Merddin, or "Merlin", armed himself with sword and shield, and lodged in the Caledonian Wood, guarding the trunk of a tree in order to gratify the goddess Bun, "the maid", who was perhaps the nymph of the tree.[39] Now this is precisely the manner in which "the ghostly priest" of the Arician grove stood sentinel over the sacred tree at Nemi. Merddin alludes to himself on this occasion as "a wild and distracted object", thus heightening the resemblance to him of Aricia. The passage, I hold, not only justifies Professor Macalister's assumption that the rite, as known at Aricia, was reflected among the Celts, but it reveals the authentic character of the Welsh poem in question, "The Avale-nau", the composer of which cannot but have been ignorant of the tradition at Nemi, with which his work reveals so striking a parallel.

If the proofs furnished in this chapter are acceptable, they would seem to make it evident that the originally Egyptian cultus of the divine king had gained a substantial settlement in Ireland. I believe that they further reveal that the Druids constituted in one respect at least the priesthood of the cult of the divine king. If this be so, the more precise nature of Druidism is at length explained. Of course one would also have to make it plain that the kingship cult was the origin of the priesthood in other lands where it flourished. But perhaps it accounts for the rise of Druidism in Gaul at a comparatively late epoch as a brotherhood appearing more or less spontaneously and suddenly at a given period. If that be so, much of Celtic mythology will be found explicable in terms of Egyptian belief, and at a later stage I will try to make it plain that such a theory is justified, at least in certain especial instances. As we shall see later, the cult of the divine king also made its way into Britain, as the whole tendency of the Grail legend shows.

That the idea of reincarnation was imbedded in certain other Celtic beliefs is also proven from such accounts as we possess respecting the Circles of Life which have come down to us in Welsh literature, which, however, appear to have little authority to recommend them. I shall refer to these circles of exist-ence more fully when we approach the subject of early British Mysticism. Here I am concerned with them only so far as they have a bearing on reincarnation. There were three spheres of Infinity: Ceugant, traversed by the Creator alone, the Circle of Felicity or Gwynvyd, and that of Abred, or Evil. If a soul were not sufficiently perfected to rise to the circle of Gwynvyd, it sank once more to that of Abred, where it assumed bestial or reptilian shapes until it was sufficiently purged to enter the sphere of Felicity. That these changes are of the nature of transmigration has been warmly contested by more than one Welsh critic, particularly by Sir John Daniel, who conceives them as penitential psychic states—if I read him aright—rather than transmigrational conditions.[40] But that the idea of the transmigration of souls was a capital one among the Celts, though strongly marked by primitive traits, and probably owing little to outside influences, I would regard as a theory sufficiently established in the circumstances.

Here a difficulty arises. It may be asked, and with good reason, why, if the Egyptian cultus of the divine kingship found its way to Ireland and to Britain, that of reincarnation, which was undoubtedly associated with it, should not also have done so. It is known that the Pythagorean doctrine of transmigration was derived in the first instance from Egyptian thought. "There is nothing in Pythagoreanism," remarks Jevons, "which is not to be found in the religion of ancient Egypt." That the Egyptian doctrine of reincarnation, as implied in the system of the divine kingship, actually did penetrate to Ireland, we have already seen. There is the likelihood that another and native belief of the lower cultus of transmigration into animal bodies also existed in Ireland, and, as some students of folk-lore believe, this inferior doctrine may have been associated with Totemism.

Perhaps D'Arbois de Jubainville sums up the case for Celtic reincarnation more appropriately than any writer who has approached it. After drawing attention to the fact that at least two forms of reincarnation are alluded to in Irish myth, that as found expressed in the story of Etain and that to be observed in the tale of Find, reborn as Mongan, he describes the first as an example of divine reincarnation, and the second as a story of transmigration. But the stories of Find and Tuan Mac Carell, he points out, are exceptions to the rule in ancient Irish literature, wherein "it is not usual for the dead to be born a second time". This kind of transmigration, he continues, may have a certain likeness to that of the Pythagorean doctrine, but it is not identical with it. In the code of the Greek philosopher transmigration into the bodies of men or animals is the wages of sin. It is not so in the Celtic system. Tuan and Find experienced it because they were exceptional. In Celtic doctrine men after death find "in another world the life and new body which their religion holds out to them". And wherefore were Tuan and Find exceptional? Simply because the composers of the Irish sagas wished to use them as mouthpieces who would, through the circumstances of a reincarnation story, describe the early mythical history of Ireland, and so justify their chronology and statements concerning that history as eye-witnesses of the several invasions of Erin, and so forth.[41]

I think that D'Arbois is justified in his conclusions. These "transmigration" myths are merely the exception which prove the general Celtic rule that it was only individuals of divine or royal origin who underwent reincarnation. The Egyptian equivalent circumstance that only the Pharaoh had such an experience practically clinches the matter and reveals that the theory of the divine kingship was associated with both the Egyptian and Celtic ideas of reincarnation, as apart from the Pythagorean view.

But—for the science of myth bristles with that preposition, and here I may say I do not quote the French Celticist—in later Egyptian belief the idea came into force that most, if not all, people might undergo reincarnation. This belief was certainly an extension of the idea of the pharaonic process of reincarnation. Because the Pharaoh underwent the process, so must the wealthy and powerful. And that such a process also took place in ancient Ireland we know. For, once the divine race of the Tuatha Dé Danann was dispossessed of its godlike qualities and was reduced to the state of mere fairyhood, dwelling in the mounds and raths, reincarnation became its general lot. The sidhe, or fairies, the "dead" god-kings, came to be regarded as the spirits of the dead awaiting reincarnation in human bodies, reincarnating, indeed, again and yet again. What had been thought of as happening in the case of the king-gods now happened to all as the dead. I have frequently described the process, and do not require to do so in these pages.[42] In this sense, then, we are justified in saying that reincarnation came to be a later general belief among the Celts, though in such a form it certainly did not partake of the Hellenic idea of an expiatory process. And, indeed, it may well have been a recrudescence of a much older and more primitive native doctrine, as I more than suspect. It is, I think, associated with that alluded to by Diodorus, with which this chapter begins, and by Lucan and Caesar. The statement of Valerius Maximus, it has not yet been made clear, is obviously a contradiction in terms. He confuses the idea of immortality, pure and simple, with that of Pythagoreanism, as is very plain.

CHAPTER X

CELTIC MYSTICISM

THE very numerous class whose chief interests lie in the direction of the arcane and the supernatural is now only too woefully familiar with that description of mystical treatise in which the most spectacular and extraordinary revelations are promised to the reader, yet invariably fail to be vouchsafed to him. Its disreputable twin is to be found in the kind of book which actually does supply thrill after occult thrill, yet which is merely either an effort of invention concocted by unprincipled ignorance, or issues from that kind of credulity which seems to exist in a continual mental haze. But why invent fictitious wonders when positive marvels actually exist and only await recording? Indeed, it seems to me that the rainbow vapours which arise from the cauldron of Celtic Mysticism hold enough of the strange and the unusual to satisfy even the most exacting neophyte of the mysterious. The Magics of Druidism, or rather the problems associated with them, are enthralling enough in themselves to attract even the most conventional among us without the invitation of drum and pan-pipes. The elfin chronicle of Celtic legend can, on its own ground, easily rival the whole gilded and bejewelled machinery of Arabian story, or the remote wonders of India and the Land of Sinim.

And these things are our very own; they constitute our most intimate racial traditional background; they were imagined and invented not by distant strangers but by men and women whose blood runs in our own arteries, by British folk in the morning of British time, while yet this magical island of ours was a demesne of enchantment cinctured by grey ramparts of sea, the very prototype of a territory under defensive spells. From the days of Pytheas to those of Ariosto—aye, and even afterward—Britain was regarded by the peoples of Europe as the very fortress of marvel and romance. The Greeks thought of it as another world to which the souls of the dead were ferried by night, as Procopius assures us, the Gauls knew it as the treasure-house of their own mysteries. To the romancers and poets of later France and Italy it was at once the birthplace and last preserve of all that appeared fascinatingly mysterious, a kingdom of sorceries and secret prodigies.

Countless works have been penned on the arcane mysteries of Britain. Many of them are fascinating to a degree, others merely revolve round their subject without approaching the heart of it. In few—very few—is any genuine attempt made to arrive at definite conclusions concerning the actual nature of the heaped and disordered legacy of tradition which has descended to us. In this chapter and that which follows it will be my aim to attempt to reduce this tangle of confused and seemingly incongruous lore to something resembling definite system and orderly conception. The initial step in a process so supreme-ly difficult is naturally associated with the examination of the material which composes this ravelled and perplexing disorder—a task in itself so involved that I must plead for the reader's patience in making the effort.

That something of philosophy inspired and underlay the Druidical system it seems most reasonable to believe. Had it been otherwise the writers of antiquity could scarcely have borne such unanimous witness to its mode of thought and its general principles as I have made it clear they did. I am not of those who contend that it reached a phase in which its doctrines can be compared with the more or less profound speculations of India or Egypt. But I do believe that the evidence we possess makes it possible for us to entertain it as holding a place not much inferior to the conceptions of early Rome or primitive Persia and somewhat more advanced than those of primeval Germany or Scandinavia. Had it been possible for the Druidic faith and philosophy to advance without extraneous interference for some centuries, they might, indeed, have rivalled the Roman system or have surpassed the indigenous faiths of many other European communities. The British mythology reveals a greatly more lofty and poetical spirit than either the Roman or Scandinavian systems, its indwelling genius is natively more mystical and attractively beautiful than anything to be encountered in these. It became the parent of a sentiment of chivalry, as expressed in its literature and all that derived from that literature, which is foreign to Roman, Scandinavian, Jewish or even Hellenic thought. And if its later results were exhibited on a plane so lofty, I imagine it to be only just and rational to suppose that the roots of thought and conception from which they sprang could scarcely have been so lowly or so primitively grovelling as certain distinguished but undiscerning authorities would have us believe. The whole colourful, heroic and highly artistic performance of Irish Celtic legend and saga, the amazingly imaginative and poetically conceived corpus of Welsh myth and fiction, the princely splendour of the Arthurian epos, the high spirituality of the legend of the Grail were as surely the later consequences of the self-same racial mentality as that which conceived the earlier principles of Druidism, as the compositions of Augustine, St. Francis and Dante owed their inception to the inspiration of Christianity. This being so, it is scarcely reason-able to conceive of a cause which initiated effects so triumphantly sublime and so aesthetically illustrious as having had its origins in a system which did not at least possess an original inspiration of lofty sentiment, even though its environment was at first humble and comparatively barbarous.

That the Druidic fraternity inculcated the worship of one God above all other gods seems possible, judging from a remark of Origen, who wrote in the first quarter of the third Christian century, while Druidism was probably still remembered in Britain.   In his homily on Ezekiel he states that the British people had worshipped "the one God" "previous to the coming of Christ", and in his Commentary on the same Scriptural book he adds that the "island had long been predisposed to Christianity through the doctrines of the Druids and the Buddhists, who had already inculcated the doctrine of the unity of the Godhead".   Whether Buddhist missionaries ever reached Britain or not is a disputed question.   But the evidence of the Christian father is of value, not only as revealing that Druidism had a monotheistic bias, but that it had existed in Britain shortly before his own day.

The Druidic faith has been associated by many writers with the oak. Maximus Tyrius says explicitly that the Celts worship "Zeus" in the form of an oak.   The Celts, as a race, appear to have regarded more than one species of tree as sacred, and Canon MacCulloch records instances where they adopted the tree-cults of other races who dwelt in their vicinity.[1]   Pliny is our main source for the belief in the Celtic adoration of the oak.   He tells us that "they esteem nothing more sacred than the mistletoe and the oak tree on which it occasionally grows".   But he adds that "they choose oak-woods for their sacred groves, and perform no sacred rite without using oak branches".   He proceeds to say that the Druids believed that everything which grows on the oak came from heaven.[2]   When Europe was covered by great oak forests in primitive times and men lived partly upon acorns, as archaeological research has revealed, the tree was probably regarded as a food-giver (as indeed it continued to be for the herds of swine which roamed the woods) and a source of fuel.   There is a tendency to worship such "beneficent" agencies, trees and plants which supply food or firing, wells which yield water, and so forth, as the friends, allies or protectors of man.   In time everything associated with them comes to be regarded as holy o: sacred; they are supposed to ensoul a guardian spirit which assumes human form, but which yet retains certain signs of his or her arboreal or aqueous character, and this spirit, in the course of generations, is magnified into the form and status of a god.   Sacrifices are rendered to it; priests, especially set apart for the purpose, guard its principal shrines.   And putatively the oak was the reservoir of fire, the fire-giver, and as such was associated with the sun.

Now the Gallic Druids were known to be priests of the oak and of the solar god.   The cult of the oak was unquestionably a most ancient one.   This being so, it would seem to follow that Druidism must have been an almost equally venerable institution.   But had it been so, it, or some cult resembling it, would have manifested itself all over Europe, wherever the oak was adored, and not in Gaul alone.   That it did not do so we know.   The cult of the oak was widespread as the Continent, but not the priesthood which served it.   It seems to me that however ancient the oak-cult may have been—and it must have had a prolonged history—the association of a priesthood with it was a much later event.   Scores of barbarous tribes today in many parts of the world venerate trees, but it is seldom that a priesthood is associated with such adoration.

But I think we can here surprise the mental tendency which made it possible for Druidism, or the cult of which it was the priesthood, to entertain and accept the idea of the divine kingship.   For both the cult of the oak and that of the divine king were concerned with the self-same principles—the adoration of such spirits as were supposed to furnish the community with the wherewithal of existence, the promoters of fertility and well-being.   As I have said, we find the sacred Kings of Ireland and Scotland associated with trees, and in this, I believe, we can realize the link which connected Druidism, the cult of the oak, with that of the sacred king.

In any case, such a phenomenon certainly took place at the grove of Aricia, in Italy, where, as Frazer has shown, a priest stood sentinel over a grove and particularly over a certain tree sacred to the goddess Diana, who was not only a patroness of the fertility of cattle, and a spirit associated with fire, but who was also given in ritual marriage to the kings of Rome on their coronation. The parallel with Druidic practice seems to be complete, but no connection between the two cults is apparent. It would seem, however, that what occurred in Italy also happened in Gaul. The cult of Nemi marks, I believe, an amalgamation between a local tree-cult and that of the divine king, the latter an immigrant complex, and I am of opinion that a similar mingling of religious and magical ideas took place in Gaul between two cults of the kind, thus initiating what is known as Druidism. We should not forget, however, that the Egyptian religion had a tree-cult of its own.

We must now consider the arcane meaning of the mistletoe, associated so closely with Druidic tradition. Pliny correctly informs us that this plant is but seldom found upon the oak, but, when discovered, it "was gathered with due religious ceremony, if possible on the sixth day of the moon", when the influence of that planet is at its height. The Druids, he remarks, called the mistletoe by a name meaning "the all-healing", and after a banquet and a sacrifice a priest cut the plant from the tree with a golden sickle, another Druid holding a white cloak for its reception. Two white bulls were then sacrificed to the god of the tree. "They believe," adds the Roman naturalist, "that the mistletoe, taken in drink, imparts fecundity to barren animals and that it is an antidote for all poisons." [3]

Mr. Kendrick indicates that in a tumulus at Gristhorpe, near Scarborough, excavated in 1834, there was found an oak coffin containing a skeleton and covered with oak branches and vegetable matter later identified as mistletoe. The burial was associated with the Bronze Age; thus the presence of "Druidical" customs was discovered on English soil of a period greatly anterior to that generally connected with Druidic belief. [4] Frazer believed that the sacrifice of white bulls at the Alban Mount at Rome invites comparison with the Celtic rite. [5]

Mistletoe was certainly regarded as an "all-heal" in England for generations. Aubrey tells us in his *History of Surrey* that at Norwood in that county there formerly stood an oak on which it clustered and that the country folk cut slips of the parasite to sell to apothecaries in London, so that the demand for it as a medicinal element must have been considerable. To cut oakwood, he adds, "is "unfortunate". People who did so fell lame or lost an eye, and when the Earl of Winchelsea, in Kent, felled a grove of oak trees on his estate, his Countess died suddenly and his eldest son "was killed by a cannon-ball" at sea. Colbatch recommends mistletoe as a cure for epilepsy. Its importance as one of the accessories of Christmastide scarcely requires to be stressed.

That the mistletoe was one and the same with the "Silver Branch" of Celtic mythology already described I am convinced. But that it had the significance of a life-giver I am also persuaded. Canon MacCulloch correctly describes it, I feel, as "the soul of the tree" which "contained the life of the divine representative". It seems to me that white bulls were slain after it was cut and removed to compensate the god for the loss of his vigour, which was thought to be contained in the berries of the plant, for the renewal of his male essence or protoplasm—a notion which would also explain the amatory exhibitions associated with mistletoe at Yuletide, which seem to have been emblematic of the plant's fertility-giving powers.

The subject of the offering up of human sacrifices by the Druids is one which has aroused considerable controversy. Caesar makes it clear that persons vexed with disease or who found themselves in danger of death on the battlefield were in the habit of vowing a human life to the gods if their own lives were spared. He adds that the gods could not be appeased unless a life were offered up for a life. Canon MacCulloch thinks that "the victims may have been offered to disease demons or diseases personified, such as Celtic imagination still believes in, rather than to gods, or, again, they may have been offered to native gods of healing". Coming danger, he thinks, was also averted on the same principle, and "though the victims were usually slaves, in times of great peril wives and children were sacrificed".[6] War captives were usually immolated outright, being either put to the sword, impaled or drowned, while, as in the case of Boadicea's Roman victims, others appear to have been suspended on the trees of sacred groves after being impaled.

But more general and extensive national or seasonal sacrifices appear to have been held, and probably those which Caesar so briefly mentions were of this nature. Great cages of withes or osiers were fashioned in the likeness of the gods and into these human victims were crowded and burnt. That such horrible hecatombs were held chiefly at the spring festival of the sun-god (*Bealltainn*) appears highly probable, and that they were held to have a definite effect upon the fertility of the soil is known. In all likelihood in the original *Bealltainn* sacrifice a human victim was offered up to the solar deity in order that he might furnish the god with renewed power, as was the case in ancient Mexico, when blood not only refreshed the gods but quickened the growth of the maize crops. Pliny refers to the practice of ceremonial cannibalism among the British Celts and Strabo mentions the custom among the ancient Irish of devouring their parents, while Diodorus Siculus says they ate the flesh of their enemies, and we know that at a much later time St. Jerome accused the Attacotti of Scotland or Ireland of such cannibalistic practices. The idea behind these horrors was not associated with the desire of flesh-famished savages to feast upon their kind, but rather to partake of the dead enemy's strength and vigour and to incorporate in themselves the virtues of their kindred. But one has little desire to dwell upon these abominations, the customs of a people emerging from a condition of gross superstition to higher forms of religious observance. And, when all is said, were these atrocities any worse than the holocausts by fire which Romans made of Protestants, or Protestants of Romans, in a later and greatly more civilized age; or those instituted by Teutonic ferocity which have imparted to war in recent years a gruesomeness which has put into the shade all previous cruelties known to human record? In my own view they were, indeed, almost naïvely innocent when compared with these latter, the perpetrations of a "civilized" diabolism, which has done more to degrade human dignity than the entire chronicle of "barbarous" devilment.

Both Tacitus and Diodorus Siculus allude to the Druidic custom of divining future events from the entrails of sacrificed victims. "The Druids," says the former, "consult the gods in the palpitating entrails of men," while Strabo tells us that they stabbed their human victim in the back with a sword and then drew omens from the convulsive movements made by him in his death-struggle. Diodorus, who describes the horrid business in much the same manner, says that they augured, from the posture in which the victim fell, his various contortions and the direction in which the blood flowed from his body. From these "they formed their predictions according to certain rules left them by their ancestors". [7]

I should add that some interesting relics of the dreadful custom of burning victims in wickerwork images seem to have survived until recently, or still survive. Thus the English "Jack-in-the-Green", who appeared on May Day in a framework of wickerwork covered with holly and ivy, and the lad who is similarly equipped in France on the same occasion, may possibly represent memories of Druidic victims. Many of the giants and monsters who appeared formerly in seasonal processions in Great Britain and on the Continent were also made of wickerwork covered with pasteboard. The figures of Gog and Magog, which anciently stood in the Guildhall at London previously to those quite recently destroyed by bombing, were of this description. [8]

There appears to be good reason for believing that after the official overthrow of Druidism in Gaul and Britain, the Bards who had been associated with the Druids and who, indeed, acted as their mouthpieces and thus composed a part of their sodality, carried on the traditions of Druidic thought and belief for some centuries. Indeed, to depart from the strict letter of setting down nothing which has not the soundest authority for its statement, and indulging for a moment in surmise, one may be forgiven if he ventures to infer that nearly the whole content of Druidic belief found its way into the repositories of Bardic tradition. As Mr. Kendrick neatly phrases it: "The supposed bardic religion [of Wales] was eventually developed into a system in which Druidism, so far as it is discoverable in the Classical sources, and the patriarchal faith of the Scriptures were ingeniously combined." He is, of course, speaking of the later bardism which began to reveal itself in Wales about the beginning of the eighteenth century. But almost the same might be said of the much earlier bardism of the twelfth century and, indeed, even of the sixth, always allowing that the documentary and traditional evidence concerning these may be regarded as authentic, a question with which I will deal in a later chapter. But Mr. Kendrick is of opinion that "the basic assumption that the mediaeval Welsh bards were a continuation of the Druidic hierarchy . . . is not by any means an extravagant or ridiculous belief". His reasons for thinking so are associated with the ancient close connection between Druid and Bard, the latter having been the professional transmitters of their lore, and that many Druids, "when their sacerdotal powers vanished", may have been "merged in the bardic class". He lays some stress upon the statement that "the survival of the calling of the professional bard is only a token of Keltic custom, and not a proof of connection with Druidism. The most that can reasonably be claimed is that some bards of special distinction may have been possessed of the Druidic doctrines." It would scarcely be possible, he thinks, "to demonstrate that any of the mediaeval Welsh poets and poetasters were the conscious possessors of a scrap of the ancient Druidic lore", even although they arrogated to themselves the name of Druid. [9]

With this dictum I agree, but I must to some extent qualify such conformity by remarking that I believe that the Druidism of the sixth and twelfth centuries was a quantity which differed decidedly in its general views and acceptances from that of the days of Caesar, or Pliny. An almost entirely novel dispensation had, as we shall see, usurped its place and dogmas. Here I must confine myself to the question as to whether the Bards actually inherited the lore of the Druids at the era of the first downfall of Druidism—that is, at some time not later than the end of the first Christian century. I am of opinion that on the whole they did so. The assumption is, indeed, a highly probable one, but I scarcely find myself in a position to proffer an absolute statement of its veracity in consideration of the slight evidence in its favour.

O'Curry says that part of the training of the Irish Bards was the learning of magical incantations, the use of which was certainly a Druidic office.[10] We find at least one bard in Ireland stopping the growth of the corn by the use of Art Magic, while another caused an enemy's life to be shortened by his incantations.[11] O'Beirne Crowe, after speaking of "the utter contempt in which the name *bard* is held in all our records", alludes to the Bards "practising incantations like the Magi of the Continent, and in religious matters holding extensive sway". I find something of superstitious dread and dislike of the Bards in old Irish literature, but nothing approaching "contempt". In Ireland the Bards held hereditary tenure of office and territory. That the Irish Bards retained at least a leaven of the ancient Druidic knowledge and practice before their art became Christianized seems, indeed, more than probable. So far as the Bards of Britain are concerned, their songs are certainly eloquent of the mythology which must have been part of the Druidic lore and religion. Even in Christian times they praise the pagan deities with a warmth and with something of the awe of devotees which makes it hard to believe that they were inspired by the same species of mock heroic and purely mythological intention as the English Augustan poets when they sang the glories of the Hellenic Olympus. That they indulged, or pretended to indulge, in magical exercises is plain from many of their compositions. But the entire question of the rightful acceptance of such evidence is inevitably bound up with the authenticity of the manuscripts which contain it, as I hope to make plain in thetproper place.

Elsewhere I have described the Druidic idea of the transmigration of the soul. Have we to our hands any material by which we can discover the Druidic or Celtic idea of the nature of the soul itself and its properties? Taliesin, the Bard, asks in a poem entitled "The Elements of Instruction":

> Knowest thou what thou art,
> In the hour of sleep—
> A mere body—a mere soul—
> Or a secret retreat of light?

Again he declares farther on:

> I marvel that in their books
> They know not with certainty
> What are the properties of the soul;
> Of what form are its members;
> In what part, and when, it takes up its abode ;
> By what wind or stream it is supplied.[12]

But he enlightens us no farther regarding his own psychic conceptions. Sir John Daniel likens the passage to the doctrines of the Swedenborgians. The soul "is the proximate receptacle of life from God", as that cultus holds. But I cannot see precisely by what train of reasoning he connects the thought of Taliesin with such a conclusion. Taliesin asks, but he refrains from answering his own question.[13] I am afraid that I can discover nothing precise in Celtic literature concerning the Druidic idea of the soul and its qualities other than those that can be gleaned from the Celtic doctrine of transmigration, which makes it pretty clear that the ancient Celts entertained much the same ideas of soul and spirit as do other peoples in a similar phase of culture to that which they possessed in the last century before the coming of Christianity—that the soul was immortal, that in it was enshrined the actual personality of the man, which might, in certain cases, resume its life in other bodies, or, alternatively, as Skene says, might dwell in the body after death in another region.[14] It might, also, as Canon MacCulloch states, live on in the grave (an idea, I think, fully justified by the doctrine of Faerie), but evidently not as a shade, nor unapart from a body of a more ethereal kind, and that the immortality thus conferred upon it was "more or less dependent on the eating or drinking of some food or drink of immortality", the food of eternal life, which was as essential to its sustenance as was ordinary food in the material world.[15]

But, as I hope to show, other and later ideas concerning the soul took shape in the Celtic mind in connection with novel imported ideas. And we may, perhaps, learn more about its development in association with the notions displayed according to the belief in the several circles of psychic life as expressed in the myths of the British Celts which deal with these.

I have already referred to these circles and have very briefly outlined their general nature. Here I must describe them a little more fully. Ceugant was the abode of deity alone, Abred the sphere of evil, while that of Gwynfyd was regarded as felicitous, a spiritual casting-off of the material frame. Now this belief in arcane life-cycles appears to have no official or historical status, but seems to have emanated almost entirely from the writings of the Rev. J. Williams ab Ithel, the author of *Barddas*, a volume which the highest Welsh authorities regard as an unmitigated forgery, but which others of less official status seem to regard as possessing certain traditional sanctions. To my way of thinking the entire scheme is much too complete and systematic not to invite suspicion, yet I think that if it is examined with due caution, certain genuine traditional ideas may be extracted from it. It tells us that the Creator is opposed in duality to Cythraul, that is darkness, or chaos, but that He united Himself with this element for the purpose of bringing forth life and intellectual existence.

Now this is nothing more or less than the purest Pythagoreanism, the action of "Determination" upon "the Unlimited", and if it is genuinely traditional it would seem to be an acceptance of comparatively late date. In any case we have no Classical authority for the appearance of such doctrines among the Celts other than those already given, and, as I have made it clear, the soundest authorities refuse to accept the view that Pythagoreanism made its way into Celtic thought. At the same time, as I have suggested, Egypt and not Greece was the earliest home of what has come to be known as the Pythagorean doctrine, and it may just be possible that this reached Britain and Gaul in its Egyptian and earlier, and not its Hellenic or later form as part of the complex associated with the cultus of the divine king. Even so, I cannot think that it was embraced by Celtic thought in its entirety, or without undergoing considerable simplification, bowdlerizing, and general alteration.

This divine interaction, we are told, began in the depths of Annwn, or the Abyss and, by virtue of it, life underwent a course of gradation from the lowliest forms, including reptilian and other shapes, to the highest spiritual conceptions. The evolutionary course through Abred, or evil, from grade to grade, continually strained towards perfection of spirit. Free choice was granted to the soul of man. Abred thus includes humanity and all below it. Annwn, indeed, (and *its* mythical existence is "officially recognized") appears as a still lower phase than Abred. From that latter state man proceeds to the circle of Gywnvyd, after death, his migration through various lower forms is at an end, he has perfected himself after many struggles, in the course of which, if he has not led a righteous existence, he may descend into Annwn once more and be doomed to experience a second period of painful upward growth. Abred is, indeed, the earth-plane, the circle of humanity, and appears to be totally separate in this respect from Annwn. These ideas, Williams claimed, are founded upon the writings of many Welsh bards and philosophers, among them Llewelyn Sion, Einion the Priest, Taliesin, and Sion Cent.[16]

Whatever the value of Williams' writings, we have much stronger authority for the tradition of Annwn itself, the literary and folk-lore background of which is admitted by most authoritative writers on Celtic faith. Annwn, sometimes spelt Annwfn, is mentioned in mediaeval Welsh poetry as lying beneath the mortal world. In mediaeval Welsh legend, however, it is spoken of as being divided into several planes or kingdoms. It was from this underworld region that man had received certain of the gifts of civilization, particularly the pig! And in the hope of taking from it what its supernatural governors did not choose to grant, it was occasionally raided by enterprising heroes with an eye to the main chance. The name Annwn appears to mean "the Not-world", and was also known to the Welsh Britons as Anghar, "the Loveless Place", Difant, "The Unrimmed Place", Affwys, "The Abyss", and Affan, "The Invisible Land".[17]

From the point of view of the Welsh Bards, if we follow Williams for the nonce, Annwn seems to denote the opposite of Gwynvyd—that is, it is a sphere of ignorance as compared with one of intellectuality. In the circle of Abred, or rebirth, it was regarded as the lowest sphere of existence, that indeed from which the human soul struggled upward through all the intermediate stages of growth until it reached the human state. If, in this world, the soul chose good, it was capable of reaching a higher circle of being after death. But in its more popular acceptation Annwn came to be regarded as the supernatural world, the world invisible, and, perhaps later, as Fairyland. Davies, a Celtic traditionalist of the early nineteenth century, describes it, however, as "figuratively the condition of the dead, or the infernal regions, which comprehends the Elysium and the Tartarus of antiquity".[18]

There seems to be good reason to believe that at least a part of Annwn was regarded as a mystical realm. A Welsh poem ascribed to the Bard Taliesin, who flourished in the sixth century, is known as "The Spoiling of Annwn", and describes a raid upon that region by Arthur and his companions, for the purpose of seizing the magic cauldron of inspiration and plenty which was one of its chiefest treasures. The piece is one of the most obscure in an obscure literature, but I need not examine it in this place, as I have already essayed to disentangle its difficulties elsewhere.[19] The poem, however, refers to the imprisonment of one of the adventurous band in a place called Caer Sidi. Now this place is alluded to in another poem by Taliesin, in which he speaks of his "chair", or place, in Caer Sidi as "perfected". In this delectable region, he tells us, plague and age can reach no one, while its attractions are heightened by three organs which play near a fire. Ocean flows around it and it possesses a mystical well which gives drink sweeter than white wine.[20] Rhys saw in this description of Caer Sidi reasons for thinking that it was "a mythical country beneath the sea".[21]

But the poem in which Taliesin speaks of the adventures in the Underworld alludes also to a place called Caer Wydyr, or the Glass Castle. Its warders would not exchange words with the invaders. Now we find a similar glass castle in Nennius, who states that its guardians refused to converse with the Irish Milesians. This castle of glass is nothing but the fortress of the dead, a place of happiness, whose inmates feast and enjoy themselves in musical entertainments.

As regards Caer Sidi, I cannot control the Brythonic etymology of this name, but ignorance may venture a guess that it may have some reference to a "fairy", or supernatural locality, as does the Gaelic *sidh*, or *side*. Indeed, Rhys has hinted at such a possibility. Kirk appears to speak of some such idea as that which was associated with the circle, or evolutionary process of the Welsh Annwn, when he tells us that his Scottish fairies held as a tenet "that nothing perisheth, but (as the Sun and Year) every Thing goes in a Circle, lesser or greater, and is renewed and refreshed in its Revolutions".[22]

The adventures of Pwyll, Prince of Dyfed, in Annwn, as set forth in the *Mabinogion*, further make it clear that in the later and more legendary sense that region was regarded as a place of enchantment, just as in its earlier acceptation it may have been imagined as a realm of the continuous development of life from lower to higher forms. Some accounts of it allude to the transformations into early forms of life, reptilian and other, which the body must undergo in its ascent to the human.

We see, then, that the idea of Annwn, at least, had a genuine popular tradition behind it, and this might appear to justify the belief that a similar tradition of Gwynvyd, the spiritual sphere, may formerly have existed as well. But the notion of the sphere of Gwynvyd, or the little we know of it, clashes rather badly with what we are told of the Brythonic Otherworld, which appears to be subterranean—Anghar, "the loveless place", Affwys, "the Abyss", Affan, "the land invisible"—anything, indeed, but a delectable region and manifestly a land of the dead based on a belief that the departed continue to lead a cheerless existence in graves and tumuli.[23] Canon MacCulloch, I may say, regards it as a reflection of the Christian hell, or as having been confused with the same, but thinks that it was originally "an over- or under-sea world in which some of the characteristics of the Irish Elysium are found". "Hence the name Annwfn has probably taken the place of some earlier pagan title of Elysium."[24] There does not appear, then, to be sufficient reason for thinking that the ancient British believed in a spiritual circle of refined souls such as Gwynvyd would seem to represent. It was, I should add, in Annwn that the famous cauldron stolen by Arthur in his descent into that region was situated, as I shall have occasion to explain in the chapter which deals with the problems associated with that hero.

CHAPTER XI

CELTIC MYSTICISM (*continued*)

ASTROLOGY seems to have formed an important feature of later Cymric Mysticism. In a poem known as the "Hanes Taliesin", or History of Taliesin the Bard, one of the more obscure productions of Welsh bardhood which is only now receiving from Welsh scholarship the critical examination it so sadly requires, we catch glimpses of allusions to astrological books, the *Llyvran seryddiaeth*, or Books of the Stars. Davies provides a description of this poem in his *Mythology and Rites of the British Druids*, but we have the warning of modern Welsh censors that his translations and elucidations are to be dealt with rather more than circumspectly. In any case, his absurd "Helio-Arkite" theory, borrowed from Jacob Bryant, has played havoc with his work. But out of the heap of nonsense we can at least glean that the three chief astrologers of ancient Britain were Idris the Giant, Gwydion ap Don, and Gwyn ap Nudd, and that these three could foretell all future events, however remote, by their skill in reading the stars. The *Historia* of Geoffrey of Monmouth mentions the existence of a college of two hundred astrologers at Caerleon-upon-Usk, in the time of Arthur, while throughout the Welsh mystical writings other allusions are made to Astrology and star-lore. Caesar certainly mentions that the Druids were addicted to this form of foretelling the future, and we know that those of Ireland forecast the appropriate time to build a house by the movements of the heavenly bodies.[1]

In groping for the remains of Druidic mysticism, we are, I think, justified in looking for a possible connection with that arcane creed in the old custom which is known as "the hunting of the wren". That this bird had a mystical association appears as not improbable, while it has been asserted that its British name, *dryw*, has reference both to a wren and a Druid. However this may be, a singular degree of popular importance certainly attached to the rite in question. In Ireland, the Isle of Man, and Scotland, the wren was hunted and killed by the peasantry either on Christmas Day or St. Stephen's Day, which follows it, and was borne round the villages to a song which hailed the creature as the king of all birds. The same ceremony was formerly recognized in some parts of France, where the youth who killed the wren was known as "king". In the Isle of Man, we read, the bird was formerly cooked and ceremonially eaten, although it was regarded as unlucky to kill it at any other season of the year. All this, as Canon MacCulloch remarks, lends support "to the idea that the Celts regarded the wren as a divine animal, or perhaps a totem animal, that it was necessary to slay it ritually and to carry it round the houses of the community to obtain its divine influence, to eat it sacramentally or to bury it".[2] If this be so, and I think the evidence points to some such conclusion, the status of the wren must have been one of high symbolical import, and one rather feels that it must have had some association with an allegory of the season—the winter solstice. Had this myth some connection with the sun in its declining stage? We have the assurance of tradition that

> The robin and the wren
> Are God Almighty's cock and hen,

and that

> He who hunts the robin and the wren
> Shall never prosper, sea nor land.

It seems to me plain that the death and burial of the wren symbolizes the decease and obsequies of the old sun; that it was, indeed, in some mythological manner associated with that death of the robin known to folk-lore. The robin's red breast would appear to have conferred upon it a solar connection, and the event in question seems to be celebrated in the well-known folk-song, "The Death of Cock Robin". Was the greedy sparrow who slew him symbolic of the season of cold and dearth? Here, I think, we are in the presence of a myth descriptive of a very ancient rite. After many years of intimate association with the minor circumstances of British Mythology I am convinced that much of it was based upon an avian or bird-like saga, or series of sagas, as the circumstances of the Arthurian cycle of gods and heroes appears to bear out—a question upon which I shall hope to touch in the chapter dealing with matters Arthurian.

Before approaching what may be called the Mythology of esoteric Druidism it is essential to clear the ground concerning the sources whence it proceeds. To my way of thinking there is nothing more extraordinary in literature than the position presently occupied by the remains of our ancient British literature as it survives in Wales. The authenticity of early Irish literature has not seriously been questioned, nor has it been the subject of prolonged and hostile attack. But the genuine character of native Welsh poetry appears to have been challenged by a host of English writers who were as vastly ignorant of the Welsh tongue as Samuel Johnson was of Gaelic when he launched his celebrated diatribe against pseudo-Ossian. And now we behold sundry Welsh critics of authority, abashed by an evident inferiority complex, addressing themselves almost in a spirit of levity to the task of pulling down the last rafters of the Welsh literary edifice.

I am, of course, referring to the criticism which has been aimed at those fairly numerous verses in the older Welsh language which make allusion to the figures of British Mythology which we discover scattered through *The Red Book of Hergest*, *The Black Book of Carmarthen*, the *Myfyrian Archaeology*, and *The Book of Taliesin*. After working for several years on the materials contained in these books and publishing his findings and translations concerning them in *The Four Ancient Books of Wales*, William Skene, a Scottish Celtic enthusiast, who lived and worked not a hundred yards from where I am now writing these lines, turned away from the topic in contemptuous disgust, with the angry remark that the poems upon whose examination he had squandered so much time were mostly incoherent nonsense. In a note to his *Math vab Mathonwy*, Professor W. J. Gruffydd, Professor of Celtic at the University College of South Wales, says of old Welsh mythological poetry, that "such translations of it as have appeared (including Rhys's, the best) are mere guess-work, and no theory of any kind may be built upon them. This warning, which the Arthurian scholars of America may well heed, applies to nearly all the translations in Skene".[3] Elsewhere in the same work, however, he says in respect of the characters in the French versions of the Arthurian romance, that "most of these Arthurian personages are known in the Welsh tales and in Welsh poetry", and he provides examples of them.[4] What I particularly wish to point out is that he takes the subject seriously and by no means flippantly, and that he does not assert that British mythological figures are not alluded to in these poems, but that the poems themselves have been badly translated. Like the majority of Welsh purists, he is legitimately nervous of the forgeries of the disreputable Iolo Morganwg, and issues a caveat concerning certain Triads which appear to have been tampered with by that worthy.

This will dismay people of a mystical propensity who have pinned their faith to the authenticity of the ancient Welsh poems. But I venture to say that certain considerations which I shall advance hereafter will demonstrate that these strictures, though well founded, are scarcely so calamitous in their effects as one might be led to think at first. I cannot, of course, deal with them from a linguistic point of view, but other factors associated with them seem to call clamantly for discussion before the controversy regarding the authenticity of the material of these poems is finally closed. In my view it is absurd to conclude that, merely because they have been inexpertly translated or bowdlerized by later scribes, they contain no genuine references to early British myth or legend. Nor have the gentlemen who deal with them in a literary sense much acquaintance with the science of folk-lore, as indeed they frankly admit.

As the whole question is one of cardinal importance to the large and growing body of those interested in British Myth and arcane belief, I make no apology for ventilating it at some length in a work devoted to the occult traditions of our island. So far as essentials are concerned, I must be guided by expert opinion, and to that end I will follow the arguments of Professor Ifor Williams, Professor of Welsh at the University College of North Wales, as summarized in his recently published *Lectures on Early Welsh Poetry*.[5] But I, in turn, must summarize his findings briefly, as my space does not permit of lengthy statement.

Unhappily, Professor Williams, although his profound knowledge of his subject and his brilliant critical treatment of it are certainly not to be gainsaid, approaches it with a levity all too characteristic of a certain school of Cambrian criticism. Here I will do my best to describe his conclusions without prejudice. Saga in early Welsh literature, he tells us, has survived merely in a vestigial form. The oldest manuscript written wholly in Welsh is *The Black Book of Carmarthen*, which dates from the late twelfth century. This contains a number of songs from the earliest sagas, among them priceless fragments of the earliest Arthurian romances. In *The Red Book of Hergest*, the date of which may be placed about the year 1400, there are many similar series of poems. It is possible to divide these into groups or units which seem to form parts of a larger scheme, and these reveal signs that they were intended to be memorized. It was not possible to modernize them much because of their intricate verse-forms, and they may be regarded "as a collection of the verse element in the oldest Welsh sagas". But before they can be understood it is necessary to discover the old prose setting of each group. It is possible to accomplish this in some degree by comparing them with such Irish compositions as reveal characteristics common to all Celtic writings. Thus the Welsh *Dream of Rhonabwy* may be compared with the story of Caoilte in Irish literature. When, at last, the old poetic forms were found to be too obscure by reason of the antiquity of their language, the stories they contained were told in prose.

The poems attributed to Llywarch Hen and contained in *The Red Book of Hergest* and elsewhere relate to a personage who appears to have lived in the sixth century. This attribution was contested by Nash, Wright, and other English critics, who were of the opinion that they had reference to events occurring in the early fifteenth century. Professor Williams, however, finds good reason for assigning them to the year 850 or thereabouts, and not to the sixth century, as some Celtic enthusiasts have asserted. Moreover, "their author was not the Llywarch Hen of history: he is merely the chief character in a play".

For the Llywarch Hen poems "are the remnants of a lost saga". Sorting out the poems relating to Llywarch contained in *The Red Book of Hergest*, Professor Williams, after very considerable thought and research, which reflect much credit on his powers of patience and concentration, concluded that they describe events as they occurred in the district of Powys, which faced the severest opposition from the Saxons of Mercia, about the middle of the ninth century, and that they contain chiefly a series of laments for the slaughtered sons of Llywarch, who fell in battle with the Saxons.

Applying his critical faculties to the alleged poems of Taliesin, another famous Welsh bard, Professor Williams lays it down that "we can discard at the outset practically every scrap of poetry ascribed to Taliesin outside *The Book of Taliesin* and one poem in *The Book of Aneurin*". All else is later than the sixth century and consists of "faked prophecy". *The Book of Taliesin* itself dates from about the year 1275. There is, however, good reason to suppose, from a passage in Nennius, that such a bard as Taliesin actually flourished in the sixth century. Profes or Williams disposes of about one-half of the material in *The Book of Taliesin* as being of later origin than the floreat of the bard. But "a hard core" of twelve historical poems remains, which refer to sixth-century personages and events.

As for the remaining material which deals with Taliesin, Professor Williams postulates the existence of a Taliesin saga, probably composed about the ninth century at the earliest. In the remains of this saga are found a strange mingling of Christian and pagan elements. The composition, he believes, was the work of a later Christian cleric who adapted older material for his own generation. But he was not the only Welsh author who had treated the Taliesin tradition or legend in such a manner, as a fragment in *The Black Book of Carmarthen*, entitled "The Dialogue of Ugnach and Taliesin", reveals. This consists of a passage in which Taliesin describes himself as knowing the origin of all things, and, as I have already mentioned in another chapter, alludes to his various transformations into many animal shapes.

In this deliverance Professor Williams discerns nothing mystical. For him Taliesin speaks merely as an actor in a play. That is quite comprehensible. The tradition of Taliesin may well have assumed a dramatic form, precisely as did the stories of the saints in mediaeval drama, or that of Oberon and Titania in "The Midsummer Night's Dream". Myth has its origin in dramatic ritual, and to its ancient form it inevitably returns. But is that to say that the passage in question possesses no mythological significance? Rhys, as we shall see, construes it differently. Professor Williams tells us that the story contained in the poems can be checked by the legend concerning the bard as found in the folk-tale known as the "Hanes Taliesin", in which his adventure of the cauldron of Ceridwen and his absorption by that goddess are related. This story, thinks Professor Williams, accounts for the omniscient attitude of Taliesin in the poems. He is "just showing off". The mythological character had become the bombastic jester of a folk-play.

Now I fully agree, acquainted as I am with similar dramatic metamorphoses of mythic figures in other literatures, that such an illustration of it in British tradition is wholly probable. But I cannot agree with Professor Williams, whose arguments I trust I have presented fairly, if all too succinctly, that such a process implies an absence of the mystical or the inherently mythological in the most primitive form of the Taliesin myth or tradition from which the "Hanes" derives, as he would appear to imagine. Indeed, the very reverse appears to me to be the case. If the "Hanes Taliesin" fortifies the theory of a Taliesin drama, it also suggests in the strongest possible manner the existence of a myth in which the bard figured as the hero. Professor Williams evades the question by saying that he is content to leave the consideration of the Taliesin folk-tale to folk-lorists, and that his only concern in connection with it is the light it casts upon the Taliesin poems. And that is precisely where modern Welsh literary criticism fails. Because of the "inferiority complex" which appears to inform it, it contents itself by a graceful dalliance with the merely literary side of its material, professing a rather amused nescience for the profounder traditional implications which that material suggests.

Professor Williams, writing on the Welsh Triads, remarks that a certain series of them "bears unmistakable signs of additions" by the obnoxious Iolo Morganwg. Surely, then, if the signs are so unmistakable, the additions can all the more easily be removed so as to compose a purified text. And surely, widespread as his depredations appear to have been, Iolo did not tamper with the standard Welsh manuscripts, *The Red Book of Hergest*, *The Black Book of*

Carmarthen, and the rest, those which Skene entitled *The Four Ancient Books of Wales*, which also contain mythological passages.

Nor was it possible for Iolo to have seriously vitiated the basic mythology with which these manuscripts teem. Apart altogether from their imperfect translation, or whatever import they may have, they appear to possess a definite mythological background and allude to certain deities whose names continually recur. These names, or some of them, are to be found also in the *Mabinogion*. Many of them appear to be those of local gods. They have a most definite relationship in some cases with the figures of Irish myth. If these gods can be proved to have had a relationship with certain localities in Wales—and such proof is occasionally forthcoming—they can scarcely be regarded as other than authentic. And if this be so, one would be interested to learn from the Welsh *literati* how, precisely, they think the names of these deities managed to insert themselves into the manuscripts unless a very definite tradition concerning them and their attributes had remained, or, alternatively, they were drawn from greatly more ancient manuscripts or traditions. What puzzles the onlooker is the attitude of the Welsh scholars to their native myths. Simply because these were vitiated and bedevilled by someone over a century ago, they appear to regard them as collectively spurious and absurd. At times, for example, Professor Gruffydd compares them seriously with cognate Irish examples. But at the least hint of "Ioloism" he obviously shudders and turns aside. Would it not be more reasonable to remove the signs of interpolation?

Composite in the extreme as parts of the *Mabinogion* certainly are, as Professor Gruffydd has made only too clear, they still reveal all the signs of careful bardic literary selection and redaction. In numerous cases Irish plots have been taken over and the Welsh equivalents of Irish gods and heroes have taken the place of the Hibernian deities. Ireland was evidently a great fictional reservoir from which the rest of the Celtic archipelago drew much of its inspiration. Almost the self-same process took place in Celtic Scotland as in Wales, the acceptance of Irish plots and characters in the western counties of Scotland having been of such a wholesale character that at long last their popular appearance in Argyll and the Western Isles, and penetration even as far east as Perthshire, precipitated the ignorant and calamitous *kulturkampf* of the Ossianic controversy. Scot and Hibernian contended as to their respective rights in a Celtic saga-series which was indeed common to both. Nor is this all. The material of much of this story-stuff, it is now apparent, penetrated to the Scottish Lowland Court at Edinburgh and Stirling, probably carried thence by Highland bards, so that we have left to us an entire series of folk-tales, 'The Red Etin", "The Well at the Warld's End", "The Black Bull of Norroway", and half a dozen others, which indubitably owe their origin to Highland-Irish plots and are eloquent of Celtic sentiment and folk-lore.

And indeed—and here I can speak from first-hand experience—the self-same process took place in the case of Mexican and Mayan myth, the tales concerning which remained utterly incomprehensible until expert linguists afforded them adequate translation and explication. When at last the Welsh poems receive similar treatment at the skilful hands of such scholars as Professor Ifor Williams and Professor Gruffydd, Welsh proficients in folk-lore will be enabled to disentangle the mythology which forms much of their background These considerations may give pause to the people who so stubbornly condemn the Welsh Triads and other compositions as nonsense. They have merely been villainously and inaccurately translated, so far. The language in which they are couched certainly appears to be almost wantonly obscure, it abounds in ornate phraseology and antique reference, but it will yield to persistent examination exercised with patience and goodwill.

It will be well to examine the *bona fides* of certain Welsh mythological figures. The goddess Arianrhod, alluded to in the *Mabinogion*, is certainly among the most obscure. The triad which mentions her is later than the *Mabinogion* and a few lines in *The Book of Taliesin* merely speak of her beauty in enthusiastic terms. But as the mother of Llew and the daughter of Beli she can scarcely be other than a deity, and she certainly passed into Arthurian romance as the sorceress Argante, Queen of Avallon, and also into Spanish story as Urganda. That she was well known to the Welsh poets of the fifteenth century Professor Gruffydd has made it amply plain.[6]

Dylan, her son, who, according to the *Mabinogion*, took to the sea whenever he was born, is rather obviously a marine deity. His name still remains that of a Welsh promontory. He is alluded to in Taliesin's poem "The Battle of the Trees". A folk-lore tale concerning him exists in the vicinity of Clynnog. One of the "Taliesin poems", the *Marwnad*, or Elegy, tells of his death at the hands of a smith, and has been carefully treated by Professor Gruffydd, who sees in him "a much more important personage than he seems to be at present . . . all that we are certain of at present is that this important figure in Welsh mythology was, though much more indefinitely than in Wales, attached to the Lugh legend in Ireland".[7] The outsider welcomes such breakings of the Cambrian ice. This is the kind of statement we require from the authentic scholarship of Wales, nor do I think we shall be disappointed in its further findings as time proceeds.

The Taliesin-Ceridwen myth appears to be a commingling of ancient stories concerning a goddess with those about Taliesin, a typical British bard. It seems to account for the manner in which he achieved bardhood. May he not be the God of Bardhood? So it would seem to me at a mere guess. Anwyl conceived the myth as having had a specific origin and development in an area to the south of Dyfi estuary, and on the shores of Lake Teyid.[8] To this appears to have been added the old folk-lore formula of the "combat" story in which magicians assume various animal forms in the course of a magical struggle. My own impression—for it is nothing more—is that it represents the myth-framing propensity of a College of Bards, or that it is fragmentary of the same, revealing as it does signs of construction by an ancient school of initiate poets who sought to explain the original manner by which *awen*, or inspiration, was conferred upon their fraternity.

As regards the mysterious Hu Gadarn, who was, perhaps, the chief prop and stay of Davies' absurd theory that the foundations of Welsh myth rested upon the legend of the Ark, we are scarcely on very safe ground. In the second volume of his *Mabinogion* M. Loth has made it abundantly clear that the triads which relate to this personage are late in date. Judging by what these triads have to say of him, he appears to have been a species of culture-hero, who came from the East, taught the Cymry the art of ploughing and divided them into septs or clans. He it was who dragged the monster Avanc from the depths of a lake which had overflowed, thus causing the primal flood, by the help of his oxen. He was also a kind of Apollo, the inventor of music and song. To his later apparent *avatar* as Darvell Gadarn I have already alluded. It may be that Hu Gadarn represents a later culture-hero, and the general resemblance of what we know of his myth to that of the Egyptian Osiris appears to me to associate him in a measure with the legend of the divine king, of which importation it may perhaps constitute a memory. Herbert imagined him as a "Neo-Druidic Bacchus", as he is styled "the giver of wine", and, drawing on references from Iolo Goch, in Davies, states that his name Gadarn (which he here spells "Cadarn") is reminiscent of war. "Hu Gadarn was the commander of the elements and the inhabitant of the Sun." He was "the concealed God", and was invoked as creator. Herbert agrees with Davies that he is a combination of Noah and Bacchus.[9] This, of course, is mere mythological guesswork, yet I think that the rough resemblance to Osiris holds good and that Herbert is correct in regarding Hu Gadarn as a deity of the Neo-Druidic cultus. Rhys regards him as a British Hercules, and surmises that he was superseded by Arthur. He points out that even in the fourteenth century the semi-pagan school, that of Taliesin, was so strong in Wales that it extracted a vigorous rebuke from a Welsh priest and poet, Sion Kent, who alluded to its personnel as "the Men of Hu, whose muse was the genius of lying, as distinguished from the better muse that was of Christ". The Men of Hu retaliated by charging the Christian poets with gross ignorance of the mysteries of bardism. What the Taliesin School meant to imply, continues Rhys, when they bragged of their transformations into various forms, was associated with the magical powers of the initiated, who could assume any form they chose and could command the elements according to their will. They knew the Otherworld, the chairs of Ceridwen and Teyrnon. Their boasts, he thought, are similar to those of the Irish seer Amergin, the Milesian prophet, as found in *The Book of Leinster*, where he specifies his arcane knowledge. M. D'Arbois de Jubainville translates and recounts the same in his *Irish Mythological Cycle*, comparing it with the Taliesin passage. This is important, for if we agree with these conclusions it follows that much of what has been thought of as referring to reincarnation or transmigration can be nothing else than allusions to a magical potency of identifying oneself with natural objects by the process of arcane will-power.

Here I am confining myself almost entirely to those personages of Welsh Mythology who are mentioned in the poems and triads. "A striking feature of all these bardic and triadic references," remarks Professor Gruffydd, "is their apparent dependence . . . on the *mabinogi* tradition." This implies that they are no older than the *Mabinogion*. The *Mabinogion*, as we have it, seems to belong to the last quarter of the eleventh century, but that it drew upon sources very much older can scarcely be questioned. Are we to understand, then, that these poems, ascribed for the most part to primitive bards, are mere *pastiche* of the *mabinogi* or story-telling tradition? If so, it is indeed curious that their mythic background is so much more closely associated with the idea of divinity than is that of the *mabinogi*, in which broken-down gods assume the parts of characters in a series of romantic stories. Judging from the atmosphere of these bardic pieces, I should unhesitatingly describe them as greatly older than the *mabinogi*, or traditional tales of Wales, both so far as their matter and spirit are concerned.

Sources of high antiquity have gone to the making of Welsh literature, still Welsh critics persist in ignoring them, or, what is worse, treating them contemptuously. This attitude, however, is not universal. Writing upon the MSS. of "the nigger in the woodpile", Iolo Morganwg, Professor Gruffydd surprisingly says: "I refer to this much suspected source with all due reserve, but it may be safely stated that *a large portion of the information given in the Iolo MSS. goes back, directly or indirectly, to genuinely ancient sources.*" Again he quotes a legend from Iolo, remarking that "he must have got it from somewhere". This somewhat naïve remark practically sums up my own attitude to the writings of the "unspeakable" Morganwg, whose work contains quite a fair proportion of genuine tradition which any competent student of folk-lore can readily extract from the rubbish with which he has interspersed it.

One observes, too, that despite his frequent warnings against the employ-ment of the triads as evidence, Professor Gruffydd does not hesitate to draw upon them himself, more particularly on page 200 of his notable work and its adjacent folios. But, indeed, he is only doing what all traditionalists sooner or later find themselves compelled to do. He finds that unless he is content to use, under due safeguards, such data as come to his hand, he will have little or nothing to draw upon. The mythologies of most post-Classical peoples resemble a patchwork quilt, and that of Wales is no exception. The one reason why it has not been worked over in a rational manner long before this late date is that certain English writers insisted on laughing it down. It was "Celtic nonsense" and "mere invention". The unhappy thing is that Welsh litterateurs should have allowed themselves to be intimidated by such ignorant and unabashed browbeating.

The principal British deities who make an appearance both in the *Mabinogion* stories and in the Welsh poems of antiquity are Beli, Llyr, Bran, Don, Teyrnon, Pryderi, Dylan, Gwydion, Rhiannon, Ceridwen, Taliesin, Hu Gadarn and Arianrhod. The recognition of these in both sources appears to me to give them a satisfactory mythic status. Beli is of importance to us as an arcane figure and with his myth Professor Gruffydd has dealt in a manner which could scarcely be surpassed by the most acute among folk-lore proficients. Indeed, he and other Welsh litterateurs are much too modest in their estimate of their own powers of traditional elucidation. Beli, he tells us, was among the most famous of the legendary kings of Britain. Rhys correctly equated him with the Irish Bile, and the correspondence between the Beli of the Cambrian annals and the Bile of the *Annals of Ulster* "makes this identification certain".[10] There also appears to be a certain equivalence betwixt him and the Irish Cyclops, Balor of the Evil Eye. In Welsh poetry he is associated with a spear of surpassing might. He is buried in "the Great Plain" Maes Mawr, which equates with the famous Irish Magh Mor, and a plain so named exists in the Benlli Gawr district in Wales, near Rhyd y Gyvarthva. In Welsh verse Beli is called the son of Benlli the Giant, concerning whom a story is told by Nennius which appears to associate him still more closely with Balor. According to Milton, St. Michael's Mount, in Cornwall, was connected with a giant, Bellerus, as Tory Island, off the north coast of Ireland, was with Balor. In popular Cornish tradition the giant of St. Michael's Mount had but one eye in the midst of his forehead, a circumstance which again links him with Balor. "Beli's own particular country seems to be Gwynedd, or even Arvon, whenever he is not mentioned in connection with the whole island of Britain." [11]

Professor Gruffydd makes little mention of the Belinus of Geoffrey of Monmouth. Geoffrey describes him as the son of Dunwallo and the brother of Brennus. The brothers strove for the crown of Britain, but Belinus proved successful. Brennus enlisted the aid of Segin of Gaul, but Conwenna, the mother of the combatants, cemented a peace between her sons. Belinus erected a marvellous gate in the city of Trinovantum, or London, which, says Geoffrey, the citizens still called Billing's gate in his day. At Belinus' death his ashes were enclosed in a golden urn and placed on the summit of this portal. Similar statements respecting the disposition of Belinus' remains at this gate are made in the Welsh *Tysilio*, a later manuscript, which appears to be a reflection of Geoffrey's *History*, in the English *Brut* and in Layamon. It was, indeed, such a burial of heroic remains as I have already alluded to in connection with Vortimer, intended to ward off foreign invasion by magic.

There is no evidence of the existence of such a gate at this site in either Roman or pre-Roman times, but in 1843 large numbers of piles were discovered on the spot, which seem to reveal evidence of a bridge at this point east of the present London Bridge. The name, too, has been referred to the Saxon family of the Billings, the royal house of the Warings. Belinus seems to be associated with the Gaulish god Belatucadros, a deity of war with a solar connection, and thus with the ancient rite of *Bealltainn*, just as his brother Brennus is probably one and the same with Bran, well known from his story in the *Mabinogion*, and as the "Bran the Blessed" of Grail legend.[12]

Beli, says Rhys, is "the King of the Brythons in the golden age of their history". As such, it may be suggested, he was well fitted to become one of the principal figures in any British renaissance, and that, I think, is what he did become. He is also associated with the realm of the dead. Indeed, as Rhys hints, he may be that Dis Pater, or Lord of the Otherworld, from whom the Druids thought the Gauls were descended, as Caesar tells us.[13] That he was the consort of Don, the eponymous ancestress of one group of the British gods, there seems to be little question. Herbert states that Beli had a caste of bards especially devoted to him, the *Beirdd Beli*, but gives no authority for the statement. But I think that it may be possible to equate Beli with the Gaulish god Cernunnos. This deity is depicted on a stela found at Paris (on the site of the Cathedral of Notre Dame), and in a statuette unearthed at Autun, as a horned god, and has been identified by M. Mowat and other French authorities with the Dis Pater, alluded to by Caesar. That his worship penetrated to Britain seems likely in view of the legend associated with "Herne the Hunter", that horned phantom which was supposed to haunt the royal forest of Windsor, the name Herne appearing as a corruption of Cerne, or Cernunnos. We have no direct evidence that Beli was a horned deity, but his close association with cattle, as in the rite of *Bealltainn*, makes such a guess a not too improbable one. In later folk-lore the devil, or Satan, of the witches almost inevitably appears as a horned being, with tail and hoofs, and that witchcraft in England was connected with the oversight (beneficent or otherwise) of cattle is an established fact. But it is possible to reach out too far in assuming such resemblances, which must be taken for what they are worth. In one ancient Welsh poem we read of "the herds of the roaring Beli", and he is elsewhere alluded to as "a bull of battle". And that Beli was connected with another Gaulish deity is revealed by the fact that Geoffrey of Monmouth tells us he was the father of Gurguntius that is Gargantua. And Gargantua was Cernunnos.

I believe that I have now covered the ground in respect of those British deities who have the most intimate associations with the arcane, and of whom I intend to treat in the chapter devoted to the cultus of Arthur. I must now confine myself for the remainder of this chapter to some account of the background of British Celtic Mysticism, its Otherworld scenery and the nature of its magical paraphernalia, its crystal fortresses and ships, and the rest of those remote marvels which still remain as baffling mysteries to those who seek to penetrate its profounder implications. In approaching these we enter a sphere which, I am convinced, has no equal in the whole range of the world's legendary tradition in respect of the sense of uncanny wonder and remote fancy it reveals. In the conception of these mysterious wildernesses, where the atmosphere may be described as a brilliant dusk, the British fancy has triumphantly outsoared the imagination of all other races, European or Asiatic, in its keen and vivid representation of a half-world populous with spiritual shapes of an indeterminate weirdness unguessed by Greek, Egyptian or Hindu. This environment in its creepy yet attractive mystery recalls the country of dream and at times the grimmest terrors of nightmare. No poet has ever captured the shadowy radiance which illumines its vast and forlorn wastes and abysses, and indeed none could hope to portray the faint and ghostly projections with which its recesses are fulfilled. Here are the desolate purple crags and windless deserts conceived by Druidism as the horizon of its abstract thought and most sublime meditations. You may laugh at its utter abnegation of all that is implied by the practical and the material if you choose, as do the modernist poets—men lost to all that is spiritual or imaginative—but you will, if you are a Celt, realize that everything which moves you most potently finds expression in this dim theatre conceived by the early Celtic soul as the stage of its psychic development.

Here, however, I am not referring so much to the Tir-nan-Og of the Gaels, that Land of the Gods and the ever-young, which lies across the misty wastes of ocean, but what is to me the even more attractive sphere of Caer Sidi, the Otherworld of the Brythons, which, after all, is, mystically speaking, vastly the more important of the twain. Tir-nan-Og is a paradise of extraordinary beauty, a loveliness so sharply defined, indeed, as to be almost material in its glittering splendour. But it has few associations with the mystical. Despite its enchanting scenery there is something of the crudeness of the mediaeval Cockaigne about this Irish paradise. Ale falls in rain upon its meadows, its rivers are of milk and its tables are loaded with pork. How different is the Brythonic Caer Sidi! The Irish Land of the Ever Young has been the theme of a whole poethood; but it cannot vie in mystical beauty and in the sentiment of remote strangeness with the British Otherworld, which only needs to be appropriately realized to arouse a furore of interest among the imaginative. It appeals to the spiritual and intellectual side of human nature. Let us hear what the Bard Taliesin has to say concerning it:

> Perfect is my chair in Caer Sidi;
> Plague and age hurt him not who's in it—
> They know Manawyddan and Pryderi;
> Three organs round a fire sing before it,
> And about its points are ocean's streams;
> And the abundant well above it—
> Sweeter than white wine the drink in it.

Where is Caer Sidi? Most authorities are agreed that it is a blessed place, a part of Annwn, which was divided into many strange satrapies—Caer Pedryvan, the Four-cornered Castle in the Isle of the Strong Door, whose folk are described as quaffing the sparkling wine in a sphere where grey twilight merges into complete darkness, a gloom spangled with the yellow flare of torches, golden-yellow against dusky silver. There, too, is Caer Vedwit, the Castle of Revelry, Caer Golud, the Castle of Riches, Caer Wydyr, the Glass Fortress, Caer Ochren, a dread neighbourhood, Caer Rigor and Caer Vandwy, of some of which we know the names only.

It was in this locality, as we shall see, that the first home of the Grail was situated. This is the true enclave of British mysticism. If we desire to penetrate the secrets nourished in the souls of our early British ancestors we shall surprise them here. How utterly necessary it appears that we should comprehend and appreciate this, the earliest mystical background of our island, if we wish to realize and understand our own psychical beginnings! But I will not labour the necessity. We are a mighty folk, mightier now than ever. Whence sprang that spirit of might? Whence arose the profound inspiration which animates it? In a matrix of early thought and imagination, an alembic of the mysterious, where the seeds of poetry and wonder were nurtured in a sacred darkness. The myth of a people is often the seed of its future greatness, it frequently projects its destiny in allegory. Our psychic beginnings were nurtured centuries ago in a vast and enchanted cavern where fatal whisperings were uttered. This utterance, this primitive assurance, grew more and more coherent, less sybilline, assumed at last the phrase of ethnic philosophy. It issued at length into the light of common life, bravely human, angelically sounding, heroically manly, trumpet-tongued, with the tones of freedom and lofty chivalry. The whole gospel of this brilliant and passionate myth of light and beauty issuing from its gestation in that darkly wonderful womb of early Celtic thought inspires our ideals today, individual and personal as well as national and communal. In that ancient dimness of the early thought-caverns of our race the first British heroes groped in search of the very virtues we now cherish most. There they found the Grail, our national palladium, the vessel which would not cook the food of a coward, the arch-symbol of righteousness and imagination, and in pursuance of this and equally perilous adventures they painfully but generously wrought out and sublimated that code of chivalry which remains as the greatest glory of our race, and to which all the nations of earth look with hope as the last remaining ordinance of human justice and mercy.

These subterranean duchies, Rhys explains, constituted "one and the same mythical region under a variety of names". One of these, the Glass Fortress, Caer Wydyr, is alluded to in the pages of Nennius, who associates it with Irish story. When certain warriors were sailing from Spain to Ireland, "there appeared to them in the middle of the sea a tower of glass, the summit of which seemed covered with men, to whom they often spoke, but received no answer". They besieged the tower, but when they landed on the shore which surrounded its base, "the sea opened and swallowed them up".[14]

In *The Book of the Dun Cow* Cuchullin is also made to tell of such a magic tower, the fort of Scatha, a Caledonian sorceress, the mistress of a shadowy land, which he attacked and took by storm. It was cinctured by seven walls, it had doors of iron, pits of serpents, a ghastly cell full of toads with sharp beaks. It could also boast of a magical cauldron and much treasure of gold and silver. The Irish mentality has coloured the myth in the shades of horror. Keating also speaks of such a stronghold, Conaing's Tower, on Tory Island, which, when it was assailed by the Irish of the mainland, was visited by a terrific inundation, so that only thirty among the invaders saved their lives.[15] Taliesin, the Welsh bard, also sings of such a fortress as having been encountered by Arthur when he raided Annwn:

> Beyond the Glass Fort Arthur's valour they had not seen.
> Three score hundreds stood on the wall;
> It was hard to converse with their watchman.[16]

In the mythologies of more than one nation the glass tower or mountain is the stronghold of the dead. "In popular belief," says Miss Marion Roalfe Cox, "the soul in its wanderings has to climb a steep hill-side, sometimes supposed to be made of hair, sometimes of glass, on the summit of which is the heavenly paradise."[17] The Norse had a glass heaven known as Gler-himinn, and tales of such glass mountains are familiar in Celtic and Balkan folk-tale. But the Caer Wydyr to which I have alluded (the Glass Place) also appears to have reference to Arthur's ship of glass in which his company set forth to raid the sphere of Annwn. Elsewhere this vessel is called "Pryderi". Merlin made a similar voyage in a similar ship. But he is also associated with a glass house or castle in the island of Bardsey, into which he took the thirteen treasures of Britain, "including among them such rarities as Arthur's tartan, that rendered its wearer invisible, Gwydno's inexhaustible basket, and other articles of equally fabulous virtues". This he did, says an old author, "to please his leman".[18]

The fortress of Caer Pedryvan, we are told, revolved ceaselessly, so that it was difficult to find its entrance. It seems to me allegorical of the ancient myth of the "churning of the ocean", associated with the Celtic god Manannan, or Manawyddan, a mythic picture of the glassy expanse of the restless ocean. A castle in the Irish tale of Saudon Og also revolves. We read also of a dreadful prison in which Arthur, like Gwydion before him, was confined when captured during his descent into this subterranean sphere —the prison of Ochren. This enclosure seems to have been constructed entirely of human bones divided into numerous cells, forming a kind of labyrinth. It had been constructed by the god Manawyddan (according to the dubious authority of Iolo Morganwg). Pwyll and Pryderi, the gods of Annwn, when they captured Gwydion the son of Don, had immured him in this charnel-house, whence he managed to escape. Now this cavern of bones, I believe, is nothing more or less than the famous "Davy Jones's locker" of modern folk-lore. "Davy Jones" is the spirit of the River Tavy, in Devonshire, and his "locker" the prison in which drowned seamen lie. Manannan, or Mana-wyddan, is the Celtic god of the sea, and the circumstance that he possesses such a "prison" in a locality described by Rhys and others as being of a sub-marine character appears to clinch the argument. Perhaps the analogy justifies Iolo, who "must have got it somewhere". W. B. Yeats mentions an Irish story in which a goblin of the sea keeps the souls of sailors in "cages".

Sir John Daniel ventures the opinion that Caer Sidi was the prototype of the Druidic temple, "the pattern, in form and order, from which all other Temples, whether large or small, were copied". The name, he thinks, was derived from the twelve constellations or signs of the zodiac, with the sun as their centre. It was "the similitude of a higher and *invisible* kingdom over which God ruled . . . the guide to their seasons and times of worship, and the corresponding quarter days in the year, as well as provincial and local meetings on the full moon, half and quarter moon days. . . . We have still in Wales many such circles known to this day as Caer Sidin. One of these is on Snowdon, and is sometimes called Gyfylchi."[19] I do not know by what authority Sir John justifies his theory of Caer Sidi as the prototypal British temple. The name is usually associated in the etymological sense with the Gaelic Celtic *sidhe*, implying "a mound", a dwelling of supernaturals or fairies. Rhys ventured to collate it with the Latin *sedes*, "a seat".[20] In any case, stone circles are not regarded by most modern archaeologists as "Druidical".

Miss Eleanor Hull was of opinion that close attention should be paid to the legends concerning Annwn, in which sentiment she was undoubtedly justified. For her, stories of the Celtic Otherworld were divided into two groups, those which describe a raid upon that place, with intent to carry off its treasures, and those in which mortals are invited to visit it by its queen. The first type was most common in Wales ("The Spoiling of Annwn", "The Battle of the Trees", "Kilhwch and Olwen", and "Math and Mathonwy"). In Ireland, as we have seen, several such myths were associated with Cuchullin, and in Scot-land we have the Scottish version of the "Wooing of Emer". These are not descents into a Hades, she maintains, but into a bright country in search of its treasures.

The earliest description of the Welsh Annwn, proceeds Miss Hull, makes it resemble Magh Mell, or the Irish paradise of the gods. Professor Morris Jones thought that the term "Annwn" replaced, under late influence, some more ancient name now lost, and that it became identified in the Christian consciousness with the Place of the Dead. It is evident that we have two overlapping conceptions. Sometimes Annwn is called "Uffern" (Inferno), a later development. Annwn, with its sweet wells of water, its cauldron, its perfect chair, and so forth, says Miss Hull, seems the Welsh doublet of the Irish Mahg Mell. With this I agree, but she fails to discern the vastly greater importance of Annwn as a spiritual sphere.[21]

While on the subject of Snowdon, I should like to refer to the somewhat neglected topic of the Pheryllt, who, says tradition, were a caste of priests associated with the mysteries of the secret city of Emrys, situated on Snowdon. In *The Book of Taliesin* we are informed that the goddess Ceridwen was determined "agreeably to the mystery of the Books of Pheryllt to prepare for her son a cauldron of water of inspiration and knowledge", with due attention to the books of astronomy, and to the hours of the planets—that cauldron which, in fact, we read of in the myth of Taliesin, the three drops of which afforded him his bardic inspiration. The Pheryllt, or "Ancients", are occasionally mentioned by the bards of Wales and an old chronicle quoted by Dr. Thomas Williams states that this brotherhood had a college at Oxford, prior to the foundation of that University. That they were perhaps regarded by tradition as an ancient caste of alchemists appears probable from the circumstance that the term for ancient chemistry and metallurgy is *Celvyddydon Pheryllt*, that is, "the arts of the Pheryllt". They seem to have been associated with the cult of Ceridwen and to have had their headquarters in Emrys, in the mountains of Snowdon, the city of the dragons of Beli, which was also known to Welsh tradition as Dinas Affaraon, or "the Place of the Higher Powers". This site is alluded to in *The Black Book of Carmarthen* as the centre of mystical rites and by Gibson, Camden's commentator, as occupying the summit of "the Panting Cliff", on Snowdon itself. It is indeed identified with the ruins of an exceedingly strong fortification encompassed by a triple wall on an eminence known as Broich y Ddinas, "the Ridge of the City", which forms part of the summit of Penmaen. If Gibson's statement be credible, this place was of immense size and solidity. It was in this city, legend assures us, that in the time of Beli and in that of Prydain, the son of Ædd the Great, those dragons were concealed which drew the car of Ceridwen and were so closely identified with certain important passages in early British legend. Here, too, were deposited by a mysterious sow the cub of a wolf and an eaglet, according to a myth contained in one of the ancient Welsh poems.[22]

All this, I need scarcely say, is by no means accountable to authority, but I think that, as in the case of all tradition, it has a background. As Professor Gruffydd remarks of Iolo's authenticity in respect of a certain tradition, the old bards "must have got it from somewhere". Even the most fantastic legends possess a modicum of fact, whatever the most exacting of mythological critics may say, and in the alchemists of Emrys, their dragons and other grotesqueries, I think I see the remains of a tradition referring to some primeval brotherhood of magical predilection highly coloured by the fictional genius of an imaginative peasantry. I do not know what modern Welsh Archaeology has pronounced concerning the "ruins of Emrys" on Snowdon, and indeed can discover nothing on that head. Its conclusions, if any, could not fail to be interesting.

The purpose of this examination into some of the elements of Celtic mysticism will be more clearly discerned in the next chapter of this book, which deals with the Cultus of Arthur and the Mystery of the Grail. I have striven to make plain the nature of the mystical environment in which the seeds of the

Arthurian legend and the later idea of the Grail were nurtured, and to afford some impression of the original mythological background of their scenery. Indeed, it is in the gloom of Annwn that we first encounter Arthur in British myth, and when we do he is seeking the cauldron of Annwn which became the prototype of the Grail.

It is to that cavern of primitive thought, then, the old British Annwn, that we can trace two of the outstanding factors which have gone to the making of that British tradition which is justly the pride of our race and the envy of the world outside these seas—the pattern of the stainless knight, inspired by the indwelling spirit of chivalry, and the sacred vessel associated with one of the most poignant passages in the chronicle of our faith. But even in their germinal form these conceptions were not degraded, as many worthy acceptances from the past have been in their initial phases. From the first we find Arthur a spiritual influence, exalted and courageous. The cauldron, for which he quests, is both a fertility vessel and one which yields inspiration in song.

> By the breath of nine maidens is it gently warmed . . .
> It will not boil the food of a coward.

It is a thing of beauty, rimmed with pearls. Here is nothing base, nothing of the savage or the obscene. These ideas are the projected shadows of that gentle if fantastic beauty and mild serenity which were to yield our race a literary and ethical tradition without parallel in the long chronicle of saga.

CHAPTER XII

THE CULTUS OF ARTHUR

THE imagination, brooding over the vast landscape of history, a perspective in which the centuries dwindle like receding counties viewed from a mountain-top, discerns in that gloom which mingles with horizon a flash and smoulder of such brilliance as the spirit of fire awakes in a thick mantling of smoke. From that dim borderland where chronicle marches with tradition is borne the echo of ghostly trumpets mingled with the thin clash of legendary steel. This luminous plot upon the margin of the chart of time arrests the fancy. The eyes of the beholder are strained in an effort to catch the bare outlines of the shadow-shapes which charge and hurtle through the almost impenetrable haze. But, as these are caught and held for a fleeting moment, the dusk of intervening ages appears to roll athwart the vision, and as the fogs of the years gather over it once again, silence quenches its elfin clamour.

Some such experience of acute disappointment and baffled hope must have been the lot of all who have endeavoured to seek a more explicit knowledge of the terrain of the Arthurian legend, to come to a closer understanding of the circumstances of Arthur's myth. For that he belongs to mythology rather than to history has been made so plainly evident by recent research that the argument for his humanity must at last be regarded as futile. The evidence in support of it is scarcely worth quotation, but, such as it is, it has been clearly set forth by Mr. E. K. Chambers in his masterly essay *Arthur of Britain*, and found to be wanting in all those factors which are associated with exact historical record.[1] To detail it here, in view of what Mr. Chambers has set down, would not only be supererogatory, but apart from my purpose. Algernon Herbert, more than a century ago, perceived the mythic nature of Arthur, who "presided over the wars of Britannia as her Quirinus or Enyalius", and whose influence he likened to that of Mars. The Britons of the North who fought against the Northumbrian Saxon ninety years after the date of Arthur's alleged death are termed by the bards as "The Warriors of Arthur", which Herbert likens to the Roman phrase, "servants of Mars". British bardhood alluded to Arthur as "the Bull of Conflict, King of the World". In one ancient Welsh poem, adds Herbert, Arthur is described as a "swiftly moving lamp", and as the sun, these terms revealing his godhead significantly enough.[2]

In a manner greatly more precise, as befits the modern exponent of folk-lore, Lord Raglan has made it abundantly clear that Arthur's nature is pre-dominantly mythological. I will not quote such evidence as he adduces in favour of the humanity of Arthur, for, as he admits, it is "almost nil", and indeed he disposes of it without much trouble. He points out that Mr. R. Briffault, in his work *The Mothers*, has derived Arthur's name from the Welsh *arrdhu*, meaning "very black", and that he has concluded that "the Black One", "leader of battles", is identical with the god Bran, "the Raven", "the leader in battle of the Celts in every war which they have fought throughout the ages". There seems no doubt, says Lord Raglan, that Bran was a god who was identified with the raven, still he considers the connection of Arthur with the derivation *arddhu* improbable, although he has been identified with the raven and also with the chough. "Arthur has none but mythological relatives," remarks Mr. Briffault. "His father is the dragon Uther, his sister the goddess Anu, his wife 'the White Lady', his mistress or sister Morgana, the fairy." The knights of the Round Table betray their mythic character by their attributes, continues Lord Raglan. Sir Kaye, Arthur's famous seneschal, could breathe nine nights and days under water, and could make himself as tall as the loftiest tree in the forest. These are scarcely the properties of ordinary men! His lordship further collates the circumstances of the myth of Arthur with those of Robin Hood, Dionysius, Theseus, Romulus and other traditional figures, revealing that all of these partake of the same qualities and that their personal histories possess the self-same story-pattern more or less.[3]

Canon MacCulloch feels constrained to "postulate a local Arthur saga fusing an old Brythonic god with the historic sixth-century Arthur". "He may have been the object of a cult."[4] Mr. E. K. Chambers, however, is of opinion that the proof adduced by certain writers for the mythic character of Arthur has been pushed too far. Particularly is this the case with that part of it worked over by Rhys, who sought on insufficient grounds to find parallels with the Arthurian legend in certain Irish myths. Many of the tales con-cerning Arthur traceable to British sources reveal him as a species of culture-hero, Chambers concludes, and some Welsh legends connect him with those heroes who slumber beneath hollow hills, awaiting the signal to deliver their kingdoms from foreign enemies, while, like Odin, he is also the leader of "the furious host", who rides the wind. But as regards the precise mythological position of Arthur, Chambers leaves us very much in the dark.[5]

For my own part I have ventured the opinion in more than one essay that Arthur was the central figure of a comparatively late British pagan cultus. I believe that he represents an older hero-god or sun-god of the Britons under a slightly altered guise, and who has had a new name accorded him to chime with the altered circumstances of his novel and more modern phase and presentation.

Tradition asserts that Arthur's father was one Uther, surnamed Pendragon, whose myth is more fully presented by Geoffrey of Monmouth than by any other writer, and is therefore rather dubious. Succeeding Aurelius as King of Britain, he fell in love with Igerna, the wife of Gorlois, Duke of Cornwall, and aided by the magic arts of Merlin was enabled to enter the castle of Tintagel in the likeness of Gorlois, and to become the father of Arthur. In a poem by Taliesin, Uther becomes a wolf (Welsh *gorlois*) for this purpose. In an ancient Welsh poem entitled "Marwnad Uthyr Pendragon", one who appears to be a priest addresses Uther as a god of war who has given a ninth part of his "giant power" to Arthur.[6] Uther is also spoken of in one of the Triads as a master of Magic, and as having taught this art to Menw, son of Teirgwaedd.[7] In dealing with such sources repeated cautions must be issued that Welsh scholarship has not yet reached the stage of an agreed and confident rendering of these early texts. But if I err in quoting them at all, I do so in the company of certain Welsh authorities who, while warning us as to their present imperfections, refer to them more or less freely themselves. Thus they can scarcely castigate others for following their example—and I may add that without these texts we should all be in limbo! As matters stand, we must be content with half-loaves where whole loaves are to seek.

Mr. E. K. Chambers remarks "that there is no evidence that anyone before Geoffrey made him [Arthur] the son of Uther Pendragon".[8] He quotes Dr. Kemp Malone as suggesting that Arthur "is really a doublet of a divine Uthyr Ben, due to a confusion between the Welsh *uthr*, 'cruel', and a variant form *aruthr*, and to an attempt in Cornwall to remedy the confusion by making Arthur the son of Uther!" Like Mr. Chambers, "I do not think that these theories are worth serious pursuit."[9]

But to return to the theory that Arthur was the deity of a particular cult in Britain: we have already seen that Canon MacCulloch suggests as much. Herbert, too, more than suspected it. He says that when the Britons had shaken off the Roman rule they began once more to cultivate many of the superstitions of their ancestors, and "resorted to secret and mysterious ceremonies", especially in connection with the worship of Beli. He even ventures so far as to say that this apostasy was first organized by Eugenius, son of Maximus, by whom, I suppose, he means that Maximus who, in the fourth quarter of the fourth century, usurped the royal power in Britain. But Arthur, he continues, "in foolhardy fanaticism proclaimed and exposed to the public gaze and adoration the most ineffable mysteries" of this restored pagan creed.[10] What precisely induced the son of a Spanish military adventurer, as was Eugenius, to attempt to relume the glories of British paganism is scarcely clear. The chief god of this new cultus, says Herbert, was Bran. Where so much is guesswork it is hardly necessary to indulge in fancy. He adds elsewhere that when the Roman Empire was tottering, "a pagan apostasy crept into Gaul and Britain", which ended in the establishment in the latter country of that Neo-Druidism "to which the fables of Ambrosius and Arthur relate". This, he tells us, was Mithraic in its doctrines.[11] It appears, so far as Herbert is concerned, that this cultus was in some manner "established on the ruins of British Christianity", which, he remarks, had an especial preference for the Johannine doctrine, as sacramental. There is evidence, he continues, of an apostatic heresy in Britain in the "Apology" of Bacharius, who, according to Gennadius of Marseilles, a writer who flourished about the year 490, was "a man of Christian philosophy", and was still living in the year 460, when Vortigern reigned in Britain. Bacharius denounces his country as the head and front of paganism, but he omits to particularize what country he is writing of! Herbert, however, will have it that it was Britain, and that the paganism he thunders against was a form of Neo-Druidism. His arguments by no means convince me.[12]

I will now endeavour to set forth my own theorizings on the subject of the cultus of Arthur as briefly and as clearly as it is possible to do so in the rather complex circumstances.

After the official departure of the Romans from Britain in the year A.D. 410, the last slender associations being definitely severed about 442, the southern part of the island was practically at the mercy of Saxon freebooters and Pictish invaders, the large drafts of her young men to the Roman armies on the Continent having depleted her powers of resistance. The entire history of Saxon invasion and advance, as we formerly accepted it from Victorian authorities, must now be regarded with dubiety, as the major portion of it certainly does not agree with the archaeological evidence, as submitted by recent authorities. In any case, Hengist and Horsa have no more claim to personal reality than Robin Hood or Herne the Hunter, although Vortigern appears a shade more substantial.

Vortigern, if an actual personality, appears to have been a prince of West British origin, untrustworthy and even disreputable, who, from motives of envy, had held aloof from the Romano-British Party, whose policy was to conserve the remains of Roman culture in the island and to incorporate this culture in a revival of British ideals. This Party was led by Ambrosius Aurelianus, the son of Constantine, brother of Conan, King of Brittany. Constantine had married a British princess, and may have been elected Emperor of the Britons after the Roman withdrawal. His son, Ambrosius, was the brother of Uther, father of Arthur, and was thus Arthur's uncle.

Out of this Romano-British Party—and that such a Party existed despite the shadowy nature of its personnel is a matter of acknowledged fact—emerged what I believe to have been the Arthurian cult, the gospel of the deliverance of Britain from Saxon invasion and oppression by a great hero-god of British origin, a supernatural deliverer capable of driving the alien invader into the sea and of restoring Britain and the Celtic race to their pristine status of independence. But it would surely seem that the relationship of this Aurelianus to Arthur the hero-god was scarcely one of ordinary tribal or family affinity. It is much more probable that it was that of the founder or re-shaper of a cult to his patron deity. Tradition, as usual, has reduced the god to human status. Arthur, the saviour of Britain, was, as I have suggested, an old Celtic hero-god restored from the ancient pre-Roman traditions of the British race rather than a Romano-British champion like Aurelius himself.

Arthur was a sun-god of the British Celts, a patron of agriculture in its early form and therefore, like most agricultural deities, a war-god, surrounded by a company of fighting retainers. The supernatural birth of Arthur reveals him as a "saviour" or national champion. He is the fruit of an amour between Uther, King of Britain, and Igerna, wife of Gorlois, Duke of Cornwall, Uther having taken the shape of Gorlois, through the magic arts of Merlin, for the express purpose of begetting the hero. In similar circumstances was the Egyptian god Osiris born of Nut, the wife of the god Ra, and of Geb, one of his companions, a coincidence which fortifies the resemblance between Arthur and Osiris.

It seems to me probable that the Old British, Irish and Gaulish faiths partially accepted the general technique of some Eastern cults at a later time, as indeed the late Mr. Alfred Nutt suggested in his notable work, *The Voyage of Bran*. Oriental cults were well known in the Britain of Roman and post-Roman times, the population of which had been reinforced by many thousands of Syrians, Moors and other Easterners. Temples and shrines of Oriental cults existed in Roman London, a fane of Isis having existed on the site of Southwark, while the rites of Mithra were celebrated in a cave beside the River Walbrook, near Bond Court. Druidism proper and the old British faith had been extirpated by the Romans, or nearly so, but the great body of its supporters, especially the more literate and advanced nucleus of them, would certainly be thrown back upon a more secret yet intense mystical form of belief, as all suppressed or "minority" religions have ever been. We have only to think of the "Vecchia Religione" in Italy and of Nagualism in Mexico. That the British pantheon had not been entirely overthrown is proved by the existence of the great Temple of Lud, or Nudd, at Lydney on the Severn and other similar fanes elsewhere, which certainly flourished in Roman times.

The Egyptian faith at an earlier period had highly fashionable acceptances in Rome and throughout Italy, where many temples of Isis and Osiris had been patronized by the élite for at least three centuries, and the introduction of Alexandrian Neo-Platonism initiated a new form of it. What more likely than that a body of British patriots educated in the manners and according to the ideals of Roman Society, and inspired by native ambitions, should accept and revive a mythical and traditionally mystical cultus which displayed a strong resemblance to that of the fashionable Egyptian rite while it yet had actual native associations?

In such an atmosphere, I think, the Arthurian ideal received revival and fresh life-impulse as "the Gospel of Britain" through the propaganda of a military and arcane cultus which had for its purpose the preservation and maintenance of the sacred isle of Britain from destruction by the invading barbarians from the North and from Germany, the conservation of British ideals and civilization and the cherishing of that Secret British Celtic Tradition which had flourished in our island from time immemorial. This, I believe, was the origin of a system of arcane-romantic wisdom and legend which was later to emerge in altered form as one of the most brilliant and chivalrous of European literatures, the Arthurian Saga, in which we can observe all the insignia of a lost culture and hidden philosophy. Indeed, we have some historical grounds for the assumption, for Gottefried of Viterbo, in his "Chronicle", assures us that Ambrosius was a "pagan" who encouraged the sect of the Manichaens and disliked the Church.

This cultus provided the new Party with a religious-mystical and political rallying-ground, its deity and hero-god becoming the hope and light of a people struggling for very existence. Later tradition came to euhemerize Arthur, to regard him as a human leader, as was inevitable under the influence of a growing Christianity. For Christianity, though it had been introduced into Britain for some considerable time before the middle of the fifth century—at which period, it seems to me, the patriotic movement I allude to must have arisen—was at that time only one among several religions struggling for foothold in our island. Five of the ancient Welsh poems allude to Arthur, practically all of them in such a manner as makes it quite clear that such allusion is arcane in its symbolism. Perhaps the most important is that entitled "The Spoils of Annwn", ascribed to the Bard Taliesin. When I wrote on this poem fourteen years ago I said that it seemed to me to refer "to a definite attempt on the part of the initiates of some mystical society to explore the

Underworld plane of Annwn". I confess to some surprise at having written in this vein, for I had not then the barest notion of the former existence of any particular Arthurian cult. The statement was at that time compelled from me by the evidence and was certainly not intended to fit any preconceived theory.

Now the several localities which Arthur and his company pass through in the Underworld of Annwn are the dwellings of Pwyll, the lord of that region, and of one Pryderi, known to later French Grail stories as Pelles and Peleur. Taliesin's poem, "The Spoils of Annwn", is an account descriptive of a raid upon an underworld locality, for the purpose of bringing back a magical vessel containing a brew or liquor a draught of which conferred the gift of wisdom or inspiration. In short, Arthur and his band of mystics make a special journey to the Underworld for the purpose of being initiated into the mysteries of the place, precisely as did Osiris, Orpheus, Thomas the Rymour, the divine brothers in Central American myth, Faust and scores of other heroes who, like the members of Egyptian and Greek mystical societies, believed that initiation was to be experienced only in the recesses of that subterranean world whither souls betake themselves after death to undergo a process of trial while awaiting rebirth.

For not only had each member of the Arthur cult to be reborn spiritually, but Britain, their country, must also be reborn through them. Where, then, should they betake themselves under the leadership of their tutelary god or hero save to the sphere in which his myth assured them the spirit and apparatus of revival and restoration were to be found and where supernatural strength awaited them?

That an Arthurian cultus of mystical-military association actually existed in Britain from the third quarter of the fifth century to, say, the middle of the sixth, and to a much later period in some of the more remote and more essentially British parts of the island such as Wales and Strathclyde, is, I think, reasonable of belief from the foregoing statements, which are capable of extended proof. Such a theory would explain the whole Arthurian "process" and make it unnecessary to credit the existence of a personal Arthur, unless, indeed, the leader of such a society symbolically or ritually took the name of its patron god. It further provides reasons for the great popularity of Arthur and his story—a popularity which has for centuries baffled Celtic students, who could not discover any god of that name in the Celtic pantheon other than a very shadowy Artaios, a minor agricultural deity of the Allobroges of Gaul.

Ambrosius Aurelianus, to whom I have alluded as the probable leader of this cultus, is mentioned by Gildas as a man of modest position, the survivor of a noble Roman family, who took up arms against the Saxons. Nennius merely mentions him as being dreaded by the Scots, Picts and Romans, although in a later passage he speaks of him as "king among all the kings of the British race". There has been confusion between the boy called Ambrosius, mentioned by Geoffrey of Monmouth as having advised Vortigern of the presence of dragons under the foundations of his castle, with the Ambrosius Aurelianus of history on the one hand and with Merlin, or Merlin Ambrosius, on the other. Leaving this phase of things apart for the moment, there is no doubt of the existence of a British-Roman family known as Aurelius in that period of British history immediately subsequent to the departure of the Romans. It is also certain that several members of this family bore official positions, that an armed force to combat the Saxons was named after it, that its most influential member was Ambrosius Aurelianus, who appears to have been in opposition both to the treacherous Vortigern and to the Saxons, and that he was slain in civil war. Such, indeed, are the conclusions of Mr. Edward Foord, with which I long ago expressed myself as being in sympathy.[13] Herbert alludes to Ambrosius as "the founder of the great sanctuary of Neo-Druidism", a magician of might and "the fountain-head of bardic doctrine". With Rhys, I believe that his story became entangled with that of Merlin, who was occasionally called "Merlin Emrys", or "Merlin Ambrosius", for I think that the tales concerning two quite separate figures, both of great prowess and associated with the magical arts, came to be fused in the popular imagination.

In the myth which arose concerning these personages, Uther came to be known as the brother of Ambrosius Aurelianus, while Arthur was regarded as his nephew. All this genealogical connection, in my belief, was the work of that class of professional story-teller who, when a cult begins to break down, invariably attempts to rationalize the material of its myth into historical narrative by humanizing its personalities, mingling them with actual personages to give their details of kinship the appearance of reality and who transform into pseudo-chronicle the drama of the gods, being probably themselves in complete or partial ignorance of the true character of the data they deal with. Such a transformation has, indeed, taken place in the case of almost every mythological system known to scholarship, and is a process too familiar to it to require amplification here. For popular appreciation is seldom satisfied without the fullest explanation of myth either in its original or later fictional form, and demands that the relationship betwixt gods and heroes shall be definitely pronounced upon.

I think that there is some reason to identify Uther with the god Beli. In "Tysilio" he is spoken of as the builder of the great Cor upon the Maes Mawr, or Plain of Salisbury. Now we are told that Beli was slain and buried at a place of that name, and that Uther was similarly interred there. The attributes and gigantic size of the two figures bespeak their close resemblance. That Beli was a sun-god there is little doubt, and that Arthur was regarded as his emanation, precisely as Cuchullin was that of the Irish sun-god Lugh, seems clear to me. The resemblance of Cuchullin to Arthur has long been apparent to me. Both are avatars of the sun-god, both are terrible in battle, both are associated with a nymph or goddess, the Morrigan or Morgan, who sometimes acts as an enemy, occasionally as a lover. The causes which initiated the Cuchullin cult in Ireland appear to be much the same as those which actuated the rise of the cult of Arthur in Britain—the necessity for the appearance of a national hero-god at a time of internecine struggle. Like Cuchullin, Arthur slays his tens of thousands. The whole question, I admit, requires a much greater degree of explication than I can afford it here, but I believe that the resemblances of the myths of the two heroes is greater than the differences which their circumstances reveal. The point is that we know precisely that Cuchullin was the son of a sun-god, and if the equation holds good, such a statement may also be made in the case of Arthur. And I think it proper to add that at least one old Welsh poem, the "Cyvoesi Merddin", pictures Beli and his warriors as a storm of wind rushing through the valleys—that is, he is described as acting precisely as did Arthur himself, as "the wild huntsman", as both Welsh and English folk-tales aver.[14]

I must here clear up one or two points concerning Arthur's personality which, as we shall see, will have a later bearing upon any decisions we may arrive at with regard to his identity. In his *Don Quixote*, Cervantes makes his quaint hero aver that "there goes an old tradition, and a common one, all over that kingdom of Great Britain, that this king [Arthur] did not die, but that by magic art he was turned into a raven; and that in process of time he shall reign again" (Book II, Chapter V). This legend was still repeated in Cornwall within the last century. A gentleman who was out shooting one day at Marazion Green saw a raven in the distance and fired at it, but was rebuked for so doing by an old man who chanced to pass at the moment, who told him that on no account should he have done so, for that King Arthur was still alive as a raven.[15] Bran, we will recall, was the raven *par excellence* in Welsh lore. The Rev. R. S. Hawker also gives one to understand that Cornish legend identified Arthur with the chough.

There is also some evidence that Artbur was identified with the divine king. He certainly appears to be one and the same with the "maimed king" of Grail romance, who lies in his Avallon, his thighs pierced with a spear-wound, awaiting the words which will bring about his disenchantment. And be it remembered that he was borne to Avallon to recover from his wounds. To this I shall revert later, but here I should like to say that his status of divine king is borne out by the circumstance that his absence and sickness are regarded in some romances as the causes of years of dearth in some localities, and that the wound in the thigh from which the maimed king snffered is characteristic of fertility deities, as Professor Krappe points out The same kind of wound is sustained by Aengus and Adonis.[16] Goronwy also suffered from such a wound. In a Taliesin poem we find that one Tyllon was cut in the thigh, evidently for some mystical reason. In another poem by Taliesin, entitled "Buarth Beirdd", "The Ox-pen of the Bards", the poet exclaims: "Let the thigh be pierced in blood." In his "Cad Goddeu", or "Battle of the Trees", we find Taliesin boasting that "To my knife a multitude of thighs have submitted." Sacrifice of blood by piercing the thigh was, as is well known, one of the methods employed by the priests of ancient Mexico when placating the gods, and had reference to the belief that blood so offered up not only sustained the lives of the deities in question but assisted the growth of the crops.

Plutarch alludes to the fact that many of the islands around Britain were uninhabited and that some of these were called after gods and heroes. Demetrius, an ancient traveller, explored one of these and found it occupied by few inhabitants, who were sacrosanct to the Britons. In another island, he was told, Cronus was imprisoned with Briareus, who kept guard over him while he slept, "for sleep is the bond forged for Cronus". Now the sickle-bearing Cronus, or Saturn, is a god of fertility, and Greek myth tells us that he reigned in the Isles of the Blessed. If Plutarch's statement is to be depended on, and I can see no reason why it should not be, its application to Britain—for the name Cronus, given by Demetrius to this sleeping deity, can only have been his own translation of a British appellative—implies that a myth startlingly resembling that of Arthur sleeping in his Avallon was current in the Britain of the first century of our era, the date of Plutarch's floreat. I am aware that the resemblance of this legend to that of Merlin has been pointed out by Rhys. But in this case, Arthur and Merlin are "in the same boat". Both slumber in magic isles off the coast of Britain, and doubtless this part of their myths harks back to some such early story as Plutarch recounts in his little work *De Defectu Oraculorum*. I mention the tradition to show that such a myth did exist in early Britain, and it would appear to cast back the original of a sleeping Arthur to a hoary past, in view of which we must regard his associations with Avallon as a comparatively modern version and application of a very much more ancient Celtic tradition.

Having regard to this legend, this is distinctly the place in which to speak of Merlin, as it certainly aids us in coming to conclusions respecting him. Mr. E. K. Chambers is of opinion that "Merlin seems to have been wholly a creation of Geoffrey [of Monmouth's] active brain". He sets aside Rhys's elucidation of Merlin as a great Celtic sky-god and states that the name is untraceable in any authentic document prior to Geoffrey's time. Nor is he that prophetic boy in the history of Nennius who expounds to Vortigern the omen of the two dragons, a person, he thinks, who was clearly Ambrosius. Nor are any of the Welsh poems which allude to him older than Geoffrey, but vernacular prophecies stimulated by his work.

Now all this may be very true, but Mr. Chambers fails to account for that part of Merlin's myth which deals with his enchantment and disappearance. The point is that nowhere does Geoffrey touch upon that topic. Merlin's enchantment by Niniane or Vivien in the forest of Broceliande finds its earliest description in the Vulgate continuation of the "Merlin" of Robert de Borron. This continuation recounts the manner in which the damsel Niniane puts him under a spell and sends him to sleep in a tower in the Forest of Broceliande

Where did the writer of the Vulgate continuation, sometimes called the *Livre d'Artus*, get the story? Geoffrey of Monmouth has no more to do with this part of the myth than had the Bards or legend-mongers who placed "Merlin's grave" on the banks of the Powsail Burn in Upper Tweeddale. But there was a source ready to the scribe's hand—the myth mentioned by Plutarch as given above. Like Osiris, Merlin has many resting-places, which I do not need to enumerate here. Such is to be expected of a god. I have already alluded to the legend that he retired to Bardsey Island with the "Thirteen Treasures of Britain". Nor does it seem essential to say much concerning the theories which divide his personality into two or three. The confusion seems to have been due to Giraldus Cambrensis, who, deriving to some extent from Geoffrey's "Vita Merlini", distinguishes two Merlins, a "Merlin Ambrosius" and a "Merlin Calidonius" of Scotland. Perhaps this may be due to a separate body of myths respecting Merlin having arisen among the North Welsh or Britons of Strathclyde, a goodly portion of whose territory was situated in what is now Scotland. I see no greater difficulty here than might be encountered in discovering a different set of myths concerning Osiris in various parts of Egypt, or two separate bodies of belief respecting Quetzalcoatl in Mexico proper and in the Zapotec country, as indeed we do. Time and distance may readily bring about such a condition of disparate myth.

But that part of Merlin's myth which tells of his disappearance was found in the Forest of Broceliande by Villemarqué in a folk-lore form, precisely as it is found in several places in Britain. The important thing is that all these forms of it can be proved, in their elements, to agree substantially with the myth of a British Cronus, as given by Plutarch. This fact should give pause to those who insist upon regarding Merlin as merely a fiction of Geoffrey of Monmouth. Geoffrey may have spun an entire web of fiction concerning Merlin, but he obviously knew nothing of this particular factor in his story, nor does he allude to it in his life of Merlin, the *Vita Merlini*. I hold that it is impossible to separate the plot and circumstances of the tale of the disappearance and enchanted slumber of Merlin from the Cronus legend of Plutarch in Britain, any more than it is possible to do so in the case of Arthur's withdrawal from the world. For me, both are most obviously derived from a very ancient myth of a British god sojourning in slumber in an insular locality, and if this does not altogether justify the rather elaborate status as a sky-god which Rhys has built up for Merlin, I plead that it goes far to class him among the deities. Cronus is the divine king, the fertility god, who, like the Mexican

Quetzalcoatl, seeks repose and refreshment from his labours in an island, and I believe that the circumstances of the myths of Merlin and Arthur reflect such an idea.

Indeed, I think we find corroboration of Plutarch's statement in a piece of modern folk-lore from the Isle of Man. Tradition says that Rushin Castle in that island stands on the site of an ancient Druidical sanctuary. A generation ago it was possible to enter its dungeons, which, says local legend, were freed by Merlin from the giants which inhabited its subterranean labyrinth. These capacious depths were said to contain many fine apartments, and the story goes that about a century ago an adventurous person resolved to explore them as did Theseus the Minoan labyrinth—by the aid of a clue of thread. After passing through a number of vaults, he observed a gleam of light, which shone from a splendid mansion, at the door of which he knocked. It was opened by a guardian, who assured him that if he wished to penetrate farther he must pass through the building, which he accordingly did. In time he arrived at a second mansion, still more magnificent, and brightly illuminated. Looking through one of its windows, he beheld a great table of black marble, on which lay at full length a man of gigantic stature, plunged in the deepest slumber, his head resting on a book and his hand upon the hilt of an immense sword. Terrified, the explorer hastily made his way back to the surface again.

To me, this legend has all the appearance of a local version of the Cronus legend alluded to by Plutarch. Indeed it may well represent that myth, and Man may have been the island it alludes to. I believe, too, that it reveals a link between that tradition and the sleeping or enchanted king of Grail story, and it certainly bears a resemblance to similar tales concerning the bespelled slumbers of Arthur. It has been recorded by Waldron in his *Description of the Isle of Man* and by Grose in his *Antiquities* (VI, p. 208).

But in Arthurian legend Merlin assumes the part of the advisory and wonder-working Druid who is ever at the elbow of the typical Celtic king of history and tradition and I have no doubt that in this particular capacity such a portrait of him was due to the popular memory of a figure of this kind. Irish saga is rich in references to such Druids who acted as companion-counsellors to monarchs, and the notices we have of them amply justify such an assumption. In my view, Merlin in this particular guise bears a strong resemblance to the Mathonwy of Welsh legend, a wielder of magic, who, again, bears a suspicious likeness to the god Beli, judging from the little we know of him.

To return to Arthur, I wish to make clear certain resemblances between him and the Egyptian god Osiris, which, strangely enough, have been almost utterly neglected by those who have hitherto reviewed Arthurian sources. It is from the circumstances surrounding the deaths of these two seemingly incongruous figures that the more startling points of resemblance in their histories emerge. Egyptian myth and funerary practice make it plain that after he was slain by his evil brother Set, the destroyer, Osiris was ferried in a sacred barque across the Nile, accompanied by his sorrowing sisters Isis and Nephthys, to the region of Aalu in the West, a paradise of plenteous fruits and grains, there to reign as god of the not-dead, awaiting a glorious resurrection.

Arthur, slain in his last battle with his treacherous nephew Mordred, is carried off by his sisters in a barque to the mystic isle of Avallon or Avallach, "the Place of Apples", in the Western Sea. There he remains, neither dead nor alive, awaiting the fateful day when Britain shall require his aid once more.

The myth of Horus, the son of Osiris, otherwise Osiris resurrected, strongly resembles that of Arthur. Both attract to themselves a large company of warriors devoted to the destruction of evil monsters. And Horus took the shape of a hawk, as did Arthur that of a raven or crow. Moreover, the name of Arthur's nephew Gwalchmai means "hawk", while his sister Morgan is probably the Morrigan, or crow-goddess, of Irish mythology.

There appears also to be a strong resemblance between those parts of the myths of Osiris and Arthur which recount their adventures in the Underworld. In old Welsh poems Arthur is described as descending to Annwn, the Celtic Underworld, in his crystal ship to despoil it of the magical cauldron of inspiration and plenty. In like manner, Osiris penetrates Amenti, the dark realm of the dead, in his barque and does battle with his demon enemies.

It is thus obvious that the points of resemblance between Arthur and Osiris are neither few nor unimportant and that their legends have parallel contacts. But still further striking and noteworthy affinities seem to be revealed when that part of the later Arthurian epic known as "The Holy Grail" comes to be considered. Rhys and other scholars have proved conclusively that the Grail vessel is to be identified with the Cauldron of Annwn already alluded to, and have brought much erudition and convincing argument to bear upon the proof that the pagan story was transformed into a later Christian legend concerning a bowl or vessel which contained the blood of the Redeemer and which was brought from Jerusalem to Britain by Joseph of Arimathea. It seems to me that the original myth of a bowl of plenty originated in Egypt, for the people of that ancient land had a very especial and logical reason for believing in the existence of such a source of alimentary affluence.

For the Egyptians looked to the Nile, the river of Osiris, with which, indeed, he was identified, as the source of all wealth and provender. Without the Nile every living creature within the borders of old Egypt would very speedily have perished. The circumstance, too, that the source of the river was unknown to the Egyptians tended to add a mystery to the character of its presiding deity. The people of the country could not comprehend the rise and fall of the river, which appeared to them to take place under supernatural auspices.

The mythic story of the Nile was found inscribed on a rock on the island of Sahal in 1890. It tells of the cavern of Querti, shaped like two breasts, from which arose the sacred flood which blessed the land with fruitfulness. Thence all good things were bestowed upon Egypt—"bread, meats, fruits and beverages". The Nile, in that phase of its flooding when it becomes red with soil, was the blood of Osiris, the rich heart-stream which quickened the banks of the river into fruitfulness, for, to the Egyptians, blood was synonymous with life.

The Grail was pre-eminently a vessel bearing a magical blood-supply from which all rich and plenteous things emanated. It was associated with food and prosperity and each of those who beheld it had meat and drink according to his desire. "Every knight," says the "Queste Saint Graal", "had such meats and drinks as he best loved in this world." It is a "rich" as well as a "holy" Grail. Indeed, the word "Grail" implies "dish" and nothing more.

There is plenty of evidence that the personages associated with the Grail legend are connected with both Osirian and Arthurian myth. The "Fisher King", or "Maimed King", whom Percival or Gawain discovers in a condition of dead-aliveness in the Grail Castle, is certainly Arthur in his Avallon waiting to be healed from his wounds by the speaking of the mystic word or the posing of the magic question, just as he is Osiris in his Aalu. The name "Fisher", or "Rich Fisher", given him in romance, is significant of his association with the symbolism of life. Osiris, in his character of the Nile, was "The Lord of Fish", and, as both Miss Weston and the late Professor Rhys declare, the whole Grail story is redolent not only of a very early nature-myth but of initiation into the mysteries of a highly elaborated nature-cult such as the worship of Osiris, in its more lofty associations, assuredly was.

I am thus of the opinion that the Grail story and many other similar cycles had their origin in a belief associated with the River Nile—a source, let us remember, which, in the geographical sense, was enshrouded in the veils of mystery until less than a generation ago. Not a few of the sources of British rivers are still known as "cauldrons", as are the sources of many other streams elsewhere, and that the expression was reminiscent of the notion of a bowl of plenty seems natural enough.

Miss Jessie Weston believed the British myth to be a memory of the rites of Adonis, the Syrian god who annually descended into Hades, and she saw in the Grail a magical food-vessel employed in his mysteries—"the central dish of a ritual feast". But Adonis is obviously a later "version" or surrogate of Osiris, a personification of the Syrian river of that name which rose out of his grave at the sacred spring of Aphaca, its sanguinary hue due to discoloration by red mud, which was regarded as his blood. His myth is substantially the same as that of Osiris. Such a fount, source or cauldron, was also known to ancient Arthurian myth as situated in "Caer Sidi", whose sacred well was "sweeter in drink than white wine". A similar cauldron or source was discovered by Arthur himself at Caer Pedryvan and, according to Sir John Rhys, it "served as a prototype of the far more famous Grail".

It would thus seem that almost the entire "machinery" of the Osirian mystery was at some distant period conveyed to British soil, and when it is added that Arthur, like Osiris, was, in one of his aspects, a patron of agriculture and tillage of the ground, little seems lacking to render the parallel complete and thus to connect it with the tradition of the divine king. Proofs both numerous and cogent appear to support it, and the further identification of several of the place-names in the Grail story with actual localities in Egypt goes far to confirm a recognition of the ancient association.

Let me now summarize as briefly as possible those other circumstances which appear to support the conclusion that the faith of Druidism had Eastern associations. In selecting the material I will adhere only to such proofs as present an aspect of authenticity and probability. Resemblances between Druidism and the religion of the Brahmins, the Persians, the Phoenicians and the cult of the Curetes of Greece have been stressed by numerous writers, ancient and modern, but as undoubted likenesses exist between all religious systems it becomes essential in dealing with such a problem as that before us to concentrate upon those which reveal more than a general similarity in their rites and structure.

One enlightening circumstance is revealed. Pausanius states that the Galatae, a Celtic people who had settled in Pessinus in Anatolia, adopted the local cult of the god Attis.[17] This god was certainly a fertility deity whose rites represented the decay and rejuvenation of vegetation and that his cult was merely a Phrygian reflection of that of Osiris appears as more than probable. It seems to me, then, that the Celts of Galatia, in accepting his worship, had taken much the same course as their brethren in Gaul and Britain.

That Neo-Platonic mysticism reached Britain and Ireland in the later Roman decades cannot be questioned, that it carried with it the entire myth of Osiris in the bowdlerized version characteristic of it and that it linked up with native myths and beliefs must be granted. The Britain of the second, third and fourth centuries was a theatre of rival cults, as was Rome herself at that period. Among these was Mithraism, and that this particular system succeeded in establishing itself both in Gaul and Britain is among the manifest things. The "Manichaeism" which Gottefrid of Viterbo attributes to Ambrosius is explained by Poste as Mithraism. We have already seen that the Gaulish Arch-Druid Chyndonax, in his burial inscription, placed his ashes under the protection of the god Mithras. Mithraism was, to describe it summarily, a cult adapted from the ancient worship of the Persian sun-god, modified by Greek influence. In at least one British sculpture, discovered in London, near Ludgate Hill, Mithras is depicted as slaying a bull, a rite which was regarded as renewing the strength of nature and of mankind through the animal's blood. Other such sculptures have been discovered at York and Housesteads, and we recall the importance of the bull in British rite.

That Mithraism powerfully influenced the Neo-Druidic or Arthurian cult there is considerable proof. That it was among those influences which in Britain made for the later complete acceptance of the Christian faith is certain. To some extent it mimicked the Christian faith when this came to be accepted by the Roman emperors and thus protected itself against persecution and extinction. The Roman Emperor Julian, known as "the Apostate" (fl. 331–363), particularly affected it, and in his day it possessed numerous apostles and converts both in Gaul and Britain. The Roman poet Ausonius, who sang the praises of the Gaulish scholars of Bayeux, and dwelt upon their descent from the Druidical worshippers of the god Beli, associates these in his verses with the Appolinarian mystics (a Christian schism), and fairly numerous allusions to ideas obviously Mithraic appear in the Welsh Triads and poems, which seem to enshrine memories of this cultus in Britain. As we have seen, a Welsh bard of the fifteenth century distinguished between "the bards of Hu" and those of Christ. Indeed, there was little in Druidism with its fire-worship and bull-sacrifice which might not be found also in Mithraic doctrine. It appears to me as highly probable that the remaining Bards of Britain in the fifth century, possessing, as they did, a fragmentary tradition of Druidic dogma, combined this with acceptances from a rather contorted species of Mithraism, and I have formed the opinion that this amalgamation is largely represented in the revived cultus of Arthur, which became the hope of that religious knighthood which sought to liberate the southern portion of Britain from the onsets of the Saxon and the Pict. Indeed, the myth appears to be Osirian, the ritual Mithraic.

Gildas seems to allude to the existence of pagan rites in Britain when he attacks the Cambrian prince, Cuneglasse, alluding to him, as he does, as "the guider of the chariot which is the receptacle of the bear".[18] Again and again he fulminates against the pagan condition of the several British kingdoms in the sixth century. Is it possible to arrive at any conclusion concerning the mysteries of the Arthurian cult, to reveal its circumstances and their significance? In treating of such a matter it is useless to seek aid from modern sources or the fantastic theories of those who are determined to read into tradition such notions as they desire to support. We must look for trustworthy evidence alone.

In the first instance, I think that the poem entitled "The Spoils of Annwn", ascribed to Taliesin, may reasonably be regarded as a myth which, as translated by Sir John Rhys, narrates the deeds of an expedition of a company of gods or divine heroes into a supernatural sphere with the intention of removing a magical cauldron the properties of which would confer arcane powers of some kind upon the raiders. It is not only symptomatic of the presence of an Arthurian cultus in Britain, but, whether its terms are presently translatable in an adequate manner or not, it is possible to glean from it its main significance. And it is obvious enough that it cannot be a thing of chicanery. The first verse refers to Annwn and to "the prison of Gwair in Caer Sidi". It tells us that after his experience in this prison, Gwair, or Gweir, who has been identified as the magician-god Gwydion, remained for ever afterwards a Bard or poet, which can only imply that during this process he received inspiration, or underwent some initiatory experience. The second stanza describes the cauldron of inspiration itself. The third appears to have reference to the island of the "quick" or "strong" door, Caer Pedryvan. In the fifth, "Taliesin" appears to denounce the ignorance of the uninitiated multitude—"They know not the day of the Ruler, nor the Speckled Ox with the strong halter." Only seven of the expedition returned.

In another poem, "The Chair of Taliesin", the bard speaks of the god Dovydd, "in behalf of the assembly of the associates qualified to treat of mysteries", and alludes to the cauldron of inspiration and its ingredients—to an offering of wheat and honey, incense, myrrh and aloes, "the precious silver", the ruddy gem, the berries, cresses and vervain. All these are certainly magical ingredients, and a few of them can be identified as Druidical elements—"the precious silver" as the fluxwort, "the ruddy gem" as the hedge-berry, known in Wales as the "Borues y Gwion", the cresses as "Taliesin's cresses", or the *Fabaria*; and the essentially Druidical plant Vervain, which was gathered at the rising of the Dog-star. The poem also alludes to a bath for the immersion of the neophyte and to the selago plant, which was gathered to the accompaniment of an intricate rite. For further details concerning this arcane poem I must ask the reader to refer to my book *The Mysteries of Britain*.[19]

In a poem quoted in *The Myvyrian Archaiology* we encounter a dialogue between Arthur and Kai, who, approaching the portal of a sanctuary, engage in a mystic conversation with its guardian. This is most obviously a passage dealing with the subject of initiation. The guardian recognizes Arthur as a personage of importance, and tells him that he may not enter the shrine unless he is ready to preserve it. Kai announces his zeal to do so at all costs, and the hierophant narrates the manner in which other of his servants have maintained the institution by arcane works. "Their Lord," he says, "preserved them and I rendered them complete." The rest of this obscure dialogue refers to the adventures of Arthur and Kai after their initiation. The text, too, alludes to three assistant ministers, each of whom appears to have impersonated a different god in the course of the rite which followed.

In the Greek mysteries, at one point, a herald summoned the initiates to embark upon the sea. In a Welsh poem attributed to Gwydno, the novice appears to follow the same course, and is assured by the hierophant that "to the brave, the ascending stones of the Bards will prove the harbour of life". He adds that only the unworthy risk the fate of being drowned. "The conduct of the water will declare thy merit." The casting away of Taliesin by Ceridwen in a coracle also appears to have reference to such a rite. The Gwydno alluded to above was, it is thought, the husband of Ceridwen, and probably the hierophant of her mysteries, and he also appears to have been connected with that group of horned gods of which I have spoken. That the mysteries of Ceridwen were closely associated with the Arthurian cult appears to me as highly probable. For this Gwyddno was said to be the father of Eidiol, or

Ambrosius, in a mystical sense, and if the association is a slight one, it may indicate still another connection of the great Romano-British hero Ambrosius with the mysteries of an ancient cultus.

The poem known as "The Dialogue of Arthur and Eliwlod" also appears to contain mystical allusions to a cultus, but, as translated by Herbert, its terms are so obscure as to make it plain that the rendering is from an unskilful hand. Here Eliwlod evidently assumes the aspect of an eagle. Arthur evidently enquires of the mystical bird what things he must abstain from doing. The eagle answers him in a spirit of Christian enlightenment, assuring him that only the Redeemer can avail him in his difficulties, and warning him against treason and to seek for repentance. The poem is indeed of the same species as that in which an ancient scribe warns the enchanter Merlin to forgo his Druidism and turn to the true God. That it is the mythological Arthur to whom the eagle speaks is made plain by the words in which the bird addresses him: "With thy host thou wert a complete huntsman," and again as "Arthur, swiftly-moving lamp," which can only have reference to his known form of the Wild Huntsman and to his solar status. The whole endeavour appears to be that of bringing a pagan deity into the Christian fold. Herbert thought that the poem dealt with Arthur in his wounded state after the battle of Camlan. He is here "the slain Arthur in his enchanted Ynys Avallon, the dead-alive Adonis of the Mysteries". By the Neo-Platonists, persons in this living-dead state were called *Biothanati*, those who supported life in death. Eliwlod, who assumes the shape of an eagle, is Arthur's nephew, son of his brother Madawg ap Uther. These more recondite personages are seldom, if ever, alluded to by students of Arthurian myth, and until we know a little more concerning them and their relationships with the hero-god we cannot expect to make much progress in the great and patriotic task of unveiling the more arcane circumstances of British mythology. A whole galaxy of talent toils vigorously in the vineyards of legendary Egypt, in those of Buddha or in the lore of the Classic lands of Mediterranean, but few are the workers in the hidden vales of ancient Britain, that most magical of all countries. To the man or woman whose eyes are dimmed by Oriental glamour nothing marvellous can come out of this our island. The wondrous spirit of ancient Britain haunts our immediate lanes, our very gardens, our hills, our rivers; it is a thing familiar, common as the soil, therefore unworthy of notice. Perhaps we are the only people who have known so glorious a present who have so ignorantly neglected an equally glorious past. We are indeed "the multitude who know not the Speckled Ox", and whose lack of enlightenment drew upon them the noble indignation of the instructed Bard.

Now we are already aware that Llew took the form of an eagle when in his dead-alive state, and after being wounded by his wife's paramour, as the *mabinogi* of "Math, son of Mathonwy" tells us. Like that eagle, the spirit of Eliwlod sits on the summit of a sacred oak tree. If we are to judge from these two instances, then, we may be justified in regarding this eagle-shape as indicative of a phase of psychic existence between life and death. This is implied by Herbert, and I think with reason. The poem, he believed, indicated that the sun of the mysteries should be superseded by a greater sun, that of the Christian Saviour. This process, he was of opinion, had reference to a Manichæan doctrine, but surely it is nothing more nor less than a function of the old Celtic dogma that sun-god emanated from sun-god, a belief which we have found to be almost constant in Irish Celtic creed.[20] In a later work Herbert advanced the theory that the semi-pagan Bards of Britain paid a more or less discreet reverence to the Christian faith, and rejected the sanguinary

rites of Beli, probably because they realized the great popular acceptance of
the novel dispensation, although they still continued to describe themselves
as the Bards of Beli.[21]

Certain mystical birds and animals appear to have been associated with
the Arthurian cultus. Predominant among these was the raven or crow,
to which I have already alluded as one of the forms of Arthur. It is noticeable
that this species of bird, the predacious, is very closely connected with the
figures of the Arthurian myth. Arthur himself is spoken of in folk-lore as
having assumed the shape of a raven or crow; Bran is the raven *par excellence*;
Ceridwen had a son whose name was Morvran, or "Sea-Raven"; the name of
Arthur's nephew, Gwalchmai, means "Falcon"; Morgan, his sister, may
possibly be connected mythically with the Irish Morrigan, the crow-goddess,
the *babdh*. We have seen that Llew and Eliwlod took eagle-shape. The
bards are occasionally styled "Ravens" and their discourse "the motley jargon
of the raven". The raven is a bird characteristic of the cultus of Mithra, and
its ministers were called Coraces and Hierocoraces, that is "Ravens" and
"Sacred Ravens". The bird is invariably depicted on those stelae of Mithra
which depict him as slaughtering the bull. As we have seen, "Raven-knowledge"
or wisdom constituted a special lore of itself in the Highlands, and in Ireland.
But the crow or raven is sufficiently well established in the mythology of Celtic
Ireland to justify its acceptance as a British-Celtic form. Indeed, I have
formed the opinion that much of our ancient myth was originally resolved
from a cultus in which the more primitive shapes of the gods were either
imagined as bird-like, and as birds of a specific class, the *Raptores*, or that this
form of them was regarded as one of their disguises. And as most of my
readers will be aware, the gods of practically every mythology were addicted
to taking avian form on occasion. It would appear, however, that in the case
of British myth the bird-shape of the gods came to have a special arcane
significance, as the continual use of verbiage revealing this in the ancient
Celtic poems and sagas seems to make clear.

The pig or sow also seems to have had an occult significance in bardic
lore. The bardic initiates were frequently addressed or known as "pigs"; a
great black sow was thought to chase the participants at the rite of *Bealltainn*
down the hill on which the holy fire burned and to claim the last of them
as a victim. The Gauls had a god known as Moccus, "the Pig", and the animal
was regarded as symbolic of the powers of fertility. Ceridwen is also associated
with the pig as an emblem of fertility. The theft of magical swine from Annwn
is a feature of one of the most outstanding of Welsh legends. Herbert has a
lengthy dissertation on the connection of swine with the mysticism of the
Neo-Druidic cult.[22] Of the association of the bull and cow with this I need
say no more than I have already done. But the horse is also an arcane animal
in Neo-Druidic lore, as continual allusion to it in the Welsh poems makes
clear. There was a mare-goddess in Gaul, known as Epona, who presided over
the breeding of steeds, and horses were sacrificed by both Continental and
insular Celts. The appearance of the horse so very frequently on ancient
British coins is eloquent of its mythical popularity among our ancestors. At
least one mythological figure in British lore, March, son of Meirchion, that is
"Horse, son of Horses", is known, who is more familiar to Arthurian legend
as King Mark of Cornwall, the husband of Iseult. Beli had a sacred horse.
The horse was a notable symbol of the Gnostic brotherhood. The effigy of the
white horse is carved gigantically on the hills of Bratton and Uffington. In
all likelihood these represent the sun in his swiftness and luminosity. Here
again we have evidence of a very ancient British association, and it would seem

that immigrant ideas from Neo-Platonic sources may have fused with native conceptions.

The mystical nature of the Round Table now falls to be considered. That this institution represents a sodality of warriors banded together for a special purpose can scarcely be questioned. The author of the *Merlin*, which continues the legend of Joseph of Arimathea, states that it was founded by Uther on the advice of Merlin, and not by Arthur. Of course he models it on the type of a Grail Table mentioned in Chretien's *Joseph of Arimathea*. If irritation arising from priestly meddling be excused, one must denounce this bowdlerizing as a mere ecclesiastical invention. The pale imprint of the monkish hand is indeed found upon every page of early romance, subduing it to a level of pious allegory and robbing it of its natural *joie de vivre* and its more primitive pagan meaning. There is a vacant seat at the Round Table, to be filled only by the champion who achieves the Grail adventure. Indeed, the Table is said in Robert de Borron's poem "Joseph of Arimathea" to have been especially founded by Joseph, a manifest wrenching of the original myth. How frequently the student of folk-lore deplores the enormous loss and damage to tradition by the blundering and ignorant interference of priestly scribes, who sought to turn everything to the advantage of their faith. With little more intelligence, Herbert seems to have conceived the Round Table as "a similitude of the world", as though in the later Middle Ages the rotundity of the globe was a recognized fact! In one of the Norman-French romances, however, Merlin so describes it. In the centre of it, he tells us, was the Seat Perilous, representing "the mundane station of the sun", to sit in which was the highest honour a knight could aspire to. Those who dared to do so unworthily met with disaster of one kind or another. In the *Conte du Graal* we are told how Perceval came to Arthur's Court at Carlion, and accomplished the adventure of the Perilous Seat "which a fairy had sent to Arthur". Only the destined finder of the Grail might sit in it. Six knights who had essayed to do so had been swallowed up in the earth. They reappeared when Perceval at last completed the Grail adventure. Perceval seats himself in the Siege Perilous, the earth gives forth a *brait*, and breaks in all directions round the seat, which, however, remains *in situ*. From the gulf which environs it the six knights who had disappeared arise unharmed. A monkish scribe has been careful to add that during their sojourn in the Underworld they beheld the torments of sinners![23]

A little knowledge of folk-lore would, I believe, have saved the commentators of this passage a good deal of trouble in their efforts to explain it. The Seat Perilous reveals some of the properties of those stones or megaliths so commonly encountered in Celtic legend. It was the gift, or shrine, of a fairy, in which it equates with the Lia Fail and numerous other standing stones. It was one of twelve seats, and that is, indeed, the almost constant number of megaliths in a stone circle. Such stones are occasionally known as "the Knights", as in the case of the Rollright Stones in Oxfordshire, which are thought by the country folk to contain or ensoul the spirits of dead warriors. These knights whispered to one another, and, at seasons, actually "danced" or "walked"! In all likelihood the idea derives from the general notion of a megalithic circle, associated with the tradition of twelve gods or heroes, the rude and primitive pantheon of the tribal deified warriors. When stripped of the pious nonsense with which it has been festooned by priestly scribes, we behold it in its true form as a legend associated with the familiar stone circle, and thus one of extraordinary antiquity, turned to the uses of a mediaeval Christianity, itself fulfilled of legend, which was actuated by an overmastering desire to construe every belief associated with paganism according to its own tenets.

Arthur revealed his heirship to the crown of Britain by the feat of drawing a certain sword from a block of stone. Once again this act associates him with the ancient megalithic tradition. In the *Mabinogion* story of "Peredur the son of Evrawc", the hero, who is Perceval in his older British form, meets with a black warrior who arises from a cromlech, or standing stone. He is mounted on a bony horse and clad in rusty armour, and arises to encounter Peredur from beneath the cromlech. He is, of course, the dead hero who lies buried underneath it. They fight, and when Peredur dismounts, the black knight vanishes. This provides us with some idea of the kind of warrior usually connected in tradition with such standing stones, and in popular ballad we encounter several such warriors.

Perhaps the knighthood of the Arthurian cultus adopted the idea dormant in the ancient tradition, beholding in it something essentially native and racy of the soil. On the other hand, it is by no means impossible, I think, that the tradition, which must have been a popular and widespread one in Britain, became fused in the national imagination with the legend of the Deliverers of Britain at a later period. It can scarcely be accounted for in any other way, I believe, unless by the acceptance of one or other of these hypotheses. It seems not improbable that in the cult of Arthur the leaders assumed the names of ancient British gods.

As revealing the manner in which extraneous pagan ideas succeeded in establishing themselves in Roman Britain, I should perhaps make a passing allusion to the circumstances which prevailed in Roman York. Established as the Roman station of Eboracum in the year A.D. 71, at one time in its history it was garrisoned by the Sixth Legion, under the Legate Claudius Hieronymianus, who is believed to have been an Egyptian. This captain erected a temple to the Egyptian god Serapis, a form of Osiris in his phase of the sacred bull Apis, at the site now occupied by Tanner Row. An inscription exists commemorating this fane, while another records the erection of an altar to Serapis in his Roman form of Jupiter-Serapis, at Appleby in Westmorland. A Mithraic sculpture has also been discovered at York, and, as I have said, one was found at London, where there was also a temple of Isis, while an altar to the Great Syrian Mother has been unearthed at Carvoran. The Roman Emperor Severus visited York in the year 208, and is known to have been an ardent devotee of Serapis. He died at York in 211, and was cremated there. The altar to Mithra was unearthed in Micklegate Hill, and the sculpture it contained displayed the usual Mithraic allegory of the sacrifice of a bull. The remains of the Roman *Sacellum*, or sacred shrine devoted to the worship of the Emperor, were found to occupy a line running through the crypt of York Minster.[24]

It is thus fully apparent that Oriental cults had already established themselves in several parts of Britain, and those the most important from a political point of view, by the period of the early third century, at a time when Christianity was scarcely known in the island. That their influence and propaganda would be readily forgotten is incredible. On the appearance of a military-religious body, at some time in the fifth century, and pledged to the deliverance of Britain from Saxon invasion, it seems not unreasonable to believe that such influences, in their allegorical aspects, would naturally form a part of the established creed and principle of that knighthood and would as naturally mingle with the older and revived British mythology which formed the basis of its general faith.

In the above pages I have endeavoured in a temperate and restrained manner to render more clear the outlines of what I believe to have been the origin and circumstances of a cultus devoted to the manumission of the British realm by a society of military heroes who adopted the worship of an ancient British god as the central figure of their patriotic venture. That this cultus partook of much that was fashionably mystical at the period, the fifth century, is, I think, fairly manifest. I fully realize that before the idea which I have set forth can attain the rank of a genuine hypothesis many years of intense research must naturally elapse. But I also feel that such evidence as I have been enabled to present in respect of it not only justifies further examination, but that on its own merits it strongly suggests, if it does not furnish in entirety, a rational explanation of the mystery which has for so long surrounded the Arthurian problem. If I have erred in so thinking, if facts can be adduced which utterly confound the theory I have sought to build up during many years of almost continuous devotion to Arthurian studies, I will be among the first to admit failure. Presently, however, although I may have blundered sadly in many respects, and may have tendered as evidence much that appears untenable, I remain convinced of the soundness of the main contention here set down.

CHAPTER XIII

THE MYSTERY OF THE GRAIL

ASSOCIATED with the Arthurian body of romance is the tradition of the Holy Grail, the legendary dish or vessel in which the Saviour is said to have celebrated the Last Supper with His apostles. Early British Christian opinion held that the sacred receptacle was conveyed to this island, and in mediaeval literature the discovery of its hidden repository was regarded as the chief quest of the knights of Arthur's Round Table. According to folk-lore theory, however, the belief in this vessel was derived from the assumed existence of the magical cauldron of a Celtic fertility cult. A great and complex literature, both narrative and expository, has gathered round the legend of the Grail. This, in its first phase, would appear to have been developed from British lays or songs founded on Celtic traditions, and orally transmitted, which at a later time were adopted as subject-matter by French poets, and brought into consonance and harmony with the general outlook of Arthurian saga.

The word "Grail" may have been derived from the Low Latin *gradale*, meaning a flat dish, or perhaps its more direct origin is to be traced in the term *San Greal*, that is "Holy Dish". Its etymology, says Skeat, "was very early falsified by an intentional change from *San Greal* (Holy Dish) to *Sang Real*, that is 'Royal Blood', perversely taken to mean 'Real Blood'." He adds that "the word was probably corrupted in various ways from the Low Latin *cratella*, a small bowl, the diminutive of *crater*, a bowl".[1]

An outline of the Christian legend of the Holy Grail as it was altered from the original pagan form into a narrative consonant with Christian belief may perhaps be most profitably extracted from that version of the story known

as the *Grand St. Graal*, written in England about the beginning of the
thirteenth century. Here I shall adhere to its main terms, and more particularly those which refer to its British associations. Its anonymous author,
manuscript copies of whose work are to be found in the British Museum and at
Cambridge, describes the manner in which the Grail vessel was brought to
Britain. One Joseph of Arimathea, it is said, was present at the crucifixion
of our Lord, and greatly desired to possess a memento of Him. He repaired
to the house where the Last Supper had been held and carried away the dish
out of which the Christ had eaten. This Joseph was a knight of Pontius Pilate
and begged the body of the Redeemer from that Roman Governor in order
to give it suitable burial. The boon was granted and Joseph placed the body
in a sepulchre, collecting the blood which still flowed from it in the aforesaid
dish, afterwards to be known as the San Greal. The Jews, on learning of this
honourable burial, were indignant and cast Joseph into prison, where, however, he was miraculously sustained in life by the holy vessel. Christ Himself
appeared to Joseph and assured him that he would ultimately be delivered
and would carry His gospel to foreign lands. Forty years passed before his
manumission from prison, when, with seventy-five followers, Joseph set out
on his journey, bearing the sacred dish in a wooden ark. When this receptacle
was opened by Josephes, the son of Joseph, he beheld the drama of the
crucifixion enacted therein. He also found within it several sacred symbols,
among them a rich and beautiful head. Joseph and his followers, we are then
told, received the sacrament from the ark in the form of a child. In passing
through various kingdoms countless adventures befell the band, with whom
a heathen king, Seraphe, now converted, joined his fortunes under his new
baptismal name of Nasciens. A marvellous lance which dripped blood was
one of the more important contents of the ark, and concerning it great things
were prophesied. The company took ship and arrived in Britain, which at that
time languished in the darkest paganism. Some of the heathen Britons were
baptized, but those who refused conversion were destroyed by a flood. Above
their bodies a tower was raised, the "Tower of Marvels", over which, it was
prophesied, a king named Arthur should reign. In connection with this tower
a series of adventures was to ensue until the last descendant of Nasciens
should end them.

Joseph's wife bore a son, whose name was Galahad. Strife with the
heathen natives arose in Britain and Joseph's friend, Mordrains, arrived in the
island to reinforce him. He overcame the pagans, but was sorely wounded.
Mordrains was later struck with blindness through approaching too closely
to the Holy Grail, and retired to a hermitage. We now hear of Brons, Joseph's
kinsman, as being in his company. The Grail Table was then constituted
and a seat was left vacant for the person who should conclude these adventures. Joseph's son, Josephes, was made keeper of the Grail. When in course
of time Josephes died, the Grail found a resting-place in the "Terre Foraine",
and a long line of keepers followed Josephes, all of whom were individually
known as "the Fisher King".

A similar account is given in Robert de Borron's poem *Joseph of
Arimathea*, which connects the story with that of Merlin to be found in
the later poem of that name. In this version the seat at the Grail table is
left vacant until a son is born to Brons, Joseph's brother-in-law, when the
child would occupy the same. The further legends of the Grail are recounted
in *The Queste del Graal* (which, perhaps, links up more accurately with the
preceding matter than any other version), and in *The Conte del Graal*, the
Didot *Perceval*, *Perceval le Gallois* and various German versions, all of which

detail at great length the adventures of Perceval, Galahad and the other heroes who go in quest of the holy vessel. As the reader will probably have noticed or suspected, the early Christian material respecting the Grail is a compound of early Christian mysticism (and a very lowly type of it at that), Neo-Platonism, and pure thaumaturgy. A Celtic element makes its appearance in the "rich head", found in the Grail ark, which is reminiscent of the head of the god Bran, usually described as occupying a sacred dish.

Other legends tell how Joseph of Arimathea and his followers came by way of Wales from the South of France and settled in Glastonbury, where they built a church of wattles and taught the people the true faith. Alfred Nutt was of opinion that the Glastonbury story was associated with a local tradition of the worship of the Celtic god Bran and his sacred head. "At some time in the course of the twelfth century," he says, "the old Christian site of Glastonbury took, as it were, the place of the Celtic Paradise" (Avallon).[2] Mr. H. L. D. Ward considered the localization a late one, and that no authority existed for it of an older date than the romances. But, as Nutt adds: "it seems far more likely that the transformation was effected in virtue of some local tradition than wholly through the medium of foreign romances," a statement which most authorities would endorse. In any case, the locality of Glastonbury was formerly known as *Ynys Witryn*, that is "the Island of Glass", a name of the Celtic Otherworld, and that the monks of Glastonbury made every endeavour to replace this title by the modern name is clear enough, although it is only a disguised version of the Celtic appellation. Again, British personal names make their appearance in Grail story. Pelles, one of the keepers of the Grail, is merely a Normanized form of Pwyll; Pellam, his son, seems to be Pryderi; Gwynn, son of Nudd, found his equivalent as "Sir Gwuinas" in later Grail story, while "Sir Melias" seems to be the Cornish Melwas. Evalach, one of the early converts of Grail legend, is almost certainly Avallach, the ruler of the Celtic Otherworld of Avallon, while Perceval is nothing but the Welsh Peredur, and, lastly, Brons may be equated with the god Bran himself.[3]

The Grail legend has been transmitted in several forms. The most celebrated of these, in a literary sense, is known as the *Conte del Graal*, and was the work of four poets in succession: Chrestien de Troyes, Gautier de Doulens, Manessier, and Gerbert. It may be said generally that its commencement dates from the last quarter of the twelfth century. The romance of *Joseph of Arimathea*, with its continuation, *Merlin*, is also in verse, and was composed by Robert de Borron. *Perceval* is a prose romance which narrates the adventures of that knight from his birth. The *Queste del Saint Graal* is also in prose, as are the *Grand Saint Graal* and *Perceval le Gallois*. In the Welsh tongue we find one of the *mabinogi* under the title of "Peredur the son of Evrawc" in the *Red Book of Hergest*, dealing with the quest for the Grail, and several German versions of the story have survived, among them the *Parzival* of Wolfram von Eschenbach, and the *Diu Krone* of Heinrich von dem Türlin. In old English we have the *Sir Perceval of Galles*, which dates from the early fifteenth century, and an adaptation of the *Grand Saint Graal* by Henry Lovelich of about the time of Henry the Sixth. It is almost unnecessary to say that the Grail legend has been the subject of more modern works from the time of Malory to that of Tennyson and Swinburne, but these do not come within the scope of this book.

The Grail legend has been divided by Alfred Nutt into two distinct portions: that which deals with its origins and wanderings, and that which treats of the adventures of those knights who went in quest of the holy vessel. In nearly all of the romances both themes are alluded to. The first portion is associated with the legends of Christian provenance which I have already outlined. As regards the second class, the main incident is the hero's quest for the Grail and his visit to the castle of a sick or maimed king, where he sees the Grail and its associated relics. He neglects to ask the meaning of what he sees, and thus brings misfortune upon himself and upon the inmates of the castle. On a second visit, however, he makes good the omission and, by putting the question, frees the sick king from the state of enchantment in which he languishes, or, in some versions, wins the Grail kingship as the reward of his constancy. The several romances differ in some respects as regards their plots and circumstances, but, on the whole, it is plain that all are inspired by one tradition, so far as the method and rationale of the quest is concerned.

If we carefully examine the elements of the romances proper, as apart from the Christian tradition which interpenetrates them, we shall find that these issue almost entirely from Celtic pagan sources. In short, they display a series of themes and ideas reflexive of Celtic pagan factors. A good deal of nonsense has been written concerning the profundity of the Christian mysticism which inspires the Grail legend, and there can be little doubt that Tennyson, Richard Wagner and others are responsible for much of the pious glamour which hangs about it. Stripped of its colours of sanctity, the Grail legend appears, in very truth, as an aggregation of Celtic mythic elements which were gradually built up into a semi-coherent whole and were seized upon by later Christian propagandist effort as suitable for its purposes. The pious folk who transformed the Grail legend into a Christian tradition caparisoned it with the trappings of Christian myth at a period when that was inspired by the most grovelling and absurd superstitions—beliefs so basely ignorant that they could be credited, then or today, only by ritualists of the most retrograde type.

I have mentioned that the two principal versions of the Christian Grail legend resemble each other in many particulars. The one recounts the circumstances of the conversion of Britain by Joseph of Arimathea, the other its enlightenment by Brons, who is succeeded as the guardian of the holy vessel by his progeny. Brons at once suggests Bran, and that recension of the story which especially "features" him is obviously the more native and older of the twain. Bran, as a Celtic deity, is the owner of a mystic dish, which later acts as a receptacle for his severed head. He also possesses a magical cauldron capable of restoring the dead to life. He is the god of the Celtic Otherworld, so far as its British associations are concerned, and Welsh tradition speaks of him as the chief figure in a legend of conversion, from which he gained the title of "Bran the Blessed", while the epithet is also conferred upon him in the *mabinogi* of "Branwen, Daughter of Llyr", the composition of which may be referred to the tenth century. Moreover, we find mention in the Hengwrt MS. of *Blessed Bran's Head*. These circumstances reveal the gradual development of the Christian saint from the pagan god. On the other hand, we do not find the Christian legend of Joseph in circulation until the latter half of the twelfth century—that is precisely at the period when the romances were beginning to take shape. There seems, however, to have been current in Britain a much older legend of Joseph and his doings, and at a time, the eighth century, when it was practically unknown on the Continent. But all this, in my view, does not, and cannot, militate against the theory of the original Celtic genesis of the Grail history, more particularly as the rival version associated with Bran or Brons reveals this Celtic origin in numerous particulars. In any case, the evidence and argument for the priority of the earlier Joseph legend are much too slight to permit of its successful adoption as the original source of the Grail story and the consequent relinquishment of the tradition associated with Brons or Bran.

Apart altogether from its inherent interest, the entire body of romance associated with the Grail story is of but secondary importance to the student of Celtic tradition, containing as it does only the broken lights of that tradition, odds and ends of Celtic material presented in a French or Norman-French form, distorted and transformed, at times almost past recognition. Indeed, so far as the Grail of chivalric romance is concerned, we seem to have little to do with it here unless to disentangle from its fantastic material those incidents and passages which appear to be associated with genuine Celtic tradition. This can only be effected with difficulty, and, if a few notable instances be excepted, the study of the Grail romances has not brought about that degree of enlightenment which might have been expected from the very great amount of research lavished upon it.

At the commencement of the *Conte du Graal* we encounter an incident which is generally held not to be the work of Chrestien de Troyes, the author of the main body of that poem. It refers to the land of Logres, the eastern portion of ancient England, and to a bevy of "damsels" who dwelt in springs, or wells, who hospitably entertained travellers with provisions. Amangons, the king of that country, did wrong to one of these nymphs, and bore away her golden cup, in consequence of which these supernatural maidens withdrew themselves from human association. Evil results followed. The springs dried up, the grass withered, the land became waste, and the Court of the "Rich Fisher", a mystical centre which emanated plenty, might no more be found. The passage can allude to nothing else than that species of royal delinquency which was thought to spell ruin for a community—the failure of the divine king to recognize and preserve his personal sanctity and the dearth which followed upon his misdeed. He had offended the genii of fertility and as a punishment his possessions were visited by famine. The Knights of the Round Table, learning of the outrage, set forth to protect the damsels, for the men of King Amangons had followed his base example. The knights resolved to seek the Court of the Rich Fisher, who is described as a magician of might. After a quest had been made, the land of the Fisher King was discovered by Gauvain, or Gawain, and Perceval, but the latter failed to enquire specifically the significance of the marvels he beheld while he sojourned there, and for that reason was unable to free the Fisher King from the enchantments which held him apart from mankind.

These latter details are more clearly set forth in the *Queste del Graal*. Galahad, Perceval and Bors come to Castle Corbenic, the seat of the Grail, definitely associated with Celtic legend. Galahad must part from his companions ere he undergoes the Grail test. A wounded and crowned man is brought into the hall, and is followed by the spirit of Joseph of Arimathea, who is borne by angels to a table on which stands the Grail. A bleeding lance appears, the drops from which fall into the Grail vessel. Galahad is told that he must not leave the land without healing the Maimed King, who, when restored by having his legs anointed with some of the blood from the lance, takes his departure to spend the rest of his life in an abbey.

This particular account says nothing concerning the question which he who assumed the adventure of the Grail must put to the sick Fisher King, if the enchantments which surrounded him were to be completely dispelled. Perceval failed to put this question when he, in his turn, came to face the test, with disastrous results. The prime arcane question, or sesame, appears to

DRUIDIC JEWEL

Found in a barrow at Kingston, Barham Downs, near Canterbury, and representing the several circles or planes of existence

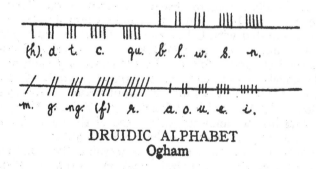

DRUIDIC ALPHABET
Ogham

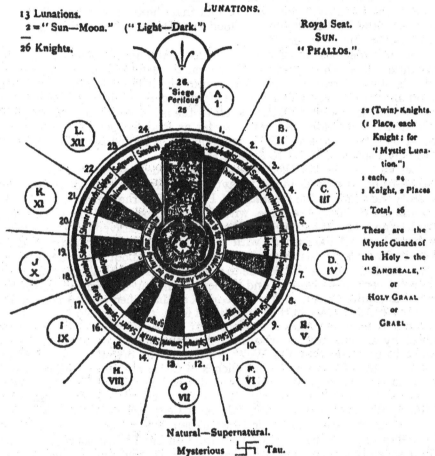

THE ROUND TABLE OF KING ARTHUR.

From the Original, preserved in the Court-House of the Castle at Winchester
"SANGREALE"— or "HOLY GRAIL."

LUNATIONS.

13 Lunations.

2 = "Sun—Moon."   ("Light—Dark.")
—
26 Knights.

Royal Seat.
SUN.
"PHALLOS."

26 "Siege Perilous" 25

22 (Twin) Knights.
(1 Place, each
Knight; for
"1 Mystic Luna-
tion.")

1 each, 24

1 Knight, 2 Places

Total, 26

These are the
Mystic Guards of
the Holy — the
"SANGREALE,"
or
HOLY GRAAL
or
GRAAL

Natural—Supernatural.

Mysterious ⌐Ⴙ Tau.

* TRADITION, that Judas Iscariot left the Table at the words of the Saviour—"What thou doest do quickly!" and had *no portion* in the Last Rite. (Refer below.)

A. I.	Saint Matthew.	G. VII.	Saint Philip.
B. II.	Saint James.	H. VIII.	Saint Libœus.
C. III.	Saint Simon.	I. IX.	Saint Andrew
D. IV.	Saint Peter.	J. X.	Saint Thomas.
E. V.	Saint James (of Alpheus).	K. XI.	Vacant.
F. VI.	Saint Bartholomew.	L. XII.	Saint John.

"After the sop, Satan entered into him.   Then said Jesus unto him, ' That thou doest, do quickly!'
Now no man at the table knew for what intent He spake this unto him.
"He" (Judas) "then having received the sop, WENT IMMEDIATELY OUT.   AND IT WAS NIGHT
S. JOHN, Chap. xiii., vers. 27, 28, 30

SEAT OF THE HOLY GRAIL AT THE ROUND TABLE

have been: "Unto whom one serveth of the Grail?" This query, it was said, would unlock the lips of the Fisher King and have permitted him to pass on to the querist certain secret words, the key to the mystery of the Grail. But on his second coming to Corbenic, Perceval does not omit this duty, with the result that he probes the hidden meaning of the mysterious syllables. Gawain, in a German version of the story, asks, but seems only to learn that he has seen the Grail, which appears to suffice him. In the *Petit Saint Graal*, the writer says that he may not tell what these words were. In Wolfram von Eschenbach's *Parzival*, again, we are told that the Grail was not a cup, but a stone, which yielded all manner of food and drink—a fact which, as we shall see, has a bearing on its origin.

In most versions the sick Fisher King is wounded through both thighs, a condition of which we have already seen the significance. Bran, wounded in the leg by an arrow, dies, or is cast into an enchanted state. His head is cut off and he remains in story as the sleeping god. In like manner his surrogate, Arthur, is wounded and borne off to the isle of Avallon in an enchanted or dead-alive condition. As much, so far as Bran is concerned, was demonstrated by Rhys long ago, his explanation was accepted by Alfred Nutt, and personally I find it difficult to dispute.[4]

Let us now discuss the evidence which would seem to show that the Grail story has it sources in Celtic myth. As Alfred Nutt made it very plain, the story-incidents in the *mabinogi* of Peredur and the romance of the *Conte du Graal* are precisely the same, with minor exceptions. This, of course, led some foreign critics to assume that the *mabinogi* was derived from the romance. We have been all too patient with foreign critics in this country and have taken it for granted that they know much more about our traditions than we do ourselves. But I should like to point out that in the *Mabinogion* version of Peredur certain expressions and similes are employed which are known to be of great antiquity among the Celtic peoples, so that when we find them appearing in the Welsh version in their traditional form, and in the old French version in such a manner as makes it obvious that the significance of them has been garbled by an alien author who did not comprehend their purport, we have a right to conclude that the Welsh version is the original and not the old French. Some of these well-worn clichés of Celtic phrase and allusion which appear in the *mabinogi* of Peredur are also to be found in Irish tales known to have descended from the eighth century—and that, I feel, clinches the matter.[5] We have here a Celtic tale on a Celtic topic, which bears on the face of it all the marks of Celtic construction, and we are asked by German scholarship to agree that it is derived from an old French source! To make such a suggestion to anyone who has been collecting and discussing Celtic folk-lore and fiction for the best part of a lifetime, and who is knowledgeable of the true spirit of Celtic saga and its idiosyncrasies, is offensive to his intelligence, and I refuse to consider further these intolerable Teutonic assumptions which would seek to reduce British tradition to the status of a re-hash of Norman-French "novelettes". To impugn the integrity of our tradition is to assault the dignity of that very source from which everything we honour most has sprung. There are wars other than that of the quick-firing gun and the bomb, and we must rebut with vigour the destructive attacks made upon our ancient literature by those who can never comprehend its indwelling spirit.

One thing is very clear. The names of deities known to British mythology and some of which have analogies with those of Irish myth, appear again and again in the French romances in a disguised form, and in the Welsh Peredur in their native orthography. And we are tacitly asked to believe that these ancient names were the inventions of French poets. For it is to such a conclusion that the entire argument of foreign invention is forced and reduced. Where, it may be asked, did the French romancers procure their knowledge of these plots and tales in the first instance? Obviously from Celtic sources. As Nutt has made abundantly clear, the Peredur story was derived from a number of older British tales dealing with the figures of British myth, and it reveals "the peculiarly weird and fantastic impress of Celtic mythic tradition". It is even positively certain that the French poets who bowdlerized the legend were totally ignorant that they were dealing with the shapes and figures of myth, which they appear to have regarded as those of early British Christian fable. To dispute this would be the final absurdity associated with a prolonged record of Continental misapprehension of British tradition.

The Grail cannot be anything else than that cauldron of abundance and inspiration so frequently alluded to in ancient Celtic literature. The Tuatha Dé Danann of Irish legend possessed four treasures: the Stone of Destiny, the sword of Lugh, his spear, and the cauldron of the god Dagda, from which no one ever went away unsatisfied. In the Irish account of the battle of Magh Rath we are told of more than one cauldron of the kind which figured in the older Irish traditions. In Welsh tale we have the analogous cauldron of Bran as described in the *mabinogi* of "Branwen", a story which can be referred in a literary sense to the eleventh or even perhaps the tenth century, but which is obviously much older. If a slain man were placed in it he was restored to life. Further, we find the cauldron of inspiration associated with the goddess Ceridwen, already alluded to. Such a cauldron is also carried away by Arthur in his descent upon Annwn. Rhys has identified this vessel with the Grail, and has revealed that the same properties were inherent in both vessels—both repel the unworthy, heal the sick and wounded and possess the quality of supernatural "uplift", giving health to the soul. That the Castle of Carbonek, or Corbenic, in French romance, where the Grail reposes, is merely the Celtic castle or fortalice of Caer Pedryvan, the seat of the cauldron of Annwn, is proved by Squire. In romance, this castle invariably lies on the other side of a river, implying that it is situated in the Otherworld, and more than one instance of such a locality has been cited by Nutt as composing the *mise en scène* of Celtic story.[6]

The name of "the Fisher King", it has been argued by German critics, associates the Grail story with the cult of Orpheus. But it is unnecessary to seek so far afield for such an analogy, for it is perfectly competent to associate that title with the ancient Celtic theme of the salmon of knowledge, which has already been discussed in these pages. In any case, it also reveals an Osirian genesis rather than a Greek.

Analogies with the Grail story are to be found in Scottish Celtic tale. The "Story of the Lay of the Great Fool", as mentioned by J. F. Campbell in his *Popular Tales of the West Highlands*, reveals striking similarities with the Grail story, more particularly with the *mabinogi* of Peredur. It tells how, like Peredur, Cumhall's son is reared in the wilderness, how he slays his father's slayer, how he captures the magic trout, the taste of which confers all knowledge, and the manner in which he wins back his father's lands. The fact that it links up with the story of Finn and the salmon of knowledge and with the *mabinogi* of Peredur renders it perfectly plain that all three derive from a common source, and that they are quite independent of the French versions.[7]

The modern legend that the Grail was actually a Christian vessel, and that it has either been discovered or awaits discovery, dies hard. When the so-called "Chalice of Antioch" was discovered in 1910 by a party of Arabs who were digging a well and who came upon a subterranean chamber believed to be a part of a great church erected at Antioch by the Emperor Constantine, it was argued that this vessel, which enclosed an inner cup, must be the Holy Grail.[8]   A wooden cup in the possession of the family of Powell, resident at Nanteos, in Wales, is said to have formerly been taken from the Abbey of Glastonbury, for its better protection, to that of Strata Florida, Cardiganshire, and is believed by many of the faithful to be the Holy Grail. It is thus that folk-lore is made. See Dunlop, *History of Fiction*, I, p. 463 ff.

That the Grail legend came to be fused with that of the divine king is, I think, beyond dispute. That the "Maimed King" is none other than Arthur, it is, I believe, reasonable to hold. The legend of Arthur asleep in some island or cavern, or beneath a mountain, awaiting the summons to return to the world of men, is a widespread one. Moreover, he is unquestionably the wounded king, who is tended by enchantresses, and in this respect he closely resembles the Grail King. Through his sin or his wounding the land had become waste and dearth, nor would it regain its prosperity until he is disenchanted. The story of Amangons provides the clue. In one myth Arthur causes seven years' sterility wherever he sets his feet, a hint that he is associated with the maimed or sinful king.[9] The circuit of evidence is plain enough.

I believe that the myth of the Grail formed part of the legend of the divine king, which, by devious paths, reached Britain at a fairly early period and that when it arrived in our island it became fused with native Celtic traditions of a similar character, such, for example, as those which deal with the "salmon of knowledge" and the Cauldron of Annwn. It is certainly part of the mythical material associated with the cultus and ritual of the divine king, nor can it be dissociated from the same.

In the previous chapter I have given my reasons for believing that the myth of Arthur was associated with the tradition of the divine king which again had its rise in the conditions anciently current in the Nile country. In the same way, the legend of the Grail seems to have had its origin in this Nilotic myth, and to have amalgamated with a British cauldron legend. The myth of the source of the Nile, which was anxiously sought at a time of famine in the island of Elephantine, just as another source was sought by Arthur at Caer Pedryvan, not only gave rise to the legend of the Grail, but was probably the source of many stories of the Fountain of Youth, the waters of which were thought to confer upon man a new lease of life. A volume might easily be filled with parallels and illustrations. In more than one version of the Grail story the land of the Fisher King is once more rendered fruitful when he revives from his trance, and in at least two versions it is stated that his return to health caused the rivers to flow again throughout the country—which seems to the writer to support his theory of an Egyptian origin for the Grail legend.

Later these conceptions came to be associated with the Christian legend of the Grail. This itself arose from beliefs already current in Britain which had for their sources the mixed conception of it arising from the fusion of Celtic and Egyptian ideas. Upon this mingled foundation the later romances in French and in English were superimposed, and these bear irrefutable evidence of the mixed "ancestry" from which they were derived. That the cultus of Arthur, itself a mingling of British and Egyptian Neo-Platonic beliefs, must have exerted a powerful influence upon Grail story appears to me as most probable, particularly when the identification of Arthur with Osiris is recalled.

That British god would indeed seem to have taken on the whole character of Osiris in the mythology of the cult in question, as nearly every portion of what we know of his myth reveals. But the more definite identification of these British and Egyptian divine forms would occupy greatly more space than can be afforded for such a discussion in a book dealing with Celtic Mysticism in its general aspects.

CHAPTER XIV

THE SECOND SIGHT

ALTHOUGH it is now known that the Second Sight is not an endowment or condition exclusively Celtic, it must be admitted that it was much more prevalent in Celtic countries than elsewhere and that its history is more prolonged and continuous among the Celtic peoples than in the case of any other race. The name "Second Sight" is in reality an inexact translation of the Gaelic term *an-da-shealladh*—that is "the two sights". The vision of the world of sense, ordinarily possessed by all, is *one* sight, while that of spirits, which is visible to certain persons only, is a *second* sight, so that such persons are spoken of as having "the two sights".[1] The Rev. J. G. Campbell, a man of great experience in Highland lore, was of opinion "that the Celtic priests had reduced the gift of seeing spectres to a system, a belief which formed part of their teaching", and that this accounts for the circumstance that the Second Sight has flourished more among the Celts than among other peoples.

The Celtic area in which the Second Sight has chiefly manifested itself is that of the Highlands of Scotland, more particularly the West Highlands and islands, but instances of its occurrence in Wales and Ireland are on record, while in Scandinavian folk-lore stories concerning it are fairly numerous. But it is by no means unknown among savage and barbarous peoples, as most anthropologists are aware.

The vision or phantasm seen is known in Highland Scotland as *taibhs* (pron. "taish") and the person who sees it as *taibhsear* (pron. "taisher"), while the gift of vision itself is known as *taibhsearachd*. Roughly speaking, the idea of Second Sight is based on the assumption that man has an astral counterpart or doppelgänger which is visible to those who have the gift of "the two sights". This phantasm, however, must be carefully distinguished from his spirit proper. Indeed, it would appear to resemble closely the Egyptian *ka*, or "double". It is this counterpart, then, which is known as the *taibhs*.

"Second Sight," says Andrew Lang, "is only a Scotch name which covers many cases called telepathy and clairvoyance by psychical students and casual or morbid hallucinations by other people. In Second Sight the percipient beholds events occurring at a distance, sees people whom he never saw with the bodily eye and who afterwards arrive in his neighbourhood; or foresees events approaching but still remote in time. The chief peculiarity of Second Sight is that the visions often, though not always, are of a *symbolical* character. A shroud is observed around the living man who is drowned; boding animals, mostly black dogs, vex the seer; funerals are witnessed before they occur and corpse-candles (some sort of light) are watched flitting above the road whereby a burial procession is to take its way."[2]

The above, though correct in statement, constitutes a remarkable instance of anthropological myopia. Out of his very considerable experience, it might have been given to Lang to realize that the symbolical nature of the visions afforded to habitual seers augurs the existence of a system of supernatural vision of great antiquity, in which the technique of vision has become, so to speak, "hieroglyphic" rather than detailed, and symbols have taken the place of more elaborate concepts. "The object," says Dalyell, "was generally represented under some dismal aspect, either in a shroud, in a condition incompatible with life, or as menaced by destruction."[3] Second Sight was, indeed, a condition of hereditary magic, in which visionaries saw, or believed they saw, prophetic pictures, which, by reason of a former (and now partly broken-down) system of familiar, frequent, and thoroughly "organized" vision, had assumed at last the character of a visual "shorthand", or symbolical typology —as, indeed, the present writer is only too dismally aware, being blessed (or afflicted) with it himself, as a hereditary legacy.

Aubrey, one of the first Englishmen to interest himself in the problem of Second Sight, lays some stress upon its symbolic character. He says that if a man is to be hanged, the seer will behold a gibbet, or a rope about his neck; if to be drowned, he will appear with water up to his throat; if he is to be beheaded, as a headless man, and so forth.[4] Such seers never behold the dead, Lord Tarbet assures us, only the fated. He adds that, so far as the time which will elapse between the vision and its sequel is concerned, they can occasionally judge of this by the position of the shroud relative to the body. If it covers the body, enveloping it more or less, early death is certain.[5] In the Isle of Man, it seems, this "symbolic" species of Second Sight also prevailed, as we gather from a passage in the Peniarth Collection of MSS. (p. 163).

Napier is somewhat more definite regarding the circumstances in which vision was granted and the implications to be drawn from it. "Sometimes," he tells us, "the seer fell into a trance, in which state he saw visions; at other times the visions were seen without the trance condition. Should the seer see in a vision a certain person dressed in a shroud, this betokened that the death of that person would surely take place within a year; should such a vision be seen in the morning, the person seen would die before that evening; should such a vision be seen in the afternoon, the person seen would die before next night; but if the vision were seen late in the evening, there was no particular time of death intimated further than that it would take place within the year. Again, if the shroud did not cover the whole body, the fulfilment of the vision was at a great distance. If the vision were that of a man with a woman standing at his left hand, then that woman will be that man's wife although they may both at the time of the vision be married to others. These seers could often foretell coming visitors to a family months before they came, and even point out places where houses would be built years before the buildings were erected. The seer could not communicate the gift to any other person, nor even to those of his own family, as he possessed it without any conscious act on his part; but if any person were near him at the time he was having a vision, and he were consciously to touch the person with his left foot, the person touched would see that particular vision."[6]

Although Second Sight is generally held to be a hereditary faculty, all writers on the subject, as we have just seen, are not in agreement with this belief. Martin, an acute observer, remarks that it "does not lineally descend in a family, as some imagine, for I know several parents who are endowed with it, but their children not, and *vice versa*".[7] In Lowland Fifeshire "a child born feet first was held to be either possessed of the gift of Second Sight, or to be born a wanderer in foreign countries".[8] That the Second Sight was, in many cases, thought to be hereditary, there can be no question, as Dalyell remarks, and as Sacheverell states in his *Account of the Isle of Man*, though that it might be acquired is equally certain. Mr. Evans Wentz alludes to the remarkable case of the late Father Allan MacDonald, who, during a residence of twenty years on the isolated isle of Eriskay, in the Western Hebrides, acquired this faculty of vision and who could exercise it freely.[9]

One of the earliest allusions to Second Sight is that of Ralph Higden, in his *Polychronicon* (I, lxiv), who wrote about the middle of the fourteenth century. Speaking of the Isle of Man he says: "There oft by daye tyme, men of that islonde seen men that bey dede to fore honde, byheded, or hole and what dethe they deyde. Alyens [aliens] setten theyr feet upon feet of the men of that londe, for to see such sightes as the men of that londe doon." At a much later period the Second Sight appears to have caused almost a furore in literary circles in England, and Robert Boyle, Henry More, Glanvil, Pepys, Aubrey and others kept up a correspondence with people in Scotland concerning its lore and circumstances. The works of Kirk, Frazer, Martin and Defoe, "Theophilus Insulanus" (Macleod) and Woodrow heightened southern interest in it, and even Dr. Johnson himself made the long journey to the Western Highlands to gratify his curiosity concerning it, although he returned only half convinced of its powers.

"I am informed by one who came last summer from the Isle of Sky," wrote a Scottish correspondent to John Aubrey, the English antiquary, in 1694, "that any person that pleases will get the second sight taught him for a pound or two of tobacco." Expensive as it is today, tobacco in the reign of Dutch William was even more costly, being vended weight for weight in the scales against silver coinage. Even so, the price for enjoying the privilege of supernatural vision appears unduly modest.

More for the sake of completeness than anything else, I append the details of a few cases of Second Sight. Most of these will probably be familiar to the reader, but I shall adhere to such instances as seem to illustrate the outstanding types of experience in respect of *da-shealladh*.

In the year 1653, says Lord Tarbet, he and Lt.-Col. Alexander Monro were walking in the neighbourhood of Ullapool, near Loch Broom, when he observed a peasant, who had been engaged in digging, suddenly pause in his work and stare into vacancy. Tarbet addressed him, and was informed that he had seen an army of English troops, leading horses, come down the hill to the plain, where they ate the barley growing in a field hard by. The gentlemen took little notice of the man's statement at the time. This happened in the month of May. In the ensuing August the Earl of Middleton, then in command of the Royal forces in Scotland, had occasion to despatch a force through the neighbourhood in question. A body of English troops descended the hill alluded to and fell to eating the barley crop at the very spot where the crofter had seen them do so in a vision. Lt.-Col. Monro, being apprised of the fulfilment of the vision, immediately sent an express letter to Lord Tarbet, then in Ross-shire, acquainting him with the circumstance.

Tarbet also tells us that he was once in company which included a well-known seer, who told him that he perceived the apparition of a stranger hovering in the neighbourhood of a young lady who was one of the party and that she would marry the person in question, who would predecease her. Two years later he again met the visionary, who chanced to have with him the identical man whose phantasm he had beheld in the proximity of the lady mentioned, and he informed Tarbet that at that very moment her apparition was standing beside this person, to whom she had been lately betrothed. A little later the pair were married, but not long afterwards the bridegroom died.[10]

One of Aubrey's Scottish correspondents told him that a gentleman of the family of MacLean and his lady found their child's nurse in tears, but on asking the cause of her distress she refused to acquaint them with it. Being pressed to do so, she told them that MacLean would die and that the lady would shortly marry another man. She had seen a gentleman with a scarlet cloak and a white hat kiss the lady "over her shoulder". All this came to pass and "the tutor [i.e. legal guardian of an heir under age] of Lovat married the lady in the same habit the woman saw him".[11]

A typical case is recorded by another of Aubrey's correspondents in the North. Andrew MacPherson, of Clunie in Badenoch, was paying his addresses to a daughter of Lord Gareloch. Her mother beheld him on a country road, when one of her attendants, who had the Second Sight, assured his mistress that unless her daughter married Clunie within six months "she would never marry him at all", for he too beheld him, and he was swathed in his winding-sheet up to the mouth. The vision was justified in the event.[12]

In his *Sketches of the Highlands*, General Stewart of Garth says that in 1773 the son of a neighbouring gentleman called at his father's house and enquired about a child of the family, a boy of three years of age. He was shown into the nursery, where the nurse was trying a pair of new shoes on the child's feet and complained that they did not fit the boy. "They will fit him before he has occasion for them," remarked the young gentleman. Being chaffed regarding his ill-omened saying by other guests in the sitting-room, he revealed to them that he had beheld, while approaching the house, a crowd of people, one of whom was carrying a small coffin. In the funeral train he recognized many individuals, among them his own father. The boy in question fell suddenly ill on the following night and died. This, adds General Stewart, was the young man's first and last experience of the Second Sight.

It would be needless to multiply such instances, of which the above are fair examples. But occasionally the Second Sight appears to have been exercised collectively, as the following account makes clear.

"In the year 1686," says Walker, in the postscript to his *Life of Peden*, "especially in the months of June and July, many yet alive can witness, that about the Crossfoord-boat, two miles beneath Lanark, especially at the Mains, on the water of Clyde, many people gathered together for several afternoons, where there were showers of bonnets, hats, guns, and swords, which covered the trees and ground; companies of men in arms marching in order upon the water-side; companies meeting companies going all through other, and then all falling to the ground and disappearing, and other companies appearing the same way. I went there three afternoons together, and, as I could observe, there were two of the people that were together saw, and a third that saw not, yet there was sich a fright and trembling upon these that did see, that was discernible to all from these that saw not. There was a gentleman standing next to me, who spake, as too many gentlemen and others speak, who said, '*A pack of damned witches and warlocks that have the second sight, the devil ha't do I see.*'"

Here I may mention that numerous tales have circulated and still circulate throughout the Highlands of Scotland with regard to a personage known as "the Brahan Seer", one Kenneth Ore, who is said to have been among the most prominent of the practitioners of the Second Sight. None of these accounts, however, is of an authentic nature. Kenneth, it is said, flourished in the seventeenth century, and was burned by the Countess of Seaforth because of an obnoxious vision which he experienced regarding her husband, at the Castle of Brahan, the family seat of the Seaforths near Dingwall. No record survives of the event, and in any case it is anachronistic, as the Seaforth family was certainly not founded until long after Kenneth's day. Many of the prophecies attributed to him are also attached to the names of Michael Scot and Thomas the Rhymer. In the Scottish Parliamentary records an order has been found giving authority to persons in Ross-shire to punish Kenneth as a wizard, and this is actually the only authentic notice we possess respecting him.

If we examine the genuine and original sources of the belief in the Second Sight, we are compelled to the conclusion that it had a spiritistic origin, that it was associated with a highly developed technique for getting *en rapport* with the spirits of the dead, who, by granting such a gift of supernatural vision, could place the living in a position to forecast the doom of persons still alive, or events still to happen. That such a technique was, in the first instance, developed by a definite caste or priesthood, I am constrained by the evidence to believe. Research has made it clear that in Scotland the spirits known as fairies were regarded as the spirits of the departed and that Second Sight, as known in Scotland, was associated with these beings there is ample proof, as I hope to be able to demonstrate.

It is clear from the account of it given by Kirk in his *Secret Commonwealth*, written in 1691, that he chiefly regarded Second Sight as a means of seeing the Fairies, for one of the sub-titles of that work sets forth that it is an essay "of the Nature and Actions of the Subterranean Invisible People, heretofoir going under the names of Elves, Faunes and Fairies, or the lyke, among the Low-Country Scots, as they are described by those who have the Second Sight". Again and again throughout the treatise the importance of the possession of Second Sight to those who desire to come into contact with the fairies is stressed. At each quarter of the year, we are told, "Seers or Men of the Second Sight (females being seldom so qualified) have very terrifying encounters with them." They were clearly seen by men of the Second Sight at funerals and banquets.[18] But that even these qualities of the Second Sight more usually associated with modern tradition also came from fairy sources is alleged by Kirk. He tells us that: "A man of the Second Sight, perceaving the Operations of these forecasting invisible People among us, told he saw a winding-sheet creeping on a walking healthful Persons Legs till it came to the Knee; and afterwards it came up to the Midle, then to the Shoulders, and at last over the Head", by which means he was enabled to tell how long the man was to live. When Kirk visited London and dined with the Bishop of Worcester elect, his Lordship made enquiries regarding the Second Sight, to be informed by the Aberfoyle parson that although some people acquired it "innocently, of their predecessors", others received it "by contact with evil men or spirits".

When the notorious Scottish witch, Isobel Sinclair, was tried in 1663, it was alleged against her that "Sex times at the reathes [quarters] of the year shoe hath been controlled with the Phairie; and that be thame shoe hath the Second Sight; quhairby shoe will know giff their be any fey bodie in the house." Elspeth Reoch of Orkney, a witch who was tried in 1616, received the Second Sight from one Johne Stewart, a fairy man who "had been slane by the McKy at the downgoing of the sone [sun] and therefore nather deid nor leiving". By virtue of this gift she saw "folk with tows [ropes] about their craigs" [necks].

Sir Walter Scott alludes to a rustic, one M'Coan, who dwelt in Appin, who told his friend, Mr. Ramsay of Ochtertyre, that he "owed his prophetic visions" to the intervention of the Fairies. But Sir Walter appears to have been none too clear regarding this communication, for Ramsay states distinctly that M'Coan not only "pretended to the Second Sight, but to a power of preventing the operations of witches and spirits, which last he affirmed he often saw and conversed with". Ramsay further states: "Those who are reputed to possess this faculty can give no account of how it was communicated to them, neither was it ever imagined to proceed from necromancy or other impious means, being esteemed an extraordinary and ineffaceable impression of futurity upon the mind." "The power of Second Sight," says Mr. Thomas Henderson, in his notes to the *Border Minstrelsy*, in which Scott made the above statement, "was not communicated by the fairies, but enabled its possessor to behold, and hold intercourse with them." The first part of Mr. Henderson's statement is, of course, erroneous, as will be seen from the evidence already given and to be adduced.

"Those who had the Sight could see fairies leave their mounds," remarks Mr. R. C. Macleod.[14] A *glaistig* encountered by a Maclachlan of Ardnamurchan, who had settled in Glennahurich, was captured by him, and offered to give him the gift of the Second Sight if he would liberate her. He agreed and let her go. Later, when he was fishing in the River Spean, he caught and cooked a fish. He pressed a blister on the side of the fish while it was cooking, burned his finger and placed it to his mouth. By this means he received the gift.[15] A young man of Nithsdale heard enchanting strains one night, was invited to partake in the fairy dance and was offered a cup of wine. He was allowed to depart, and was ever after endowed with the Second Sight. He boasted of having seen and conversed with several of his earthly acquaintances whom the fairies had taken and admitted as "brothers".

In his essay, "An Accurate Account of Second Sighted Men in Scotland", published in his *Miscellanies*, John Aubrey says that he dispatched a questionnaire on the subject to certain persons in Scotland as regards the manner in which people came by the Second Sight. To this one correspondent stated in reply: "Some say by compact with the devil; some say by converse with those daemons we call fairies. I have heard that those that have the faculty of the Second Sight have offered to teach it to such as were curious to know it." Another correspondent stated that one percipient, James Mac Coilvicalaster, alias Grant, used to make room for invisible beings at his fireside. "But whether the man saw any more than Brownie and Meg Mulloch, I am not very sure . . . others affirm he saw these two continually and sometimes many more. . . . They assigned it [the Second Sight] to Bogles or Ghosts so that *Taishtar* is as much as one that converses with ghosts or spirits, or, as they commonly call them, the Fairies or Fairy-Folks."[16]

An Irishman told Lady Gregory that his dead sister appeared to him and gave him the Second Sight. She had been carried off to Fairyland.[17] The Macglashens of Creaganich had the "Sight". On going to church, they left one of their boys at Allt Aogain, a fairy place, and the fairies gave him the gift.[18]

The province of Scottish ballad is productive of other recollections of ancient methods for inducing clairvoyance granted by the fairies. In the ballad of "Thomas the Rhymer", which describes his meeting with the Fairy Queen, Thomas places his head on her knee, and she reveals to him four paths leading to different planes: one to Heaven, another to Paradise, a third to a place of pain for sinful souls, and a fourth to the fire of hell. As will be seen, this laying of the head on the sorceress's knee is analogous to the ritual mentioned by Kirk, in which the person desirous of the vision of faerie places his left foot under the wizard's right, while the seer's hand is put on the wizard's head. We discover, too, some such process in the old ballad of "The Queen of Elfland's Nourice". The Queen hears her nurse moaning for her son in Christendie (she is evidently one of those mortal nurses who were kidnapped to attend on fairy ladies) and the elfin queen requests her to nurse her newly born infant until it can walk, after which she may return to her own son. She asks the mortal woman to place her head upon her knee, when she shows her the several roads to heaven, to hell, and that which "wins from Elfland", where she must "wait to gae". The process of laying the head on the knee was therefore a recognized ritual by which it was believed one could at least trace the path to Fairyland.

Kirk enumerates the solemnities employed in investing a man with the mysteries of the Second Sight, in making him a "Privado to the Airt", as he calls it. He must gird a tether of hair which had bound a corpse to the bier about his middle, then bow his head downward and look back through his legs until he espies a funeral advancing. Or he must peer through a hole from which a knot of fir had been taken. If the wind changed while he had the tether about him he was in danger of his life. A second method was to place his foot under the right foot of a wizard or wise man, who should place his hand upon the percipient's head. He must then look over the wizard's right shoulder, when he will behold "a Multitude of Wight's, like furious hardie Men, flocking at him hastily from all quarters, as thick as Atoms on the Air".[19] These "solemnities", it seems to me, have all the appearance of the elements of a broken-down ritual.

It remains to investigate the significance of such material as we possess which may seem to suggest the existence of a cultus or society for the cultivation of Second Sight as a means of communication with the Spirit or Fairy world. This particular aspect of the subject has been unaccountably neglected by those writers who have dealt with it, though Andrew Lang, who knew most things, once lightly touched upon its cult-like tendency. It certainly appears to have been thought possible to acquire Second Sight by certain definite acts which look uncommonly like those of a magical ritual abraded, or in course of breaking down. Indeed, the facts appear to make it plain that Second Sight was not only an endowment with which certain people were born, or which they inherited from their ancestors, but a quality or psychic sense which might be awakened and enhanced in those who were not originally gifted with it, but who were at the same time predisposed to it.

If my conclusions are correct, it follows that the prevailing ideas regarding Second Sight must be rather drastically revised, and that it will have to be regarded not only as a "gift", cropping up in isolated instances, but as the result of a definite cultus instituted and pursued by a caste or school or other body of mystics at a distant period. As we behold it now, and have witnessed it during the last century or so, it is, and was, of an isolated nature, but that it was formerly the outcome of "dogma", and a special technique issuing from a definite centre or centres, I cannot doubt.

Second Sight differs from trance or divination. As Lang put it: "It is not a hallucination 'suggested' to a hypnotized subject, but an impression produced by a remote person or event on a subject who has not been hypnotized at all." It has thus little in common with the visions induced in the Sibyls of ancient Greece by the use of drugs and gases, or in the Shamans of the Siberian Kalmucks by trance. At the same time, the apparitions or phantasms beheld under its influence are of the self-same occult character. Its visions, though now reduced to the symbolic apparitions of "winding-sheets round the candle", and so forth, were formerly greatly more ambitious, and were experienced by persons apparently in their ordinary waking senses, and by virtue of a genuine occult gift of sight which "normal" people did not possess.

The evidence already produced appears to me to be conclusive as bearing upon the belief that Second Sight was primarily and originally regarded as a means of seeing the fairies, otherwise the dead, and that it was thought to be a gift especially granted by them to certain individuals for that specific purpose.

Kirk speaks of making a man "a Privado to the Airt", which, I think, indicates that in his time, the close of the seventeenth century, a belief still existed that it was possible to initiate people into its secrets, and that the means for this initiation were at hand in many parts of the country. It should be noted that in this particular regard he says nothing of the Second Sight being a gift, for he writes: "There be odd Solemnities at investing a Man with the Priviledges of the whole Mistery of this Second Sight", but elsewhere he speaks of other prognostications of the kind more popularly known as associated with it, which are experienced by "the Minor Sort of Seers", thus differentiating between those who confined themselves to the ominous part of seeing and those who practised the secret art as a means of beholding the fairies or spirits and communicating with them.[20] From this we may infer that in his day the older and more genuine description of Second Sight was still in vogue, as well as the more popular.

At times he stresses the point of initiation in a manner which seems to convey the impression that he had satisfied himself concerning its actuality. He admits that a man can "come by it unawares, and without his consent". But he adds: "The Seers avouch, that severalls who go to the Siths or Fairies [or People at Rest and, in respect of us, in Peace] before the natural Period of their Lyfe expyre, do frequently appear to them." (That is, people who had been carried off by the fairies and who were thought to be dead, appeared to them.) "A Vehement Desyre to attain this Airt is very helpful to the Inquyrer."[21] It was thus a possible and harmless method of correspondence between men and spirits "even in this lyfe". He is of the opinion that the Sight is native to Scotland alone, for "all other people wanted the right Key of their Cabinet, and that exact Method of Correspondence with them, except the sagacious, active Scots, as many of them have retained it of a long Time".[22]

He adds that if invited and earnestly requested, "These Companions [the fairies] make themselves known and familiar to men; otherwise being in a different State and Element, they neither can nor will easily converse with them." This would seem to reveal that a certain ritual of invocation was employed to get en rapport with the Fairy World. He also made it clear that men occasionally employed stratagems "for procuring a Privacy to any of these Mysteries". This is surely a further indication that mysteries were actually held and that they were frequented and continued by people who were the initiates of some arcane body or society.

Second Sight, wrote the late Mr. J. G. Campbell, "is a Celtic belief, and the suggestion that it is the remains of the magic of the Druids is not unreasonable. . . . It is probable enough that the sage Celtic priests, assuming the spectres to be external [he means objective] reduced the means of seeing them to a system, a belief in which formed part of their teaching." It is indeed, "probable enough", for in so doing the Celtic sages would only have been acting in a manner similar to that found among practically all peoples in an early stage of culture who cultivate a method of correspondence with the spirit world of one sort or another, as indeed the entire literature of folk-lore eloquently proves.

Sacheverell remarks that it is not for him to determine "whether these fancies proceed from ignorance, superstition, or prejudice of education, or from any *traditional or heritable magic, which is the opinion of the Scotch diviners, concerning their Second Sight*". So that it appears that a tradition of hereditary Magic in connection with the Second Sight actually existed. Mr. J. G. Campbell, alluded to above, an authority of great weight, remarked that persons gifted with Second Sight could see the fairies where others could not.[23]

We are now, I think, enabled to arrive at the following conclusions regarding the Second Sight. It was believed to be granted by the fairies, and was used as a means of beholding them. The fairies, we know, were the more modern representatives of some of the old gods of Britain and Ireland, as the tradition concerning the Tuatha Dé Danann makes plain. We know, also, that the Tuatha Dé Danann were served by the Druids, as were their kindred deities in Britain. It therefore follows that Second Sight, which is so closely associated with the fairies, can be nothing else than the remains of a technique employed by the Druids and others for getting in touch with the gods. If it was associated with these gods in the phase of their deterioration, it must also have been associated with them in their heyday. Among many barbarous and savage peoples today the "doubles" of the gods are beheld only by the priestly caste, which receives from them a knowledge of the past and the future.[24] I believe, then, that the origin of the whole technique of Second Sight is capable of being referred back to such a caste, and as the only caste of the kind we have any tradition of in Britain was the Druidic, that it was in its earliest phase a Druidic conception, a means of beholding and getting *en rapport* with the gods.

As I have already stated in the Seventh Chapter of this book, there exist quite a number of traditional bonds between the fairies and the Druids, while it is notable that, so far as Scotland is concerned, a fair proportion of those who have given thought and study to the problem of fairy origins definitely associate it with the Druidical caste. Such was the opinion of the Rev. J. G. Campbell, one of the foremost authorities upon Celtic superstition, while his even more famous namesake, J. F. Campbell of Islay, actually believed certain classes of fairies, such as the *gruagach*, to represent the Druidical caste—which, of course, was to confuse that worshipped with the hierophant who served it. The Rev. P. Graham, in his *Sketches of Perthshire*, also arrived at a similar, if errant, conclusion, which at least makes it evident that he regarded the association between fairies and Druids as having been a very intimate one. It is also a remarkable circumstance that so many of the Scottish peasants who furnished J. F. Campbell with the tales which he collected and edited should have borne witness to a living tradition that a close association existed between fairies and the Druidic class, while, as I have said, a belief equally vivid existed among the Irish peasantry that Druid and fairy were linked in the closest traditional bonds.

I think we may conclude, then, that the visions of death or disaster and the "seeing" of persons at a distance, which are apparently the most important developments in what might be called the more "modern" phase of Second Sight, are rather its natural concomitants and consequences than inherent in its earliest idea and intention, which was to devise a means by which men might communicate with and behold his gods and the spirits of his ancestors. At a later period this gift of supernatural vision came to include foreshadowings of death and the perception of persons at a distance, until at length, under the influence of Christianity, the visionary beholding of the gods came to be sternly discouraged, while that relating to death, accident, or distant perception were alone tolerated as having no religious association.

From a general view of the material presented in the foregoing pages it may, I think, be concluded that the Magic Arts as cultivated among the Celtic peoples of the British Isles very closely resembled those practised in almost every area where humanity has concerned itself with occult belief and its practical observance. This makes it self-evident, if it be necessary to say so, that the Magic Art in all its branches is of an antiquity so great as to be practically unfathomable. Even so, the spirit which inspired Celtic Magic reveals the existence of a sharply different temperament in certain aspects from that of other arcane systems. Few races have developed a spirit-world so fantastically beautiful or have peopled it with shapes so attractive, or at times so terrific. Perhaps, too, no race which had not yet approached the full stature of civilization has brought forth a religious-magical caste at once so distinctive and so richly garbed in the trappings of mystery as the Druidic. Moreover, if the spells and charms of the Celt resemble in their nature those of other races, they are usually couched in a vein of poetry the exalted genius of which is seldom to be encountered in that of the Teuton or the Slav. There are depths still unplumbed and heights still unconquered in the imaginative descents and flights of Celtic Magic which baffle the scientific enquirer and the significance of which is, perhaps, only to be guessed at by the poet or the inspired seer. I believe that, as research in Celtic affairs proceeds and the mysterious places of the Celtic soul are gradually unveiled, it will be given to us to realize that our British ancestors, shackled as they were by the grievous bonds of superstition and perplexed by those baffling difficulties which surround the primitive thinker, stood up boldly and fearlessly to the problems of life and religion and approached them in that spirit of resolute confidence which has from the first distinguished the British race. If the tradition which they reared was challenged by another it was never altogether superseded, but was rather merged in that of the later ascendancy, to which, indeed, it contributed a legacy of saga which, in its sublime and matchless fantasy, no less than in its moral example, remains among the most potent forces which have served to make the island of Britain the shrine and temple of those virtues to the achievement of which the soul of man has painfully striven through ages of strife and shadow. Were the Empire of Britain to be overthrown and its history to be forgotten, this, the legacy of our Celtic fathers, would still remain because of the exalted spirit inherent in its legend, and men ten thousand years away, forgetful or ignorant of kings and triumphs, prosperities and policies, would still speak of the chivalry and freedom of Britain begotten by that legend as among the divine things of an otherwise unknown antiquity.

LIST OF WORKS CONSULTED

Ammianus Marcellinus: History of Rome (trans. by C. D. Yonge). London, 1862.
Annals of the Kingdom of Ireland, by the Four Masters (ed. J. O'Donovan). Dublin, 1856.
Anwyl, E.: *Celtic Religion in Pre-Christian Times.* London, 1906.
Baring-Gould, S.: *Curious Myths of the Middle Ages.* London, 1884.
Bertrand, A.: *Religion des gaulois.* Paris, 1897.
Boece, Hector: *The History and Chronicles of Scotland* (trans. by John Bellenden), 2 vols. 1821.
Bonwick, J.: *Irish Druids and Old Irish Religions.* London, 1894.
Book of the Conquests of Ireland (Leabhar Gabhala) (ed. R. A. S. Macalister and J. MacNeill). Dublin, N.D.
Brand, J.: *Popular Antiquities of Great Britain*, 2 vols. London, 1813.
Briffault, R.: *The Mothers.* London, 1927.
Brown, A. C. L.: *The Round Table Before Wace.* Boston, U.S.A., 1900.
Bruce, J. D.: *The Evolution of Arthurian Romance.* 1923.
Brut y Tywysogion, or The Chronicle of the Princes (ed. and trans. by J. Williams Ithel, Rolls Series). London, 1860.
Daniel, J.: *The Philosophy of Ancient Britain.* London, 1927.
Evans, J. G.: *The Text of the Book of Taliesin.* Llanbedrog, 1910.
Evans, J. G.: *The Poetry of the Red Book of Hergest.* Llanbedrog, 1911.
Foord, E.: *The Last Age of Roman Britain.* London, 1925.
Frazer, J. G.: *The Magic Art*, 2 vols. London, 1917.
Geoffrey of Monmouth: *History of the Kings of Britain* (trans. by A. Thompson). London, 1718.
Geoffrey of Monmouth: *Vita Merlini* (ed. and trans. by J. J. Parry). Chicago, 1925.
Gildas; *In Six Old English Chronicles* (Bohn's Antiquarian Library). London, 1848.
Giraldus Cambrensis: *The Topography of Ireland and the Itinerary Through Wales* (trans. by T. Forester). London, 1863.
Glennie, A. S. Stuart: *Arthurian Localities.* Edinburgh, 1869.
Gomme, Sir G. L.: *Ethnology in Folklore.* London, 1892.
Gruffydd, W. J.: *Math vab Mathonwy.* Cardiff, 1928.
Guenebauld, I.: *Le Reveil de Chyndonax.* Dijon, 1621.
Guest, Lady Charlotte: *The Mabinogion*, 3 vols. London, 1838–43.
Gwynn, E.: *The Metrical Dindshenchas*, 3 parts. Dublin, 1903–13.
Haigh, D. H.: *The Conquest of Britain by the Saxons.* London, 1861.
Henderson, G.: *Survivals in Belief Among the Celts.* Glasgow, 1911.
Herbert, A.: *Britannia after the Romans*, 2 vols. London, 1836–41.
Herbert, A.: *An Essay on the Neo-Druidic Heresy.* London, 1838.
Higgins, G.: *The Celtic Druids.* London, 1829.
Holmes, T. Rice: *Ancient Britain and the Invasions of Julius Caesar.* Oxford, 1907.
Hubert, H.: *The Greatness and Decline of the Celts* (trans. by M. R. Dobie). London, 1943
Hull, Eleanor: *Folklore of the British Isles.* London, 1928.
Hull, Eleanor: *The Cuchullin Saga.* London, 1898.
Hunt, R.: *Popular Romances of the West of England.* London, 1923.
Hyde, Douglas: *Beside the Fire.* London, 1910.
Hyde, Douglas: *The Literary History of Ireland.* London, 1910.
Irish Texts Society, Vols. I to XXV. Dublin 1899–1924.
Jones, W. L.: *King Arthur in History and Legend.* Cambridge, 1914.
Joyce, P. W.: *Old Celtic Romances.* London, 1920.
Jullian, C.: *Recherches sur la religion gauloise.* Bordeaux, 1903.
Keating G.: *The General History of Ireland* (trans. by D. O'Connor). Dublin, 1941.
Kendrick, T. D.: *The Druids.* London, 1927.
Kennedy, P.: *Legendary Fictions of the Irish Celts.* London, 1891.
Kirk, Robert: *The Secret Commonwealth of Elves, Fauns and Fairies.* Stirling, 1933.
Kittredge, G. L.: *Gawaine and the Green Knight.* Harvard, U.S.A., 1916.
Krappe, A. H.: *The Science of Folklore.* London, 1930.
Larminie, W.: *West Irish Folk-Tales and Romances.* London, 1893.
Lewis, J.: *History of Great Britain.* London, 1729.
Lloyd, Humphrey: *The Breviary of Britaine.* London, 1729.
Loomis, R. S.: *Celtic Myth and Arthurian Romance.* New York, 1927.

Mabinogion: *The Text of the Mabinogion and other Welsh Tales from The Red Book of Hergest* (ed. by J. Rhys and J. G. Evans). Oxford, 1887.
Macalister, R. A. S.: *The Archaeology of Ireland*. Dublin, 1928.
MacBain, A.: *Celtic Mythology and Religion*. Stirling, 1917.
MacCallum, M. W.: *Tennyson's Idylls of the King and Arthurian Story from the XVIth Century*. Glasgow, 1894.
MacCulloch, J. A.: *The Religion of the Ancient Celts*. Edinburgh, 1911.
MacDougall, J., and Calder, G.: *Folk-Tales and Fairy Lore*. Edinburgh, 1910.
MacGregor, A. A.: *The Peat Fire Flame*. Edinburgh, 1937.
MacInnes, D.: *Folk and Hero Tales from Argyllshire*. London, 1891.
Maclagan, R. C.: *The Evil Eye in the Western Highlands*. London, 1902.
McPherson, J. M.: *Primitive Beliefs in the North-East of Scotland*. London, 1929.
Malory, Sir Thomas: *Le Morte d'Arthur*, 2 vols. (Library of English Classics.) London, 1900.
Meyer, K., and Nutt, A.: *The Voyage of Bran*, 2 vols. London, 1895.
Milton, John: *History of Britain*. London, 1677.
Morris, Lewis: *Celtic Remains*. London, 1878.
Myvyrian Archaiology of Wales (collected by O. Jones, E. Williams and W. Owen). Denbigh, 1870.
Nennius: *Historia Britonum* (ed. W. Gunn). London, 1819.
Nutt, A.: *Studies on the Legend of the Holy Grail*. London, 1888.
O'Curry, E.: *Lectures on the Manuscript Materials of Ancient Irish History*. Dublin, 1878.
O'Curry, E.: *Manners and Customs of the Ancient Irish*, 3 vols. Dublin, 1873.
O'Grady, S. H.: *Silva Gadelica*. London, 1892.
Parry, J. H.: *The Cambrian Plutarch*. London, 1824.
Pokorny, J.: *Origin of Druidism* (In the Annual Report of the Smithsonian Institution, 1910, and in *The Celtic Review*, Vol. V, 1908–9).
Poste, Beale: *Britannia Antiqua*. London, 1853.
Raglan, Lord: *The Hero*. London, 1936.
Reinach, Salomon: *Cultes, Mythes et Religions*, 2 vols. Paris, 1905.
Rhys, John: *Hibbert Lectures on Celtic Heathendom*. London, 1886.
Rhys, John: *Studies in the Arthurian Legend*. Oxford, 1891.
Rhys, John: *Celtic Folk-Lore, Welsh and Manx*, 2 vols. Oxford, 1901.
Roberts, P.: *The Chronicles of the Kings of Britain* (trans. of the *Brut Tysilio*). London, 1811.
Sayce, A. H.: "The Legend of King Bladud" (in *Y Cymmrodor*, Vol. X, pp. 207–21). London, 1889.
Sheldon, G.: *The Transition of Roman Britain to Christian England*. London, 1932.
Sikes, Wirt: *British Goblins*. London, 1880.
Skene, W. F.: *The Four Ancient Books of Wales*, 2 vols. Edinburgh, 1868.
Skene, W. F.: *Celtic Scotland*, 3 vols. Edinburgh, 1876–80.
Spence, Lewis: *The Mysteries of Britain*. London, 1931.
Spence, Lewis: *Legendary London*. London, 1937.
Spence, Lewis: *Boadicea*. London, 1937.
Squire, C.: *Mythology of the British Islands*. London, N.D.
Stokes, W., and Windisch, E.: *Irische Texte*. Leipzig, 1891.
Strabo (trans. by Hamilton and Falconer). London, 1854–7.
Tacitus; *Agricola* (trans. Church and Brodribb). London, 1876.
Toland, John: *A Critical History of the Celtic Religion and Learning: Containing an Acccunt of the Druids*. Edinburgh, 1815.
"Tysilio": (*see* Roberts, P).
Waldron, G. A.: *Description of the Isle of Man*. Douglas, 1865.
Wentz, W. Y. Evans: *The Fairy Faith in Celtic Countries*. Oxford, 1911.
Weston, J. L.: *The Quest of the Holy Grail*. London, 1913.
Weston, J. L.: *From Ritual to Romance*. Cambridge, 1920.
Wilde, Lady F. S.: *Ancient Legends and Superstitions of Ireland*, 2 vols. London, 1887.
Williams ap Ithel: *Barddas* (Welsh Manuscript Society). Llandovery, 1862.
Williams, E.: ("Iolo Morganwg"), *The Iolo Manuscripts*. Llandovery, 1848.
Williams, Ifor: *Lectures on Early Welsh Poetry*. (Published by Dublin Institute for Advanced Studies.) Dublin, 1944.
Wimberley, L. C.: *Folk-Lore in the English and Scottish Ballads*. Chicago, 1928.
Wise, T. A.: *History of Paganism in Caledonia*. London, 1887.
Wood-Martin, W. G.: *Pagan Ireland*. London, 1895.
Wood-Martin, W. G.: *Elder Faiths of Ireland*, 2 vols. London, 1903.
Wright, Dudley: *Druidism, the Ancient Faith of Britain*. London, 1924.

REFERENCES

CHAPTER I

THE MAGIC ART AMONG THE CELTS

1. Osthoff, *Allerhand Zauber etymologisch beleuchtet*, p. 113.
2. N. MacLeod and D. Dewar, *Gaelic and English Dictionary*, p. 819.
3. E. O'Curry, *MS. Materials of Ancient Irish History*.
4. Owen Connellan, *Transactions of the Ossianic Society*, V.
5. A. MacBain, *Celtic Mythology and Religion*, p. 80.
6. A. MacBain, op. cit., p. 80.
7. C. Squire, *Mythology of the British Islands*, pp. 201–2.
8. For a full discussion of tales of this type see L. Spence, *British Fairy Origins*, Chap. ii.
9. J. Rhys, *Hibbert Lectures*, pp. 338 ff.
10. D'Arbois de Jubainville, *The Irish Mythological Cycle* (trans. by R. J. Best), pp. 136 ff.
11. D'Arbois de Jubainville, op. cit., p. 138.
12. D'Arbois de Jubainville, op. cit., pp. 139–40.
13. J. Rhys, op. cit., pp. 544 ff.
14. W. J. Gruffydd, *Math vab Mathonwy*, pp. 15 ff.
15. J. F. Campbell, *Popular Tales of the West Highlands*, I, pp. 176 ff.; II, p. 307: G. Henderson, *Survivals in Belief among the Celts*, Chap. ii; *Trans. of the Gaelic Society of Inverness*, XIV, p. 214; J. G. Campbell, *Superstitions of the Scottish Highlands*, p. 109; and see "Folk-Lore", XLIII, p. 144; J. G. McKay, *More West-Highland Tales*, p. 209; D. Hyde, *Beside the Fire*, p. 89; J. MacDougall and G. Calder, *Folk-Tales and Fairy Lore*, p. 204; Lady Gregory, *Gods and Fighting Men*, p. 274; Wirt Sikes, *British Goblins*, pp. 108–9.
16. J. Rhys, *Hibbert Lectures*, pp. 33–4.
17. J. F. Campbell, *Popular Tales of the West Highlands*, II, pp. 421 ff.
18. D. MacInnes, *Folk and Hero-Tales of Argyll*, pp. 207 ff.
19. Pliny, *Natural History*, Bks. III, Chap. xii; XVI, Chap. xliv; and XXVIII, Chap. iv.
20. A. Herbert, *An Essay on the Neo-Druidic Heresy*, p. 61; *see* also A. MacBain, op. cit., pp. 76–7; Forbes-Leslie, *Early Races of Scotland*, pp. 74, 77, 409 and 508; J. Wylie, *History of the Scottish Nation*, I, pp. 108–9; O. Pughe, *Llywarch Hen*, p. 5.
21. D'Arbois de Jubainville, op. cit., pp. 79–83.
22. P. W. Joyce, *Old Celtic Romances*, pp. 106–9.
23. C. Squire, op. cit., p. 202.
24. J. Bonwick, *Irish Druids*, p. 14.
25. Giraldus Cambrensis, *The Topography of Ireland* (trans. by T. Wright), p. 97.
26. J. Bonwick, op. cit., pp. 15–16.
27. E. Hull, *The Cuchullin Saga*, pp. 252 ff.

CHAPTER II

THE MAGIC ART AMONG THE CELTS (*continued*)

1. J. Rhys, *Hibbert Lectures*, pp. 509–10.
2. Windisch, *Irische Texte*, pp. 222–7.
3. J. F. Campbell, *Popular Tales of the West Highlands*, III, pp. 436 ff.
4. P. Kennedy, *Popular Fictions of the Irish Celts*, pp. 15–16.
5. E. O'Curry, *Atlantis*, IV.
6. A. MacBain, *Celtic Mythology and Religion*, p. 81.
7. D. MacInnes, *Folk and Hero-Tales of Argyll*, pp. 3 ff.
8. J. F. Campbell, op. cit., I, p. 266.
9. J. Jacobs, *English Fairy Tales*, p. 57.
10. D'Arbois de Jubainville, *The Irish Mythological Cycle* (trans. by R. I. Best), pp. 185 ff.
11. A. Nutt, *Studies in the Legend of the Holy Grail*, pp. 192–3.
12. A. Lang, *Magic and Religion*, pp. 207 ff.
13. E. O'Curry, *MS. Materials of Ancient Irish History*, pp. 491, 618 ff; Hennessy, *The Book of Fenach*, pp. 322–3.

14. J. Rhys, op. cit., pp. 206–7, 575–7.
15. A. Herbert, *Britannia After the Romans*, p. 96.
16. R. Briffault, *The Mothers* III, pp. 432–3.
17. E. K. Chambers, *Arthur of Britain*, p. 206.
18. Lady C. Guest, *The Mabinogion* (Tale of "Branwen, the Daughter of Llyr").
19. C. Squire, *Mythology of the British Isles*, p. 273.
20. C. Squire, op. cit., p. 260.
21. J. Rhys, op. cit., pp. 223–4.
22. J. Rhys, op. cit., p. 260.
23. A Skene, *The Four Ancient Books of Wales*, I, pp. 79–80.
24. E. Hull, *Folklore of the British Isles*, p. 36.
25. J. Rhys, op. cit., pp. 666–7.
26. P. W. Joyce, *Old Celtic Romances*, pp. 37 ff.
27. J. Toland, *A Critical History of the Celtic Religion*, pp. 142–3.
28. J. G. Dalyell, *The Darker Superstitions of Scotland*, pp. 456–7.
29. J. G. Dalyell, op. cit., pp. 458 ff.
30. J. Rhys, op. cit., 210 ff.
31. D. MacInnes, op. cit., p. 45.
32. J. F. Campbell, op. cit., II, p. 97.
33. Train, *Account of the Isle of Man*, II, p. 154.
34. Boethius (Hector Boece), *Scotorum Historia*, Bk. XI, p. 221.
35. J. MacDonald, *Religion and Myth*, p. 3.
36. J. Rhys, "Folk-Lore", II, p. 385.
37. J. F. Campbell, op. cit. I, pp. 181 ff.
38. D. MacInnes, op. cit., pp. 23, 173. (For list of such tales, both British and Continental, *see* M. R. Cox, *Cinderella*, p. 473, Appendix.)

CHAPTER III

THE PROBLEM OF DRUIDISM

1. Pliny, *Natural History*, XVI, p. 95.
2. J. Rhys, *Hibbert Lectures*, pp. 221–2.
3. G. Henderson, *Survivals in Belief Among the Celts*, pp. 220–1.
4. A. MacBain, *Celtic Mythology and Religion*, p. 75.
5. J. A. Wylie, *Early History of the Scottish Nation*, I, p. 95 (note).
6. E. Anwyl, *Celtic Religion*, p. 44.
7. E. Davies, *Celtic Researches*, p. 139.
8. J. Toland, *A Critical History of the Celtic Religion*, p. 222.
9. MacLeod and Dewar, *Gaelic and English Dictionary*; MacAlpine, *Gaelic and English Dictionary*.
10. A. Herbert, *Essay on the Neo-Druidic Heresy*, p. 5.
11. E. Anwyl, op. cit., p. 47.
12. Diogenes Laertius, *Vitae*, Intro. I.
13. Diodorus Siculus, *Histories*, xxxi, pp. 2–5.
14. Julius Caesar, *Gallic War*, Bk. VI, Chap. xiii.
15. Tacitus, *Agricola*, Chap. xxx (*cf.* Strabo, *Geographica*, IV, 4, Chap. cxcviii).
16. *Origen Against Celsus*, Bk. VI.
17. E. Hull, *Folklore of the British Isles*, p. 289.
18. C. Squire, *The Mythology of the British Islands*, p. 35.
19. Julius Caesar, op. cit., Bk. I, Chaps. xix, xx, xxxi: Bk. VI, Chap. xiii.
20. Julius Caesar, op. cit., Bk. VI, Chap. xiv.
21. Julius Caesar, op. cit., Bk. VI, Chap. xvi.
22. Strabo, *Geographica*, Bk. IV.
23. Julius Caesar, op. cit., Bk. VI, Chap. xiii: Tacitus, *Histories*, IV, 54; Toland, op. cit., pp. 105 ff.
24. J. Rhys, *Hibbert Lectures*, pp. 233–4.
25. Ausonius, *Commen. professorum*, Chap. v, 12; Chap. xi, 17.
26. A. E. Waite, *The Hidden Church of the Holy Grail*, pp. 176 ff.

CHAPTER IV

THE PROBLEM OF DRUIDISM (*continued*)

1. W. F. Skene, *Chronicles of the Picts and Scots*, p. 31.
2. Adamnan, *Life of St. Columba*, Bk. II, Chap. xxxiii.
3. A. B. Cook, "Folk-Lore", vol. XVII, p. 332; Sir A. Mitchell, *The Past in the Present*, p. 147.
4. C. F. Gordon Cumming, *In the Hebrides*, pp. 194–5.
5. W. Beaufort, *Collectanea Hibernica*, II, p. 208.
6. J. Rhys, *Hibbert Lectures*, p. 222.
7. A. MacBain, *Celtic Mythology and Religion*, pp. 69, 79, 82.
8. W. F. Skene, *Celtic Scotland*, II, p. 3.
9. T. D. Kendrick, *The Druids*, pp. 132 ff.
10. G. Keating, *The General History of Ireland* (trans. by D. O'Connor), II, p. 33.
11. W. C. Mackenzie, *The Races of Scotland and Ireland*, p. 55.
12. E. Hull, *Folklore of the British Isles*, pp. 291–3.
13. Ammianus Marcellinus (quoting Timagenes), *History of Rome*, XV.
14. Vopiscus, *Numerianus*, XIV; *Aurelianus*, XLIII.
15. Strabo, *Geographica*, IV, pars. 4, 6.
16. Pomponius Mela, *De Chorographia*, III, Chap. vi.
17. T. D. Kendrick, op. cit., p. 140; J. A. MacCulloch, *Religion of the Ancient Celts*, p. 317.
18. Consult: O'Curry, *Manners and Customs of the Ancient Irish*; Ledwich, *Antiquities of Ireland*: Vallencey, *Vindication of the Ancient History of Ireland*.
19. Julius Caesar, *Gallic War*, Chap. xiii.
20. Lucan, *Pharsalia*, I, par. 451.
21. Diodorus Siculus, *Histories*, V, par. 31.
22. E. Hull, op. cit., pp. 194–5.
23. T. D. Kendrick, op. cit., p. 114.
24. D'Arbois de Jubainville, *Les Druides*, p. 12.
25. J. Rhys, *Celtic Britain*, pp. 69 ff.
26. J. A. MacCulloch, op. cit., p. 295.
27. T. D. Kendrick, op. cit., p. 199.
28. T. D. Kendrick, op. cit., Chap. v. passim.
29. A. MacBain, op. cit., p. 69.
30. L. Spence, *Boadicea*, pp. 150 ff.
31. E. Davies, *The Mythology and Rites of the British Druids*, p. 617.

CHAPTER V

CELTIC SPELLS AND CHARMS

1. G. Henderson, *Survivals in Belief Among the Celts*, pp. 10 ff.
2. E. Hull, *Folklore of the British Isles*, pp. 272–3.
3. E. Hull, op. cit., p. 281.
4. "Revue Celtique", xxi, pp. 149, 312, 388.
5. W. J. Gruffydd, *Math vab Mathonwy*, passim.
6. G. Henderson, *Norse Influence in Celtic Scotland*, p. 73.
7. Consult: G. Henderson, *Survivals in Belief Among the Celts*, p. 12; E. Hull, op. cit., p. 179, note 1.
8. A. Carmichael, *Carmina Gadelica*.
9. W. Mackenzie, *Gaelic Incantations*, pp. 48 ff.
10. E. O'Curry *Atlantis*, III, pp. 386–8, and note 13.
11. C. Squire, *Mythology of the British Islands*, pp. 83, 87, 174.
12. J. G. McKay, *More West Highland Tales*, p. 231.
13. A. Carmichael, op. cit., I, p. 289.
14. J. G. Campbell, *The Fians*, p. 233.
15. R. C. Maclagan, *The Evil Eye in the Western Highlands*, passim.
16. J. M. McPherson, *Primitive Beliefs in the North-East of Scotland*, p. 193.
17. J. G. Dalyell, *The Darker Superstitions of Scotland*, p. 7.

18. Glanvil, *Sadducismus Triumphatus*, pp. 319–25.
19. C. Squire, op. cit., pp. 48–9.
20. G. Henderson, op. cit., p. 17.
21. Sir Walter Scott, *The Minstrelsy of the Scottish Border*, II, p. 278.
22. R. Bovet, *Pandemonium, or the Devil's Cloister*, p. 217.
23. J. Jackson, *The Originall of Unbelief*.
24. See also: J. Frazer, *The Golden Bough*, II, p. 287.
25. See *Irische Texte*, III, Pt. I, pp. 51–3, 95–7.
26. E. Hull, op. cit., pp. 42, 206.
27. C. Squire, op. cit, p. 210.
28. J. Rhys, *Hibbert Lectures*, pp. 553 ff.
29. D'Arbois de Jubainville, *The Irish Mythological Cycle* (trans. by R. I. Best), pp. 228–9, additional notes.
30. L. C. Wimberley, *Folk-Lore in the English and Scottish Ballads*, pp. 325 ff.
31. L. C. Wimberley, op. cit., p. 365.
32. F. J. Child, *English and Scottish Ballads*, I, p. 338.
33. F. J. Child, op. cit., I, p. 336.
34. E. Hull, op. cit., p. 200.
35. J. M. McPherson, op. cit., p. 101.
36. R. C. Maclagan, op. cit., p. 172.
37. P. Kennedy, *Legendary Fictions of the Irish Celts*, pp. 135 ff.
38. J. MacDougall and G. Calder, *Folk-Tales and Fairy Lore*, pp. 260–1.
39. A. Carmichael, op. cit., II, p. 45.
40. E. Hull, op. cit., p. 169.
41. J. G. Dalyell, op. cit., p. 60.
42. G. Henderson, op. cit., pp. 310–7.
43. Sir A. Mitchell, *The Past in the Present*, p. 265.
44. Consult: J. G. Dalyell, op. cit., Chaps. ii and iii : G. Henderson, op. cit., pp. 334 ff.: J. M. McPherson, op. cit., Chap. viii.
45. J. Rhys, op. cit., p. 273.
46. W. Mackenzie, op. cit., p. 32.
47. R. Hunt, *Popular Romances of the West of England*, pp. 107–8.
48. L. Broadwood, "Journal of the Folk-Song Society, III, p. 12.
49. Consult: R. Rhys, op. cit., pp. 518–9; E. Hull, op. cit., pp. 229–31, 235–8, 246–7.
50. J. McPherson, op. cit., pp. 19 ff., 23.
51. *The Book of Leinster*, pp. 17, 156; E. Hull, op. cit.. p. 129.
52. J. G. Dalyell, op. cit., pp. 210–11.
53. J. G. Dalyell, op. cit., pp. 211–12.   (For other similar cases, see p. 305.)
54. G. F. Black, "Scottish Charms and Amulets", *Proc. Soc. Ant. Scot.*, XXVII, pp. 433–526.
55. G. Henderson, op. cit., pp. 263–6.
56. L. Spence, *The Gods of Mexico*, p. 218.

CHAPTER VI

MAGICAL BOOKS OF THE CELTS

1. A. Herbert, *Britannia After the Romans*, I, p. 92.
2. W. F. Skene, *The Four Ancient Books of Wales*, I, pp. 277–8; II, p. 138.
3. See L. Spence, *The Mysteries of Britain*, Chap. iv passim; and J. Williams ap Ithel, *Barddas* (Welsh Manuscript Society).
4. A. Griscom, *The Historia Regum Brittaniae of Geoffrey of Monmouth*, passim; and see my remarks in *Legendary London*, pp. 135 ff.
5. E. K. Chambers, *Arthur of Britain*, pp. 24–9.
6. See Windisch and Stokes, *Irische Texte*, III, Pt. I, text 2, pp. 51 ff.
7. J. F. Campbell, *Popular Tales of the West Highlands*, II, pp. 99 ff.
8. M. Summers, *History of Witchcraft*, pp. 86–7.
9. J. G. Dalyell, *The Darker Superstitions of Scotland*, p. 235.
10. W. Scott, Notes to *The Lay of the Last Minstrel*, note 2c.

CHAPTER VII

THE CELTIC SPIRIT WORLD

1. D'Arbois de Jubainville, *The Irish Mythological Cycle*, pp. 201 ff.
2. Walter Map, Dist. I, Chap. ii.
3. Sir Thomas Malory, *Morte d'Arthur*, III, p. 339.
4. R. Kirk, *The Secret Commonwealth*, p. 70.
5. R. Kennedy, *Legendary Fictions of the Irish Celts*, pp. 168–70.
6. E. Hull, *Folklore of the British Isles*, pp. 209–10.
7. T. T. Westropp, "A Folk-Lore Survey of County Clare", in "Folk-Lore", XXI, p. 191.
8. T. T. Westropp, "Folk-Lore", XXIX, p. 309.
9. T. T. Westropp, "Folk-Lore", XXI, p. 187.
10. T. Crofton Croker, *Traditions of the South of Ireland*, p. 102.
11. T. Crofton Croker, op. cit., p. 120.
12. T. T. Westropp, in "Folk-Lore," XXI, p. 188.
13. J. G. Campbell, *The Fians*, p. 45.
14. Wood-Martin, *Pagan Ireland*, p. 135.
15. T. T. Westropp, in "Folk-Lore", XXI, p. 190.
16. D'Arbois de Jubainville, op. cit., p. 110.
17. *The Dethe and False Murdure of James Stewarde, Kyng of Scots.* (Glasgow, 1818.)
18. R. Law, *Memorialls*, pp. 74 ff.
19. "Choice Notes", from *Notes and Queries*, p. 69.
20. P. Fraser Tytler, *History of Scotland*, III, p. 417.
21. J. Rhys, *Celtic Folk-Lore*, II, p. 453.
22. Wirt Sikes, *British Goblins*, pp. 219 ff.
23. Wirt Sikes, op. cit., pp. 216 ff.
24. J. G. Campbell, *Superstitions of the Scottish Highlands*, pp. 45, 191.
25. S. Grieve, *The Book of Colonsay and Oronsay*, pp. 176–9. For the *glaistig*, see J. G. Campbell, op. cit., Index; and A. A. MacGregor, *The Peat Fire Flame*, pp. 59–66.
26. A. A. MacGregor, op. cit., p. 298.
27. M. MacPhail, "Folk-Lore", IX, p. 91.
28. E. Hull, *The Cuchullin Saga*, p. 247.
29. J. G. Campbell, *The Fians*, p. 33.
30. F. S. Copeland, "Folk-Lore", XLII, pp. 405 ff.
31. E. Hull, quoted by Wentz in *The Fairy Faith in Celtic Countries*, p. 70.
32. A. H. Krappe, *The Science of Folk-Lore*, pp. 87–9.
33. L. C. Wimberley, *Folk-lore of the English and Scottish Ballads*, pp. 165, 225, 240–1, 280.
34. R. Kirk, op. cit., p. 79.
35. E. S. Hartland, *Primitive Paternity*, pp. 236 ff.; J. Frazer, *The Belief in Immortality*, I, pp. 93 ff.
36. J. C. Daniels, "Notes on Welsh Folk-Lore", "Folk-Lore", XXX, p. 157.
37. L. F. A. Maury, *Les Fées du Moyen Age*, pp. 55, 62.
38. Wirt Sikes, op. cit., pp. 127–31.
39. R. Hunt, *Popular Romances of the West of England*, p. 81.
40. P. Graham, *Sketches of Perthshire*, p. 263.
41. J. W. Joyce, *Social History of Ancient Ireland*, I, p. 228.
42. W. Y. Evans Wentz, *The Fairy Faith in Celtic Countries*, p. 432.
43. P. Kennedy, op. cit., p. 228.
44. J. F. Campbell, *Popular Tales of the West Highlands*, I, pp. 86 ff.
45. J. F. Campbell, op. cit., II, pp. 101 ff.
46. M. Martin, *A Description of the Western Isles of Scotland*, pp. 28–9.
47. K. W. Grant, *Myth, Tradition and Story from Western Argyll*, p. 13.
48. J. G. Campbell, op. cit., pp. 199 ff.
49. J. Rhys, *Arthurian Legend* (see Index).
50. T. Crofton Croker, op. cit., pp. 278 ff.
51. Wirt Sikes, op. cit., pp. 30 ff.
52. W. Henderson, *Folk-Lore of the Northern Counties of England and the Borders*, p. 129.

CHAPTER VIII

NECROMANCY, PROPHECY AND DIVINATION

1. M. Martin, *Description of the Western Isles*, pp. 110–12.
2. J. G. Campbell, *Superstitions of the Scottish Highlands*, pp. 304 ff.
3. D'Arbois de Jubainville, *The Irish Mythological Cycle* (trans. by R. I. Best), pp. 118 ff.
4. D'Arbois de Jubainville, op. cit., pp. 144 ff.
5. W. F. Skene, *Celtic Scotland*, I, p. 282.
6. Diodorus Siculus, *Historical Library*, Bk. V, Chap. xxxi.
7. E. Hull, *Folklore of the British Isles*, p. 177.
8. G. Henderson, *Survivals in Belief Among the Celts*, p. 89.
9. G. Henderson, op. cit., pp. 90–1.
10. J. Toland, *A Critical History of the Celtic Religion*, pp. 174 ff
11. Cicero, *De Divinatione*, Bk. I, Chap. xli.
12. C. Hardwick, *Traditions, Superstitions and Folklore*, p. 245.
13. W. Gregor, *Folk-Lore of the North-East of Scotland*, p. 136 ff.
14. Trevelyan, *Folk-Lore and Folk-stories of Wales*, pp. 81–2.
15. Giraldus Cambrensis, *Itinerarium Cambriae*, Bk. I, Chap. ii.
16. G. Henderson, op. cit., p. 96.
17. L. Spence, *Boadicea*, pp. 192–4.
18. J. Rhys, *Hibbert Lectures*, p. 199; N. W. Thomas, "Survivance du Culte des Animaux dans la Pays de Galles", *Revue de l'Histoire des Religions*, XXXVIII, pp. 295 ff.
19. G. L. Gomme, *Folk-Lore as an Historical Science*, p. 288.
20. W. Henderson, *Folk-Lore of the Northern Counties*, p. 309.
21. J. G. Dalyell, *Darker Superstitions of Scotland*, pp. 506–7.
22. J. G. Dalyell, op. cit., p. 506.
23. J. G. Campbell, op. cit., pp. 264 ff.
24. J. G. Dalyell, op. cit., pp. 515 ff.
25. MacLeod ("Theophilus Insulanus"), *On the Second Sight*, p. 77.
26. John of Salisbury, *De Nugis Curialium*, Bk. II, Chap. xxvii.
27. W. Camden, *Britannia*, IV, p. 469.
28. E. Davies, *Celtic Researches*, p. 300.
29. J. Brand, *Popular Antiquities*, I, p. 389; Owen, "Account of the Bards" in R. Hoare's *Itinerary of Archbishop Baldwin*, II, pp. 315 ff.
30. G. Henderson, op. cit., p. 261.
31. E. Hull, *Folklore of the British Isles*, pp. 178–9.
32. J. G. Dalyell, op. cit., p. 523.
33. W. Camden, op. cit., IV, p. 470.
34. J. Daniel, *The Philosophy of Ancient Britain*, p. 87.
35. D. Wright, *Druidism*, p. 108.
36. E. Davies, op. cit., p. 248.
37. E. Davies, op. cit., pp. 249–53.
38. E. Davies, op. cit., pp. 274–6.

CHAPTER IX

THE CELTIC BELIEF IN REINCARNATION

1. Clement of Alexandria, *Stromata*, I, xv, 70, 1.
2. Valerius Maximus, *Factorum et Dictorum*, II, 6, 10.
3. Lucan, *Pharsalia*, I, 450–8.
4. Hippolytus, *Philosophumena*, I, Chap. xxv.
5. T. D. Kendrick, *The Druids*, pp. 106 ff.
6. T. D. Kendrick, op. cit., pp. 107–8.
7. J. Rhys, *Hibbert Lectures*, p. 431.
8. W. Y. Evans Wentz, *The Fairy Faith in Celtic Countries*, p. 368.
9. D. Hyde, *A Literary History of Ireland*, p. 95.
10. E. S. Hartland, *Primitive Paternity*, I, pp. 194 ff.
11. D'Arbois de Jubainville, *The Irish Mythological Cycle*, pp. 25-35.

12. E. Windisch, *Irische Texte*, pp. 136 ff.
13. K. Meyer, "The Wooing of Emer", in *Archaeological Review*, I, p. 70.
14. D'Arbois de Jubainville, op. cit., pp. 191 ff.
15. E. Hull, *The Cuchullin Saga*, p. 82.
16. E. O'Curry, *Manners and Customs of the Ancient Irish*, pp. 192 ff.
17. A. Nutt, *The Mabinogion*, p. 307.
18. W. J. Perry, *The Children of the Sun*, pp. 180 ff.
19. See J. G. Frazer, *The Golden Bough*, Vols. I and II, passim.; also A. M. Hocart, *Kingship*, for a general review of the subject.
20. E. Hull, *The Cuchullin Saga*, pp. 271–3.
21. W. Y. Evans Wentz, *The Fairy Faith in Celtic Countries*, p. 413.
22. W. G. Wood-Martin, *Pagan Ireland*, p. 352.
23. G. Keating, *The General History of Ireland*, I, p. 231 (edn. of 1841).
24. Dion Chrysostom, *Orations*, xlix.
25. *The Antient Laws of Ireland*, I, p. 22.
26. G. Keating, op. cit., p. 241 ff. (Irish Text Society's edn.).
27. E. Hull, *Folklore of the British Isles*, pp. 92 ff.
28. E. Hull, op. cit., pp. 276–8.
29. J. A. MacCulloch, *The Religion of the Ancient Celts*, p. 160, note 2.
30. Wheatley Stokes, *The Academy* (1892), pp. 23 ff.
31. S. H. O'Grady, *Silva Gadelica*.
32. D'Arbois de Jubainville, op. cit., p. 143.
33. E. Hull, op. cit., pp. 270–1; R. A. S. Macalister, *Tara*, passim.
34. E. Windisch and W. Stokes, *Irische Texte*, I, p. 213.
35. L. Spence, *The Myths of Ancient Egypt*, pp. 298 ff.
36. J. G. Frazer, *The Magic Art*, II, p. 47.
37. J. A. MacCulloch, op. cit., pp. 201–2.
38. J. A. MacCulloch, op. cit., p. 244.
39. E. Davies, *The Mythology and Rites of the British Druids*, p. 484.
40. J. Daniel, *The Philosophy of Ancient Britain*, pp. 193–202.
41. D'Arbois de Jubainville, op. cit., pp. 26, 196–7.
42. L. Spence, *British Fairy Origins*, passim.

CHAPTER X

CELTIC MYSTICISM

1. J. A. MacCulloch, *The Religion of the Ancient Celts*, p. 198.
2. Pliny, *Natural History*, Bk. XVI, Chap. 44.
3. Pliny, op. cit., Bk. xvi, Chap. 249.
4. T. D. Kendrick, *The Druids*, pp. 124–5.
5. J. G. Frazer, *The Magic Art*, II, p. 189.
6. J. A. MacCulloch, op. cit., p. 233.
7. Tacitus, *Annals*, XIV, 30; Strabo, *Geographica*, IV, 4, 4 : Diodorus Siculus, *Histories*, V, 32.
8. L. Spence, *Legendary London*, p. 150.
9. T. D. Kendrick, op. cit., pp. 27–8.
10. E. O'Curry, *Lectures on MS. Materials of Ancient Irish History*, p. 240.
11. J. Bonwick, *Irish Druids*, p. 39.
12. E. Davies, *The Mythology and Rites of the British Druids*, pp. 50–1.
13. J. Daniel, *The Philosophy of Ancient Britain*, pp. 185 ff.
14. W. F. Skene, *Four Ancient Books of Wales*, I, p. 370.
15. J. A. MacCulloch, op. cit., pp. 333, 376 ff.
16. J. Williams ap Ithel, *Barddas* (Welsh Manuscript Society), passim.
17. E. Anwyl, *Celtic Religion in Pre-Christian Times*, pp. 60–1.
18. E. Davies, *Celtic Researches*, p. 175.
19. L. Spence, *The Mysteries of Britain*, pp. 121 ff.
20. W. F. Skene, op. cit., poem xiv.
21. J. Rhys, *Hibbert Lectures*, p. 249.
22. R. Kirk, *The Secret Commonwealth*, p. 74.
23. E. Anwyl, op. cit., p. 62.
24. J. A. MacCulloch, op. cit., pp. 367–8,

CHAPTER XI

CELTIC MYSTICISM (*continued*)

1. E. O'Curry, *Manners and Customs of the Ancient Irish*, II, p. 46.
2. J. A. MacCulloch, *The Religion of the Ancient Celts*, p. 221.
3. W. J. Gruffydd, *Math vab Mathonwy*, p. 266, note 88.
4. W. J. Gruffydd, op. cit., p. 205, note 92.
5. Ifor Williams, *Lectures on Early Welsh Poetry* (Dublin Institute of Advanced Studies), passim.
6. W. J. Gruffydd, op. cit., pp. 187 ff.
7. W. J. Gruffydd, op. cit., p. 222.
8. E. Anwyl, *Zeitschrift für Celtische Philologie*.
9. A. Herbert, *An Essay on the Neo-Druidic Heresy*, p. 97.
10. J. Rhys, *Hibbert Lectures*, pp. 91 ff.
11. W. J. Gruffydd, op. cit., pp. 174 ff.
12. L. Spence, *Legendary London*, pp. 184 ff.
13. J. Rhys, op. cit., pp. 90–1.
14. Nennius, Par. 13.
15. G. Keating, *General History of Ireland*, pp. 87–91.
16. W. F. Skene, *The Four Ancient Books of Wales*, II, p. 182.
17. M. R. Cox, *An Introduction to Folk-Lore*, pp. 180–1.
18. J. Rhys, op. cit., pp. 155–6.
19. Sir J. Daniel, *The Philosophy of Ancient Britain*, pp. 104–5.
20. J. Rhys, *Celtic Folk-Lore, Welsh and Manx*, pp. 677–8.
21. E. Hull, "The Development of the Idea of Hades in Celtic Literature", "Folk-Lore", XVIII, pp. 121 ff.
22. E. Davies, *The Mythology of the British Druids*, pp. 213–15, 435–6; *The Myvyrian Archaiology*, II, pp. 9, 11, 59, 65, 66, 78.

CHAPTER XII

THE CULTUS OF ARTHUR

1. E. K. Chambers, *Arthur of Britain*, Chap. vi, pp. 168–204.
2. A. Herbert, *Britannia After the Romans* I, pp. 85–8.
3. Lord Raglan, *The Hero*, pp. 73–81.
4. J. A. MacCulloch, *The Religion of the Ancient Celts*, pp. 118–21.
5. E. K. Chambers, op. cit., Chap. vii, pp. 205 ff.
6. E. Davies, *The Mythology and Rites of the British Druids*, pp. 577 ff.
7. W. J. Gruffydd, *Math vab Mathonwy*, p. 166.
8. E. K. Chambers, op. cit., p. 87.
9. E. K. Chambers, op. cit., p. 206.
10. A. Herbert, op. cit., I, p. 131.
11. A. Herbert, *An Essay on the Neo-Druidic Heresy*, p. 29.
12. A. Herbert, *Britannia After the Romans*, pp. 103 ff.
13. E. Foord, *The Last Age of Roman Britain*, pp. 186 ff.; L. Spence, *Legendary London*, pp. 110–11.
14. E. S. Hartland, *The Science of Fairy Tales*, pp. 234 ff.
15. "Choice Notes" from *Notes and Queries*, pp. 69–70.
16. A. H. Krappe, "Folk-Lore", xlvii, pp. 358–61.
17. Pausanius, vii, 17.
18. Gildas, III, 32.
19. L. Spence, *The Mysteries of Britain*, pp. 194–8. (See also *The Myvyrian Archaiology*, pp. 37 ff.)
20. A. Herbert, op. cit., pp. 28–39.
21. A. Herbert, *An Essay on the Neo-Druidic Heresy*, pp. 80–1.
22. A. Herbert, op. cit., pp. 118 ff.
23. J. L. Weston, *Legend of Sir Perceval*, II, pp. 140–1.
24. J. Ward, *The Roman Empire in Britain*, Chap. vi, pp. 101 ff.; A. B. Gosse, "The City of York", *The Speculative Mason*, xxv (July, 1933).

CHAPTER XIII

THE MYSTERY OF THE GRAIL

1. W. W. Skeat, *Concise Etymological Dictionary*, p. 183.
2. A. Nutt, *Studies on the Legend of the Holy Grail*, p. 233 and note.
3. C. Squire, *The Mythology of the British Isles*, pp. 357 ff.
4. J. Rhys, *Hibbert Lectures*, pp. 85–95 ; A. Nutt, op. cit., pp. 208–14.
5. A. Nutt, op. cit., pp. 137 ff.
6. A. Nutt, op. cit., pp. 190 ff.
7. J. F. Campbell, *Popular Tales of the West Highlands*, II, p. 152.
8. R. Jaffray, *King Arthur and the Holy Grail*; S. W. Gentle-Cackett, *The Antioch Cup*.
9. F. Loth, *Le Mabinogion*, II, p. 231

CHAPTER XIV

THE SECOND SIGHT

1. J. G. Campbell, *Witchcraft in the Highlands and Islands of Scotland*, pp. 121 ff.
2. A. Lang, *Cock Lane and Common-Sense*, pp. 227–8.
3. J. G. Dalyell, *The Darker Superstitions of Scotland*, pp. 472–3.
4. J. Aubrey, *Miscellanies*, p. 176 (edn. of 1890).
5. Lord Tarbet, *A Succinct Accompt*, in R. Kirk's *Secret Commonwealth*, p. 92.
6. J. Napier, *Folk-Lore in the West of Scotland*, pp. 71–2.
7. M. Martin, *A Description of the Western Isles of Scotland*, p. 321.
8. D. Rorie, in Simpkins' *Folk-Lore of Fife*, p. 396
9. W. Y. Evans Wentz, *The Fairy Faith in Celtic Countries*, p. 91, note 1.
10. Lord Tarbet, in R. Kirk, op. cit., pp. 94–6.
11. J. Aubrey, op. cit., pp. 175–6.
12. J. Aubrey, op. cit., pp. 185–6.
13. R. Kirk, op. cit., pp. 69–70.
14. R. C. MacLeod, *The Island Clans*, p. 166.
15. J. MacDougall and G. Calder, *Folk-Tales and Fairy Lore*, p. 251.
16. J. Aubrey, op. cit., p. 191.
17. Lady Gregory, *Visions and Beliefs*, p. 109.
18. J. G. McKay, *More West Highland Tales*, p. 182, note.
19. R. Kirk, op. cit., p. 82.
20. R. Kirk, op. cit., p. 85.
21. R. Kirk, op. cit., p. 99.
22. R. Kirk, op. cit., p. 103.
23. J. G. Campbell, *Superstitions of the Scottish Highlands*, p. 21.
24. J. G. Frazer, *Taboo and Perils of the Soul*, p. 28.

INDEX

A

Abred, the circle of, 129 f.

Aderyn y corph, bird of death-warning in Wales, 84

Amangons, King of Logres: and the Grail-cup, 167

Ambrosianus Aurelianus (or Ambrosius Aurelius), a British leader: alleged uncle of Arthur, 150–1

Amergin, an Irish Druid: his transformation, 15; boasts of his arcane knowledge, 138

Amulets, magical, in Scotland, 72

Aneurin, a Welsh bard, 44

Anglesey, Suetonius attacks Druids in, 42, 52

Angus, Irish god of youth: his magical abilities, 33

Annwn, the circle of, 129–31; "The Spoils of" (poem on), 130, 143–4

Arthur, a British deity: as a raven or chough, 83, 151–2; supersedes Hu Gadarn as god of the Neo-Druidic cultus, 138; his ship of glass, 142; his cultus in general, 145 ff.; an emanation of the sun-god Beli, 151; his resemblance to Cuchullin, 151; not a historical figure, 145–6; derivation of his name, 146; his mythic relationships, 146; central figure of a late British pagan cultus, 146 f.; Uther as his father, 147; probabilities concerning the cult of, 148; a sun-god of the British Celts, 148; revival of his cult, 149; as "divine king", 152; as "the Maimed King" of the Grail legend, 152; and the myth of Cronus, 152–3; Compared with Osiris, 154 f.; his dialogue with a mystical eagle, 159; mystical birds and animals associated with his cult, 160; his footsteps cause sterility, 172; as the Grail King, 172

Astrology, Celtic, 131–2

Avanc, a Welsh water-monster, 93

Avellenau, the, a Welsh mystical poem, 74

Awenydhyon, a divinatory caste in early Wales, 98

B

Badbs, war spirits of the ancient Irish, 82

Balor, god of the Fomorians, tale of, 16, 26; death of, 35; his evil eye, 63; prophecy concerning him, 98

Banshee, the, in Scotland and Ireland: her several forms, 81 f.; of the royal House of Stuart, 82 f.; and the spirit called Huthart, 83

Barddas, writings of Williams ap Ithal, 129

Bards, Druidic, 46; charms studied by, 64; preserved Druidic belief, 127; training of the Irish, 128

Barnacle goose, beliefs concerning the, 94

Battle of the Trees, 74

Bean-nighe, or "Washing woman", a form of banshee, 84–5; in Ireland, 85–6; similar spirit in Brittany, 86

Beli, a British deity, 139–40: his resemblance to the Gaulish god Cernunnos, 140; his association with Gargantua, 140; identified with Uther, 151

Biasd na srogaig, a horned monster of Skye, 95

Black Book of Carmarthen, 74

Bloddeuwedd, her legend, 32 f.

Blue Men of the Minch, sea-spirits of the W. Highlands, 92

Bocan, a Highland spirit, 91

Boobrie, a gigantic water-bird of the Highlands, 93–4

Book of Ballymote, 77

Book of Taliesin, 74

Book of the Four Masters, 77

Book of the Grail, 76–7

Books, magical, 73 ff.

Brahan Seer, the, 176–7

Bran, a British god, 74; the deity of a late pagan cult in Britain, 147

British mythological figures: examination of their *bona fides*, 137 ff.

Broichan, a Caledonian Druid, 14, 48–9

Brons, a character in Grail legend, 164; identified with the god Bran, 166–7

Brownie, a spirit, 90–1

Bwbach, a Welsh fairy, 92

C

Caer Pedryvan, "the Revolving Castle", 143

Caer Sidi, a mythical locality, 130–1, 141 f., 143

Caer Wydyr, "The Glass Castle", 130, 142

Caesar, Julius, on Druidism in Gaul, 45 f.

Calatin, an Irish wizard, his clan, 24

Cauldron of Inspiration, 17, 130, 144, 158

Ceridwen, a British goddess: transformation story of, 17; her association with the Pheryllt, 144; mysteries of, 159

Ceugant, the circle of, 129 f.

Charms, studied by the Irish bards, 64; Iron as a charm against Magic, 67; horseshoe as a protective, 67; leaves and twigs as, 68; love-charms, 71–2; the *caisean-uchd*, or sheepskin strip, 72

Children of Don, the, a company of British deities, 23

Children of Tuirenn, legend of the, 34

Chyndonax, a Gaulish Druid, discovery of his tomb, 47

Ciothruadh, an Irish Druid, his magical contest, 50